ECONOMICS OF MAHATMA GANDHI
Challenges and Development

ECONOMICS OF MAHATMA GANDHI

Challenges and Development

Edited by

DR. ANIL KUMAR THAKUR

and

DR. MITHILESH KUMAR SINHA

Published on behalf of
THE INDIAN ECONOMIC ASSOCIATION

DEEP & DEEP PUBLICATIONS PVT. LTD.
F-159, Rajouri Garden, New Delhi-110027

ECONOMICS OF MAHATMA GANDHI
Challenges and Development

ISBN 978-81-8450-158-2

Typeset by S.S. COMPOSERS
3190, Mohindra Park, Shakur Basti, Delhi-110034.

Printed in India at NEW ELEGANT PRINTERS,
A-49/1, Maya Puri, Phase-I, New Delhi-110064.

Published by DEEP & DEEP PUBLICATIONS PVT. LTD.
F-159, Rajouri Garden, New Delhi-110027.
Phones: 25435369, 25440916
E-mail: ddpbooks@yahoo.co.in • ddpubs@gmail.com
Showroom:
2/13, Ansari Road, Daryaganj, New Delhi-110002 • Telefax: 23245122

Contents

Preface

Relevancy of Gandhian approach is a matter of debate among intelligentsia. Some believe that we have gone too far to implement Gandhian economic thought. They argue that Gandhian model seems to be old-fashioned in an age of computer, internet, and space. However, this clearly reveals that they have not been able to comprehend the essence of Gandhian approach.

Gandhian model of growth which is based on spirituality, morality and ethical background and so, it is Gandhian prescriptions for economic diseases found in India was relevant, is relevant and will be relevant for the future generation. Between blood-thirsty capitalism and freedom-thirsty socialism Gandhian philosophy is the only practical and rational solution of various ills that harass the modern world. The Gandhian perspective of sustainable development is non-materialistic, non-violent, harmonistic, egalitarian, and value-driven. Gandhian concept of Swadeshi has once again to the fore. These days there is the environment of global unrest, i.e. terrorism, corruption, communal rift. Modern world is faced with a multi-faced economic crisis entailing poverty in the midst of plenty, insecurity of employment, alienation, erosion of moral values, uncontrolled urbanisation, environmental pollution, depletion of resources, ecological imbalance, inflation and other monetary and economic problems. The efforts to solve the problem by technological progress and exploitation of natural resources are further aggravating the situation. In these circumstances to chose the proper path for economic development is a need-based question. Our circumstances do not allow us to ignore Gandhiji. That is why recognizing Gandhian thoughts and deeds, the U.N.O. paid homage to the great soul by celebrating his 168th birthday as the "International Non-Violence Day."

With the objective of bringing Gandhian thoughts to fore the Indian Economic Association declared, "Economics of Mahatma Gandhi: Challenges and Development" as one of the themes for deliberations during its 90th Annual Conference, held at University of Kashmir, Srinagar under the presidentship of Prof. B.B. Bhattacharya during October 25-27, 2007. Out of several scholarly papers submitted and presented on this theme during the conference 35 papers have been selected for inclusion in this book. There is an introduction added for the convenience of the readers, which outlines main issues, and the central tenet of the book along with a brief summary of each paper.

The editors would like to place on record their thanks and gratitude to Indian Economic Association as well as Conference President Prof. B.B. Bhattachrya for providing this excellent opportunity. Each one of the contributors of this book deserves praise for their brilliant piece of work and the editors would like to thank each one of them. Editors alone would be responsible for any mistake that has remained in the book.

ANIL KUMAR THAKUR
MITHILESH KUMAR SINHA

List of Contributors

A. Sangamithra, Lecturer, Department of Economics, Bharathiar University, Coimbatore.

Amrendra Kumar Singh, Deptt. of Sociology, Sabour College, Sabour, Bhagalpur.

Aniruddha Kumar, Lecturer in Geography, D.A.V College, Siwan.

Arjun Singh, Professor, Deptt. of Agricultural Economics, CCSHAU, Hisar, Haryana.

Arun Kumar Thakur, Head, Deptt. of Economics, R.D.S. College, Muzaffarpur, Bihar.

Birendra Kumar Jha, Reader and Head, Department of Economics, R.B. College, Narhan, Samastipur, Bihar.

Bishwanath Singh, Professor of Economics, M.U. Bodh Gaya.

D.M. Diwakar, The author is Professor of Economics at Giri Institute of Development Studies, Lucknow.

Dalip Kumar, Manager (Projects), National Council of Applied Economic Research, New Delhi.

G.M. Bhat, Professor and Head, Post-Graduate Department of Economics, University of Kashmir, Srinagar.

Harindra Kishor Mishra, Department of Economics, Nagendra Jha Mahila College, Laheriasarai, Darbhanga-846003.

I.D. Gupta, Professor of Economics, Lucknow.

K. Mahesh Naidu, Ph.D. Scholar (part-time), Schoversity, Tirupati, A.P.

K. Srinivasulu Naidu, Professor, Department of Economics, Sri Venkateswara University, Tirupati, A.P.

K.M. Naidu, U.G.C. Emeritus Fellow: Department of Economics, Sri Venkateswara University, Tirupati, A.P.

K.S. Rajashekar, Professor, Deptt. of Economics, J.S.S. P.G. Centre, Mysore.

L.K. Mohan Rao, Professor and Head, School of Economics, Andhra University, Visakhapatnam, A.P.

M.G. Basava Raja, Professor, Division of Economics, University of Mysore, Sir M. Visvesvaraya P.G. Centre, Mandya, Karnataka.

M.M. Goel, The author is Professor and Chairman, Department of Economics, Kurukshetra University, Kurukshetra (Haryana).

Mahesh V. Joshi, Professor and Head, Department of Economics, Saurashtra University, Rajkot.

Maheshwar Goit, Department of Political Science, A.S. College, Deoghar, Jharkhand

Mithilesh Kumar Sinha, Reader in Economics, Nagaland University HQS. Lumami, Mokokchung, Nagaland.

Mohan Bhai Patel, Principal, N.S. Patel Arts College, Anand.

Mrinal Kumar Dasgupta, 289, Jodhpur Park, Kolkata, W.B.

N. Sharma, Principal, A.S. College, Deoghar, S.K.M. University, Dumka.

Niraj Kumar, H.N.K. Inter College, Ara.

Nisha Bhargav, Senior Lecturer, D.A.V. College, Hoshiarpur.

Pushpa Sinha, Lecturer, Deptt. of Economics, Patna Women's College, Patna

R. Arunachalam, Professor, Deptt. of Economics, University of Madras, Chennai.

R. Raj Kumar, Reader in Economics, Department of Economics, IDE, University of Madras, Chennai-5.

R. Sreenivasan, Research Scholar, Deptt. of Economics, University of Madras, Chennai.

R.P. Sarma, Director, Institute of Economic Studies, Brahmapur.

R.P. Singh, Professor of Economics, M.U. Bodh Gaya.

R.S. Bawa, Professor of Economics, G.N.D. University, Amritsar, Punjab.

R.S. Gadage, Chintamanrao College of Commerce, Sangli (M.S.).

R.U. Singh, Department of Commerce, College of Commerce, Patna, Bihar.

Raghubansh Singh, Ex-Principal, S.S. College, Jehanabad, Bihar.

Rajesh Pal, Lecturer in Economics, Mahatma Gandhi Kashi Vidyapeeth, Varanasi.

Rakesh K. Singh, Deptt. of Economics, R.D.S. College, Muzaffarpur, Bihar.

Ram Naresh Thakur, H.O.D. P.G. Centre of Economic Studies and Gandhian Study Centre, Samastipur College, Samastipur, Bihar.

Ratan Lal Basu, Reader in Economics, Bhairab Ganguly College, Kolkata.

Ratna Mitra, Lecturer, Deptt. of Economics, Patna Women's College, Patna

S. Ramachandran, Research Officer, Dr. Ambedkar Centre for Economic Studies, University of Madras.

S. Rengarajan, Reader in Economics, PG and Research Department of Economics, Sir Theagaraya College, Chennai 600 021.

Sachinandan Sau, Professor of Economics, Department of Economics with Rural Development, Vidyasagar University, Midnapore, West Bengal.

Sandhyarani Das, Department of Economics, Brahmapur University.

Shabir Ahmad Padder, Project Fellow-UGC Major Research Project, Post-Graduate Department of Economics, University of Kashmir, Srinagar.

Shakuntla Gupta, Professor, Department of Economics, Punjabi University, Patiala.

Sharad Tiwari, Professor in Economics, Govt. Hamidiya College, Bhopal.

Sunil Kumar, Rajput Colony, Alalpatti, Post-DMC, Benta Darbhanga, Bihar.

Sudakshina Gupta, Reader, Department of Economics, Ramakrishna Sarada Mission Vivekananda Vidyabhavan, Kolkata.

Ugra Mohan Jha, Former Director, Agro-Economic Research Centre for Bihar and Jharkhand, Bhagalpur.

Urmila Vijayvargiya, Professor and H.O.D., Economics Department, Govt. Sarojani Naidu Girls P.G. College, Bhopal.

Venkatesh Sharma, Block Supply Officer, Bokaro, Jharkhand.

Yogendra Kumar, Deptt. of L.S.W., A.N. College, Patna.

Introduction

Mahatma Gandhi was a complex, many-sided personality. He was a religious saint, a politician, a patriot and a nationalist, and economist, and a great freedom fighter, all in one. He was also one of the most profound and original thinkers that the modern age has produced. He has expressed his views practically on every sphere of life, and invariably what he has said is of far reaching significance even today after 60 years of his death.

To Gandhi, education does not mean a mere knowledge of alphabets. To him, 'education implies child's learning, how to put his mind and all his senses to good use that is to say, he really learns his hands, feet and other organs of action and his nose, ears and other organs of sense'. The purpose of education is to establish a non-violent, non-exploiting, human and social order, i.e. all round development of mind, body and soul. The concept of 'Basic Education' propounded by Gandhiji was a revolutionary concept and directed to create Thinking Hands.

Gandhi was one of the greatest champions of women's rights and equality. To him, women are the incarnation of Ahinsa, to call women a weaker sex is a libel, it is man's injustice to women. 'If I were born a woman I would rise in rebellion against man's cruelty to women. I have mentally become a woman to steal into her heart. I could not steal into my wife's heart until I decided to treat her differently than I used to do, and so, I restored to her all her rights, by dispossessing myself of all my so-called rights as her husband'. Gandhi, in a way, started the first feminist movement in India.

It was Gandhi who drew the Indian women in the freedom struggle. 'The British rule in the India', he said, 'could end in the minutes if the women of India wanted and understood it'. If the history of mankind is conceived in terms of women's empowerment Gandhi occupies a very high position in it. Sarojini Naidu called him 'The Micky Mouse of History' from the paper tigers of England were literally scared. He made Indian women fearless and brave and honourable. When a British office tried to push Sarojini Naidu at Dandi during the Salt Satyagrah, she shouted: 'don't touch me. I am the Agni of India. I will consume you if you move an inch.'

Gandhi gave due thought to economic problems that faced the country and suggested his own solution. He saw that the Indian masses were groaning under the crushing heels of poverty. They could not even enjoy two square meals a day. Their poverty was largely owing to their exploitation by the British imperialists. Spinning of the Charkha and Swadeshi were Gandhi's ways to Self-dependent. They must lead a simple life. They must spin and weave their cloth, and they shun the use of foreign cloth. They must wear only swadeshi. His economics was the economics of the Charkha. This would not only give employment to the Indian farmer who is under-employed during the greater part of the year, but would also strike at the very roots of the British rule in India.

Gandhiji's concept of trusteeship is the genuine dream of a historic personality with stunning simplicity and moral grandeur who inspired the non-violence movement as the political way for settling problems for humanity in modern times. Gandhiji's life was an amazing adventure of morality and ethics. For Gandhiji, morality or ethics was the very foundation of life. The moral conscience, according to him, should be man's inner guide to his actions. Truth and non-violence were the basic philosophy of Gandhi's life. These two concepts are the essence of morality.

According to Gandhian scheme of things, each capitalist and industrialist should consider himself to be a trustee of the wealth that he possesses. He should consider himself to be a custodian of the industry, resources, labour and wealth that he uses for his business purposes. If all capitalists and all industrialists begin to believe themselves as such custodians of their own wealth, then collectively, they would become the custodian of wealth of the society. And that would transform the capitalist order of society into an egalitarian one, where the 'greatest good of all' could be achieved.

Gandhiji's doctrine of trusteeship does not recognize the right of the individual ownership. The right to individual or private ownership is abolished and permitted only to the extent that it is needed for one's own welfare of the society. To quote Gandhiji:

"Supposing, I have come by a fair amount of wealth either by way of legacy, or by means of trade and industry. I must know that all that wealth does not belong to me; what belongs to me is the right to an honourable livelihood, no better than that enjoyed by millions of others. The rest of my wealth belongs to the community and must be used for the welfare of the community."

Gandhiji opined that business should be people-friendly. In order to come up the expectations of the society, business in modern times envisages bridging the gap between what the society wants and what the business makes it available. Gandhiji while working out a formula for trusteeship advocated for exactly the same model of behaviour on the part of the business. "What they produce in their industries and release to the society should be determined by social necessity with the optimum utilisation of the scarce resources of society. What they produce should not be determined by personal whim or personal greed."

Gandhiji wanted an economic order where labour and management were to live in a state of peaceful co-existence, supporting and supplementing each other. He observed: "My ideal is that capital and labour should supplement and help each other. They should be a great family living in unity and harmony; capital not only looking to the material welfare of the laboureres, but their moral welfare also, capitalists being trustees of the welfare of the labouring classes under them." Hence, Gandhiji sought paternalist role from the part of management in their dealings with labour.

Gandhiji advocated 'Mutual Trusteeship'. He suggests "The owner should look after the workers and the workers should look after the institution's productivity and profit. Both the owners and the workers should work for the true benefit of consumers."

Mahatma Gandhi understood the dynamics of Social Change that could be executed only through Youth Power, which he tried successfully during the Independence movement. He had realised the tremendous potentialities in the youth. Youth have by nature greater fellow feeling and sympathy, which makes them, fit instruments of social change. Ethical and spiritual values can only provide a sure basis for a creative social order.

Analyzing the social milieu, Gandhi must have thought that students and youth are the only sections where idealism is still a force to reckon with. The first and the foremost reason for according such high priority to youth power as a vehicle of social change lay in Gandhi's perception that the youth have got the least vested interest of all.

Gandhiji had a dream for India. Realizing this dream has become a nightmare. Today, we are living in a constant adjustment to changing conditions, which requires a different kind of discipline. Now it rests on our shoulders, yours and mine to see that the democratic values in our country remains intact and that social justice, equity, gender equality is achieved for all. Rights should follow duties. If we are able to achieve this, we shall be helping to reinstate Mahatma Gandhi's dream. I firmly believe it can be done. Gandhi's unfinished task is the biggest challenge before the youth. After all it is their future. It is their world. Does not look like it? But it is.

Gandhiji was the great communicator and journalist. More than any one else, he recognized that communication is the most effective tool to shape opinion and mobilize popular support. He was successful because he had a talent skill in communication that surfaced in South Africa where he had gone initially to set-up practice as a lawyer. The practice of communication started by him in South Africa gave him the clue to rally millions of his countrymen when he returned to India.

Gandhiji was associated with six journals, for two of which he was the editor. To Mahatma Gandhi, journalism is not the means of earning a living. He observed: "In my humble opinion, it is wrong to use a newspaper as a means of earning a living. There are certain spheres of work which are of such consequence and have such bearing on public welfare that to undertake them for earning one's livelihood will defeat the primary aim behind them. When, further a newspaper is treated as a means of making profits, the result is likely to be serious malpractices. It is not necessary to prove to those who have some experience of journalism that such malpractices do prevail on a large scale."

In the fast changing modern world equipped with scientific and technological advancements we may find people putting question mark on the relevance of Gandhian thought in present context. Such questions point out to the level of ignorance of the person otherwise well equipped with scientific and technical knowledge only. One may also ask how can a person who has not seen 'Gandhiji' relate oneself with the vision of nurtured, followed and envisaged as the guiding force of the people of India? Mahatma, as a mortal being, may not be present among us, but he has been constantly guiding as an inspiration, an illuminated light on almost all the diversified issues that an individual, a society or the state may come across. Mahatma Gandhi need not be seen as an individual, but as a movement, a phenomenon and a light removing darkness from each and every walk of life. Wherever there is a struggle for survival, wherever there is injustice, poverty, hunger, illiteracy, inequality, and darkness, Gandhi showed a road light.

In 21st century, all over the world we find the atmosphere of competition, conflict and fear, clash of civilisation, warfare in the name of religion, diminution and erosion of values in life, insecurity of employment, alienation, environmental pollution, depletion of resources, ecological imbalance, poverty in the midst of plenty and other economic problems. The efforts to solve the problem by technological progress and exploitation of natural resources are further aggravating the situation. As a matter of fact, the problems are becoming more and more complex and gigantic day-by-day. One of the most important characteristics of the world economic problems of today is their interconnectedness and inter-dependence. The problems act and interact upon each other, have positive feedback loops, and are not restricted to national boundaries. All these factors have gone a long way in increasing the magnitude and complexity of the problems. As a result, the traditional fragmentary economic solutions have been rendered quite ineffective in tackling these problems of a complex and global nature.

The current economic crisis with all its complexity calls into question the very foundations of economics. The nature of the pressing economic problems that the world is facing today and the failure of the traditional economics to find a solution to them, necessitates a deep examination of the world-view undertaking the entire economic thought. The solution to our problems cannot be found from within the existing theoretical framework, as the roots of the problems lie somewhere outside the system in the paradigm that bears upon the basic values and concepts of economics. In Schumacher's language, a deep study of meta-economics is required. "The study of economics is too narrow and too fragmentary to lead to valid insights, unless complemented, and completed by a study meta-economics."

The present economic system contains the seeds of its own destruction. If the economic activity continues with the old methodology motivated by the traditional economic drives, the entire economic system is likely to meet a disastrous end. A study team at MIT (USA) under the guidance of Prof. Dennis Meadows, has concluded, "If the present growth trends in world population, industrialisation, pollution, food production and resource depletion continue unchanged, the limits to growth on the planet will be reached sometimes within the next one hundred years." The restructuring of economics based on a new vision of reality is urgently required. It is in this connection that Gandhian Economics based on a fundamentally different paradigm becomes most relevant. Dr. V.K.R.V. Rao has observed, "Gandhiji's ideas are beginning to command increasing attention in a world that is disillusioned by the working of both capitalism and communism and attracted by possibility that the circle can be squared with economic growth, social justice, full employment, economic and social equality, political democracy, and individual freedoms all forming components of a harmonious new social order"

According to Gandhiji, "the economic constitution of India and for the matter of that of the world, should be such that no one under it should suffer for want of food and clothing." But he did not favour giving alms or doles and instead advocated 'Gospel of Work' or 'Bread Labour' described in the Gita as Yajna. He tried to combine the secular and immediate needs with his philosophical approach to the entire development problem. He had a holistic conception of development—material, social, cultural and moral development. Hence, he wanted to create moral basis for economic progress. To him, "true economics never militates against the highest ethical standard." In Gandhi, man emerges at the centre of all economic and political development. Hence, he challenged the technological basis of modern civilisation, which has caused environmental pollution. Where population pressure is too high to sustain on the per capita land available, it should not displace human labour. Where heavy and large-scale industries are inevitable it should be under producer's control. All production should be for consumption and not for profit. Production and Consumption should be localised.

Global system makes common people completely helpless in the matter of production and distribution. The capitalist avatar of globalisation creates more and more unemployment and poverty. Globalisation and market economy is concerned about price while Gandhi's global vision was concerned about value.

As regards Gandhi's development philosophy, it revolves round a man, his society, nature, and their respective and simultaneous development. He had a philosophy of work, wealth and happiness of man in line with the religious and ethical philosophies of the East as well as the West. Today in India, his vision of life, society, and civilisation has been increasingly shared and practice in various parts of the country and the world refers to several basic and contingent problems, like poverty, violence, terrorism, discrimination based on caste and religion, ecology, centralisation of wealth and power. This has created a tremendous interest in the people of India and the whole world to know and understand his philosophy of living and development.

Thus, Gandhi remains extremely relevant in the context of development in the 21st century. His Life's Message will lead a new path of Universal Love and Harmony.

Today, Gandhi is the sign at the World's crossroads. Gandhian thoughts are economically viable, politically sound, and sociologically sustainable and Gandhiji is as relevant to India and the world as Sun to the solar system.

I.D. Gupta's analytical paper deals with issues of market economy and consumerism, excess of industrialisation and its sustainability, the issues of rising disparity and its repercussions in the form of rising crime and naxalism in the country and evaluates Gandhi's economic thinking and its relevance in the new millennium.

Mrinal Kumar Dasgupta in his paper has tries to search for the relevance of M.K. Gandhi's idea on equity and social justice in comparison to those ideas in the economic framework.

In his analytical paper Harindra Kishor Mishra depicts ten economic constituents of Gandhi's economic philosophy—Machinery, Decentralisation, Trusteeship, Swadeshi, Population, Prohibition, Food problem, Bread labour, Village republic and Environment—that are important constituents for balanced and human-faced development. He emphasizes that only by following Gandhian economic thought predicaments arising due to globalisation might be overcome.

Sandhyarani Das and R.P. Sharma formulate Gandhi's approach for empowerment of women into a logical triangular model—Education, Employment, and Social Structure. They advocate following the Gandhian model to empower the women that was experienced by Gandhi century ago.

Sudakshina Gupta in her paper uses econometric tools and equation related to welfare economics to show that turning agricultural lands into industrial hubs will not necessarily increase the welfare of society. She points out that by violating Gandhian principles, society's welfare may not be increased.

Sangamithra's paper analyses six constituents of Gandhian philosophy and suggests that Gandhian economics must be viewed from a historical and dynamic perspective not in a historical and static terms.

R. Arunachalam and R. Seenivasan's paper covers Gandhian approach of the participatory democracy. Arunachalam and Seenivasan stress the Gandhian philosophy of Panchyat Raj to be translated into action using the provisions of New Panchayat Raj for social transformation as well as rural development in India.

Mithilesh Kumar Sinha and Rakesh K. Singh's paper discusses Gandhian economic vision along with Gandhian perception on quality of life and approach of women empowerment. Sinha and Singh show the contribution of Gandhi to evolution and growth of modern corporate ethics. Lastly, they assert without hesitation that Gandhian economic philosophy remains extremely relevant in the context of development in the 21st century.

S. Ramachandran's paper evaluates the Government's efforts to develop Gandhi's vision on industries after independence and its relevance in the present globalisation era. This paper suggests the policy-makers to follow Gandhian economic ideas of industrialisation to transform the society in the positive direction.

R.S. Bawa's paper divides the resources of a country based on Gandhian thought into two groups—one set of resources Gandhi referred to as current economy resources and second as reservoir economy resources. Bawa asserts that the guidelines by the Gandhian thought can give us reasonable ground from which to raise our economic policies and to build up the economic super-structure.

Bishwanath Singh and R.P. Singh's paper advocates that growth strategy should be formulated following Gandhian marg (route). Only through Gandhian route poverty may be removed providing the rural and poor people employment.

Urmila Vijayvargiya and Sharad Tiwari in their paper highlights the Gandhian vision of villages as self-sufficient units and shows through data that PMSGY connectivity opens door for enhancement of the quality of rural life and has a positive impact on them. They prove that PMGSY is an entry point for Gandhian vision.

S.S. Gadage's paper includes indigenous model of Gandhian thought and concludes that if indigenous model of Gandhian thought had been adopted right from beginning, socio-economic problems could have been avoided.

M.G. Basava Raja and K.S. Rajashekhar's paper covers the concept of Gandhian industrial model especially Khadi and Village Industries and concludes that Gandhian Industrial Model alone is able to solve the problems of unemployment, poverty, and pollutions facing developing countries.

V. Mahesh Joshi and Mohan Bhai Patel's paper pinpoints the problem of unemployment and asserts that unemployment problem may be overrun through the Gandhian thought.

Rajesh Pal in his paper highlights Gandhian views on Economics of Khadi and he stresses the need for honest acceptance of Gandhian pro-poor growth model which was relevant, is relevant and will be relevant in Indian context in the near future.

In another paper by Birendra Kumar and Arun Kumar Thakur it is discussed that globalisation adds fuel to the fire through making human community more greedy and commercial in outlook and in the global era 'Market is the temple and money is God'. If the present trend is allowed to continue, the world will be loser in all fronts in general. In this scenario Gandhian model of economic development appears to be only alternative and more relevant.

K.M. Naidu, L.K. Mohan Rao, K. Srinivasulu Naidu and K. Mahesh Naidu in their paper presents the positive picture of Gandhi as a global man mainly interested in the prosperous development of villages in India. Explaining the difference between Pandit Jawahar Lal Nehru and Mahatma Gandhi covering present position of India they conclude that Gandhi and his economic ideas are relevant to globalisation and in 21st century.

M.M. Goel in his paper tries to investigate the relevancy of Gandhian thoughts in 21st century and concludes giving his submission to his fellow citizens. "Let's follow the great Mahatma's ideals in our life."

In the paper by Sachinandan Sau many issues—technical, institutional, inequality—of present globalisation age, are discussed and it is concluded that sustainable development is possible only through the adoption of Gandhian thoughts.

Ratan Lal Basu in his paper examines the Gandhian concept of Swadeshi and concludes that Gandhian concept of Swadeshi is relevant as devising the correct path of industrialisation catering to the well-being of the masses and generating adequate employment opportunities.

D.M. Diwakar's paper deals with the idea of Gandhi on equity and land relations. The paper also focuses that Gandhi's views on the issues of land questions may provide important insight towards understanding the land questions in India.

In his paper Niraj Kumar deals with the Gandhian theory of humanistic economics and asserts that this theory is lasting solution to all the fundamental problems facing not merely India but the entire humanity.

The paper by Ram Naresh Thakur and Yogendra Kumar deals with the Gandhian concept of 'Satyagraha' and correlates Satyagraha with development. It concludes that Satyagraha of Mahatma Gandhi is more relevant than other principles or theories in this environment of global unrest.

In their paper, R.U. Singh and Maheshwar Goit interpret Gandhian thought as a practical attempt to relieve the poverty and uplift the standards of the Indian villages.

In his paper G.M. Bhat and Shabir Ahmad Padder feature the modern world facing poverty in the midst of plenty, insecurity of employment, alienation, erosion of moral values, uncontrolled urbanisation, environmental pollution, depletion of resources, ecological imbalance, inflation and other monetary and economic problems and seeks the restructuring of economics based on a new vision of reality. Explaining different economic thoughts of Gandhi they epitomize that Gandhian Economics based on a fundamentally different paradigm becomes most relevant.

The paper by Shakuntla Gupta and Nisha Bhargav

assays Gandhian economic thoughts and asseverate that Gandhian thoughts have relevance for modern India as well the world.

The paper, by Pushpa Sinha and Ratan Mitra inquests three concepts of Gandhi—Swadeshi, Sarvodaya and Swaraj. After assaying these three concepts they reach on epitome that in the present scenario where the prevalence of corruption raise strong obstacles and inhibition to development India is highly in need of moral boost up for which it has to adopt Gandhian model of growth.

In their paper Dalip Kumar and Venkatesh Sharma tries to reflect the ideas of social justice in the contemporary contexts. The paper contains themes which explain the thoughts on Gandhian Perspective of justice and equity, justice for gender equity, justice for Indigo Peasants in Champaran, justice against untouchability and justice related to communal conflagration.

The paper by Arjun Singh puts forward Gandhian ideas about democracy, non-violence and governance and advocates that the gap between the poor and the rich may be reduced or bridged by following the Gandhian ideas.

In his paper Sunil Kumar deals with the question of relevance of Gandhian thoughts and asserts that Gandhian ideas are universal and relevant for all times to come.

The paper by N. Sharma and Anirudha Kumar makes attempt to enquire into the causes of the present miserable state of affairs of the weaker sections of the population. They conclude that Gandhian economic thought may be described as pragmatic humanistic economy because it is based on realistic approach of life with emphasis on human value and human dignity.

In their paper Ugra Mohan Jha and Amrendra Kumar Singh emblazons Gandhian economic thoughts and considering from all points of views they conclude that Gandhian approach is the only way-out of poverty, inequality and threat to humanity itself.

The paper by S. Rengarajan and R. Raj Kumar highlights the Gandhian rural economic philosophy and for rural uplift they stress the need for adopting his rural economic philosophy.

In another paper by Raghubansh Singh establishes Gandhiji a journalist of the first rank and a great editor and concludes Gandhiji through his journalistic venture is immortal.

ANIL KUMAR THAKUR
MITHILESH KUMAR SINHA

1

Gandhian Economic Thinking

It's Relevance in 21st Century India

I.D. GUPTA

At the outset we should acknowledge that Mohan Das Karamchand Gandhi was not an Economist as such. He was much more than that. He was a saint, a Mahatma and the Father of the Nation. His economic ideas were a part of his general crusade against exploitation, poverty, social and economic injustices prevailing in India. His whole approach is rooted in human dignity. He wanted to elevate economic philosophy from its materialistic base to high spiritual plane where actions are by social objectives rather than self-considerations

Gandhi is not a name. It is a philosophy—the philosophy which is firmly rooted in Vedic philosophy. He gave the world message of truth and non-violence. In economics, he presented the approach of trusteeship. The message of trusteeship emerges from Ishopanishad where it has been established that whatever is there in this world is the property of God. And He has created all this for all His creatures. There is plenty for everyone's need in this world. Man should consume things with the sense of sacrifice and he should not take other's share. Upanishad says one should not be greedy and should always remember that it is not his property. This has been given to him for proper utilisation. He is only a trustee of God's property.

Gandhi gave the message to the humanity that sacrifice in consumption and non-possession of material wealth is the basic thing to be understood. There is enough for everyone's need in this world but all the wealth of this world is not sufficient for one man's greed. Had this been understood properly world wars would have been avoided and Hitler had not come into being. In the world community ridden with terrorism, violence and racial strife, today in the Twenty first century, Gandhi's message of Non-Violence in resolving the problems has become much more relevant than ever before.

The present paper is organized in three parts. The first part seeks the original roots of Gandhi's spiritualism and Satya (Truth) and Ahimsa (Non-violence). The second part makes a brief review of development of Indian economy during the past sixty years and the rise and decline of Gandhian economic ideology during that. The third part is concerned with the developmental issues before world economy and India in the post-reform period. This will deal precisely with issues of market economy and consumerism, excess of industrialisation and its sustainability, the issue of rising disparity and its repercussions in the form of rising crime and naxalism in the country. And finally an attempt will be made to evaluate Gandhi's economic thinking and its relevance in the new millennium.

PART I

Gandhi regarded economics as a moral science and laid tremendous emphasis on its ethical aspect. Economics that hurts the moral well-being of an individual or a nation is immoral and therefore sinful. Its goal is not pure material benefit but advancement of humanity on its road to progress by strengthening the character and the development of personality of each individual engaged in such activity. He formulated economic principles in the context of his design of an ideal social order: a non-violent, non-exploitative, humanistic and egalitarian society.

Today the economic thinkers are trying to find out the meaning and purpose of economic development. Economic development was defined in terms of growth of gross national product and per capita income not so long ago. During sixties, Physical Quality of Life was the basic concern, and then came the Human Development approach. Mahbubul Haq and others in the World Bank found out in nineties that Man is in the centre of development and he should live a long and healthy life. As in most of the poor countries life is short and miserable the concept was well attended.

Years later it was found out that the purpose of development should be happiness and happiness index was prepared world over. Then it was found that people in Bangla Desh, one among the poorest countries, are the happiest people in the world. Some more attempts are made in recent time to give credential to this approach. This is akin to defining an elephant by the four blind fold persons.

The basic question still stands what is the objective of economic development. Western view has no answer to it. Money, more money then still more money. Then what? Life of stress, frustrations and miserable death. The example of happiness attained by the poor people living in an underdeveloped country like Bangladesh, and not in possession of material wealth, disapproves the very basic tenet of this materialistic approach to happiness in life. As happiness is a state of mind, it does not have much concern with accumulation of money after a point. Rather more and more of income and wealth make life more miserable. Here money commands man rather than man commanding money. It is slavery. So the western economic philosophy becomes indeterminate.

Here comes Mahatma Gandhi who proclaims: the root of happiness is righteousness,

"Sukhasya mool Dharmah"

Dharma is righteousness in action, thought and words. The basic criterion of judging what is right and what is wrong is, what you consider not good for yourself, do not do that to others. That is the basic test. Dharma prescribes the duty of a man.

In Manusmriti, Manu has given ten characteristics of dharma:

Dhriti, kshama, damoasteyam, shaucham, indriya nigraha;
Dhirvidya, satyam, akrodhah dashkam dharma lakshanam.

Dhriti is patience, kshama is forgiveness, dam is controlling own mind, shauch is purity of body and thought. Indriya nigraha is controlling the five jnana indriyas (sense organs) and five karma indriyas, dhee is intellect and vidya is acquiring knowledge, satya is truth and akrodha is not to be angry. These are the ten elements or characters of dharma.

In Yogadarshan, Maharshi Patanjali has suggested eight steps to realizing happiness and God, who is happiness (Anand) incarnate, *vis-a-vis* Sat and Chit, truth incarnate and the very basic source of life (Chaitanya). The first and the second steps of this Ashthangyoga are yama and niyama. The discipline of yama is five-fold: ahimsa (non-violence), satya (Truth), asteya (not to steal), brahmcharya (celibacy) and aparigraha (non-possession). Niyama, as per Maharshi Patanjali, too has five disciplines: shauch (purity), santosh (contentment), tapa (to brave difficulties in fulfilling duty), swadhyay (knowing ownself), and Ishwar pranidhana (to delve in Him through meditation).

Purity (shauch) has three dimensions—kayik, vachic and manasic—physical purity, purity of words and purity of thought. According to Maharshi Manu, physical purity comes through water, source of mental purity is truth (satya), and jnana, knowledge, refines intellect, by tapa and vidya together 'self 'is refined.

Adbhir gatrani shudhyanti, manah satyen shudhyate;
Vidya tapobhyam bhutatmah, budhhir jnanen shudhyati.

Gandhi's derivation of non-violence, truth, purity of body and thought, contentment, hard work, non-possession, and celibacy owe to these sources of Vedic philosophy.

The core of Gandhian philosophy is grounded in non-violence and truth. Truth (satya) is an attribute of the Almighty. Truth is eternal. These are the norms which are for man's benefit for all times. They are based on dharma. Gandhi's interpretation of dharma is truth-bound (satya-moolak) dharma.

According to Nyaya sutra:

Pramanyenartha parikshanam

(1/1 Nyaya Bhashya)

What stands at the alter of justice is truth. This also interprets what is unjust can never be true.

Maharshi Manu describes three forms of truth: satya bhava (true attitude), satya vachan (true speech), and satya acharan (truthful action). This represents three things—mind, speech and action (man, vani and karma).

In Vedic philosophy the three basic attributes of God are satyam, shivam and sundaram. What is to the benefit of all (read 'welfare') is shivam. That which incorporates 'welfare of all' (Pareto optimality) is shiva tatva. Here shivam (welfare of all) is attached with truth or the sense of what is just and what is not just or unjust. Then, these two attributes of godliness are attended by the concept of beauty (sundaram). That only could be beautiful which is true and beneficial to all. This "Trinity" concept is the crux of the Vedic philosophy wherefrom dharma has been derived.

Economic ideas of Gandhi flow from the perspective of satya, dharma and ahimsa. It puts man and his overall upliftment in the centre. Dignity of man was in the centre of Gandhi's movement against untouchability, which had divided Indian society for hundreds of years.

Another word attached with Gandhi is Ahimsa—to desist violence (even at the cost of physical sufferings). Ahimsa according to Maharshi Vyasa is:

Sarvatha sarvada sarvabhutanamaanabhidrohah ahimsa gyeyah.

(2/30 Yoga darshan)

Ahimsa is not only non-brutality towards animals, in its wider perspective it is relinquishing enemity. By one's actions the other one should not feel hurt is ahimsa. Himsa may be physical as well as mental both, says Maharshi Manu. Even thinking of one's harm is violence.

Manasa anisthachintanam,

Satya and ahimsa became the basic tools of Gandhi to fight with rulers in South Africa and the British rule in India. It was new to the world. These were the Gandhian experiments with truth.

Obviously Gandhi's whole life and philosophy and his high order spirituality has drawn heavily from Vedic scriptures, Upanishads, Geeta and Mahabharatha. He had been a firm believer in God. His message was that to achieve anything (swaraj inclusive) the path, the way of doing things, should be righteous. He believed in purity of instruments involved in attaining a right thing. There he was above Bal Gangadhar Tilak for whom "end justifies the means." Gandhi differed.

Among others whose works and who influenced Gandhi was the works of Ruskin's Unto the Last, Marxian egalitarianism and Leo Tolstoy's contentment. It is said, Gandhi's Antyodaya yojana is taken from Ruskin's concept of Unto the Last. Gandhi and Karl Marx both believed in revolution to change the existing economic and social order but they differed in their approach. Marx's revolution was violent but Gandhi's revolution was peaceful. His tools were Satyagraha and Civil disobedience. He wanted to penetrate the heart of the enemy, howsoever mighty he was.

His strategy and approach was new to the world which had been fighting battles and wars to win over the enemy to achieve objectives. Never before, the world has seen a frail mortal with immense spiritual power of heart in finding out solution this way. This was something revolutionary.

On his martyrdom Andrew Ewart writes, "Thus blind and unreasoning violence ended a life dedicated to denouncing its use in the affairs of mankind, and the world lost the counsel of a wise and selfless being whose deeds and words still guide the destinies of his vast nation and will continue so to do long after those who live by the sword have perished by the sword."

PART II

RISE AND DECLINE OF GANDHI'S ECONOMIC IDEOLOGY IN INDEPENDENT INDIA

Gandhi dreamt of self-sufficient villages, developed cottage and village industries, co-operation and a life based on simple living and contentment. Country was in poverty and more than half of its people were living a miserable life at the time it became free. In today's terminology they were living below poverty line. The country was divided into two nations. The economy was shattered. As India was the country of villages, more than seventy percent of its population was living in villages. They were dependent upon agriculture. Country was facing big problem of settlement of those who had come from Pakistan after partition. There were no developed industries worth the name except cotton textile and steel industry. There was chaos all round. A daunting challenge was present before the nation-builders.

Gandhi never liked machines as they replaced labour and were the basic cause of unemployment. He was not in favour of industrialisation. Industrialisation gives rise to Capitalism and exploitation of the working class and consumers in the market.

At the time of Independence in 1947, there were two competing ideologies of economic development in the world. One was Capitalistic market economy model and the other was the Communist or Socialist model. The first was based on private property rights and free market. The other was Communist model where all the property belonged to the state and there was no individual choice. State was responsible for providing employment and every other thing needed to its people. Equity and egalitarianism in distribution were basic to the model. It was a reaction to the capitalistic exploitation and economic disparity created by the system.

Indian leaders wanted to bring an ideal model of development which would be free from exploitation and ensure freedom of choice to its individuals. As the socialist model developed into a 'regimented society' model we wanted to take only its best part, of developmental planning and avoid un-freedom part. India adopted Mixed Economic system for development. In polity, we opted for Parliamentary Democracy.

Gandhi could not live long to see his dreams come true in independent India as his voice was silenced by the forces of communal hatred against which he struggled whole life. On 30th January 1948, he was shot dead while going to evening prayer in Delhi.

The Gandhi-Nehru model of growth aimed at establishment of a Socialistic Pattern of Society based on equity, justice and co-operation. The orientation of Five Year Plans since the beginning was rural development and speedy industrialisation in the country. Community Development Projects were started and Land Reforms were undertaken. The objective was to raise productivity of the farm sector and remove injustices from the existing system. The motto was land to the tiller. It was hoped that this will remove rural poverty and establish an order.

Soon the departure from Gandhian path became eminent as the country started on the path of large scale industrialisation since the second Five Year Plan in 1956. By the Industrial Policy Resolution 1949 and Industrial Policy 1956 the responsibility of speedy industrial development came on the shoulders of the government. The commanding heights of the economy came in the public sector and the private sector was given a supportive role. Nehru was considered 'modernizer par-excellence' by many. He chose the path of rapid industrialisation to modernize India. At that time economic development was synonym to industrial development. It was industrial revolution which has brought prosperity in the developed countries of the world.

Realities were harsh, however, and soon the economy had to face resource crunch on all sides. Population was rising at a fast pace and food shortages became perceptible.

Foreign exchange reserve of the country was exhausted and private capital—resident as well as overseas—was slow to come.

During the first decade of planning in the country the objectives of five per cent per annum growth rate was not realised. Per capita income growth was slightly above one per cent. Consequently poverty persisted at a vast scale.

Sixties brought insurmountable difficulties in the form of Chinese aggression in 1962 and yet another war with Pakistan in 1965. Death of Prime Minister Jawahar Lal Nehru on May 27th, 1964 was another big upset. Years 1966 and 67 were years of drought and the country was pushed into severe food crisis. The lesson of China war drew our attention towards neglect of defense sector. Subsequently, the next five year plan's objective became Defense and Development. A large part of the budget allocation was made for defense sector.

Food crisis was the result of neglect of farm sector and low investment in agriculture. Fast growing population and hence rising demand for food was another factor precipitating the crisis. Community Development Projects and National Extension Services did not bring desired results and farm productivity was slow to rise. Land Reforms too went into the quagmire of court cases.

Food rationing was introduced in the country. Wheat was imported in large scale from the USA, Canada, Australia and other countries. With shortages and control of essential items flourished black marketing and black money generation which changed the entire politico-economic-socio scenario of the country in the coming decades. This was the beginning of the downfall of Gandhian values and morality.

By the start of seventies a new generation took command of economy and politics in India and its various offices and institutions. They completely forgot who Gandhi was and what his values were. The institutions of governance came into the hands of people uncommitted to social values. Self-interest in politics and economic fields began to dominate the scenario. Politico-economic forces and institutions were being made corrupt by money power and muscle power.

Yet another war with Pakistan in 1971 further made the economy go back several years. Notwithstanding, rays of hope came in the form of the Green Revolution whose seeds were planted in the form of a 'new strategy of agricultural development' in the mid-sixties. We got success in Pakistan war. On the farm front too, we succeeded in breaking the food crisis to a large extent. However, much of the seventies faced double digit inflationary pressure, large scale unemployment and rampant poverty. Much of the inflation was owing to quadrupling of petroleum price by the OPEC. The objective of our Five Year Plan attempted to address the above problems.

Early seventies is regarded by many thinkers as the period of sharp decline of nationalism and Gandhian economic ideology and domination of self-interest in public life. Powered by economy of controls and authoritarianism, rampant corruption, and black money a parallel economy was flourishing side by side. The growth rate of parallel economy far exceeded the growth rate of real economy.

While Gandhi regarded economics a moral science and has laid tremendous emphasis on its ethical aspect, the people of new generation, born and brought up in Free India, completely neglected those values of Gandhian era. The system was fast moving in the opposite direction.

By eighties Indian economy was described as "Tiger in the cage." Attempts to liberalize started during this period and economy picked up. The rate of growth of gross domestic product crossed the barrier of 3 to 3.5 per cent and moved ahead of five per cent.

Political scenario in the country greatly changed after the death of Pandit Nehru and subsequent down fall of the Congress party which erstwhile had been commanding single party majority in Parliament and Council houses of the states. It was partly due to the authoritarian attitude of Indira Gandhi and partly due to the rise of the peasant class which attained economic power as a result of the Green Revolution. They wanted to share the political power too which was by now understood as the 'real' power. The rise of Janata Party and other regional parties could be attributed to this factor.

This time will also be remembered for the beginning of criminal's entry into politics.

Eighties will also be remembered for Mandal divide and reservations in government jobs. This was another death knell to Gandhi's way of achieving things. Gandhi and other senior leaders in Congress party wanted elimination of the caste system from the country. Caste system in India had divided the whole population in the country and had given rise to hatred and feelings of superiority and inferiority not based on merit or qualifications but on birth. Untouchability was the result of this very system.

During mid-eighties certain developments in other countries of the world also greatly affected the entire scenario. The USSR disintegrated and the Cold war between Communist and Capitalist ideologies ended in favour of the latter. Arguments of "egalitarianism" faded before competition and "efficiency" of the market economy system. There was a virtual revolt for freedom in so-called Socialist countries of the world against authoritarian regimentation, economic inefficiency and widespread poverty.

In India too people were fed up, by the time, with inefficiency of the government sector and performance of the public sector undertakings, which had started loosing heavily. "Weariness from planning" had started emerging among people. The country was in the grip of large scale unemployment.

In the beginning of the nineteen nineties, Indian economy was in serious foreign exchange crisis and its credibility had dipped. In the circumstances, Narasimha Rao government introduced Economic Reforms in the form of liberalisation, marketisation and privatisation. This period is also marked by rise of money power in politics and economics. Money bags started descending upon New Delhi to make and unmake the governments in the centre. Situation in the states was much worse with the large scale entry of criminal elements in Council houses. Even Parliament was not untouched with it. Election Commission of India had got full records of criminal cases pending against parliamentarians and members of legislative assemblies. The situation completely negates Gandhi's social values, economic ideologies and his code of self-less service in public life. Politics is good in isolation. So is economics. But when politics enters into the realm of economics and/or economics enters into politics the downfall becomes limitless.

In the present scenario people come into politics not only for political power or to serve people but mainly for economic power attached with it. Political power generates income. And income is needed to win elections. So the money power propels the political power. It ensures political power. As there is no income without political power it is necessary to somehow remain in power. This politico-economic nexus was unthinkable at the time of Gandhi.

PART III

DEVELOPMENTAL ISSUES BEFORE INDIA IN THE POST-REFORM PERIOD AND GANDHI'S RELEVANCE

In India of 21st century we visualize a dichotomy. The realities are conflicting and much harsh than at the time of Gandhi. The economy is growing at a high rate of eight to nine per cent, the stock market is booming, our foreign exchange reserve is at a comfortably high level, and free trade is bringing to our homes a variety of goods and services simply unimaginable even a couple of decades ago as a mark of the benefit of globalisation. We are every day reminded that India is poised economically and politically as an emergent world power.

Once one step outside the charmed circle of privileged minority expounding the virtues of globalisation and liberalisation we enter into an India of despair and grief. It is a world of those wretched ones living below poverty line where growth has not reached. It is a world of rising farmer suicides, naxalism, terrorism, hatred, communal violence and widespread squalor. There are families who do not have access to safe drinking water. There are no toilets in the house and the inhabitants are compelled to ease themselves in open fields and around railway tracks. Ladies feel shy and come out only when darkness descends. This is dark India without basics of life.

Looking at a conservative official statistics, between 2001 and 2006 in four states of Andhra, Karnataka, Kerala, and Maharasthra more than 9000 farmers committed suicide. According to another estimate of the Ministry of Home Affairs, some 120 to 160 out of total of 607 districts in 14 states are Naxal infested. Supported by a disgruntled and dispossessed peasantry, the movement has spread to nearly one-fourth of Indian territory. Of the affected districts the revolutionary movement is intense in 90 districts while the remaining districts have seen mass organisation activity/ underground squad movement, but not revolutionary violence.

The unrest in society indicates towards large income disparity prevailing in economy. Had the fruits of economic development trickled to the bottom rung of society the crisis situation would not have arisen.

Besides, we may address the problems with another angle and include some more issues. Here the problems pertain to three Ps: poverty, population and pollution. Though poverty had come down significantly over the past decades it is still sizeable. Around 260 million people as per official estimates are below the poverty line. And this size matches the entire population of India at the start of the 20th century. It is much more than the entire population of many countries in the world. Hence we find not one but two or three India living simultaneously. One is poor and the other is rich. A poverty curtain divides them. One is poised to jet age the other one still languishing in bullock cart age. One is rural and backward the other is urban and modern. In one India income level is very high and there are problems to manage money. In the other one people are starving and desperately looking for some gainful employment for survival. In one India there is talk about higher and higher quality of life; in other for life itself.

At the same time the excess of industrial growth in the developed countries of the world has presented yet another problem of Environmental pollution and Global Warming. They talk about its 'sustainability'. There is concern about 'limits to growth'. As a result of rising environmental pollution level life sustenance itself is threatened. The developed countries are returning back to nature. Their consumption pattern is heading increasingly towards natural products.

In India we are following western model of economic development and still lean on industrial development to raise the rate of growth and ignore the farm sector. The rate of growth of farm sector is around 2.7 per cent and there is condition of somewhat stagnation. Rural income is consequently not rising. This is when the dependence on agriculture is still substantial. More than 60 per cent of population still live in rural areas and are dependent upon agriculture and allied industries. But in the wake of our emphasis on industry we ignored this sector. Problem of "food security" is looming large before the country.

Ideologically we are in a state of vacuum. Our objective of a Socialistic Pattern of Society has already lost steam. Our Mixed Economy is dissipating and public sector is increasingly giving way to private sector. And now our policy-makers are under the pressure of Crony Capitalism of market. We have not yet developed our own model of development. We ignored Gandhi since the beginning and reached a state of frustrating materialism. We are following the way of consumerism and heading towards the quagmire of materialism. This is a path towards frustration and strife and violence. We can not avoid confrontation and it could be violent whose signals are already coming in.

In the 21st century Gandhi and his economic philosophy is relevant for two reasons. One for showing the path of survival to human beings which is threatened due to misutilisation of natural endowments and disturbing natural order; and secondly, to establish economic and social justice for the poor and destitute living in India and other poor countries of the world.

The world today is threatened by terrorism, hatred and violence. Even the mighty countries do not consider themselves safe. Gandhi is remembered by the world community for his universal message of Non-Violence and Truth. We may not like his tools of Charkha or his emphasis for cottage industries in the changed circumstances of 21st century India. But his basic objectives of "work to every hand

and food to every mouth" have to be ensured to check confrontation.

The message of Gandhi can never be obsolete. They are the message from Vedic philosophy whose objective is to upgrade the man itself. Vedas have asked man "manur bhavah." Be Human. And spread humanity. People will return to this ultimate path of peace and happiness when they would be exhausted of consumerism and materialism.

2

Gandhian Equity and Justice

A Comparative Study with the Neo-classical and Rawlsian Approach

MRINAL KUMAR DASGUPTA

From ancient days the words like justice, equity, fairness, equality, etc. were repeatedly included in the writings of many renowned authors. We find that these concepts were abstract in nature and thus the term social justice which included economic justice and many others that were not at all quantifiable was considered very important. In this paper we have tried to search for the relevance of M.K. Gandhi's idea on equity and social justice in comparison to those ideas in the economic framework. The ideas on justice and equity in the neo-classical writing often bring incompatibility against the rules and laws of economics as has been explained by them. As for example accepting the neo-classical assumptions of uncontrolled capitalism, absolute individual freedom and the impartial character of the state bring tremendous distortions. Thus the growth of economic justice (horizontal, vertical and distributive justice) have become incompatible with the prevailing feature of economic studies, viz. the existence of inequality, alienation, destruction of environment, the subjugation of women and so on. Further, to have the distributive justice attempted by John Rawls by augmenting inequality also brings non-commensurable and conflicting results. Economic justice, therefore, can be accommodated with respect to several condition, viz. time, space and social groups. Under such circumstances Gandhian approach with the concepts of 'Trusteeship', 'Non-Possession', 'Non-violence' and 'Decentralisation' would raise new hope for bringing equity and justice to all sections of people. However, even in Gandhian case the practicability of his ideas against the astonishing technological growth in the 21st century has brought a question mark.

I. INTRODUCTION

The concepts of 'Justice', 'Equity', 'Equality', etc. are more philosophical in nature than economics. The abstract nature of these terms seems to be incompatible and conflicting against the rigorous nature of economic analysis which always seeks to quantify the economic variables that are related to human behavior. The economists particularly the classical and the neo-classical ones elaborated endlessly the terms utility, consumer sovereignty and marginal products. They adopted the overall perspectives of commodity society as the unquestionable limits of their own aspirations which led them being sycophants of inequality, alienation, destruction of the environment, imperialism, racism and the subjugation of women. Thus arise the monotonous recitation of the concepts of free choice, competition and the market. Private property is taken as a beneficial sociological necessity. Everything outside the absolute efficient productive engine, every aspect of human relations is taken as outside economics. Under the circumstances the inclusion of Justice and Equity is the economic analysis brings vagueness in drawing the preference pattern as utility maximisation is the guiding principle of individual behavioral pattern. If the society is reduced to privatized self-seeking individuals what type of justice or equity would work in the economic analysis? Still in the

Adamsmithian academic economics by virtue of invisible hand the market is cleared and the system is stable and self-reproducing. Thus there is no conflict, no social tensions, no exploitation, no imperialism or wars and as a result justice and equity are automatic phenomena. Thus the classical and the neo-classical writers have often talked about equity principle and justice in terms of price and distribution.

But Gandhi basically was a social reformer in the political framework and he was never a formal economist. Thus his ideas on justice and equity are more philosophical than economic. He did not interpret justice and equity in terms of Economic Laws and Rules. However, Gandhi in his writing in *Harijan* (October 1937) mentioned that true economics would stand for social justice which would promote good of all equally including the weakest. Further, in his opinion justice and equity are indispensable for decent life. Gandhi interpreted social justice in the domain of economic equality. Gandhi's idea of equity and justice are not inconformity with the idea of automatic process of equilibrium and stability through invisible hand as has been interpreted in the 'Wealth of Nation' written by Adam Smith. Further, the neo-classicists under the leadership of Marshall (1842-1924) and A.C. Pigou (1877-1959) though advocated economics of welfare yet they were skeptical about the socialist proposal of reducing income and wealth disparities for justice and equity. H.D. Hunderson and L. Robbins in their writing demanded certain postulates for reducing inequality. In their opinion the basket of national income should be increased for doing justice. If necessary they advocated an extension of the state sector. Similarly, Keynes suggested increase of public investment on larger scale. In his writings emphasis was not directly on economic justice but on full employment as an essential component for justice and equity. The classical and neo-classical ideas of equity are mostly concentrated to horizontal and vertical equity[1] which they described as source of justice and fairness. But the Harvard University philosopher John Rawls advocated the distributive justice for fairness and equity. From the above facts we understand that the concepts of justice, equity, fairness, etc. are considered by the economists for stability and welfare. However, they differ in their conceptual framework of the term and sometimes certain paradoxical situation arises by accepting their ideas on justice and equity.

Gandhiji, however, interpreted economic equality and social justice in a very broad sense. He actually introduced the concept of 'Trusteeship' for reducing inequality and bringing justice to the vast poor mass particularly in the context of backwardness of so-called low caste and 'Dalit community' in India. Gandhiji's concept of equal distribution is quite different from that of socialist concept. Gandhiji collaborated the principles of trusteeship for equal distribution.[2] Gandhiji envisaged trusteeship as the protector of equity and justice in an ideal state which was his basic political philosophy. In Gandhian ideal state everything is voluntary—no force, no coercion but all people having property should hold it in trust for society willingly. But in socialist state, state becomes the supreme authority for production and distribution. Individual entrepreneurship with profit motive is considered to be non-commensurate and conflicting to social justice. Thus voluntary action of individual propertied class in Gandhian sense can never achieve the goal of bringing justice and equity.

II. JUSTICE: NEOCLASSICAL ECONOMICS, GANDHIAN TRUSTEESHIP AND THE ROLE OF STATE

During the late 19th century and the beginning of the 20th century, free enterprise economy invaded the markets in Europe and North America. Economists shifted their focus of attention from fundamental social issues to efficient resource allocation. The essential social and economic institutions of capitalism were assumed, generally with a very little argument or justification, to be natural and inevitable. Thus fierce competition would force the people towards rat race and ultimately equity and justice become non-commensurable with the basic objectives of neo-classical school. Marshall's attempt to synthestise the various conflicting tendencies in the economic thought at the beginning of the 20th century confirms the idea. In his 'Principles' he mentioned, "The present treatise is an attempt to present a modern version of the old doctrines with the aid of new work and with reference to the new problems of our own age." Actually the welfare aspect of Marshallian economics was developed by A. C. Pigou and from his writings it is understood that Marshall had much to say on the influence of 'progress' on the standards of life, but he did not see that such progress might increase the poverty of the working classes and increases unemployment contradicting Marxian view. However, Marshall regarded government ownership as desirable when monopoly was unavoidable, but was in general against public enterprise.

Marshall thought that government should actively participate in the fields like advance urban planning, training of farmers, running the post offices, etc. Again in regard to equality in distribution, Marshall indents to support government intervention cautiously. His greatest worry was about the impact of income redistribution on the rate of saving in the economy.

Unlike Marshall, Gandhi was totally silent on state's role. His total thrust was on voluntary activities of the propertied class. In this regard the theory of trusteeship puts forth the novel idea of justice and equity. In the concept of trusteeship he ruled out the ownership of natural resources by individual. He mentioned "all lands belong to Gopal" which indicates that ownership of land is not compatible with equity and justice. Under trusteeship people should shun the instincts like greed, accumulation of wealth, etc. and be satisfied with basic needs. They should not demand more than what they need for living. Thus under Neo-classical Economics the idea of profit maximisation policy under free enterprise is totally non-commensurable and conflicting to Gandhian idea of complete cessation of accumulation of private riches and private property. Thus as everything is voluntarily done under trusteeship, there is neither violence nor bloodshed and just society will automatically come to be evolved. Equity and justice will prevail under propertyless and exploitation-free society. The competitive market in neo-classical society is replaced by cooperative society in Gandhian system. He expected that there should be complete harmony and cooperation between producer and consumer.

One of the leaders of neo-classical economics A.C. Pigou (1877-1959) who was almost a contemporary of M.K Gandhi (1869-1948) applied himself to the fundamental problem of economic action, e.g. Laissez Faire. His original 'Wealth and Welfare' (1911) developed into the 'Economics of Welfare' in 1921. 'Wealth and Welfare' may be described as a systematic and ordered enquiry into all cases where government may be justified in intervening in the workings of the economic system. In his presentation of the theory of welfare economics, Pigou deviating from Marshall's analysis contends that man's object is not wealth as such but welfare.

Pigou's greatest dilemma was the relationship between the economic interests of individuals on one hand, and those of the community, on the other. Some times to fulfill the requirements for justice to individuals it may bring injustice to community and/or vice versa. Pigou was very much concerned with the extent to which the pursuance of the economic interests of individuals will occasion an improvement in the economic conditions of the community. Further, to bring justice to future generation Pigou believed that economic welfare could be increased by a discriminatory taxation in favour of saving. However, Pigou was mainly concerned with competitive conditions where private and social marginal products automatically became equal. The optimum point (maxi minimisation of social justice) can be attained by equating the marginal private product of an industry to its marginal social product by a tax or a subsidy. Here state intervention is a requirement for social justice and equity. Gandhi, however, did not agree with the suggestion, he only stressed on voluntary individual selfless attitude which would bring justice to society.

Pigou's idea of justice stems from his 'marginal analyses' in case of social net product which is defined as "the aggregate contribution made to the national dividend" and the private net product as "the contribution that is capable of being sold and the proceeds added to the earnings of the person responsible for the unit of investment." Further, this theory of employment in conformity with the Keynesian one added the welfare of the people and thus would bring the justice to the backward section. Pigou's primary question was whether any important causes could be distinguished which would affect not only the size of the national dividend but the share going to the poor also. In explaining the effect of additional national dividend and employment on economic justice Pigou reached the Paretian conclusion on the law of the unchanging pattern of income distribution.[3]

But all these theoretical economic criteria were fulfilled by humanistic point on welfare of mankind by Gandhi through his economic philosophy of Gram Swaraj. He religiously emphasized on the development of Khadi and cottage industries particularly on spinning of yarn with the aid of Charkha. By adopting complete decentralizing policy he advocated 'Gram Swaraj' through Khadi and cottage industries to absorb surplus agricultural labour which at length would create sustainable growth of employment opportunity to reduce poverty and thus bring equity and justice. It is very simplified prescription. In his analysis the intricacies and incompatibility of neo-classical economics is absent. Gandhi emphasized on non-possession by which he meant possession by all. Neo-classical idea of additional profit through large scale industry was unacceptable to Gandhiji. He always emphasized re-distribution of income and assets in favour of the poor. Thus the concentration of economic power in the hands of a few is 'fait-accompli' in case of neo-classical economic idea and from that point justice and equity are tried to be achieved. But Gandhi condemned such concentration of economic power in the hands of a few which is the basic source of injustice and inequality. In his simplistic view Gandhi considered accumulation of wealth and the concentration of economic power which are mainly due to the centralisation of large scale production would bring injustice to the society. As a solution he advocated decentralisation in the field of small scale production units.

III. ECONOMIC JUSTICE UNDER FORMAL WELFARE ECONOMICS IN COMPARISON TO GANDHIAN WELFARE CONCEPT

Gandhian welfare concept stems from humanistic point of view. He considered welfare of mankind from 'Non-possession' aspect which is the result of his outstanding contribution of 'Trusteeship' and 'Non-violence'. Thus equity and justice are automatic phenomena under his idea of general welfare of mankind. But in the new welfare economics the basic idea was converted into a policy postulate of the gainers from a change compensating the losers. There are two extreme cases. First, the gainers are fully and/or just fully compensating the losers and still remaining gainer. Secondly, the gainer over compensate the losers without any worsening of their position below the pre-change situation. Doing justices to all levels, the criteria of new welfare economics, however, bring certain difficulties in measuring gains and losses, identifying them and devising an actual method of transfer. Again theoretically a paradoxical situation arises when we consider a corner point of Edgworth-Bowley box where a single individual possesses all the incomes and others nothing. Any redistribution of income at that point will violate Paretian optimum. And after redistribution the poor will be gainers and the rich losers and ascending to new welfare criterion the poor should compensate the rich. So in the initial condition social desirability of distributional pattern should be considered in the presumption of compensation criterion. In the new welfare economics economic justice can be obtained provided optimality is reached and a distribution hypothesis can be brought into the picture in which the various conditions of optimality have been satisfied. Alternatively, one may start with social welfare function which may be adopted by some democratic political process or given certain conditions regarding the peakedness of the individual preferences derived from them. However, there is the difficulty that the individual preferences are not known and are not revealed except in certain conditions.

Thus in welfare economics economic justice is received through optimisation technique, even accepting the hazards of externalities. But if individual preference pattern is not known or if there is vagueness in the preference pattern, there are alternative methods of modeling vague preference, viz. Stochastic Orderings,[4] Binary Probabilities[5] and Fuzzy Representation.[6] Still it is difficult to have a conclusive answer to the question of vague preference. Hence to draw economic justice from the above criteria, subjective, philosophical and abstract conditions overrule the objective conditions. Thus ultimately Gandhian philosophical interpretation of Justice and Equity through the parameters of "non-possession" and "non-stealing" is considered to be quite relevant in case of welfare economics. In case of Gandhiji welfare of mankind comes through societal relation between different groups. Equitable distribution is possible through trusteeship under which he saw divinity in man that helps in relinquishing pride, greed and lust. Thus comes social justice which is in no way connected with the rigorous theoretical exercise of welfare economics as has been described previously. Practically Gandhiji believed not in unlimited material advancement, but in a well ordered society where securing livelihood for each individual should be the principal objective. So his concept of social justice and equity is related to lead a simple life in the framework of non-possession.

IV. GANDHI AND RAWLS

In case of both Gandhi and Rawls justice and equity are interpreted more philosophically than economically. To Gandhi the supreme consideration has always been man. His ideas were based on love, truth and non-violence and sacrifice. But Rawls' interpreted his ideas on justice and equity in rigorous economic framework particularly through the tools of welfare economics initiated by Pareto.

John Rawls, in his book, 'A Theory of Justice' argues that a just arrangement of society is that in which individuals would choose if they were uninfluenced by their own purely personal vested interests. As a metaphor for this disinterested state, individuals are imagined to enter into an agreement or social contract, about the nature of society while behind a "veil of ignorance" which prevents them from knowing what position (in terms of sex, race, ability and so on) they will occupy in the society. The characteristics of Rawlsian institution are such as:

(a) each individual would enjoy equal rights to maximum amount of personal freedom compatible with the freedom of other individuals,

(b) all inequalities in society would—

  (i) be derived from positions open to free competition; and

  (ii) be justified only in so far as the inequalities operated to everyone's advantage.

Rawls in his 'A Theory of Justice' (1972) mentioned two principles. The first principle states, "Each person is to have an equal right to the most extensive total system of equal basic liberties, compatible with a similar system of liberty for all." The second principle accepted inequality and held that "social and economic inequalities are to be so arranged that are both—

(a) to the greatest benefit of the least advantaged, consistent with the just saving principles; and

(b) attached to offices and positions open to all under conditions of fair equality of opportunity."

The characteristic related to inequalities operated to everyone's advantage is called as "difference principle" by Rawls and from this the optimisation techniques in economics can be interpreted.

The adoption of the difference principle by individuals in the original position may be explained in terms of the 'Maxmin' Strategy which is used in 'Game Theory'. Further the principle ensures each individual of the greatest possible protection against the risk being the poorest member of the society. The Rawlsian system recognizes the imperfections of the market which is at every point a deviation from the perfect competitive model, but still feels that the actual system is more or less competitive and is, therefore, not only efficient but also is consistent with equal liberties and a fair equality of opportunities. Gandhi laid stress on individual behavior through attitudinal change so that individuals are ready to sacrifice their belongings to accept voluntary poverty. Justice through income inequality is not acceptable to Gandhi where as Rawls' difference principle allows unequal positions which may be better for the society. The principle can be explained by the use of standard diagrammatic apparatus of elementary welfare economics.

FIG 1

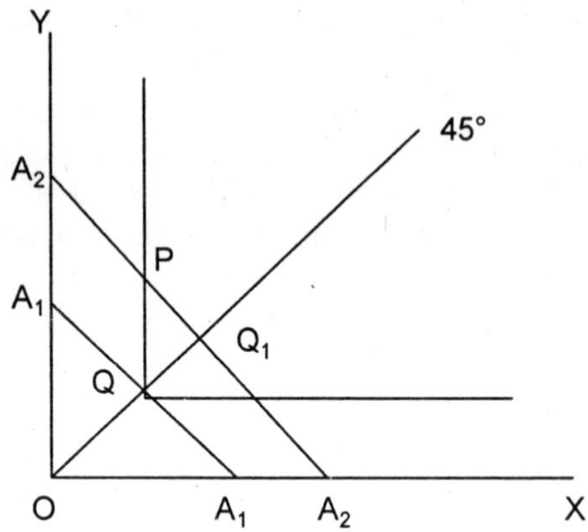

FIG 2

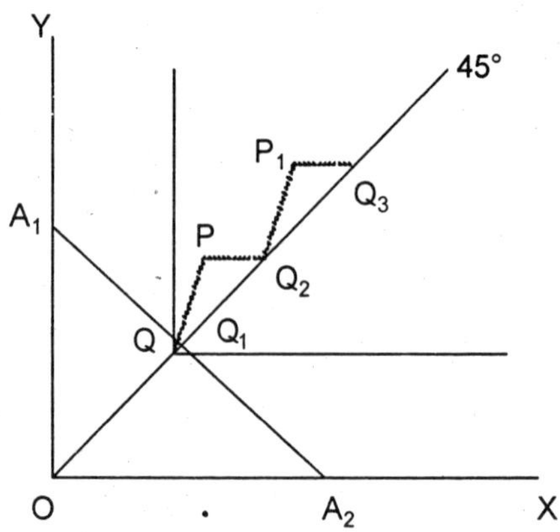

Supposing a two individual society with a stock of homogeneous goods which could be distributed between the individuals. We may draw a distribution-possibility line A_1A_1, total stock being OA_1. The 45° line in the Fig. 1 represents equal distribution and the relevant point on A_1A_1 is Q. Then the subquadrant with origin Q will represent an improved position for both individuals X and Y or in the Paratian sense at least one enjoys improved position without any loss of the other. With a rise in the total stock (shown by the distribution possibility line A_2 A_2). Now if this rise is possible only under conditions that P is the new equilibrium position drifting from Q_1 on 45° line such that Y enjoys relatively better position though both reach to higher stock bracket. Now whether shifting of Q to P keeps social justice intact or not. According to Rawls it is justified. But in case of Gandhi if from Q it reaches to P instead of Q_1 (as shown in Fig. 2), then in view of acceptance of trusteeship and non-possession, Y individual will move from P to Q_2 at a higher distribution possibility line. In this way whatever inequality comes, the equilibrium converges with 45° line.

V. CONCLUSION

From the foregoing analysis we may observe that equality of opportunity in the strict economic framework is based on competitiveness in the classical sense. It makes competitiveness into a virtue and tends to subvert other values such as those of tolerance, amity, generosity,, etc. Theoretically, economic laws are tried to be framed avoiding any sort of value judgment in the economic analysis. In the absence of level playing field equality of opportunity, however, is abandoned and the concept of welfare state is accepted. Thus we see that there is always some confusion and anomaly in interpreting economic justice in the neo-classical and Rawlsian cases.

In case of neo-classical school we have seen that through uncontrolled capitalism the basic objective, i.e. the efficient allocation of resources is achieved. Thus, there is some sort of trade-off between the basic objective and the restoration of economic justice for the greater section of population. In case of welfare economics normative approach assumes valuc judgments which are impossibility in positive economics.

Rawls' just society is characterized by the fact that each individual would enjoy equal rights to the maximum amount of personal freedom compatible with the freedom of other individuals. In his opinion equality of opportunity carried to its limits leads to callous meritocratic society. But Rawls' emphasis on acceptability for socially desirable inequality has very little operational meaning. The basic feature of Rawlsian system is the efficiency of the competitive system and on the basis he laid down his two main principles viz.,

(a) equal rights and equal basic liberties,
(b) social and economic inequalities are to be arranged so that—
   (i) a less intensive liberty must strengthen the total system of liberty shared by all, and
   (ii) a less than equal liberty must be accepted to those with "lesser liberty."

Thus the words like "less intensive liberty", "lesser liberty" can in no way be quantified in economic sense and thus confusing.

Under such circumstances arises the relevance of Gandhian concepts of justice and equity. He does not formalize his ideas on justice in the framework of economic laws and rules. In a very simple approach his basic idea depends on certain human values namely honesty, love, truth, non-violence, etc. his supreme condition has always been welfare of mankind through trusteeship based on non-possession. Thus his economic thinking on justice is limited with individual response towards society's good. Further, the behavioral pattern of various groups of the society is considered to be ideally sympathetic, non-possessional character and full of contentment. The result is that the property owners would utilize their property for the benefit of the society. The result is that the property owners would utilize their property for the benefit of the society. The voluntary approach of the people is responsible for converting exploitative class to non-possessional attitude-oriented class who will ultimately help in bringing justice to society.

Thus in case of Gandhian thought everything depends not on economic laws but on change of heart of people. He sincerely believed that divine intention of man would bring real justice. So moral and spiritual forces are the guiding principles for the restoration of justice and equity. Gandhiji himself practiced these guiding principles all through his life.

It is however, a very debatable point that whether one or two person's change of heart brings such change to the man's character or that of a community or class. So whether Gandhian philosophical idea will be considered as wishful thinking or a reality could be judged by the posterity in view of vast and astonishing technological invention.

Notes and References

1. Horizontal equity: Equity may be horizontal, vertical and distributional. Horizontal equity, in general, is the principal that like individuals should be treated in like manner where economic arrangements are concerned. The concept is most frequently used with regard to tax and income, thus horizontal equity is held to be attained if individuals with same income face the same tax burden. With regard to the benefits of public expenditure, horizontal equity may be said to require that individual with similar income or need should receive the same benefit. Vertical equity is mainly related to taxation and distribution of benefits.
2. "Indeed at the root of the doctrine of equal distribution must lie that of the trusteeship of the wealthy for the superfluous wealth possessed by them. For according to the doctrine they may not possess a rupee more than their neighbours. The rich man will be left in possession of wealth of which he will use what he reasonably requires for his personal needs and will act as a trustee for the remainder to be used for the society."
3. Pigou in his "The Economic of Welfare" reached the Paretian conclusion that "While in general and apart from special exceptions, anything that either increases the dividend without injuring the absolute share of the poor, or increases the absolute share without injuring the dividend must increase economic welfare..."
4. Stochasting orderings, or, more generally, stochastic binary relations may be used in modeling vague preferences and is defined over the universal set of alternatives under consideration. The framework is familiar enough from the large literature on: stochastic preferences and stochastic choice functions, but the formal framework was developed for a different purpose, and if it is to be used for modeling vague preferences, one needs to be careful about the interpretation of the formal theory.

5. For modeling vague preferences when stochastic binary relations defined over the universal set, are used by pair-wise stochastic preferences, it is known binary probability (B.P. Method).
6. Another way of modeling vague preference is fuzzy set theory which accommodate inherently in precise concepts.

REFERENCES

Arrow, K.J (1963): Social choice and individual values; 2nd edition, New York, John Wiley and Sons.

Betaille, Andre (1983): The Idea of Natural Inequality and other Essays. Oxford University Press.

Datta, B (1982): Social Justice in Mixed Economy – University of Calcutta.

Harijan (1937, October 9).

Harijan (1940, August 25).

Mishra, Baidyanath (1998): "Man at Centre of Development", *Yojna,* Vol. 42(10).

Rawls, J (1972): A Theory of Justice. Oxford University Press.

3

Relevance of Economic Ideas of Gandhi in 21st Century

HARINDRA KISHOR MISHRA

Gandhi in his living, thinking, teaching, and in his death is, an inexhaustible subject, with no beginning and no end. For a proper appreciation of the economic ideas of Gandhi, it is essential to bear in mind that he was not an economist in the technical sense of the term. As J.B. Kripalani puts it: "if ever there was a planner without elaborate blue prints Gandhi was one."

Gandhi is larger than economic science. He had not studied economics as a subject in the curriculum nor had he the opportunity of reading standard books on modern economics. He drew his thoughts on economic affairs from three sources. The first was his ethical and spiritual conviction, the second was his close involvement with the economic conditions of the people, particularly the rural people who formed over 80% of the country in his day, and the third was his reading and reflection and the results of his putting into action what he read of the Utopian Ruskin's 'Unto This Last' and Tolstoy's 'The Kingdom of God is within' you. The Bible also shaped his thoughts on social and economic matters. While in detention during the quit India movement, he found some time to read Marx's Das Capital.

The fullest statement of his views about ultimate criterion in the economic sphere is to be found in his December 22, 1916 speech at the Muir College, Economics Society in Allahabad. In that speech he declared: "I venture to think that the scriptures of the world are far safer and sounder treatises on laws of economics than many modern text-books... He (Jesus) is himself the greatest economist of his time." (Tendulkar, 1961, p. 195).

For him, real progress was "moral progress" and to use his somewhat startling words, "true economics stands for social justice and moral values." His ideal of true economics which was to "manufacture souls" and not material plenitude is also expressed in his unique language: "Let us seek first the kingdom of God and His righteousness and the irrevocable promise is that everything will be added to us. These are the real economics."

But we economists should realise that even as Gandhi thought and expressed himself thus, he was adhering to one of the two streams from which economics has flowed and grown—the ethical on the one hand and the engineering on the other—as one of the recent economic treatises reminds us. The ethical tradition as pointed out is the ancient Indian way of approaching any human problem, a tradition which includes Kautilya and Valluvar and more recently Vivekananda and Tagore in India, and Mill, Marx, and Marshall outside India. The engineering tradition is more recent and goes back to the French physiocrat, Quesnay, and our own Dadabhai Naoroji, and more recently to Leon Walras and the mathematical economists who have followed him.

Gandhi belonged to the ethical tradition and alleged his belief that economics is related to metaphysics and other human sciences with the reverberating words: "I must confess that I do not draw sharp or any distinction between economics and ethics. Ethics that hurts the moral well-being of an individual or a nation are immoral and therefore sinful. Thus the economics that permit one country to prey upon another are immoral." Eventually, I should say that I belong to the ethical tradition, because I am concerned with the ends as much as with the means of living.

Gandhi was of the confirmed view that economic development must precede other developments. We live in a world dominated by economic forces and economic ideas. Professor Marshall has observed: "Man's character has been moulded by his everyday work, and the material resources which he thereby procures more than by any other influence unless it be that of his religious ideals; and the two great forming agencies of the world's history have been the religious and economic... Undoubtedly, religious motives are more intense than economic but their direct action seldom extends over to large part of life (Marshall, 1948, p. 1).

According to Prof. C.N. Vakil, "One has to interpret Gandhiji's economic ideas and build-up what may be described as Gandhian Economic thought from what he did and said in this connection. Gandhian economic thought is based on four fundamental Principles: Truth, Non-violence, Dignity of Labour and Simplicity. One principle that played significant role in Gandhi's life was: simple living and high thinking. Gandhi was a practical idealist. The economics of Gandhi might also be described as the economics of non-violence. Gandhi opposed modern capitalism because it is based on the exploitation of human labour. To Gandhi, moral progress is more important than material progress."

There is an utter disregard of tradition, authority and moral precepts. Standards, aims and institutions which were generally accepted even a generation ago are now challenged and changing. Social distempers and tensions fill the atmosphere in place of mutual love, friendliness and sympathy. The whole world is driven by mutual distrust, jealousy, fear and suspicion. Poverty, violence and intolerance are on the increase. People, on one hand, clamour for the greater autonomy of individual, while on the other, demand an egalitarian society of the highest order. Social Scientists visualize no escape from the dilemma; "make man free and they become unequal, make them equal and they cease to be free." The outer uniformity produced by science and civilisation has not resulted in any inner unity of mind (Arora, 1981, p. 65).

The main problem is that centralised political and economic power has failed. Capitalist economy and society are based on profit motive and the productive machinery remains in the hands of a few. The existing order is at the dead-end and the humanity is anxiously waiting for a new world order. The question arises how to build a good society in such a bad condition? In this context, the Gandhian economic thought has a relevance and presents a proper diagnosis to meet the challenges of the suffering of human-being.

His multifaceted life and personality, I want to limit myself rather narrowly to only one facet, that is Gandhiji's economic thoughts.

MACHINERY

It is sometimes thought that Gandhi was against machinery and modern technology as such. Industrialisation leads to excessive mechanisation. He described machinery as 'great sin'. He said that "Books could be written to demonstrate its evils...it is necessary to realise that machinery is bad. If instead of welcoming machinery as a boon, we should look upon it as an evil, it would ultimately cease." According to Gandhi, machinery is rooted in man's desire for bodily comforts at the cost of everything else, and ultimately it destroys the body itself by displacing it from the scheme of life. In other words, if craze for machinery continues, a time may come when man will be incapacitated and weak that he will begin to curse himself for forgetting the use of living machine human being itself.

This is an erroneous notion and has caused unnecessary misgivings about Gandhian economic thought. The idea that Gandhi was opposed to machinery on large scale production as such is one of the many superstitions about Gandhi. He was not against machinery in general. All machines are acceptable to Gandhi as long as they operate and function as 'servants' and not 'masters' of men and are beneficial to the whole society. He prized "every invention of science for the benefit of all and that he would welcome the machine that lightness the burden of crores of men living in Cottages. " As he put it," The spinning wheel itself is a machine, a little toothpick is a machine, what I object to is the craze for labour saving machinery. Men go on saving labour, till thousands are without work and thrown on the open streets to die of starvation... Today machinery merely helps a few to ride on the back of millions." He was against "the craze for machinery" and "its indiscriminate multiplication." To Gandhiji, "the supreme consideration is man."

Gandhiji felt the ground realities that sophisticated machinery is not just possible in India because of the availability of abundant unemployed labour force. He wrote in 1934, "Mechanisation is good when the hands are too few for the work intended to be accomplished. It is an evil when there are more hands than required for the work, as is the case in India." In 1938, in *Harijan* he wrote, "If I could produce all my country's wants by means of 30,000 people instead of 30 million, I should not mind it, provided that the thirty million are not rendered idle and unemployed." He was aware of the threat of technological unemployment. He stressed the need for labour-intensive methods of production in a country with surplus labour.

Mahatma's objection to the machine was not to machine *per se* but to the use of the machine for displacement or exploitation of human labour: "I am uncompromisingly against all destructive machinery. But simple tools and instruments and such machinery as saves individual labour and lightens the burden of millions of cottagers I should welcome."

Replying to Rabindranath Tagore, who criticised him for rejecting machinery with all its potentialities for alleviating the hard economic lot of man, Gandhi wrote: "I do want growth, I do want self-determination, I do want freedom, but I want all these for the soul. I doubt if the steel age is an advance upon the flint age. I am indifferent. It is the evolution of the soul to which the intellect and all our faculties have to be devoted."

His ideas on machinery are still relevant. In spite of approximately six decades of planned and machine using and power driven economic development in India, unemployment is still existing and is growing in abundant proportion. Prof. Arthur Lewis has also deprecated the "high capital-intensity of the modern sector" and has condemned "irrational preferences for spending lavishly on structures for using the latest techniques, and for large rather than small units of operation."

It is usually claimed that modern mechanisation would ultimately provide larger volume of employment through its spread effects. This assumption has also been rejected by Prof. Myrdal. He has definitely asserted that the 'spread effects' of large-scale industries are more than neutralised and negatived by the 'backwash effects:' "There is a real risk that the slight increase in demand for labour on new modern enterprises will be more than offset by reductions in labour demands in traditional manufacturing." The learned economist concludes: "There was an essential element of rationality in Gandhiji's social and economic gospel, and the programmes for promoting cottage industry as they have been evolved in the post-war era, have come more to represent purposeful and realistic planning for development."

Several modern thinkers in western countries have termed the existing economic situation in developing countries as 'the tragedy of mere affluence.' The modern industrial structure, with large-scale mechanisation, has given birth to a few giant business corporations which tend to reduce even the state to a subservient position and bind the Establishment to, what Prof. Galbraith calls, a "Technostructure," consisting of specialists, planners and technicians. In order to avoid the perils of such an industrial system, the professor recommends the strong assertion of "other goals" so that the new industrial state would become "responsive to the larger purposes of the society." These "goals" must essentially be cultural and spiritual in accordance with Gandhiji's ideals and programmes. We have to develop 'middle' or 'intermediate' technology according to the needs of underdeveloped regions. Machine has to subserve the interests of man, it should not be permitted to make man merely a cog in its wheel. Renowned American Sociologist, Lewis Mumford, terms in a different context, a 'megamachine' or 'labour machine'. In this way we can generate employment for enormous physical labour in developing countries to meet the challenges of the 21st century, is the need of the hour. The Government has decided to establish SEZ to imitate on the pattern of highly developed countries. SEZ is a means to achieve growth and employment, which industry is eager to utilize effectively. Whatever the future or impact to generate employment may be is uncertain but on the issue of land acquisition, it is opposed by common masses on the path of Gandhian way in initial stage.

Gandhi emphatically declared his ideas about the use of machinery: "I entertain no fads in this regard. All that I desire is that every citizen of India who is willing to work should be provided with employment to earn his livelihood. If electricity or even atomic energy could be used without ousting human labour and creating unemployment I will not raise any little finger against it. I am, however, still to be convinced that this would be possible in a country like ours where population is large and capital scarce."

Gopalkrishnan asserts that Gandhiji would have heavy machinery as well provided the state owned it on behalf of the community. There was, however, to be no place for the use of machinery meant to enrich some individuals at the cost of others. He wanted production by masses and not mass production of the modern industrial type.

Technology has entered now irrational phase of making society subject to all-pervading technological determinism. While widening choices, it is reducing human capacity to choose because of man-machine imbalance. By plundering and destroying nature, technology is ironically bringing man back to the position of man-nature conflict. While creating a strong possibility for a world view, it is distorting man's view of himself. Technology in a few hands is becoming a barrier to the solution of the human problems. Having removed poverty in some areas, it has now launched man on to the ocean of greed, avarice, selfishness, and imperialism. Technology is shrinking the world but widening the gap between human beings. It is creating a synthetic civilisation of human robots making it possible for one set of men to manipulate others through psychoanalytical devices. Technology is providing all the needed instruments for destroying human freedom (Sethi, 1979, pp. 37-38).

DECENTRALISATION

Like Karl Marx, Gandhi was a philosopher, a great social thinker, a prophet and an economist. Adam Smith built up a system of free economy, Karl Marx a system of 'Violent Socialist Economy,' whereas Gandhi built a system of decentralised non-violent economy. The Gandhian model of decentralised economy and planning centers round his ideas about economic philosophy, decentralisation, machinery, emphasis on agriculture and tiny sector, cooperatives, distributive justice, employment, mixed economy and the doctrine of trusteeship,, etc.

The old order is cracking, none of the burning problems affecting mankind are finding a solution in the existing order. Suffering of the humanity with the increase in population has aggravated. Traditional economics have made earnest efforts to find some kind of a relief. No practical solution is visible. The real cause is that centralised political and economic power has failed. Capitalist economy and society are based on profit motive and the productive machinery remains in the hands of a few. In this context, the Gandhian doctrine of decentralisation becomes effective and relevant in changing scenario.

Gandhiji believed that mechanised economy model is no longer valid model and salvation of masses lies in a decentralised organic economy. A centralised economy leads to the concentration of population in the cities, leading to many problems of urbanisation, gangesterism, alienation from society and natural surroundings leading to slums, pollution of the atmosphere, problems of housing and water supply, acceptance of material values as against spiritual, violence and crimes and many other social values are its natural consequences, centralisation has caused inequalities among the people, conflicting interest, warring classes, wasteful competitions, dehumanized markets, over-production of luxurious and harmful articles while the basic needs are starving and the degradation of skilled workers. It is owing to centralisation that western Europe practiced the colonial exploitation of the countries of Asia, Africa and Latin America and greatly divided the world between rich countries comprising of the nations of western Europe, North America and Australia and the poor countries of Asia, Africa and Latin America. Gandhiji's economic critique of imperialism is non-Marxist in origin tracing back to the influences of Naoroji, Rusking, Gokhale and Tolstoy. Gandhiji visualised a decentralised economic order where there would be no exploitation social or economic of man by man.

Decentralisation of productive activity is an other essential element of Gandhian Economic Thought. It favours widely dispersed cottage and, small industry using labour-intensive techniques as a solution to the problems of a labour surplus economy and does not see any sense in pushing through gigantic programmes of industrialisation which might increase material wealth but do impoverish the masses. Large scale industry leads to concentration, greed, exploitation, inequality and slums. In this respect, there is much confusion about the place of modern technology and industry in the Gandhian Economic thought. This theory is not an uncompromising opponent of power-driven machinery and modern large scale industry. It is opposed to craze for machinery and not to machinery as such if it does not render labour surplus. Gandhi said, "If we could have electricity in every village home, I should not mind villagers using their implements and tools with the help of electricity.... But where there is no machinery, no electricity what are the idle hands to do? Will you not give them work..?" (Ganguli, 1977, p. 254)

In his philosophy of Sarvodaya, Gandhi gives an integrated approach to decentralisation and seeks to decentralise life in all its aspects—political, economic and social. According to Gandhiji, decentralisation is one of the means to create classless unexploited and egalitarian society. The word decentralised sector in economics is used to refer the cottage industries, located in the rural areas, but infact, the Gandhian concept of decentralisation is related to the rural economy as a whole. When Gandhiji used the term khadi village industries, swadeshi and the like, he meant decentralisation of production and direct corelation between consumption, production and utilisation of locally available resources. The quintessence of Gandhian socialism is a bold and planned decentralisation of economic and political power all along the line.

The basic idea behind the Gandhian development strategy are two-fold. On the one hand, the strategy is one of redirection of investment flows towards the more labour-intensive sectors of activity and the adoption of certain criteria concerning technological innovations. On the other hand, it is also a strategy of progress towards a collaborative economic order. This approach leads to an elaborate development strategy which specifies the content of development programmes, the agency structure for the implementation of these programmes, the instruments of development policy, the proper use of foreign trade opportunities, and the modus operandi through which the instruments of economic policy are to be coordinated (Das, 1979, p. 96).

Many Countries of the world are thinking in terms of decentralisation. Even from the standpoint of defence and foreign aggression, decentralisation and ruralisation of industries is a necessity. The centralised industries provide an easy target for air-bombing, and the destruction of a few industrial centers not only makes the country militarily more vulnerable but also throws the whole economic life of the country completely out of gear. As a result, the industrialised countries like Germany, Japan and Great Britain are now planning to decentralize their production with a view to strengthening their defensive capacity on the economic front. The real secret of Chinese success against Japanese powerful aggression lies in the wonderful organisation of the industrial cooperatives. Since India has yet to plan for the future, will it not be foolish to repeat the mistakes of other countries.

TRUSTEESHIP

Trusteeship provides the *modus operandi* to proceed in the direction of desired social transformation. Gandhiji says, "Trusteeship avoids the evils of violence, regimentation and suppression of individual liberty. Even if large sectors of industry were nationalised and put under state ownership the existence of individual enterprise alongside of it under a trusteeship system would prove a healthy antidote to slackness, inefficiency, corruption, lack of enterprise and bureaucratic autocracy which very often characterize state enterprise (Pyarelal, 1958, p. 15).

He was attempting to evolve something very big, namely, a comprehensive system which eliminated both capitalism and bureaucratic statism. No wonder, trusteeship was considered by many dogmatists as most fanciful or makeshift. Both Marxists and capitalists considered it as a camouflage in favour of the latter without their realising that Gandhi had aimed at quite the opposite. But Gandhi stood firm and said: "My theory of trusteeship is no makeshift, certainly no camouflage, I am confident it will survive all other theories."

He categorically states that: "...There is no other choice than between voluntary surrender on the part of the capitalists of superfluities and consequent acquisition of the real happiness of all on the one hand, and on the other the impending chaos into which, if the capitalist does not wake up betimes, awakened but ignorant, famishing millions will plunge the country and which, not even the armed forces, that a powerful government can bring into play can avert."

He made a distinction between "possession and Possessiveness." In his view, the evil lay not in possession as such but in the attitude of possessiveness. He desired the capitalists to become trustees of the nation by running their business with integrity and efficiency and for the welfare of the people.

The basic idea underlying trusteeship is quite simple. The rich man will be left in possession of his wealth, of which he will use what he reasonably requires for his present needs and will act as a trustee of the remaining to be used for the society. He allowed the people with talent to earn more but asked them to utilise their talent for the good of the poor people: "I would allow a man of talent to earn more. I would not cramp his talent. But the bulk of his greater earnings must be used for the good of the state, just as the income of all earning sons of the father go to the common family fund. They would have their earnings only as trustees,...i.e. owners not in their own right but owners, in the right of those whom they have exploited. I will not dictate to them what commission to take, but ask them to take what is fair, e.g., I would ask a man who possesses Rs. 100 to take Rs. 50 give the other Rs. 50 to the workers. But to him who possesses Rs. 100, 000, 000 I would perhaps say take one percent for yourself, so you see that my commission would not be fixed figure that would result in atrocious injustice."

He had so great faith in the doctrine of trusteeship that he believed that it would help the realisation of a state of equality on earth. His entire ideology is summed up in one phrase, i.e. a trustee has no heir but the public. The trusteeship formula, as approved of by Gandhi meant:

1. Trusteeship provides a means of transforming the present capitalist order of society into an egalitarian one. It gives no quarters to capitalism, but gives the present owning class a chance of reforming itself. It is based on the faith that human nature is never beyond redemption.
2. It does not recognize any right of private ownership of property, except so far as it may be permitted by society for its own welfare.
3. It does not exclude legislative regulation of the ownership and use of wealth.
4. Thus, under state regulated trusteeship, an individual will not be free to hold or use his wealth for selfish satisfaction or in disregard to the interest of the society.
5. Just. as it proposed to fix a decent minimum wage, even so a limit should be fixed for the maximum income that could be allowed to any person in society. The difference between such much minimum and maximum incomes should be reasonable and equitable and variable from time to time, so much so that the tendency would be towards obliteration of the difference.
6. Under the Gandhian economic order, the character of production would be determined by social necessity and not by personal whim or greed.

One day a multi-millionaire said to Gandhiji "I am prepared to renounce my millions and give up my business to follow you." Gandhi replied, "I do not want you to renounce either your millions or your business. I want to make use of both for the service of the poor." The most important thing in his trusteeship is his infinite faith in the goodness of an individual. According to him, each and every individual, whether he is rich or poor, has inherent goodness, and if given opportunity, he will certainly realise his responsibility and behave like a social being. Like Socialists, Gandhiji wanted to build a classless society by ending all exploitation. He wanted to avail an opportunity even to the worst exploiter to change his heart and mend his ways. Once he said, "My fundamental difference with socialists is well known. I believe in the conversion of human nature and am striving for it. They do not believe in this...." There must be voluntary conversion of the exploiting classes to the socio-economic justice. But if they do not, they cannot be allowed to own their property for their own benefit. Speaking about zamindars, he says, "I do not mean to destroy the zamindar, but neither do I feel that zamindars are indispensable." If zamindars do not change, "They will die a natural death."

After Indian independence, a significant step in the direction of trusteeship is Acharya Vinoba Bhave's Gramdan movement which has made considerable headway during the last few years. According to Professor D.R. Gadgil, "This Gramdan movement is an unprecedented movement with many and complex implications and very great potentialities." Louis Fischer has described it as "the most creative thought coming out of the East." Acharya Vinoba has often Called Gramdan a "defence measure," in so far as it tends to strengthen democracy at the grass roots and makes people self-reliant and conscious of their obligations to the community. But sorry to say that this great movement has not yet been able to create a visible impact on our national life, despite its immense potentialities in several spheres.

Critics often demur to the conception of trusteeship of which, they think, the capitalists take advantage in relation to their workers. To Gandhiji, however, the theory was a necessary corollary of non-violence; for "It was in order to avoid confiscation that the doctrine of trusteeship came into play, retaining for society the ability of the original owner in his own right (Das, 1999, p. 101).

Commenting on his ideas of trusteeship V.P. Patil and I.A. Lokopur writes, "the world will not implement his ideas for the simple reason that it is too late to change the path it has bestowed upon itself. When the world has reached a high state of industrialisation, how can it put the clock-back and embrace industrial primitivism? Moreover, there are many inconsistencies and gaps in his theory of trusteeship and it would require a great deal of expertise and thought on the part of contemporary scholars to develop a viable and relevant theory of trusteeship applicable to the modern period.

SWADESHI

Swadeshi is one of the most important principles of Gandhi's economic thought, as there exists a relationship between this doctrine and others, which are fundamental doctrines of Gandhian economics. In fact, to understand Gandhi's view of Swadeshi, one has to go through the entire gamut of his thought—social, political, economic and religious. Etimologically the term may mean 'of one's own country,' however, country's component is not its connotation but a sub-characteristics called 'Uplakshan' in Hindi. Accordingly, Swadeshi includes all indigenous things both abstract and concrete, namely, native language, wisdom, culture, dress and other products also. The core of the concept, however, is 'self-reliance' and 'self-governance' (Sharma, 2003, p. 99).

In the field of economics, the Principle of Swadeshi means that a person basically uses those things, which are produced, in his immediate neighbourhood and serves those industries by making them efficient and meaningful. By giving the best illustration, Gandhi explains: "Swadeshi is that spirit in us which restricts us to the use and service of our immediate surroundings to the exclusion of the more remote... In the domain of politics, I should make use of the indigenous institutions and serve them by curing them of their proved defects. In that of economics, I should use only things that are produced by my immediate neighbours and serve those industries by making them efficient and complete where they might be found wanting."

He defines swadeshi as the: "spirit which dictates man to serve his next door neighbour to the exclusion of any other." He further states that: "The neighbour thus served had in his turn to serve his own neighbour." In this sense swadeshi is never exclusive. It recognizes the scientific limitations of human capacity for service.

It might appear that by defining swadeshi as the spirit which restricts us to the use and service of our immediate surroundings and one who serves his immediate neighbour serve the world as a whole. Further Gandhi writes: "Our capacity for service has obvious limits. We can serve even our neighbours with some difficulty. If everyone of us duly performed his duty to his neighbour, no one in the world who needed assistance would be left unattended to. In this way one who serves his neighbours sees all the world."

Gandhiji had to take into consideration all these factors to devise a method by which the grinding poverty of the Indian masses could be mitigated, if not altogether removed. The only way was to revive the Swadeshi movement. The new movement had not only to solve the problem of consumption but also that of production. After all, it is production which would increase the quantum of employment. The object of the movement during the time of the Partition agitation was defeated by the Indian mill-owners. As the demand increased, they increased the price of cloth, and even passed off foreign cloth as made in India. In this respect Gandhiji was put right by a patriotic mill-owner in Bombay, who told him, "You are aware that in the days of partition (of Bengal), the mill-owners fully exploited the swadeshi movement. When it was at its height, they raised the price of cloth and did even worse things. We are not conducting our business out of philanthropy. We do it for profit (Kripalani, 2005, p. 381). He fully believed that a man could serve his neighbours and humanity at the same time, the condition being that the service of the neighbour was in no way selfish or exclusive, i.e. did not in any way involved the exploitation of any other human being.

The principle of Swadeshi demands that a person must give preference to local manufacturers even if they are of inferior quality or more costly than articles of foreign-made, they should try to search remedy these defects but not give up the use of those things. This is true swadeshi, is thus very helpful. There is no place for hatred for the foreign-made things also. He did not reject a foreign-made things simply because of its being foreign, he gladly used foreign-made things but only when there were no Indian substitute for them and it would have been a criminal waste of time and energy to try to produce them locally, for such swadeshi some times he used old swadeshi and new swadeshi, i.e. in old swadeshi goods must be produced in India and village and cottage industries must produce alternative goods for foreign goods is new swadeshi. He used the term real swadeshi for swadeshi which is 100% Indian.

There is a moral obligation for Indians to use products made in India whenever they can get them, even though these may be inferior to their counterparts. Gandhi pleaded: "there are several swadeshi things on the market which are in danger of disappearance for want of patronage. They may not be up to the mark. It is up to us to use them and require the makers to improve them whenever improvement is possible."

He has permitted international trade and exchange of commodities if this meant an exchange of equal advantages and did not involve injustice. However, if it was to be a question of choice, he would have preferred self-sufficiency. But as a matter of practical policy he did not think that India should stand aloof in the matter of trade: "I would not wish India to live a life of complete isolation whereby it would live in water-tight compartments and allow nobody to enter her borders or to trade within her border." He has also very beautifully presented his ideas in the following words: "I do not want my house to be walled in on all sides, and my windows to be stuffed. I want the cultures of all lands to blow about my house as freely as possible. But I refuse to be blown off my feet by any. Mine is not a religion of the prison house."

Swadeshi is dynamic concept and it is much more

relevant and significant in the present context in which multinational companies have already entered in every nook and corner all-around the world. India is not an exception. Swadeshi cannot be minimized or underestimated even in the era of Globalisation. We can generate employment and help to reduce poverty of the millions through rural industrialisation and village arts and crafts. It is right time to rebuild the spirit of swadeshi and self-reliance to defeat the evil design of neo-imperialistic economic vested interests of multinationals. There is an urgent need to understand the meaning of true swadeshi which means lesser dependence on foreign goods and maximum use of our own resources keeping in view the basic needs of our immediate surroundings without neglecting the universal human element. In this way, swadeshi is the best remedy to solve the problem of exploitation and inequality caused by globalisation. Gandhi declared rightly in the forties "cut down your wants and at once all your economic problems will be solved. A life of simplicity with self-respect is anything better than a life of luxury for the few bought with loss of self-esteem and independence to other nations." Undoubtedly, swadeshi will be the greatest weapon for solving the economic problems of the 21st centuary and our objective should be simple living and high thinking.

POPULATION

The most important method of self-discipline and self-control recommended by Gandhi was Brahmacharya, or the practice of celibacy and purity—not mere abstinence from sex indulgence but the attainment of purity of thought and emotion. It is this aspect of Gandhi's teachings which has been most argued about and most misunderstood. But what is necessary to note is that Gandhi made Brahmacharya—the conquest of self an indispensable preparation for the larger task of attaining freedom and selfhood for the nation. "The first thing", he said, "is to know what true Brahmacharya is then to realize its value and lastly to try to cultivate this priceless virtue. I hold that the true service of the country demands this observance (Sarma, 1980, pp. 221-22).

Gandhi opposed the method of population control through contraceptives. In his opinion, the use of contraceptives in India would make the middle-class male population imbecile through abuse of the creative function. He wanted the propagation of sex education, the object of which was to conquer the sex passion. He did not agree with the view that food shortage was caused by excessive growth of population. He believed that "by a proper land system, better agriculture and a supplementary industry the country is capable of supporting twice as many people as there are today." Since Gandhi believed that man must earn his own living by his own labour, he thought that this law was more applicable to agriculture. But since every body could not be a cultivator, he could do some other work for earning his living. And if all the people in a country work and earn their bread, there may not be any shortage of food and clothing, people would be more wealthy and happy, there would be no misery and no problem of food shortage. According to him, the obedience to this law would lead to the minimisation of human wants. If the intellectual labour satisfies our soul, the physical labour satisfies our belly. And therefore, he advised the rich people also to do some sort of physical labour for earning their living. In fact, the law of bread labour has been universally recognized as the most fundamental in all religious books.

Gandhi was against the sterilisation of women, since to him, it was inhuman. But he was not against vasectomy, especially in the case of those men who suffer from chronic diseases, because he thought that it were men who were the aggressors.

As regards population control, Vinoba made some trenchant observations: "Family planning is a question of altering the basic values of life. Artificial methods may control births, but do not change the mode of living. On the contrary, they erode moral values. If the planning commission cares a trifle for these values, I have nothing to say... In my view, it is not the weight of numbers but of sin that is a real burden on earth. If the offspring is devoid of physical and mental stamina, it is bound to be a dead weight on the country. While God has given one mouth to eat, he has provided two hands and ten fingers to feed it (Narayan, 1978, p. 72).

Our Five Year Plans have been according a very high priority to the family welfare programme for the checking the 'Population explosion.' Gandhiji was fully alive to the urgent need for birth control. Even so, he viewed with distress the tendency of the people and the state to resort to artificial methods, without emphasizing the supreme importance of self-restraint and trying to create a healthy atmosphere for it. The Third Five Year Plan did underscore the need for placing "the greatest emphasis on moral and psychological elements, on restraint and on such social polices as education of women, opening up of new employment opportunities for them, and raising of the age of marriage."

While the use of modern birth-control under specified conditions could not be ruled out, it is imperative to highlight the primary importance of self-restraint in the nation-wide campaign for family planning. If we succeed in creating a strong public opinion in favour of having smaller families through education programmes and by raising the age of marriage, the impact of family planning programmes would be much greater and more lasting. We must also take particular care to ensure that the propagation of artificial devices is not misused by the younger generation for self indulgence, leading to the erosion of fundamental values of social morality (Narayan, 1969, p. 28).

PROHIBITION

Gandhi advocated cent per cent prohibition. According to Gandhi the use coffee, tea, tobacco, and alcohol was detrimental to the mental, physical, and moral development of an individual. He regarded the use of liquor as a disease rather than a vice. He had no objection to the use of liquor if taken under medical advice. He felt that it was better for India to be poor than to have thousands of drunkards. He had gone to the extent of saying: "If he were appointed dictator of India, only for an hour, he would, in the first instance, close all the liquor shops without compensation, and compel the mill-owners to start refreshment rooms to provide harmless drinks to the workmen."

He further remarked: 'Liquor is not a matter of trifle with. No soft and easy-going policy will cope with the tremendous evil. Nothing short of total prohibition can save the people from the curse.' I want to quote well-known Chinese proverb: 'First, the man takes the drink, then, the drink takes the drink and, in the end, the drink takes the man.'

Nehru had also remarked on the problem, "I will, indeed, be very sorry if the evil of drinking spreads in India. Any argument against prohibition on financial grounds is meaningless. Nevertheless, we should try to plug various loopholes in order to implement the prohibition programme more effectively.

Gandhi thought that the evil of drinking liquor could not be eradicated by legislative measures alone. He did not agree with those who held the view that the introduction of prohibition would cause a steep fall in the revenue of the state and that enough funds would not be available for social service expenditure on items such as education.

Gandhi was, however, of the definite view that the prohibition policy could not be enforced successfully without the fullest cooperation of a large number of devoted social workers in the field. With a view to creating the necessary climate and strengthening the national will to make prohibition a success, there is need of proper coordination of official as well non-official agencies to introduce complete prohibition throughout India with a sense of mission.

I want to quote the following inspiring words of Mahatma Gandhi: "We have the right to expect the sympathy and support not only of all the parties in India, but the best mind of the whole world in this, perhaps, the greatest moral movement of the century."

FOOD PROBLEM

Gandhiji had seen the worst famine of his life during 1943-44, when Bengal suffered heavily owing to the country-wide shortage of food. To start with, he thought that this scarcity of food had been artificially created. But after visiting Madras, Bengal and Assam, he arrived at the conclusion that the shortage of food was real and not artificial. He suggested the following measures for solving the problem of food shortage in India:

(i) every individual should curtail his or her requirements of food to the minimum and as far as possible, the consumption of food grains and pulses should be reduced to the minimum by substituting vegetables, milk, fruits,, etc., for them;
(ii) every flower garden should be utilised for cultivation purposes;
(iii) the consumption of food grains and pulses by the army personnel should be economized,
(iv) black marketing should be stopped; and
(v) deep wells should be sunk by the government so as to provide irrigational facilities; and
(vi) export of oil-seeds, oil–cakes,, etc. should be stopped (Hajela, 1994, pp. 646-47).

He was against any sort of food controls. He thought that it not only created artificial scarcity, but made the people to depend upon others. They become spoonfed. That is why, in November 1947, he asked the Government of India to remove food controls.

BREAD LABOUR

Gandhi realised the dignity of human labour. To him, labour was the law of nature and its violation was the pivotal cause of our present economic muddle. "It is a tragedy of the first magnitude that millions have ceased to use their hands as hands. Nature is revenging herself upon us with terrible effect for this criminal waste of the gift she has bestowed upon us as human beings. We are destroying the matchless living machines, i.e. our own bodies by leaving them to rust and trying to substitute lifeless machinery for them."

Bread Labor means that every man should labour with his body for his food and clothing. J.D. Sethi, a well known Gandhian economist explains the principle of 'Bread labour' in this line—"Bread labour in simple terms implied that amount of physical labour, given the arts of production and the society determined necessities. That much labour time must be spent by everybody in physical labour. Any one who does not work with his hands or other limbs runs the risk of being a parasite. Even the greatest thinker, poet or philosopher is likely to be misled by his own ideas and plagues of sophistication, if he is not involved in some physical action."

Gandhi's man, however, was more than just a mental or a physical machine. The man that Gandhi brought into the center of things as a loving man, making Labour and Love the two irreducible conditions which ensure that man will remain at the center of things. In the Gandhian scheme of things, love and cooperation without labour is only sheer romanticism while labour without love cannot but lead to new forms of expliotation and greed. The Gandhian insistence on Bread Labour is an expression both of man's responsibility to labour for his own basic needs and to cooperate with his fellow men. Given the unity of theory and action that is characteristic of Gandhi, bread-labour is both an essential principle of Gandhian economics and an essential part of his moral philosophy.

Gandhi believed that God created man to eat his bread by the sweat of his brow. Bread labour or body labour was the expression that Gandhi used to mean manual labour. He did not regard all manual labour as the "Curse of Adam." He said: "it is only when a man or woman has done bodily labour for the sake of service that he or she gets any right to live." He asserted that "man cannot develop his mind by simply writing or reading or making speeches all day long. Gandhi made use of the concept of 'bread labour' to tell people to utilize their idle hours which in villages are equal to the working days of six months in the year. Gandhi preached and practised the gospel of manual work. On account of his emphasis on manual labour and oppisition to machinery, some critics have dubbed Gandhi as a mediaeval mystic who was trying to put back the clock of human progress (Lokanathan, 1995, p. 286).

To Gandhiji, economics could not be divorced from ethical and human values of life. He observed: "I must confess that I do not draw a sharp or any distinction between economics and ethics. Economics that hurts the moral well-being of an individual or a nation is immoral, and, therefore, sinful. Thus the economics that permits one country to prey upon another is immoral. It is sinful to buy and use articles made by 'sweated labour'. It is sinful to eat American wheat and let my neighbour, the grain-dealer, starve for want of customer. Similarly, it is sinful for me to wear the latest finery of Regent Street when I know that if I had worn the things woven by the neighbouring spinners and weavers, that would have clothed me, and fed and clothed them."

He added: "The value of an industry should be gauged less by the dividends it pays to sleeping shareholders that by its effects on the bodies, souls and spirits of the people employed in it. Cloth is dear which saves a few annas to the buyer, while it cheapens the lives of the men, women and children who live in the Bombay chawls."

Gandhiji regarded man as 'the supreme consideration' and to him 'life was more important than money'. "It is cheaper to kill our aged parents who can do not work and who are a drag on our slender resources. It is also cheaper to kill our children whom we have to maintain without getting anything in return. But we kill neither our parents nor our children, but consider it a privilege to maintain them, no matter what their maintenance costs us."

VILLAGE REPUBLIC

Gandhi wanted the revival of ancient village communities with prosperous agriculture, decentralised industry and small scale co-operative organisations. He also wanted that there should be participation of people at all levels. He declared that the real India was to be found in the villages and not in the towns and he accepted the remark that an Indian village was "a collection of insanitary dwellings constructed on a dunghill." His desire was that every Indian village may be converted into a little self-sufficient republic. He said: "My idea of an ideal village is that of a complete republic, independent of its neighbour for its own vital wants, and yet dependent for many others in which dependence is a necessity." Such a village will contain intelligent people. First concern of the village should be to grow its own food. Then only, all communities will live together in harmony. The curse of untochability, intoxicating drinks and drugs will not exist. Women will live together in harmony. The curse of untouchability, intoxicating drinks and drugs will not exist. Women will enjoy the same rights as men. People in villages will not live in dirt and darkness as animals. No one wallow in luxury. The village community should take up the responsibility for providing work to all able bodied people and every one will have to contribute his quota of manual labour. There will be neither plague, nor cholera, nor small-pox and no one will be hungry. There would be improvement in education, electricity, post and telegraph, railways, etc.—all of which improve the quality of life.

Indeed, Gandhi was of the view that "independence must begin at the bottom. Thus every village will be a Republic or Panchayat with full powers.... The villagers will be the main repository of power." He was aware that by presenting a picture of republican village India he was exposing himself to ridicule in a political atmosphere in which politicians of the urban classes were dreaming of power-politics and power-structure of the usual run of democracies, while reflecting on the content of independence in conventional terms.

Gandhi's conception of an "oceanic circle" as opposed to a pyramidal structure of society, and his almost mystical idea of ever-ending, but never-ascending, concentric circles that signify interdependence, mutual support, and solidarity, without there being any relation of coercion, on the one hand, and dependence, on the other, as between the periphery and the inner circles.

Gandhi opposed extensive use of machinery, urbanisation and industrialisation of machinery on the ground that it led to pauperisation of villages and large scale unemployment in the countryside. He thought that industrialisation on a large scale would "necessarily lead to passive or active exploitation of the villages as the problems of marketing and competition come in." Later on, he added, "under my scheme, nothing will be allowed to be produced by the cities which can equally well be produced by villages. The proper function of cities is to serve as clearing houses for village products." He knew that it was not easy to establish ideal village and therefore, he emphasized the revival of village industries. He opposed modern industrial civilisation because he wanted to protect the rural civilisation.

ENVIRONMENT

Gandhiji's whole life was his message and a lesson on "Protecting and Conserving Environment along with the Development process," not only for Indians, but also for the whole world to follow at large. Man has exploited the nature to the extent that it has seriously disturbed the ecological balance. He must learn to live in harmony with the nature rather than compete with it. Moonis Raza said, "The essentiality of man and nature is based on man as a natural being and nature as a human reality."

Similar views have been expressed by T.S. Ananthu while analyzing the 'Future Survey Annual' and yearly report released on june, 24, 1990. The report paints a very grim picture of our future because of the damage being caused to our environment by modern gadgets and technologies. The following alarm signals are listed as a cause of this pessimistic outlook:

(i) The growing green house effect;
(ii) Unexpected and unpredictable climate changes;
(iii) Widespread deforestation;
(iv) Loss of several species necessary to maintain ecological balance;
(v) The menace of acid rains;
(vi) The problem of disposing toxic waste;
(vii) Depleting ozone layer; and
(viii) Increasing air and water pollution.

Gandhiji felt that industrialisation is going to be a curse for mankind. It cannot provide jobs for its millions of citizens and in addition, it would be creating pollution problems, whereas, developing thousands of cottage and village industries would provide an outlet for the creative faculties and resourcefulness of the people. It would also usefully employ many persons, who are in need of employment, which in return, in fact would add to the national wealth too.

Gandhi without consciously attempting at a systematic theory explained the phenomena of the exploitation of natural resources through alienation also. He was of the opinion that the more nature was overpowered, the more alienated man will become from nature. He simultaneously wanted to focus on the relationship between man and his natural environment which would end exploitation, which in turn is the very cause of exploitation of nature. But this alientation of man from nature has also paved the way of alienation from himself also. His trueself is what man can discover through the search for truth following the path of non-violence. Gandhi has a full view of man, his spiritual, cultural and social aspects as much as his economic needs. This led him to advocate that man must adjust himself to nature and not the other way round. He would not permit imbalance to be created between man and his environment (Chauhan, 2001, pp. 304-05).

According to Mr. Mustafa Jolba, Former Executive Director (UNEP)—"Unless we begin to use our natural resources rationally and fairly, the world would face an environmental catastrophe as complete and irreversible is any nuclear holocaust." Gandhi felt, we can use the bounties of nature, but not with an element of greed. He was a vegetarian and had compassion for all norms of life.

Infact, he advocated—"Man has no power to create life, therefore, has no right to kill any life also." According to Gandhi, no civilisation is worthwhile unless it saves nature and provides full opportunity for the fullest development of human beings. He, therefore, says, "Nature produces enough for our wants from day to day and if everybody took enough for himself and nothing more, there would be no pauperism in this world, there would be no man dying for starvaton in this world.

Gandhiji's philosophy of life can be an immense help in resolving conflicts between man and man and between man and nature, which are bound to come up during the process of development. According to Gandhi, our country has plenty of natural resources, which must be properly expressed and utilised. In a similar tune our modern economists opine that in present situation natural resources are either not put in use or put in wrong uses. His love for nature made his ideas the very antidote to the problem of pollution.

If we compare between the Gandhian model of bottom-up rural development and Nehruvian model of top-down industrial development; we can visualize that Gandhian model, leads to an economy of permanence and is based largely on renewable, where the damage to the environment is minimum and manageable,while the latter is based on non-renewable and causes environmental pollution. And depollution is far more expensive. Morevoer, in reality what we find today even after the six decades of our independence is the rich have become richer and the poor have become poorer.

Entirely new approach would be required to redirect the human social involving a supreme effort of understanding imagination and political and moral resolve. There is no other avenue but man has to explore himself his goals and values as much as he seeks the world to change. There need be unending commitment to ensure that man will survive without falling into a state of worthless existence. More and more people all over the world should look for the ways to redirect economic and ecological system 'as if people mattered' (Schumacher, 1989, p. 163).

CONCLUSION

We break the word Gandhi into six constituents. The First 'G' stands for Generosity; Second 'A' for Affection; Third 'N' for Non-violence; Fourth 'D' for Dedication; Fifth 'H' for Honesty and Sixth 'I' for Integration. These six values and lessons will bring down man-made fences that segregate us. The acid test lies in Practising these virtues. It will require on our part steadfastness, self-discipline, patience and faith.

If the 19th century belonged to Carlyle and Ruskin and the twentieth to Russel and Huxley, the 21st century belongs to Gandhi alone. Gandhi dreamed of a world without wars, a society without caste or class, factories without forced or child labour, infact a non-violent, non-exploiting social order where the mind is free and the head is held high. Gandhi is universal. He does not belong to any particular country, he belongs to whole of humanity.

Some one asked Bernad shaw, "What do you think of Gandhiji as a man?" He returned, "Gandhiji was not a man, he was a phenomenon. "Once, the great Nobel prize winning Scientist, Sir Albert Einstein spoke on Gandhiji—"Generations to come, will scarcely believe that, such a one as this, ever in flesh and blood, walked upon this earth."

Pandit Nehru cried on Jan. 30th 1948: "the light has gone out of our lives." Then he corrected himself and said, "Yet, I am wrong for the light that shone in this country was no ordinary light and a thousand years later; that light will be seen in the country and the world will see it.... For the light represented the living truth."

It appears that the four challenges of the twenty-first century will be:

(a) Ensuring equitable distribution of wealth and natural resources; also to cry a halt to the exploitation and insensitivity shown in preserving balance in nature.
(b) Taming the monster of violence and keeping it within limits.
(c) Decline of moral, spiritual and ethnic considerations.
(d) Increasing reliance of rulers and politicians on religious fundamentalist elements and forces to capture power and sustain themselves in power by exploiting religious sentiments.

His economic texts, as is the case with most of his other writings, are about struggle. Believing that inequality and domination are always ready to assert themselves and that efforts to achieve equality and freedom will always find resistance, he argues that it is essential to dispute claims that economics has its own internal standards and is not subject to external standards of evaluation. In his interrogation, he is worried about remainders: not only what is neglected but also who is neglected because they do not contribute to the economic process and have become irrelevant in the modern economy (Terchek, 2000, pp. 128-29).

It is significant that the International Seminar on Gandhian Thought held in New Delhi from January 30 to February 5, 1970 generally agreed that "Gandhian thought has significant relevance for the modern world and that many things which have happened since he passed away have not diminished but heightened its relevance." The 'message' issued by the Seminar at the end of its deliberations, added: "The crisis that Gandhiji faced is obviously not over but has been deepening, and the solutions that he proposed have not become outdated..." Gandhi is still a living challenge to the economic thinking, planning and action not only in his own country but in all the countries of the world."

Gandhi has made it abundantly clear that growth alone cannot confer benefit to all the sections of the community. Joan Robinson has said, "a growth in wealth is not at all the same thing as reducing poverty. As growth goes on at the top, more and more families are thrown out at the bottom. Absolute misery grows while wealth increased." J.K. Galbraith also points out that along with significant economic growth, there is persistence of gross inequality in the distribution of income and wealth. That is why Gandhi has said, "there may be work, there may be men to do the work and tools with which to do it, yet in my view a system that admits poverty and unemployment is not fit to survive even for a day."

Gandhi had to make a compromise with machinery and the human civilisation will have to develop on such compromises, as we find in Gandhi's reply to Ram Manohar Lohia: "I do visualize electricity, ship-building, iron works machine-making and the like existing side by side with village handicrafts. But the order of dependence will be reversed. Hitherto the industrialisation has been so planned as to destroy villages and their crafts. In the state of future, it will subserve the villages and their crafts." He wanted removal of poverty and unemployment and in the 21st century both these problems are confronting each and every nation. He was a firm believer that western method of large scale industries could not solve these problems. He wanted the problem must be tackled with less capital outlay and with more labour-intensive scheme. The twenty-first century will certainly lay emphasis to revive small and cottage industries. It will certainly lead to peace, prosperity and full employment to each and all.

Gandhi brought out a synthesis between science and religion. He is not opposed to science. According to him, "I am not opposed to the progress of science as such. On the contrary, the scientific spirit of the west commands my appreciation." But what he emphasizes is that science should not be "concerned itself with the exploration of laws and methods conducing to the merely material advancement of its clientele." Gandhi would be happy if science is moralised. Great thinkers like A.N. Whitehead has also remarked, "The future civilisation depends on the degree to which we can balance the forces of science and religion." Pandit Nehru has also realised the importance of linking science with spirituality to improve the quality of life of human beings.

Development must be woven around all the people without any distinction between different races, cultures,, etc. and not people around development. In other words, the center of the development should be man. And the society should develop harmoniously in moral, spiritual and economic field on the principle of equality.

In the age of globalisation, the world is becoming one unit and hence the need for sharing at every level, a concern for food, clothing, shelter, employment, education, healthcare, etc. for every inhabitant of the globe. The present world order based on exploitation, injustice, disparities, cannot and shouldnot be allowed to last long. Hence, a change in the lifestyle is required. A life of simplicity, austerity, sharing, which leads to happiness and inner peace, as envisaged by Gandhi, may help us in overcoming present predicaments. His concept of voluntary limitation of wants can save us from the epidemic of consumerism. One of the basic principles of ecology, is limitation, besides complexity and inter-dependence. As all the resources on this planet earth are limited, man cannot survive, if goes on exploiting them the way he is doing now these days.

Although Gandhi was not an economist in the professional sense of the term, we must candidly and assertively recognize that his economic ideas, instead of being old-fashioned and utopian, are very much relevant to our times, and, in a sense, even far ahead of us. No age or no society can fade its brightness and usefulness and these ideas are essentially a process, continuation and culmination of years old civilisation. Romain Rolland regarded Gandhiji's spirit as "the perfect manifestation of the principle of life which will lead a new humanity on to a new path."

Vincent sheean calls him "The wisest and the best—a man who had no equal in our time. "Gandhi belongs to the future, and not the past. His message is eternal. He once wrote,"…. So long as my faith burns bright, as I hope it will even if I stand alone, I shall be alive in the grave and what is more, speaking from it." I want to conclude with the words of Louis Fischer, a great admirer of Gandhi: "If man is to survive, if civilisation is to survive and flower in freedom, truth and decency, the remainder of the twentieth century and what lies beyond must belong not to Lenin or Trotsky, not to Marx or Mao or Ho or Che ... but to Mahatma Gandhi."

REFERENCES

Arora, V.K. (1981), "The Relevance of the Gandhian Socio-Economic Philosophy to Contemporary Reality," *The Indian Journal of Political Science*, Vol. XLII, No. 4, October-December.

Chauhan, Sandeep (2001), "GATT to WTO Gandhian Alternative to New International Economic Order," Deep & Deep Publications Pvt. Ltd., New Delhi

Das, Amritananda (1979), "Foundations of Gandhian Economics," Allied Publishers Private Limited, New Delhi.

Das, P.K. (1999), "Philosophy of Mahatma Gandhi and the Future Ideologist," Anu Books, Merrut.

Ganguli, B.N. (1977), "Indian Economic Thought," Tata McGraw Hill, New Delhi.

Hajela, T.N. (1991), "History of Economic Thought", Konark Publishers Pvt. Ltd., Delhi.

Kripalani, J.B. (2005), "Gandhi: His Life and Thought," Publication Division, Ministry of Information and Broadcasting, Government of India.

Lokanathan, V. (1995), "A History of Economic Thought," S. Chand and Company Ltd., New Delhi.

Marshall, Alfred (1948), "Principles of Economics," The Macmillan Company, New Delhi

Narayan, Shriman (1969), "Gandhi: The Man and His Thought," Publication Division, Ministry of Information and Broadcasting, Government of India.

——— (1978), "Towards the Gandhian Plan," S. Chand and Company Ltd., New Delhi

Pyarelal (1958), "Mahatma Gandhi: The Last Phase," Navjivan Press, Ahmedabad.

Sarma, G.N. (1980), "Gandhi's Concept of Duty," *Indian Journal of Political Science*, Vol. 41, No. 2.

Schumacher, E.F. (1989), "Small is Beautiful: A Study of Economics if People Mattered," London: Abacus.

Sethi, J.D. (1979), "Gandhian Values and 20th Century Challenges," Publication Division, Ministry of Information and Broadcasting, Government of India.

Sharma, M.L. (2003), "Scope and Significance of Swadeshi under Globalisation," *Journal of Gandhian Studies*, Vol. 1, No. 1.

Tendulkar, D.G. (1961), "Mahatma: Life of Mohan Das Karamchand Gandhi," Vol. I, Publication Division, Ministry of Information and Broadcasting, Govt. of India.

Terchek, Ronald J. (2000), "Gandhi Struggling for Autonomy," Vistaar Publications, New Delhi.

4

Employment of Women
The Gandhian Model

SANDHYARANI DAS AND R.P. SARMA

Mohandas Karamchand Gandhi, who is affectionately called by the people of India as Mahatma Gandhi or Bapu, was a great practical philosopher who aimed at socio-economic development of the country, and for that the development of mankind. His key philosophical point was "Gram Swaraj" or the freedom at the level of villages. Even today one has to accept that about 70 per cent of the people are living in the villages, and without their development one cannot think of the over all development of the country. Mahatma was not a pure economist; his intention was to develop the society. For him, economics is certainly an important factor in this direction, but not the sole factor. Of course now it is accepted by the economists that the ultimate aim of economic development is social development, building up a happy and healthy society.

A society which intends to develop rapidly has to take all section of the people together into its fold, rich and poor, high society people and low caste people and both men and women. It was realised by Mahatma Gandhi and he sincerely experimented for a "free society." Of course he could not live to see it, as he was assassinated. Gandhi had his original vision and propagated a novel way of thinking in science of economics. He integrated economic aims and activities with morality and non-violence. He synthesised our successful past experiences with the recent development process. He laid emphasis on labour force, livestocks and rural economy for the nation's smooth progress. He was the first man in the world who provided a practical alternative for the then economic system. The village based economy of China and Israel, the small-scale industry based economy of Japan are nearer to Gandhian concept of *Sarvodaya* or the welfare of all.

THE CONCEPT OF *SARVODAYA*

In a society all should have equal rights and also have equal duties towards it. But there are certain unprivileged classes in the society. The lower class people (Harijans) and the female folk in all the classes of society were considered as unprivileged. As the females are almost fifty per cent of the population and if they remained powerless and downtrodden in the society one cannot think of the development of the society or of the economy. Hence empowerment of women has to be the ultimate goal to improve the quality of the society and development of the economy. Gandhiji's vision for this is *Sarvodaya,* welfare of all through co-operation and trusteeship in the economic sphere, equal participation in the political sphere and mutual aid in the social sphere without regard to caste, class and gender.

Since majority of people in the country live in the rural sector, Gandhiji specially emphasised the empowerment of village women. In the agricultural operations the women folk equally engaged in the field with men apart from their household job. Mostly illiterate, they are the worst sufferers in the society as they have to bear and rear children many a time against their wish that enhances poverty for the family and the economy at large.

The three most important factors which promotes empowerment of women are as follows:

1. Education

In ancient India there were good lady scholars at par with the male scholars, but they were limited in number and belonged to rich royal or Brahmin families. Majority of the women folk remained illiterates because the higher community people were not allowing the lower class people to learn alphabets and read books. The lawgivers defined the duties of the females to do household chores and upkeep the babies in the family and serve the husband as the *avatar* of God.

Gandhi wanted the mass education to both men and women and emphasis was given to the female folk as he believed that the female is moulder of the family and the society. Once she is empowered with education she can fight for her rights in the family and in the society and can obtain equal status in the social life. Unless they are educated they cannot actively participate in the social, political or economic life as a citizen and cannot establish their status in the society. Even after about six decades of India's independence the combined rate of literacy according to Census of India, 2001, is 64.84 per cent and the female literacy is 54.16 per cent; in some parts of India in the remote *adivasi* areas the female literacy is as low as 6 per cent. One cannot think of empowerment of women without making them literate and educated.

Even today after more than seven decades after Gandhiji's concept of empowerment of women through education, the main obstacle to empowerment has been the dismal educational level among women. (Rao, 2001) Education that inculcates human values is of great significance for the empowerment of women. Poverty, education and income are interlinked. It is a vicious circle. Because they are poor they are not able to pursue education and because of lack of education, employment opportunities are limited consequently income is limited and they rot in poverty.

2. Employment

Participation in economic activity of the nation requires education. Since literacy and educational qualification of the females are low their employment opportunity is also limited. In the organised sector their participation is very low. Even though in all walks of life the females now entered into higher positions, but the majority of females are still working in the unorganised sector. Unless they are educated and employed the loud talk of empowerment of women is meaningless.

The problem of unemployment according to Gandhi can be tackled only by developing village and cottage industries. Moreover, they take the employment opportunities to the doors of unemployed and ideally fit in the rural conditions. Gandhiji advocated for the engagement of female folk in the cottage and smalls scale industries of the village such as *gur,* broom, basket and rope making and oil processing so that the rural women can supplement to the family income.

Gandhi was not a theoretical economist. He was a socio-economic applied economist. Gandhiji gave priority to *khadi* industry; according to him "*khadi* is the sun of the village system." It is the central industry on which all other village industries revolve. He not only advocated for women's employment but he practically started experiment of Charkha to produce cloth for the people at the same time employment at the family level. He proposed several measures to provide employment opportunities in the rural sector which would help both men and women of which the important ones are as follows:

1. Cultivation of cotton in areas where it was not grown.
2. Organisation of weaving by the multi-purpose co-operative societies.
3. Compulsory introduction of spinning in all primary and secondary school, so that the boys and girls can learn the technique.
4. Use of hand-spun cloth in all government and textile and weaving departments.

He was not opposed to heavy industries but he believed that heavy industries cannot provide employment to the people in the villages, both men and women; hence some form of family engagement has to be created to earn income by the family where women can also participate which in turn will empower them in the society.

3. Psychological Trap

Education and employment are no doubt important factors for women empowerment, but the main obstacle is our traditional social system. The society has to change its social attitude with regards to the participation of females in all walks of life. No doubt in the urban sector the attitude is gradually changing but in the rural sector the female folk even the educated ones are not coming out of the social traditional trap, with regards to education, employment, household work, and public participation as well as participation in the political activities of the country.

Mahatma Gandhi was a ceaseless crusader of women's equality. He brought the women out of their homes and made them equal participants in all walks of life—social as well as political. Under Gandhi's leadership thousands of women took leading roles in national movement. Gandhi never considered women to be unfit for any position or task. Because of Gandhi's support, women's groups were formed all over India and there was hardly a week when Gandhi did not address a women's group.

Gandhi did not like Indian society's preference for a boy child. For this reason about four million women risk their lives and get illegal abortions every year in the country. Gandhi was totally opposed to gender discrimination. He described women as "embodiment of sacrifice and *ahimsa*." He firmly believed that "woman is weak in striking and strong in suffering." He advocated that daughter's share must be equal to that of a son. He opined that the slavery in the kitchen of women is a remnant of barbarism. In his policy of empowerment he advised men to participate in the household work and reduce the drudgery of woman's home work.

This is the most difficult part of empowerment. It is possible to expand educational institutions and establish small and cottage industries in the villages but to compel the females to go to school and for work leaving the household chore. is not an easy task. Hence Gangarde believes that the goal of empowerment of women requires threefold revolution in the society.

1. Change of the people's heart; that is, change in the attitude of the people towards women to accept modern role for them in the family and in the society.
2. To create change in the lives of females in the family discarding to some extent the traditional duties of the female and accepting some other duties in addition to it performed by the male members of the society.
3. The traditional social structure is another factor that hinders empowerment of women. The society divided into several classes traditionally requires change. The class instead of classifying on the basis of caste and religion it should be classified according to the work performed by person.

As early as in 18th century with the coming of the British merchants, the social leaders in India thought of reforming the society on modern lines. Raja Rammohan Ray was pioneer in taking up social reforms with an aim of emancipating the Indian women from family slavery. Even though he was not succeeded fully during his lifetime but he started the social revolution and wanted radical changes in the Hindu society on the fowling aspects:

(1) Abolition of child marriages.
(2) Abolition of *Sati* by the wife after the death of husband.
(3) Widow remarriage.
(4) Development of schools for the girl child.

Mahatma Gandhi also stressed the above reforms and towards the end of nineteenth century he firmly advocated for social change of the traditional customs which are against the development of a healthy society. He never hesitated to criticize the evils which had griped the Indian society and tried to mobilize public opinion against such evils. He was against the deep-rooted customs like child marriage, not allowing widows for remarriage, atrocities on women and *purdah* system. He was also advocated inter-caste marriage for better social integration.

Even today child marriage and *Sati* have not been completely abolished, though legally prohibited. Gandhiji has stressed all these and equal right for sons and daughters is yet to be successfully implemented in the country. Unless social attitude towards women changes, nothing can be done for the empowerment of women. And social changes require long time. After independence of India a silent social revolution is gradually coming up. The system operating for centuries in the country cannot be changed in few decades.

THE GANDHIAN MODEL

Mahatma Gandhi's approach for empowerment of women in India can be formulated into a logical triangular model. The three important components explained above are fitted into a graphical model and presented in Fig. 1.

The three important factors that promote women empowerment are: education, employment and change in social structure. All the three components are equally important and mutually related. Simply development of education of the women would not automatically empower them. The case in point is Kerala. The state has hundred per cent literacy but the women folk are not free from exploitation. This is because of the fact that the traditional Keralite society is yet to be reformed to provide equal rights to the women in *de facto* terms.

Employment of women is still restricted, even though not in legal terms, the females are not allowed to enter into certain jobs, beyond, doctors, nurses, teachers and clerical jobs. In the family and in the society the women are still treated inferior to men, even though they are now entering into some challenging jobs in a limited manner. The dignity of labour is still not given in proper perspective.

FIG I

The Gandhian Model

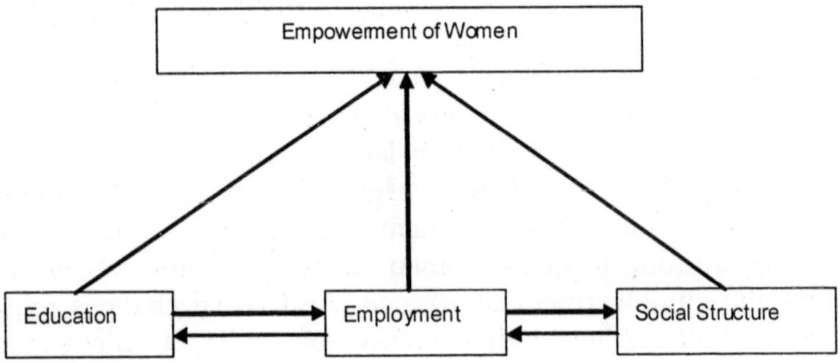

CONCLUSION

The three important factors that influence the empowerment of women are education, employment and the changing of the social structure. They are interdependent and have to be promoted simultaneously to realise effective empowerment of women. Mahatma Gandhi experimented in all these three fields a century ago and shown the way for the empowerment of women. Even today at the beginning of the 21st century his vision remains unfulfilled.

REFERENCES

Bharati, K.S. (1998), *Political Thought of Mahatma Gandhi*, Concept Publishing Co., New Delhi.

Bharati, K.S. (2000), *Mahatma Gandhi, Man of the Millennium*, S. Chand and Co., New Delhi.

Bimani, Anil, Relavance of M.K. Gandhi's Ideas of Self-sufficient Village Economy (Internet: www.mkgandhi.org/articles.htm)

Chattopadhyay, Kamaladevi, *Woman the Comrade* (Internet: www. mkgandhi. org/articles.htm)

Chaturvedi, Usha Arun., *Gandhi: A Unique Practical Economist* (Internet: www.mkgandhi.org/articles.htm)

Gangrade, K.D. (2001), "Gandhi and Empowerment of Women—Miles to Go", in *Empowering the Indian Women*, Ed. Promila Kapur, Publication Division, Government of India, Delhi.

Grover, Verinder (1997) Ed., *Mohandas Karamchand Gandhi: A Biography of His Vision and Ideas*, Deep and Deep, New Delhi,

Jaitly, Jaya, *Gandhi and Women's Empowerment* (Retrieved from Internet).

Kaur, Rajkumari Amrit, Gandhi and Women (Retrieved from Internet).

Paul, R.R., (1964) Ed., *Gandhi: His Relevance for Our Times*, Kalyani Publishers, Ludhiana.

Rao, P.H. Sethumadhavan (2001), "Education for Women's Empowerment" in *Empowering the Indian Women*, Ed. Promila Kapur, Publication Division, Government of India, Delhi,

Saxena, Kiran, *Gandhi's Feminist Politics, Gender Equity and Patriarchal Values* (Internet: www.mkgandhi.org/articles/kiran saxena.htm)

Sinha, Shall, *Mahatma Gandhi: A Crusader of Women's Equality* (Internet: www.mkgandhi.org/articles/shall sinha.htm).

5

Gandhi and Welfare

Takeover of Agricultural Land for Industry

SUDAKSHINA GUPTA

INTRODUCTION

Mahatma Gandhi, the apostle of peace was a leader of the masses. Not being a professional economist, he did not develop a formal model of economic growth. In 1944, Acharya S.N. Agarwala brought out the "Gandhian Plan" which was reaffirmed in 1948. These were formulated into a "Gandhian Model of Planning."

SUMMARY OF GANDHIAN PLAN

Gandhi, as everyone knows, was an advocate of development of agriculture and small scale and cottage industries. He wanted the Indian villages to develop as self-sufficient units of the economy, not as appendages to the urban centres. Gandhi's idea was to make the country self-sufficient in food crops and the regions self-sufficient in food. So land reforms were to be accompanied by changes in the system of tenure, abolition of the proprietary rights of land, consolidation of holdings, organisation of cooperative farms,, etc., abolition of money-lending and increased rural credit for farmers. Dairy farming was another occupation to be developed as an auxiliary to agriculture.

He emphasised the development of cottage industries with foremost importance being given to spinning and weaving of cloth.

Gandhi was not against setting up of large scale industries but he detested its random and indiscriminate development. He recognised the need for growth of defence industries, hydro-electric and thermal power generation, mining and metallurgy, machinery and machine tools, heavy engineering and heavy chemicals. The Gandhian model emphasised the idea of developing these industries in the public sector. Gandhi was not against all machinery but was against those which would not benefit all but only a few. He supported the introduction of machinery only when it would "lighten the burden of villagers without displacing human labour."

Gandhi wanted an integrated development of agriculture and industries with an emphasis on handicrafts and cottage industries. He stressed on employment-oriented growth and equitable distribution of resources. In a nutshell, the Gandhian Plan stressed the importance of making Indian villages self-sufficient with development of small and cottage industries, agriculture and auxiliary industries like dairy farming and handicrafts,, etc.

ECONOMIC POLICY OF INDIAN GOVERNMENT

In the background of this, one has to explore how far the principles of the "Father of the Nation" have been followed.

Industry

Since Independence, India has stridden on the path of "mixed economy" with emphasis on heavy and basic industries in the public sector, leaving the consumer goods industries to the private sector. The Second Plan strategy of Mahalanobis, initiated in 1956, advocated large-scale industrialisation in a socialist context. After more than three decades, however, with the introduction of economic reforms, liberalisation, privatisation and globalisation, the policy has been tilted towards denationalisation of industries and no further setting up of industries in the Government sector.

A few items were reserved exclusively for production in the small scale sector. Upward revision of investment limit has been done quite often. Credit, technical and marketing assistance have been given to this sector. Value of output per employee and capital labour ratio have shown impressive growth. Since liberalisation, however, this sector has not been given due importance. Instead of being given protection, they are now made to compete.

For handloom and handicrafts in the cottage industries sector, the Khadi and Village Industries Commission and the State Khadi and Village Industries Boards were set-up for development.

Agriculture

The agricultural sector was not touched by socialism and cooperative farming in the Soviet style was not attempted at all. On the other hand, some steps were taken to strengthen the rural credit market by opening branches of the nationalised banking network in the rural areas along with the establishment of Regional Rural Banks and revamping the cooperative credit system. A lot has been done to improve the lot of the poor and marginal farmers. NABARD has been an important step towards agricultural credit. Everything said and done, the power of the Mahajans could not be curbed, specially in the interior, where the banks do not operate efficiently and sincerely.

Land reform was initiated in the mid fifties, with abolition of intemediaries, security given to tenure, imposition of land ceiling and distribution of surplus land to the landless. Local governance at the grassroots level through the *Panchayat* system has been introduced following Gandhi's ideas, which dreamt of self-sufficient, peaceful, economically and politically strong villages to form the base of the Indian economy

PRESENT SITUATION

Half-heartedly following the Gandhian principles with a gradual shift towards becoming an international player has led the Indian economy nowhere. The advantage of self-sufficiency achieved in agricultural production in the 1980s, the creation of a buffer stock to avoid imports has been destroyed in the recent past with no growth registered in the agricultural sector in the last decade. Growth in industries has been impressive, especially in the non-manufacturing activities. The service sector is also progressing well. According to Government officials, the growth rate of GDP is between 7-8 per cent per year, which is unprecedented and spectacular. This, however has not been followed by an equitable distribution of income.

CHANGING THE BASIC STRUCTURE AND ITS EFFECTS

The main philosophy behind Gandhian economics was self-sufficiency of villages through rapid growth of agriculture and cottage and small-scale industries. This would not only boost the village economy, but also push the Indian economy towards achieving self-sufficiency in every respect. Following his ideals India would also move towards securing an important position in the international sphere.

The gradual shift towards a more liberalised and globalised economy with more emphasis on private sector industries than on public sector ones has started to change the structure of the Indian economy. In a haste to compete with the global powers and to become part of the global game, the very basic framework is being broken down. The World Bank loans and the WTO conditions have forced the Government to walk down a path not followed so far. In the name of development, the village structure is being changed. It is not a process of urbanisation that has been started but a kind of destruction.

Private industrialists, dubbed as "monopolists" till a decade ago, are being helped and given cooperation to set-up large-scale industries on small farmers' land. The Special Economic Zones (SEZ) are being set-up throughout the country on farmers' land. Foreign investment with all kinds of facilities like tax exemptions are being invited to these Zones. These foreign and Indian players are getting land from state governments, agriculture and agricultural land being state subjects. The most interesting and important point is that even the Marxist state governments are not lagging behind in this project. How much benefit will this act of grabbing land from the poor and giving it away to the rich without giving adequate compensation to the farmers bring to the society is doubtful. These industrial powers cater to the rich and the middle class in turn, not to the displaced, and the Government earn their due revenue. The helpless people become refugees in their own country as their land, owned for generations, is taken away and they get jobs nowhere! The fertile multi-crop lands, acre after acre, will be occupied by giant factories, which would work mainly for individual profits. The effect will be manifold—social, economic, political, administrative. The serene atmosphere of villages will be ridden with pollution—air, noise and visual. The exponents of this group, advocates of "Development" are advancing ideas of employment, improved technology, generation of social resources and money. The question is, however, of destroying agriculture. Agriculture has already stopped registering growth in the last decade because of inadequate attention. This step to change the very basic structure so that India can fast become a global player raises questions about the ethics of forcefully taking away one's land and giving it to someone else. One should remember in this context that Gandhi was against all kinds of corruption and unethical acts.

The main effects of the entire process can be enumerated below:

1. The farmers, rich, poor and marginal, have lost their land, not by the forces of the market, but by sheer power of the elected government and the money power of the big industrial houses. The industries have not bought their land, the Government has grabbed it forcefully and that too without proper compensation everywhere. Not

only that, the forces have been so brutal that they are even hurting personal integrity. There would have been much less opposition and criticism if the industrialists would have bought land from intending farmers at market prices.

2. This move will not only leave thousands of farmers landless, it will also make them jobless. It is not easy for people to get absorbed in jobs alien to them, for they have specialised in farming for generations. The industrial power, on the other hand, will not be interested in employing unskilled labour. So, these people will not only lose their livelihood, but also add to the millions of unemployed jobless Indians.
3. These village residents will add to millions of homeless refugees as these villages will cease to exist.
4. This move, even if practised in small isolated pockets, tends to have ripple effects on the whole economy as farmers in other places will also lose incentives to pursue agriculture as a living.
5. Destroying the village economy by industrial intrusion in the name of Development and Employment will lead, ultimately, to a further loss in agricultural production. If this policy is practised on a larger scale, the prime position of agriculture in the Indian economy is sure to lose ground. Not only that, it will undo the advantage that India has gathered through the years in agriculture—self-reliance in food grain production. This had happened because of the introduction of intensive agriculture with New Agriculture Technology, popularly known as the "Green Revolution." India, in the nineties, could even do without regular imports of food grains and create a buffer stock instead. This position is already on the verge of being lost. The situation will become critical and the crisis aggravated if this policy is followed further.
6. As a party to the global process of playing the

game and as a signatory to the WTO-GATT, India has to remove subsidy on her agricultural goods, whereas many developed countries are continuing with it. This is already hampering the Indian position in agriculture; and what will happen if, in the name of development, acres of multi-crop farmland are turned into industrial hubs, is only to guess!

7. Agricultural land, especially deltaic alluvial areas, may not be technically suitable and financially viable for construction of factories and other industrial structures and subsequent production.
8. Creating Special Economic Zones to attract foreign investment will play as a disincentive to the aspiring domestic economic powers—small or big. Discrimination of this type will do no good to the country's economy. It is already becoming difficult for many domestic companies to survive the international competition since the opening up of the economy. This policy of selling farmland to foreigners without the farmers' consent will only add to their woe.

This way, the Gandhian model of strengthening the village economy with increased production of agriculture and development of small-scale and cottage industries has been abandoned by Gandhi's own countrymen, who want to turn the villages into cities and introduce all kinds of social, economic and administrative evils associated with urban centres to the rural areas. The very basic structure which could not be destroyed even by the colonial powers, is on the verge of being destroyed by the very Indians!

PURPOSE OF THE PAPER

In the backdrop of such a crisis, a theoretical study can be done to see if this move of turning agricultural lands into industrial hubs is increasing the welfare of the society. With this purpose in mind an analysis has been done depending on a few assumptions.

DIFFERENT WELFARE CRITERIA

Society is said to be better-off when, due to a change, the utility gained by one is more than the utility lost by the other, i.e. interpersonal comparison of utility is required, which is very difficult.

There are a few methods which determine whether a particular policy increases social welfare or not. They can be enumerated as follows:

1. The Pareto Criterion says that a policy increases social welfare if it benefits some members of society (in their own judgement) without harming anyone.
2. The Kaldor-Hicks Criterion says that a change is an improvement if those who can gain from the change can fully compensate the losers and still retain some gain. The gain and loss in utility are measured in monetary terms and it also involves interpersonal utility comparison.
3. According to the Scitovsky Criterion, a change in policy improves welfare if it satisfies the Kaldor-Hicks Criterion and a movement back to the original position does not satisfy the Kaldor-Hicks Criterion.
4. The Bergson Social Welfare Function can be constructed from the explicit value judgement of society. A particular policy increases social welfare if society moves to a higher social indifference curve. Construction of a social welfare function is extremely difficult.

Arrow, through his Impossibility Theorem, proved that a social welfare function cannot be constructed by democratic vote (i.e. reflecting the preferences of all the individuals of society).

THE THEORETICAL STUDY

The Assumptions

1. Agricultural products are homogeneous and are sold at dictated price.
2. Cost of production is different for different farmers because of difference of technology used and difference in holding size.
3. Price-marginal cost equality does not take place.

The Analysis

Let:

1. The amount of total arable land in the area be S.
2. The amount of land taken away for industry be s, where s = aS, a<1
3. Total earning from land through agriculture and other activities per acre be r.
4. The average earning by people engaged in agriculture and other activities on S per head before land take-over be w.
5. Number of people engaged in agriculture on S before land takeover be L.
6. Number of people displaced due to land take-over be □•, where •=bL, b<1.
7. After industrialisation, average earning of people per head engaged in industry on s be w¢.
8. Number of people engaged in industry on s be L¢.
9. Total earning from s after industrialisation be E.

From the above, the following can be obtained:

Land left for cultivation is

$$S - \alpha S = S(1 - \alpha),\ 1 - \alpha > 0 \quad (1)$$

Earning from s through agriculture and other activities before land takeover is

$$rs = r\alpha S \tag{2}$$

Total earning by L on S before land take-over is

$$wL \tag{3}$$

People left on S for agriculture after land take-over is

$$L\text{-}\beta L = L(1\text{-}\beta),\ (1\text{-}\beta)>0 \tag{4}$$

Earning of bL before land take-over is

$$wbL \tag{5}$$

Earning of people left on S for agriculture is

$$wL\text{-}wbL = wL(1\text{-}\beta),\ 1\text{-}\beta>0 \tag{6}$$

Earning by L¢ is

$$w'L' \tag{7}$$

As per claim, since industries will generate more income and employment than agriculture on s, so,

$$w'>w \text{ and } L'>bL,$$

hence

$$w'L'>wbL, \text{ i.e. } w'L'\text{-}wbL>0 \tag{8}$$

Let this

$$w'L'\text{-}wbL = Y,\ Y>0 \tag{9}$$

It is derived from the above that because of industrialisation,

1. Total earning from land through agriculture and other activities is reduced, i.e. $rS - rS(1\text{-}\alpha)>0$.

2. Earning by people from land through agriculture and other activities is reduced, i.e. $wL(1-\beta)>0$.
3. Total earning from s increases, $E>r\alpha S$
4. Earning of people in industry is more than earning of people displaced, i.e.. $w'L'>w\beta L$.

The above derivations may be discussed in the light of the different welfare criteria.

Naming the group of displaced labour A and the newly employed labour in industry B, derivation 4 suggests that the utility of group B, UB is more than utility of Group A, UA, i.e. UB>UA, if utility is measured in terms of money. However, whether utility gained by B is more than utility lost by A is not clear as comparison of (inter-personal) utility between two groups cannot be done. The utility here not only involves money income but also the trauma of losing jobs and homes. So whether welfare of society has increased or not cannot be determined.

Considering the Pareto Criterion, society's welfare has not increased at all as Group B has been benefited only by harming Group A, if the loss in money income is considered. Whether the compensation given will be greater than what they earned from land for years is can not be determined in money terms only.

Considering the Kaldor-Hicks Criterion, the compensation to be paid to the losing group should be determined. Here, w¢L¢-wbL=Y is the total increase in money income in s. So a part of that should be paid as compensation by group B to group A. C = ¡Y, where ¡>0, may be defined as this compensation and Y-¡Y should be the net increase in income of Group B. This Y-¡Y = Y(1-¡), ¡>0 must be more than what group B earned before they joined this industry. Similarly, ¡Y should be more than wbL, but a stock of money can never be the substitute for a flow of income. One question here is that whether Group B would be willing to pay compensation to Group A. In all probability, they would not and there would be an administrative problem. The Government has arranged for compensation to Group A but the criterion on which this has been done is not clear. Whatever be the amount of compensation, livelihood can not be replaced by that. So Kaldor-Hicks Criterion of social welfare also fails here.

The Scitovsky Criterion becomes irrelevant as once the industry is set-up and labour are employed, it is not possible to revert to the old agricultural practices in the same region.

The Bergson Criterion is also not applicable in this case as a social welfare function is difficult to achieve with inter-personal utility comparison not being easy.

According to Arrow's Impossibility Theorem, democratic vote (reflecting all individuals' preferences) cannot determine the social welfare function. This, therefore, calls for a dictatorial decision, which, in a democratic set-up like India, itself goes against welfare policies.

In fact, the Government's role may be questioned in the entire process.

CONCLUSION

So, it can be concluded that, displacing farmers from their own land cultivated for generations and setting up big industries by private entrepreneurs, domestic or foreign, may increase income and employment and bring about development through other external factors in the region but welfare of society does not necessarily increase through such a step.

Private investment is welcome in the economy, so is foreign investment but destroying agriculture for that purpose complicates the matter. By violating Gandhian principles, thus, society's welfare does not increase, not even sixty years after he left this world.

REFERENCES

Gandhian Plan, 1944.

Mahalanobis Plan, 1956.

Datt, R. and Sundharam, K.P.M. (1995), *Indian Economy*, S. Chand and Co, New Delhi, pp. 131-3.

Website of the Indian Government, http.//indiabudget.nic.in/es2004-05/chapt2005/tab32.pdf

Datt, R. and Sundharam, K.P.M. (1995), *Indian Economy*, S. Chand and Co, New Delhi, pp. 680.

Salvatore, D. (2003), *Microeconomics: Theory and Application*, OUP, New York, p. 588.

Pareto, V. (1909), *Manual of Political Economy* (trans. W. Jaffe, 1971), August Kelly, New York.

Kalder, N. (1939), Welfare Propositions in Economics and Inter-personal Comparisons of Utility.

Economic Journal, December, pp. 549-52.

Hicks. J.R. (1939), The Foundation of Welfare Economics, *Economic Journal*, December, pp. 696-712.

Scitovsky, T. (1941), A Note on Welfare Propositions in Economics, *Review of Economics and Statistics*, November, pp. 77-8.

Bergson, A. (1938), A Reformulation of Certain Aspects of Welfare Economics, *Quarterly Journal of Economics*, February, pp. 310-34.

Arrow, K.J. (1951), "Social Choice and Individual Values", Wiley, New York, *The Statesman*, July 7th 2007, Calcutta.

6

Gandhi: The Pioneer of an Alternative and Parallel Tradition in Indian Economic Thought

A. SANGAMITHRA

INTRODUCTION

The revival of interest in Gandhi's thought and specially in Gandhi's economics is one of the major intellectual developments in the contemporary world. It is also a significant trend in contemporary India. For long there existed a wide chasm between professional economics and Gandhian economics. Economists for long smugly dismissed Gandhi as anti-technology and anti-growth, as an advocate of technological primates and of return to a natural economy (i.e. a simple and non-competitive, pre-industrial economy). The contributions by India's eminent social scientists of the older generation like J.J. Anjaria, D.P. Mukerji, N.K. Bose, M.L. Dantwala, B.N. Ganguli, Bhabatosh Dutta, Raj Krishna and many others inaugurated an era of serious study of Gandhi as a creative economic philosopher and development thinker of the modern period. "When the history of economic thought in India in recent times comes to be written," wrote J.J. Anjaria, "Gandhi's name will certainly occupy a place of honour in it." He further remarked: "It does not matter in this context whether we call Gandhi an economist or not: that is partly, at any rate, a question of definition of terms" (J.J. Anjaria, 1941-42: 357).

SOME BASIC CONCEPTS

The Gandhian system has never been fully articulated. Most of the ideas presented to us by Gandhi were practiced by himself. In practice, these ideas appeared fully immersed in the situation of the time. Those ideas, thus, need to be separated from the historical context in which they were developed. Since this has not been done, any formulation of his ideas and propositions needs to be subjected to a serious debate. Such a debate will analyze, refine, and hopefully also develop a consensus. In this section we propose a few concepts relevant to the economic systems. These are our interpretations and we offer these basically as an agenda for discussion and debate.

In our view there are six basic concepts that are essential in Gandhi an economics. These are all related to each other. There is no hierarchy among them. In other words, these all have equal importance. The order in which these are presented is irrelevant. We feel that these six concepts come in pairs of two. They are: (i) *swadeshi* (ii) bread labour, (iii) *aparigraha* or non-possession, (iv) trusteeship, (v) non-exploitation, and (vi) equality.

Swadeshi may be translated as self-reliance. It follows from the concept of *swaraj.* There are various interpretations of *swadeshi.* Some interpret it narrowly as "autarky" or self-sufficiency. The question is: how does one apply the concept of *swadeshi* to a nation? The problems and misunderstandings arise from the question itself. A more meaningful question is: how should *swaraj* look like with or without *swadeshi*? *if swadeshi* is essential to *swaraj,* then how does one go about introducing it in the transitional state? The interpretation of *swadeshi* as "self-reliance" provides a clue to this question.

Bread labour provides the ethical dimension to *swadeshi* at the level of personal action. One cannot be self-reliant if one cannot produce the necessities of living by ones own labour. It is possible that one can obtain ones necessities from other persons. However this is possible only under two different conditions: (a) one can become dependent upon others; or (b) one can exploit others. Both are unacceptable since they involve violence, alienation, and dehumanisation. Hence the importance of bread labours. The question is what is bread labour? Is it the time spent by one person in obtaining goods that can be later exchanged for the desired necessities themselves? The earlier concept of *swadeshi* would favour second interpretation.

Non-possession follows from truth and non-violence. It involves that a person should not possess any thing that one does not need. The Gandhian concept of theft is based on *aparigraha*. Accordingly, any one who possess things and objects not needed by oneself but needed by others is a thief. This is an essential concept in *swaraj*, because it brings to it the most coveted state: "to each according to ones need." This also implies institutional forms. The whole concept of private ownership of property—where property is distinguished from tools—comes under sharp questioning. We feel that non-possession is not compatible with capitalism.

Trusteeship follows from and is built on the concept of non-possession. Non-possession may also be considered as a form of non-violence, if possession involves violence. By trusteeship is meant that all those people who possess things as well as "capabilities, abilities, or other natural gifts" must hold these possessions as trustees for all others. In other words they should not derive the benefits from these possessions for themselves. On the contrary, the possession brings immediately an obligation. Possession is an burden.

Non-exploitation follows straight forwardly from the concept and principle of non-violence. One cannot exploit without doing violence. It is both simple and a complex concept. The complexity arises particularly from the nature of the society all the world over today. Some people maintain that both Marxist and Capitalisms society, as constituted today, have institutionalised exploitation, particularly in the production of goods and services. In view of the inequalities and the prevalence of alienation, the very concept of market may be exploitative.

Equality follows from and ensures non-exploitation. Exploitation among equals is not possible. Questions have been raised: What is equality? Is it equality of opportunity only? Looking at the other concepts, we feel that equality in the Gandhian system involves "all possible achievable quality." It is some thing more than equality of opportunity. It does accept differences in natural gifts. But this is a part of diversity and not a question of equality.

Why Gandhian economics did not find a place in economics text books?

Anjaria (1941) had provided a clue why Gandhian economics did not find a place in economics text books dealing with "mainstream" development thought and development thinkers." Gandhi was the pioneer of "an alternative and parallel tradition in Indian economic thought." According to Anjaria, "the Gandhian system of economic thought cannot be adequately appraised in terms of current economic theory which rests on certain limited assumptions. It is a challenge to those assumptions themselves." (J.J. Anajaria, 1941-42, 358)

In Dasgupta's view "what really differentiates Gandhi's approach to economic issues from the main stream tradition is his extra ordinary emphasis on the ethical aspects of economic behaviour. Indeed, Gandhi belived that economic and ethical question were inseparable" (Ajit K. Dasgupta, 1993:133) further, Gandhi "never relinquished a belief in the possibility that a less narrowly focused and more relevant economics could be developed. He never gave up entirely, never ceased to ask: can we evolve a new kind of economics?" (Ajit K. Dasgupta, 1993:134)

Perhaps the most important source of Gandhi's appeal lies in his integrated view of economics and ethics. In the western centers of learning we witness a new trend; we find leading economists turning to ethics and to philosophy. We also find that what were earlier treated as purely economic questions are now being defined as moral and ethical questions. (Amarthya Sen, 1987)

We also find economists recognizing those questions as highly legitimate which were first raised by Gandhi and anticipated by Gandhi. The most important questions in this category compelling attention of economists today are the issue of overall disharmony between man and nature created by the march of industrialism and aggravated by post-industrial transition towards the consumer society; the growing anxiety and alarm over the rapid exhaustion of non-renewable natural resources; the ecological destruction and environmental degradation seriously effecting the quality of life; the widening gap between rich and poor nations and between rich elites and poor masses with in under developed nations; and above all, the channelisation of the forces of scientific and technological progress towards aggressive consumerism and the arms-race leading to the growth of violence and to the danger of nuclear holocaust which has put the very existence of both nature and mankind in total jeopardy. (A.K. Dasgupta in S.R. Sen, 1992; p. 135; V. Gowrikar, 1993; Vasant, K. Bawa, 1994; John Pronk, 1991)

In the limited context of the study of Gandhi's economics, it must be recognized that a purely academic restatement of this economics presents formidable difficulties and problems. Gandhi was neither an academic economists himself nor was he, like his predecessors (for instance, Dadabhai Nauroji, R.C. Dutt or M.G. Ranade) fully rooted in the concepts and categories of modern economics. Gandhi himself made a candid admission of his ignorance of well known modern economic thinkers in a speech delivered on December 22, 1916 before the Munir Central College Economic Society at Allahabad. As part of his address on "Does economic progress clash with real progress?"

Gandhi had observed as follows:

> "Frankly and truly, I know very little of economics, as you naturally understand them. Only the other day, sitting at my evening meal, a civilian friend deluged me with a series of questions on my crankisms. As he proceeded on his cross-examination, I being a willing victim, he found no difficulty in discovering my gross ignorance of the matters. I appeared to him to be

> handling with cocksureness worthy only of a man who knows not that he knows not. To his horror and even indignation suppose, he found that I had not even read books on economics by such well-known authorities as Mill, Marshall, Adam Smith and a host of such other authors. In despair he ended by advising me to read these works before experimenting in matters economic at the expense of the public. He little knew that I was a sinner past redemption."
>
> "My experiments continue at the expense of trusting friends. For, there come to us moments in life when about some things we need no proof from without. A little voice within us tell us, you are on the right track, 'move neither to left nor right, but keep to the straight and narrow way'. With such help we march forward slowly indeed, but surely and steadily. That is my position. It can be satisfactory enough for me, but it can no way answer the requirements of a society such as yours." (M.K. Gandhi in Raghavan Iyer, 1990:93-94)

The question arises: from which source did Gandhi derive the sense of self-assurance that he could grope for an understanding of India's economic problems and for experimenting with their solutions without borrowing concepts from text books of modern economics or without borrowing prescriptions from the practitioners of modern economic theory? This is a question which has neither been asked nor a satisfactory answer been given to it. On serious reflection one finds that Gandhi's quiet self-assurance did not illustrate the classic truth "ignorance is bliss." On the contrary, Gandhi's denigration by his critics for not knowing modern economics showed that the critics had equated "half knowledge" or "borrowed knowledge" with true knowledge. The critics did not realize that "half knowledge" did incalculable harm when put to practice. Gandhi was on very firm ground when he had refused to go in for such "half knowledge" and had followed a different route for forming his basic perceptions or ideas relating to India's economic situation and its problems.

Firstly, Gandhi might not have read books from the mainstream economic thinkers like Adam Smith, Mill and Marshall. But he was very well conversant with the dissident and critical tradition in modern economic and political thinking. The ideas of Ruskin, Emerson and Thoreau had left a lasting impression in his mind and had confirmed his own intuitive perception about the evils of "progress" and "modernisation" (M.L. Dantwalla, 1995:2793-97: H.D. Thoreau, 1993; R.W. Emerson, 1990)

Secondly, modern economics had assumed a particular type of economic structure based on the marginalisation of the country side and the preponderance of urban centers. Gandhi had derived his distrust of modern economics from his intuitive grasp of the fundamental fact about Indian economic life, viz. its predominantly rural character. Gandhi thus was more "scientific" in his judgment regarding the extremely limited relevance of economic concepts derived from a town-dominated Western milieu. Gandhi had thus intuitively grasped the basic weakness of modern economic concepts much before it had caught the discerning eye of distinguished professional economists like Alfred Marshall which had recorded it in following words:

> "The same bent of mind that led our lawyers to impose English civil law on the Hindus, led our economists to work out their theories on the supposition that the world was made of city men." (Alfred Marshall, 1956:630)

Let us explore further the basic distinction between academic economics and Gandhian economics. It must be noted that modern economics had been the product of the secularisation process, i.e. the complete disassociation of thinking of economic issues from religious categories and religious institutions. Gandhi's economic approach was in contrast still rooted in a semi-religious world view. It was in fact, a bled of the sacred and secular. It is not easy, therefore for economists, wholly unfamiliar with religious categories, to understand or appreciate Gandhi's economic ideas and their deeper meanings and implications. In his work "Gandhi reconsidered", M.L. Dantwalla showed an awareness of the difficulties in deciphering the hard core of Gandhi's economic insights from the religious colouring and the didactic tone of his voluminous writings. Dantawalla had observed as follows:

> "we must avoid the temptation to exploit the inconsistencies and pre-scientific phraseology so obvious in Gandhiji's writings, transcend the prejudice against the all-pervading religious and moral atmosphere and with as much scientific detachment as we can lay claim to, dive for the core of Gandhian ideology. I am impelled to emphasis these because I find that reactions favorable or otherwise to Gandhiji's writings are still in the emotional stage, the usual fate of all contemporaneous thought." (M.L. Dantwala, 1944:7)

Further Gandhiji was essentially a man of action. He did not try to offer any systematized intellectual approach or a scientific exposition of his economic philosophy. Nor did he attempt a serious enquiry into the "economic formation" of India as Karl Marx had done for western Europe in *capital* and his other scientific writings.

N.K. Bose had explained very lucidly the method of Gandhi's thought and the difficulties of fully understanding the Gandhian phenomena in the following words.

> "Gandhi perhaps never wrote for the pleasure of writing. Thought and writing were merely tools with him for more efficient action. They were used either to clear up a knotty problem in his own mind or in that of his co-workers. His writings therefore do not exactly give a correct representation of what he actually was, but what he always try to be. It is record of ideals and aspirations and of critics events and situations in the light of those ideals. By their very nature they reflect the difficulties which confronted him from time to time, and also he was able to meet them more or less, successfully in the course of life's experiments." (N.K. Bose, 1958:14)

What was Gandhian economics? It is important to note that for various reasons Gandhian economics had been equated much more with specific policies and prescriptions which Gandhi had advocated and very much less with a distinctive and basic approach. The operational aspects had got precedence over the philosophical or the theoretical aspects. The following comments from Ajith Das Gupta are therefore extremely pertinent from the point of view understanding Gandhiji's permanent contributions to Indian economic thought. To quote:

> "Writings on Gandhian economics have usually focused attention on the specific policies that he proposed. Opposition to modern manufacturing, production-based on the use of machinery, advocacy of village industries, in particular, the spinning wheel, boycott of foreign goods, it is with such policies as these that Gandhi's name is associated. The structure of his arguments, the assumptions he made, and the principles of his conduct that he appealed must be regarded as of central importance, it is these, we believe, that makes his specific policy proposals comprehensible, not the other way round" (Ajith Das Gupta, 1993:133). It is obvious that in Gandhian's view his economic approach was neither new nor was it embodied in any of his statements which could be treated as valid "for all times and all climes" his economic approach was continuously evolving and had to be derived from the changing forms of his thought and his action which had emerged in response to the problems thrown up by the social situations confronting him from time to time.

CONCLUSION

Gandhian economics must be viewed, therefore, not in a historical and static terms but from a historical and dynamic perspective. Gandhian economics must be creatively adapted to the challenges of the period after the end of colonial rule. In this new historical context creative Gandhism could neither be anti-state nor anti-technology, nor anti-growth. It must help to explore new forms of state power suited to the diversities and specifics of India. It must also help to innovate new forms to technology and of economic growth suited to Indian conditions of land and capital scarcity and labour surplus and to the goals of promoting self-respect, self-reliance and eradication of mass poverty. There were several clues and suggestions in Gandhi's writings and speeches which showed that Gandhi was not at all an economic fundamentalist; he was all the time deeply involved in finding practical and implementable solutions to people's problems. Any technology, traditional or modern, and any pattern of economic growth based on the utilisation of this technology, which was in accord with the criteria of economic *swaraj* and uplift of *Daridranarayanan* and had a non-acquisitive orientation was acceptable to Gandhi.

References

J.J. Anjaria, "The Gandhian Approach to Indian Economics", *Indian Journal of Economics*, Vol. 22, 1941-42.

Ajit K. Dasgupta, "A History of Indian Economics Thought", Routledge, London, 1993.

M.L. Dantwala, "Gandhi Reconsidered", Padma Publications, Bombay, 1994.

D.P. Mukerji, "An Economic Theory for India", Diversities, Peoples' Publishing House, New Delhi, 1958.

J.S. Mathur and A.S. Mathur (edited), "Economic Thought of Mahatma Gandhi."

V.B. Singh, "Essays in Indian Political Economy", Essays No. 2 (Gandhism: An Interpretation), *Sarvodaya*, Chaps. 4 to 6.

Gray and Parekh, "Mahatma Gandhi: An Essay in Appreciation."

7

Gandhiji's View on Panchayat Raj and New Panchayati Raj System

R. ARUNACHALAM AND R. SREENIVASAN

Mahatma Gandhiji strongly believed in participatory democracy at the grass root level. The 73rd amendment to constitution is a step in the right direction to fulfil the aspirations of the lower rungs of people. He advocated the decentralised governance to enable the poor people to participate in nation building and at the same time to preclude the intervention of the state in the routine life of people. Gandhiji wanted to see villages as "Ling gardens of Eden" from "Clung heap." During his Non-Cooperation Movement Panchayati Raj system acquired greater significance. It aimed at replacement of courts by Panchayats. He did believe that real democracy could be realised by Panchayats and not by some number of men sitting at the Centre. He was convinced that Panchayats could render useful, cheap, speedy and efficient justice. For development of rural areas Gandhiji advocated hard work of villagers. People in the village should be aware of "Eleven Views" namely, non-violence, truth, non-stealing, celibacy, non-possession, manual labour, control of palate, fearlessness and equal respect to all religions.

He believed in a proper institutional framework such as Self-help. The Women Self-help Group is a good example in India. Panchayats have to be basic units of democratic decentralisation and the higher units need to cooperate with them. Referring to the functions of Panchayat Gandhiji emphasized administration of justice, education, village environment and uplift of the poor.

The New Panchayati Raj System aims at decentralisation of governance at the grass root level and empowerment of rural men and women. According a constitutional status, it has a 3-tier system—District, Middle and Gram Panchayats. The District level Planning Committee is empowered to take decisions including the conduct of elections to the local bodies. Harnessing the local resources optimally and preserving the environment are crucial. The Gram Sabha has to ensure participation of people at the village level. It has to promote rural development programmes. Jayaprakash Narayan, the Sarvodaya Leader regarded Gram Sabha as a grass root organisation of democracy. To conclude: The Gandhian Philosophy of Panchayati Raj has to be translated into action using the provisions of the New Panchayati Raj for social transformation as well as rural development in Indian villages.

Gandhiji's View on Panchayati Raj and New Panchayati Raj System

Mahatma Gandhiji was a great genius and a visionary of 20th century who predicted the need of involvement of the people in every act of the Government. He had a very clear perception that people in the villages and cities have the capacity to solve their own problems without much intervention by the Government by its actions. The 73rd Constitutional Amendment has rightly claimed that it is a revolutionary legislation that takes power to the people. We have to see that the spirit of the said amendment is not lost. It is the people who breath life into any act of the state. Therefore, it is imperative to educate the people at large and village leaders in particular about the implications and expectations of the Panchayati Raj Act, so that necessary foundation for participatory democracy at the grass roots is well laid.[1] The credit for reviving this grass root democratic institution goes to Rajiv Gandhiji who introduced the 73rd Amendment to the constitution, which made Panchayat elections mandatory and in particular recognising gram sabha as a basic institution of the new Panchayati Raj system. When Panchayati Raj was introduced in the country in 1959 the then Prime Minister Nehru said that it was the greatest revolution in the country and the system worked well till 1964.

The Father of our nation Mahatma Gandhiji has been considered a great advocate of Panchayati Raj in India. He wanted to reorientate village life through the institution of Panchayat. In his view, villages are the backbone of a nation. Villages of India, according to him, are the real India. In his own words, "If the village perished India will perish too. It will be no more India. Her own mission in the world will get lost."[2] Again, for Gandhiji, the real significance of `Swaraj' was opportunity to shape India's rural development in accordance with her own tradition and needs. So he remarked: "To serve our villages is to establish Swaraj. Everything else is but an ideal dream."[3] Gandhiji took keen interest in the development of the rural society. He contributed a great deal in raising the Panchayats to their rightful place in a democratic country. He emphasised that this was the medium through which his ideal of decentralisation of power could be realised. To Gandhiji, decentralisation, is the basic requirement for the success of democracy. And, a decentralised democracy based on non-violence must consist of groups settled in small communities or villages in which voluntary cooperation is the condition of dignified and peaceful existence. For, it is the only way to realize the value of democracy from the grass root level as it will enable the people to participate in taking and implementing decisions without a rigid and strict control of any higher authority. Moreover, it is the only alternative to reduce the intervention and interference of the state in day-to-day affairs of the people.

Evolution or Development of Gandhiji's Views on Panchayati Raj

It can be said that the first reference of Gandhiji wanted to turn the villages from "Clung heap" into "Model village" or into "Ling gardens of Eden", on Panchayats sometimes in February, 1916, while appreciating the working of the ancient `Indian Panchayat system'.[4] He was sure that the problem of village sanitation would have been solved long ago and India would have been enjoying self-government suited to its requirements, had village Panchayats been acting as a living force in administration.

However, during the Non-Cooperation Movement the Panchayat system acquired greater significance as it offered an alternative to the English Judicial System. It represented the positive aspect of the programme of boycott of courts. It aimed at the replacement of courts by Panchayats for the settlement of the dispute between individuals. Unlike the British courts in India, these Panchayats were to function as arbitration courts in order to dispense speedy justice to the parties. As a result, several thousand Panchayats were established throughout the country during non-cooperation movement and Gandhiji said, "I would therefore strongly advise the Panchayats to continue their very useful work of giving people, cheap, speedy, and efficient justice."[5]

In New Delhi, on January 6, 1948, in a reference to Panchayats of Aundh State, Gandhiji explained: "There was no law which could stop a Panchayat from functioning wherever the people wanted it. Aundh may cease to be a special group of villages named Aundh. The Panchayat was there to serve the people. In the true democracy of India the unit was the village. Even if one village wanted Panchayati Raj which was called republic in English, no one could be stupid. True democracy could not be worked by twenty men sitting at the centre. It had to be worked from below by the people of every village."[6] He believed that true democracy could be realised through Panchayati Raj in India.

Gandhiji referred to the Panchayats till the last moments of his life. Even a few days before his death he said that the ideal of the freedom of the country would not be realised without village autonomy. He reminded on 25th

January, 1948 that the character of India's independence as conceived by the congress was based on village autonomy.

In fact, Gandhiji emphasised on 'Panchayati Raj' till the last moment of his life. Even, only some hours before his martyrdom, he signed a document (the last document of his life) on Panchayats.

Gandhiji's Involvement in Panchayati Raj

Gandhiji does not advocate decentralisation only because of its economic and political advantages. The decentralisation envisions and upholds the cultural and spiritual ideal of 'simple living and high thinking'. It means that he does not hanker after raising merely the 'standard of living' but as a matter of fact, he wants to raise the standard of life, and improve the social status. In other words, he trusts that society should be organized in such a manner that individual recovers the maximum freedom and opportunity to strengthen his personality and character to the fullest extent.

As a result, Gandhiji is opposed to centralisation of power as it could be a danger to democracy. Centralisation of power, in his view can distort all democratic values. He argues, "possession of power makes men blind and deaf. They cannot see things which are under their very nose, and cannot hear things which invade their ears."[7] As a result, he pleads for decentralisation. He again emphasizes, "If India is to evolve along non-violent lines, it will have to decentralize many things. Centralisation cannot be sustained and defended without adequate force."[8] He affirms that without decentralisation it is impossible to ensure individual liberty and mental and moral growth of man. Similarly, it is equally essential for the realisation of the ideal of democracy for, the rule of the people, which it stands for, is not possible without adequate opportunities to individuals to participate in the management of their own affairs.

According to Gandhiji the first, the power state structure of the west. Primarily he rejects it on the ground that it leads to centralisation of power, exploitation of the weak, denial of individual freedom and moral degradation. His apprehension is that it is democratic only in its external frame but dictatorial in actual practice.

Second is the Panchayati Raj model building up from below. In other words, it can be called democratic decentralisation. As a matter of fact, Gandhiji is drawn towards this model. Though Gandhiji may not be considered, as a model builder, yet his ideas definitely orientate towards a model.

In Gandhiji's scheme, the foundation of rural development is based on the solid work of the workers. A worker should not be power hungry and he should remain a political, i.e. away from power politics. He should be above village factions and should not expect any rewards or gratitude for his work. He should work courageously and 'intelligently' with local help us for as possible. He should work as a village scavenger, train others in values of sanitation and health care and import health education with an emphasis on nature cure and such simple medicines as castor oil, quimine, etc. He should be a master spinner, habitual user of khadi, should take interest in encouraging and reviving village industries. He should be engaged in a craft so that he may earn his own livelihood. He should be a model of industry, fully utilizing all working hours. He should maintain a diary in which he should write a complete account of the daily work done by him. He prescribed 'Eleven Views' viz. "non-violence, truth, non-stealing, celibacy (brahmcharya), non-possession, manual or body-labour, control of the palate, fearlessness, equal respect for all religions, swadeshi (restricting oneself to the use and service of one's nearest surroundings in preference to those more remote) and spirit of exclusive brotherhood."[9]

Institutional Frame

Till 1936, Gandhiji had not made up his mind or he was not clear about the character of the structure of Indian polity. At the Faizpur Congress Session in 1936, he expressed that India must have a polity suited to her genuis. But he could not give its blue print. This shows that he was clear about the spirit but not of the form of Indian polity.

Gandhiji's mind was working in the direction of a broad institutional structure of administration based on the principle of democratic decentralisation. It means that village

Panchayat must be elected by the adult population of the village. Since at that time there was no regular assembly of the village he advised the election of Panchayats though public meetings called by beating of the drums.

Gandhiji emphasized the importance of the development of each village on the basis of the principle of self-help without any government assistance.

Gandhiji wrote, "To those who are hungry, unemployed, God can dare reveal himself only as work and wages as the assurance of food."[10] But he was against giving free food to those poor people who were capable of earning their livelihood provided they were given work or did 'honest labour'. He was all for giving such work which could lead to productive self-employment on a regular basis to these people. He was advocating opening of self-employment avenues based on local skills, technical know how and raw materials. He wrote, "I feel convinced that the revival of hard-spinning and hand-weaving will make the largest contribution to the economic and the moral regeneration of India. The millions must have a simple industry to supplement agriculture. Spinning was the cottage industry years ago and if the millions are to be saved from starvation, they must be enabled to reintroduce spinning in their homes, and every village must repossess its own weaver."[11]

He was of the firm conviction that Khadi, Swadeshi and spinning wheel could provide alternative and supplementary employment to rural poor, and it is through this way that rural masses could get income and there was no other way of eradicating India's poverty.

In 1934, at Gandhiji Seva Sangh meeting, Gandhiji delivered his speech and said, "we must promote every useful industry that was existent a short while ago and the extinction of which has now resulted in unemployment."[12] Without revival of village industries the 'increasing poverty' and unemployment will be difficult to stop. "Village economy cannot be complete without the essential village industries such as hand grinding, hand pounding, soap making, paper making, match making, tanning, oil pressing, etc."[13] The other village industries cover cattle farming, dairying, farming and compost manure.

Working of Panchayati Raj

Gandhiji wanted the Panchayats to end exploitation and to carry out their functions and responsibilities with the cooperation of the villages. For him, self-reliance had become the keystone of the whole system. Voluntary participation in the process of realizing the social ends was a fundamental requirement. The members of the Panchayat, therefore, must carry the people with them through persuasion and education for the proper functioning of the village Panchayat.

The relations of the village Panchayat to the higher units of organisation of the country, according to him, should not be based on any principle of subordination. This follows from his concept of oceanic circles. The innumerable villages are bound together not in pyramidal order related to each other in oceanic circles whose centre will be the individual always ready to perish for the village, the latter ready to perish for the circle of villages till at last the whole becomes one life composed of individuals, never aggressive in their arrogance but ever humble, sharing the majesty of the oceanic circle of which they are integral units.

Further, the outermost circumstance will not wield power to crush the inner circle but will give strength to all within and derive its own strength from it.

As a result, in Gandhiji's conception of Panchayati Raj, the higher units do not coerce or dictate the Panchayats. But higher units set their strength and power from the lower units. Accordingly, the Panchayat has to be basic unit of democratic decentralisation and the higher units will have to tender sound advice, give expect guidance and information, and coordinate the activities of the village Panchayats with a view to increase the efficiency and skill of administration and public service.

It seems that the whole plain is turned upside down, the village becomes the real and moving unit of administration. Gandhiji wants every village to be a republic having full powers, self-sustained and capable of managing its own affairs. However, this does not mean that it excludes dependence on the willing help from the neighbours or even from the world where dependence is a necessity.

Functions and Powers of Village Panchayati Raj

In fact, Gandhiji did not dwell upon the functions of village Panchayats systematically. He only laid down the broad principles of the functions and role to be played by the Panchayats in response to different situations and circumstances. He was essential because these could vary from time to time, and place to place. However, he was fully convinced that the local bodies must have the power to manage the affairs of their localities because no central government could understand and solve the problems of a far away area.

One of its most important functions, according to him, under the jurisdiction of institutions like Panchayats, was the settlement of the disputes between individuals. Its object was to make justice available to the villagers without incurring much cost or inconvenience so, he said in his presidential address at the Belgaum Congress, "Administration of justice should be cheapened and with that end in view the final court of appeal should not be in London but in Delhi. Parties to civil suits trust be compelled in the majority of cases to refer their dispute to arbitration, the decisions of those Panchayats to be final except in cases of corruption or obvious misapplication of law. Municipality of intermediatic courts should be avoided."[14] Similarly, he emphasised that Panchayats could be very effective instruments for the uplift of the village. So, he laid down that every Panchayat will be expected to attend to—

(a) The education of boys and girls in its village.
(b) Its sanitation.
(c) Its medical needs
(d) The upkeep and cleanliness of village wells or ponds.
(e) The uplift of and the daily wants of the so-called untouchables.

In brief, Gandhiji wants village Panchayats to perform a variety of functions covering practically all aspects of the welfare of the villagers. The Panchayats of his view hold a good deal of autonomy and this become an effective instrument for the diffusion and decentralisation of power and authority.

Gandhiji's view point here is, that development is an effort which has to be shouldered by myraid segments of people. They can work hand in glove and become complementary to each other only when they have 'mutual trust'. The political as well as economic problems of a country can be solved only when local bodies are no longer the agents or slaves, but the partners and planners of the development. It has been felt that things imposed from above, do not educate the people, not can they convince them. The people must have the feeling that they are participating in their own programmes. More important is that they should manage their development programme and it is possible only in decentralised set-up of Government where local bodies like village Panchayats enjoy genuine and real-power of decision-making and decision-implementation.

The New Panchayati Raj System

Nowadays people are very fast in the competitive environment. Today Multinational companies entered into India. So, the Government has to take care of rural and urban population. Because of this the new Panchayati Raj system got enough importance. The new Panchayati Raj system is the outcome of the world-wide movement to liberate the people from the clutches of the big government and the total state system. It is also one of the new policy options of Rajiv Gandhiji to integrate our system of political and economic activities with the activities of the developed societies. The new arrangement of decentralisation of power or devolution of power or empowerment of people is equated to developing resourcefulness of the people or entrustment of move responsibilities to the people and to turn the Government from the role of a provider to facilitator and by which the role and function of the government will be reduced and the role of the government in the present context has to be redefined. Success of any system needs a thorough understanding of the system by the operator. Hence, to make the new Panchayati Raj system vibrant and active the people are to be made aware of the full implications of the new system. The new system envisages more of responsibilities rather than powers and authority.

Characteristics of the New System

The concept, Panchayat has its own antiquity and ambiguity in the minds of all as it is seen from the backdrop of historiography. It should be seen contextually and more particularly in the background of the policy packages of the federal and state governments and the ongoing development process of the world. The new system has been given a constitutional status and by which it has got permanence in the Indian Political System as a third government. It has a three-tier structural arrangement namely, District Panchayat, middle level Panchayat and Gram Panchayat. The new system has been vested with the power of taking decision on twenty-nine subjects in the 11th schedule. To alter the planning process of the country, a statutory planning body, District planning committee has been created at the district level. To maintain periodicity in conducting election to local bodies, state election commission has been created and by which it is declared that election will be conducted to local bodies regularly in every five years and even if the local bodies are dissolved and dismissed, election would be conducted within six months. Local body institutions are not merely to carry out schemes evolved by central and state governments with the resources allocated by the federal and state governments. They have more responsibilities than the assigned and they have to chalk out various programmes based on the local needs peculiar to the local areas with the resources available locally. Their activities are not so rigid. Harnessing the local resources at the optimum level without causing any damage to environment is yet another important function. Yet in the present context to meet the basic minimum needs of the local areas they need more resources from the state and central governments. To make the local body institutions sound in financial resources to meet the requirements, a State Finance Commission has been constituted to make recommendations. The inherent weakness in the previous Panchayati Raj system with regard to finance has been eliminated by this provision through the new act.

People's participation is *sine qua non* for development and it has been realised through the creation of a body at grass root level called "Gram Sabha." All eligible registered voters are members of Gram Sabha. The Gram Sabha has many functions. Though it seems that the concept of Gram Sabha is an unworkable proposition in the villages in the present context of caste and communal clashes among communities, somehow or other, it has to be made workable to perform certain specific functions to bring peace, harmony, development and to nurture democracy at the grass root level. The unutilised resources have been put to use for the well-being of the society. Likewise the reservation of seats for SC/ST draws the attention of all. Reservation of seats is propostion to the population of SC/ST. In Tamil Nadu near about 24 percent seats have been earmarked for SC/ST in the local bodies. Thus the characteristics mentioned above do not amplify that it is not only an act by itself but it demonstrates that it is a mass movement for peace, prosperity, equity and democracy. Thus the new Panchayati Raj system will have for reaching implications in the lifestyle of the people. It needs proper understanding of the whole system by the people.

Gram Sabha and its Significance

Gram Sabha is one of the most important three basic institutions of the new direct democracy at the village level. The other two are (Gram-Kosh), a village fund (Gram Shanti Seva), a village peace corps. Therefore, it must be made successful. Gram Sabha is a village assembly of all adults, men and women, which would resulted and develop village life and function automatically. This was a structure based entirely on people's power (Lokshakti) expressing itself in the form of village power (Gram Shakti). Thus the village would emerge as an organised unit to look after its internal administration, development, and agro-industrial economy. This was a model for democracy at the grass roots based on direct participation by the people.[15] Democracy has been defined as 'a government where everybody has a say'. A democratic administration by a Panchayat cannot be a good substitute for it.[16]

Gram Sabha is an institutional approach to popular

participation. It provides a base for the three-tier structure of the Panchayati Raj institutions. It is regarded as the grassroot organisation of democracy. To J.P. Narayan, the sarvodaya thinker, Gram Sabha signifies village democracy. To him, representative government from the village to Delhi was no good substitute for direct democracy.[17] Gram Sabhas could be set-up on a de facto basis. Speed was the essence of the strategy and people's participation would be the index of its success.[18] The idea of Gram Sabha, by and large, has not struck roots in the minds of the people. It has so far reached the prominent persons in the village. The positive outlook of the prominent persons in the village on the Gram Sabha has to be tapped and activised to bring the common people in large numbers, within the fold of the Gram Sabha."[19] To enlist the people's active cooperation in the national campaign to secure the proper distribution of foodgrains and other necessities, it is necessary to organise Gram Sabhas in the villages and ward sabhas in towns and cities.[20] Gram Sabha, being a primary body would be face-to-face organ, of direct democracy, not made up of representatives but comprising all adult residents. Similar bodies, which he called "communities of work" should be founded in factories offices, educational institutions and other work places. The primary body of people's democracy had to be active body. Meeting regularly, discussing common problems and evolving cooperative and collective forms of action to manage their affairs. Jayaprakash Narayan emphasized that no one who belonged to a political party should be elected by the Gram Sabhas or other primary bodies to any office, since a member of a political party was by definition controlled by his party hierarchy.[21]

It is the 'birth-right' of every village to conduct its own affairs. The Gram Sabha should therefore take into its hands the management of village lands and forests, settle disputes, plan and carry out schemes for its own welfare, and exercise supervision over the village level officials. While pressing for the necessary constitutional changes to empower them to perform those tasks, the Gram Sabha should start exercising these functions. People in the cities should similarly take the initiative in assuming responsibility for local service.[22] We have to make every village a complete and a thorough state in miniature. Thus, in every village there would the departments of health, industries, agriculture, education, justice, etc. As there is a Foreign affairs department with respect to the relations with other countries, there will be in every village a special department which would handle the affairs pertaining to other villages.[23]

In December 1970, a seminar on "The citizen and democracy" was held at the Gandhiji's peace foundation in New Delhi. At the seminar, JP recalled that societies for the defence of democracy should be set-up in every city and voter's education societies established throughout the country. As suggested by JP, many people in the sarvodaya movement preferred to devote themselves to the objectives of Gramdan and Gram Swarajya and were opposed to frittering away energy in voters' education campaigns. In this context, Gram Sabhas, no doubt could be used as a centre for voters' education and to educate the people about the Sarvodaya Polity.[24]

By mid-1972, in July, at Bangalore, a small group of leading Sarvodaya workers and some sympathetic social scientists met to discuss ways to broaden the sarvodaya movement and to make it more effective. Some of the ideas they discussed related to Gramdan work. In the same meeting, JP proposed the idea of encouraging to set-up sub-committees within the Gram Sabha to discuss their own problems. It was in the course of this meeting that plans were also made to launch a new journal of political commentary—*Every Man's Weekly*, beginning July, 1973.[25]

At grass root level, the immediate task is to create a faith in the village people regarding the social utility of the institution of Gram Sabha and make that institution based on the village community as such. For its efficient working a committee system may be introduced. The defeated function should be encouraged to co-operate with it. This would give it a wider base. The presence of the sarpanch should be made compulsory and the panchas could remain absent only with prior permission. This would establish a vital link between the Gram Sabha and the Gram Panchayat. Proceedings of the Gram Sabhas should be recorded and approved by the village

Panchayats in their subsequent meetings. There should be a regular follow-up of these resolutions. This would increase the stature of the Gram Sabha.

Gram Sabha is a basic tier to popularize development programmes. In doing so, it tries to fill in the gap between the two roles of the Zila Parishads as a local government body and as a district development organisation. The Gram Sabha would establish an active dialogue between the village people and their elected leaders at the village Panchayat level regarding development programmes to be undertaken. This would involve the village community in the decision-making process and would develop a supporting structure for the village Panchayat. As the Gram Sabha would act as a galvanizer on behalf of the people, it would to a certain extent, remedy the defects in popular participation caused by the failure of Shramdan. Faith and interest are the two sides of the same problem and have a direct bearing on the functional efficiency of the institution. These two would operate for the success of Gram Sabha and such a Gram Sabha would further the cause of development26.

Notes and References

1. Letter from Sri K.M. Natarajan, Tamilnadu Sarvodaya Mandal, Gandhi Museum, Madurai, dated 02.06.1993.
2. *Harijan*, 29.8.1936, Vol. IV, p. 226.
3. *Young India*, 26.12.1929.
4. The collected works of Mahatma Gandhi, Vol. XIII, pp. 210-16.
5. *Ibid.*, Vol. XIX, p. 431.
6. *Harijan*, January 18, 1948, Vol. XI, p. 519.
7. The collected works of Mahatma Gandhi, Vol. XX, p. 505.
8. *Harijan*, 30.12.1939, Vol. VII, p. 391.
9. Tendulkar, D.G., The Mahatma, *op. cit.*, 1957, Vol. IV, pp. 90-91, See also Vol. VIII, pp. 91-100 and *Harijan*, 31.8.1934, Vol. II, No. 29, p. 229, 29.2.1936, Vol. IV, No. 3, pp. 7-12, 18.8.1940, Vol. VIII, No. 27, p. 252 and 2.3.1947, Vol. XI, No. 5, p. 48.
10. Gandhi, M.K., The Collected Works, Vol. 68, p. 446.
11. *Young India*, 21.7.1920, Vol. II, No. 29, p. 4.
12. Gandhi, M.K., The collected works, Vol. 59, p. 411.
13. Gandhi, M.K., Constructive programme. Its meaning and place, (Ahmedabad: Navajivan Publishing House, 1981), p. 18.
14. The collected works of Mahatma Gandhi, Vol. XXV, p. 480.

15. Diwakar, R.R., Mahendra Agrawal, Vinoba: The spiritual revolutionary Gandhi Peace Foundation, New Delhi, 1984, p. 73.
16. Nandedkar, V.G. Local Government. It's Role in Development : administration, Concept Publishing Company, New Delhi, 1979, p. 167.
17. Seminar on Fundamental Problems of Panchayati Raj (New Delhi. All India Panchayat Parishad, 1964), p. 69.
18. Geoffrey ostergaard, Non-violent revolution in India, Gandhi Peace Foundation, New Delhi 1985, p. 31.
19. Inamdar, N.R. Functioning of Village Panchayats (Bombay: Popular Prakashan, 1970), pp. 76-77.
20. Geoffrey Ostergarrd, *op. cit*, p. 55.
21. Geoffrey ostergarrd, *op. cit.*, p. 67.
22. Geoffrey Ostergarrd, *op. cit.*, p. 343.
23. Viswanath Tandon, Selections from Vinoba, Sarva Seva Sangh Prakashan, Rajghat Varanasi 1981, p. 185.
24. See Note 9, p. 44.
25. Geoffrey Ostergarrd, *op. cit.*, p. 47.
26. See Note 7, pp. 167-69.

8

The Relevance of Gandhian Economic Philosophy in 21st Century

Mithilesh Kumar Sinha and Rakesh K. Singh

Mahatma Gandhiji was never regarded as an economist by the intelligentsia though his basics of economics was sound than most. If socialist economies collapsed then their binary opposite, free market liberalism too is found wanting, resulting in violence, misery and sense of inner discontent. In the age of globalisation, there is the persistence of disparity, poverty, unemployment and a myriad socio-economic injustices that the modern development processes have brought about. All economists today agree the 'trusteeship's the practical solution of present-day malpractices in property and maldistribution of wealth. In fact trusteeship is the only way to end capitalism without ending the capitalist who could be a trustee of his own wealth. For his own household he would be entitled to a reasonable share. Twentieth century is hailed as the 'people's century' but where are the women in this crowd of people. Standing on the threshold of the 21st century as one looks back, a question that confronts us is where indeed, are the women in India in terms of empowerment and socio-economic emancipation? Mahatma Gandhi is the foremost name in the small list of those illustrious and sensitive men of the twentieth century if not down the ages who have spontaneously empathized with the women's cause. In the name of development and globalisation, dependency, under-development, etc. are increasing at a galloping pace. Why this backdrop? Is it because we have strayed away from the Gandhian path of planning and rural development? Or is it because we have not properly interpreted the essence of Gandhian philosophy? In fact, rural India is poor. It needs a special kind of attention. Therefore, at this juncture, we need to rediscover Gandhian paths of development which would lead us to march on the roads of progress and prosperity.

Thus, Gandhian economic thought is a good economics that concentrates on the even distribution of economic opportunities and benefits. Gandhiji is relevant wherever there is injustice, poverty, hunger, inequality. His economic thought is the only alternative for social justice-based development.

The objective of this paper is to discuss the relevance of Gandhian economic philosophy in 21st century therein jobless, voiceless, rootless, futureless, and ruthless growth is likely to take place.

PROLOGUE

It is an irony that relevance of Gandhi in the context of development has to be re-examined and explained in the context of development today in the era of globalisation. Perhaps this is due to the definition of development that we often accept without much thought. Development, most of the time, is taken to be just economic development and the Western model of industrialisation is believed to be the only viable option. This idea has gain strength after the decline and disintegration of the Soviet Union and the apparent defeat of the socialist system. Only those who subscribe to this ask natïve questions about relevance of Gandhiji's thought. It is true that Gandhiji was not in favour reckless industrialisation and urbanisation and certainly opposed mechanisation, this does not mean what he preached and practised have become obsolete. As a matter of fact it is his insights and strategies that can help us to contend with strong gusts of neocolonialism that threaten to blow us off our feet (Pant: 2005).

Gandhian economic philosophy is becoming increasingly relevant to the world today, particularly the Third World countries. True Economics, according to Gandhiji, must be life-oriented and a servant of humanity at large. In the words of Martin Luther King (Jr): "If humanity is to progress, Gandhi is inescapable...we may ignore him at our own risk." Gandhi is relevant wherever there is struggle for freedom, wherever there is struggle for justice, wherever there is oppression, wherever there is poverty, hunger, inequality, unemployment. The greatest tribute to Gandhi was paid by UNESCO when it adopted in its preamble the Gandhian thought. If the 19th century belonged to Carlyle and Ruskin and the twentieth to Russel and Huxley, the 21st century belongs to Gandhi alone. Actually Gandhian economic philosophy is the road to prosperity, social justice and balanced growth because it is panacea for all economic and social problems, arising in recent years due to the growing violence, beginning wars in the minds of men and the occurrence of jobless, ruthless, rootless, voiceless, and futureless growth. Gandhiji declared: 'Earth provides enough to satisfy every man's need but not for every man's greed."

With a view to examine the relevance of Gandhian economic philosophy in 21st century this paper is divided into five sections. In section I, Gandhian economic vision is discussed. In section II, the Gandhian perception on quality of life is analysed, in section III, Gandhian view of women empowerment is described, in section IV, the contribution of Mahatma Gandhi to the evolution and growth of modern corporate ethics, Gandhiji's look at the *inter-se* relationship between the business and the society and holding the key of Gandhian philosophy for unfolding the new vistas in corporate ethics are discussed. Last section examines the relevance of Gandhian economic philosophy in 21st century.

I. GANDHIAN ECONOMIC VISION

Spinning, weaving and farming were the most important features of Gandhian economics. Gandhi introduces the spinning wheel not because of he wants to bring about a social and economic revolution, but deep in his heart. He feels that self-dependence and self-activity are also assured foundations of the inherent dignity and discipline in every human being. As a matter of fact, his vision of the spinning wheel, even now belittled and ignored more often than not, has he promise and perfection at its root of a bewildered and camouflaged humanity seeking solace and substances in respectable and decent living anywhere and everywhere. "The Charkha is, as he categorically asserts on the spinning wheel, a useful and indispensable article for every home. It is the symbol of the nation's prosperity and, therefore, freedom." (Chakrabarti: 2004)

Gandhi's 'Swadeshi' (use of things produced locally) was the bed-rock of freedom. His life mission was to made India self-reliant and self-sufficient. Before the British rule India used to export 30 lakh rupees worth of hand-woven cloth every year. During the British rule all export came to a halt and, as in a reverse process, India spent 60 crore rupees every year to buy British export. The Indian weavers lost their occupation, became tillers of soil and were totally impoverished. A viceroy was appalled at this situation and remarked that the bones of cotton weavers are bleaching the plains of India. "The misery hardly finds a parallel in the history of commerce." Gandhi decided to stop the import of alien cloth. He decided to revive hand-weaving.

He revived the handloom, the Charkha and made cloth known as Khadi. "It is my conviction that with every thread I draw, I am spinning the destiny of India. Without the spinning wheel there is no salvation for this country of ours." He formed the Charkha Sangh which contributed lakhs of rupees to the national wealthy every month.

Charkha for him stood for dignity of labour, mutual co-operation, its music soother the ears as against the noise of the mill. Charkha, he said, was like the sun around which all village handicrafts revolved. Besides it was a wheel of freedom.

Trusteeship was the economic term Gandhiji gave to the idea that all wealth should be treated as a national trust. The idea was born during the train journey from Johannesburg to St. Martizburg on the night of 7th June, 1893 while reading Ruskin's 'Unto this Last'. The book changed the economic vision of 'Coolie Barrister' who was thrown out of the 1st Class compartment bag and baggage. The incident changed the destinies of half of the people of the world.

The Phoenix Farm Settlement and the Tolstoy Farms were based on the principle of trusteeship. Gandhi said there should be minimum wage and ceiling on maximum the capitalist's property. Minimum has no meaning unless there is a ceiling on maximum. All economists today agree that trusteeship is the practical solution of present-day malpractices in property and maldistribution of wealth. In fact trusteeship is the only way to end capitalism without ending the capitalist who could be a trustee of his own wealth.

For his own household expenses he would be entitled to a reasonable share.

Gandhiji always drew a distinction between the man and the system, it was an essential part of his non-violent approach. It was this approach which made him view his own short-comings rigorously and to be charitable in judging others. People accused Gandhiji that he was the friend of the capitalists but the fact remains that nobody fought them harder. All he expected the rich to hold their riches and talents in trust and use them in the service of society. 'To insist on more', he said with a smile, 'would be to kill the goose than laid the golden eggs'.

GANDHIAN PHILOSOPHY ON RURAL DEVELOPMENT

It was Gandhiji who first understood the importance, role and place of Indian villages in the whole country. The rural character of the economy and the need for regeneration of rural life was stressed by Mahatma Gandhi. He wrote in *Harijan* (4, April, 1936):

"India is to be found not in few cities but in its 700,000 villages. But we town dwellers have believed that India is to be found in its towns and the villages were created to minister to our needs. We have hardly paused to inquire if those poor get sufficient to eat and clothe themselves with and whether they have a roof to shelter themselves from sun and rain."

Gandhiji's approach to rural development was practical and productive. He wanted to develop a 'New Social Order' based on the foundation of non-violence and truth where economic upliftment and rural progress go together focussing on 'Development of Man'. As he had stated to Jawaharlal Nehru in his letter, Gandhiji wanted to have a programme of rural reconstruction so that 'Dung Hill' villages could be converted into 'village republics'. Removal of poverty and unemployment from rural India was the ultimate desire of Gandhiji. His heart was crying for the toiling millions, who were constantly exploited and expropriated. Therefore, he was rightly remarked "exploiting the village itself is organized violence...." The blood of the village is the cement with which the edifice of cities is built. I want this blood that is today inflating the arteries of cities to run once again in the blood vessels of the villages. He wanted each village should be self-sufficient and self-reliant. In Gandhiji's words, "My idea of self-sufficiency is that village must be sufficient in regard to food, cloth and other basic necessities (Gandhi). The village as 'community' should be a production and consumption unit. Such logic moved him to prefer Khadi and other village industries. The rationale behind the choice of Khadhi was his anxiety—'work to all'. Accepting the reality Gandhiji also had a pragmatic choice of industry for rural development. "Those who do not see Khadi as the centre of village activities, they are welcome to concentrate their efforts only on other industries." (Gandhi)

Gandhiji once said, "I want to prevent our villagers from catching infection of industrialism." (Gandhi: 1940) He was not opposed to machines but what he objects 'is the craze for machinery not machinery as such. The craze is for what they call labour saving machinery. Man goes on saving labour, till thousands are without work and thrown in the open streets to die of starvation'. Thus Gandhiji had elaborate plan for labour intensive production which would generate more employment opportunities and would suit to the rural community. In this context, his views are worth-mentioning "I have no partiality for return to primitive method of grinding and husking for the sake of them. I suggest the return because there is no other way of giving employment to the millions of villagers who are living in idleness. (*Ibid.*)

Gandhiji wanted "development to be related to human scale: handicrafts instead of gigantic industries, village habitats instead of megalopolies, swadeshi in place of imported technology, a decentralised economy instead of centralised one (Indireson: 1994). Gandhiji also realised the need for an integrated rural development, though a different type. He believed that craft-art, health and education should be integrated into one. His development approach was integrated with education and he elaborately explained why 'Naitalism' should be integrated with village reconstruction programme (Gandhi).

The above paradigms of development portend a bright ray of hope for the toiling millions in rural India. Alvin Toffler in his celebrated volume, 'Third Wave', makes a very objective analysis of the various options available to modern man. In a critical appraisal of the three waves, i.e. the Capitalist, Marxist and Gandhian. Toffler prefers Gandhian model as the best alternative for the whole world. Therefore, it is high time for our policy-makers, bureaucrats and academicians, to make a reappraisal of our development strategies and programmes on Gandhian lines which would give us proper insight and broad vision to rethink and redesign our planning perspective, allowing India to live in villages not in cities. In so far as the self-sufficiency of village life of 75 per cent of India's population is concerned, the best recourse is to rediscover the Gandhian paths of development. We can achieve, what we had tended to achieve if we are willing to follow Gandhiji not in theory but in practice.

II. THE GANDHIAN PERCEPTION OF QUALITY OF LIFE

Quality of life in economic jargons has by and large been used to denote the availability of economic opportunities to the people. But this is only a partial connotation of the term. Availability of economic opportunities by itself cannot improve the quality of life. Quality of life also aims at promotion of both equity and excellence. Looked at from this angle, quality of life appears to be a multi-dimensional term encompassing not only the economic opportunities available to the people, but also their ability to take advantage of living conditions which permit a healthy and productive life.

To be more specific, quality of life includes:

- Availability of adequate nutritious food at an affordable price;
- Housing and healthy living environment including sanitation, garbage disposal and drainage;
- Availability of adequate and safe drinking water;
- Clothing affordable to the teeming millions;
- Employment for all able bodied human being;
- Universal primary education;
- Basic health services to all, especially preventive medicine geared particularly for the rural areas;
- Access to media of communication and other sources of information, education and entertainment;
- Steady means of sustenance, self-protection and self-preservation; and
- Equal opportunities for individual and social development including the right to information, freedom of speech, of sustenance and expression, and so on.

The Gandhian perception: Having discussed the concept and components of quality of life let us now attempt to understand the Gandhian perception of it. Be it stated at the very outset that no where did Gandhi speak or write about the 'quality of life' as such—the way modern economists have been using this term, of late. However, the Gandhian scheme of things that constitute the core of this seemingly modern concept.

Gandhi did not study economics in any University nor did he go to any school of economics or propound any economic theory. His economics was based on his personal experiences starting from his days in South Africa where he founded two settlements namely the 'Phoenix Ashram Settlement' and 'The Tolstoy Farm'. It is there that he developed his famous doctrine of trusteeship which alone can be the solution of the present day problem of concentration of economic power in a few hands.

Gandhi dreamed of a world without wars, a society without caste or class, factories without forced labour, in fact a non-violent, non-exploiting social and economic order built on the foundations of universal education, basic morality and the principles of nature, a society marked by plenty and prosperity. As he put it, *'In the new millennium also, there will be enough for everybody's need—but not for everybody's greed'.*

Mahatma Gandhi's ideas of economic and social development are intimately intertwined with his ideas of human rights and religious or spiritual approach to all the problems including the problems of starvation (food), shelter, education, an environmental degradation, concentration of economic power and the like. He once said,

> "I have found it impossible to soothe suffering patients with a song. The hungry millions ask for one poem-invigorating food."

The same humanitarian approach to everything can be seen in his statement. When all around me are dying for want of food, the only occupation permissible for me is to feed the hungry.... To a people famishing and idle, the only acceptable form in which God can dare appear is work and promise of food as wages!.

EDUCATION

In the field of education Gandhi's legacy is even richer. His basic education in fact was another name of education for all. It was not mere literacy but it was an all round development of mind, body and spirit. It was craft-based education which was an insurance against unemployment (Singh: 2004). The craft-centered education was in keeping with the principles of non-violence where the individuality of every learner was kept alive and where values such as dignity of labour and team work were taught. This was also called 'Nai Talim' or Wardha Scheme of Education. In 1936, he founded the Hindustani Talimi Sangh. Gandhi stood for universalisation of primary education and the total eradication of illiteracy, which he said was a shame. It is rather sad that these two goals have yet to be fulfilled in spite of Constitutional Directives and 52 years of development through Five Year Plans. It is only recently that Gandhian techniques have been adopted in executing the programme of adult literacy through National Literacy Mission.

> "The adult education of my conception," wrote Gandhi, "must make men and women better citizens all round. Agriculture will play an important part in adult education in the Basic Scheme-literacy instruction will be there, much instruction will be given orally. There will be books, more for the teachers than for the taught. We must teach the majority how to behave towards the minority and *vice-versa*. The right type of adult education should cut at the very root of untouchability and communalism."

All his life Gandhi concentrated on two issues: non-violence and communal harmony. And both these could be best achieved by proper education and training. In fact, he laid down his life for these goals.

HEALTHCARE

As far as health-care is concerned, Gandhi was in favour of preventive measures instead of the curative medicines. Unfortunately, very little attention is given today on preventive measures. The new creative five star hospital culture that has sprung up in different metropolitan cities and large towns of India are all catering very well to the affluent sections. Gandhiji wanted people to take charge of their own health instead of entrusting it to the medical men.

> "We labour under the fatal illusion that no disease can be cured without medicine. Those who take medicines are really rendering the task of nature doubly difficult."

Gandhi's attitudes to sex and medicine were formulated perhaps on the morality of his time. But there is much sense in de-emphasizing the role of medicine and medical personnel in the healthy life of an individual especially in an age where the greed for quick money is motivating even the brightest of medical minds to order unnecessary test for diagnosing insignificant illness. This can better be avoided in order to lessen the cost of treatment, reduce the mental misery of patients who are poor and also widen the services to all sections of the population.

What emerges out of the above analysis is that although Gandhi did not touch upon the quality of life as being put to use by modern economists, his philosophy does touch upon the frontiers of almost all issues that constitute the contours of the term: His all-encompassing vision includes as diversified subjects as food for teeming millions, universal primary education, decentralisation of economic power, preventive health-care, environmental and ecological considerations, employment for all and so on. In fact, Gandhi was not an individual, he was an inspiration. He was not a man, he was a movement. He was not an episode, he was a phenomenon. In any area of darkness he is the light (Singh: 2004).

III. GANDHI AND WOMEN'S EMPOWERMENT

Gandhiji has indicated the path to reach the goal of women's empowerment. He always had as he admits "a passion to serve womankind. I hold radical views about the emancipation of women from their fetters, which they mistake for adornment. If God wills it, I hope one day to place some of my conclusions before the public when my researches are completed. My experience has confirmed me in that real advancement of women can come only and through their own efforts."

Gandhiji is the foremost name in the small list of those illustrious and sensitive men of the twentieth century if not down the ages who have spontaneously empathized with the women's cause. Way back in the early twenties of the last century, the world learnt of a son and a husband who poured his heart out in the pages of his autobiography, which he called 'The Story of My Experiment with Truth', regarded as one of the most outstanding book of all times. It is replete with-natural women-friendly spirit that softens the stark realities of gender relations in our society. In his writings and outpourings, Gandhi transcends the boundaries, which hide private from public. He acknowledged the debt of his mother, wife and the black women in South Africa as influences on the evolution of his concept of Satyagraha.

Efforts to understand and analyze the roots of social perversion have been on for the last several decades. Mahatma Gandhi's endeavor to bring about the regeneration of women in India and his search for the causes of its degeneration led him to question the existing Indian social structure with its entrenched prejudices and biases of several millennia. "The point", said Gandhi, "for us to consider is the degeneration of our women relatively to our men, and man has not always been fair and discriminate in forming that self-appointed task." Gandhiji was emphatic on the issue of equality of women as integral to founding a just society. His advocacy of women's rights was a step forward from the nineteenth century consciousness of the women's problem, which was confined to their status within the traditional family structure. No social reformer before Gandhi had expressed the concern about the fundamental inequality and social injustice that were women's lot—socially, economically and politically in-depth. He understood that before any talk of economic or political power, our women needed courage and self-confidence, a sense of self-respect to break free from the slavish mentality developed over centuries of boundage. He saw that if the conditions of the women were to change, education, social reform, economics and politics had to suit the genius of the soil.

To understand Gandhi's evolution as an emancipation of women, it is imperative to know that his faith in the capability of women to control their own destiny formed part of his world view. He had an open mind. A shrewd observer of people and events he could not have remained unaffected by the happenings at home and around the world and grasp their impact on future development. Tracing the origins and circumstances in which Gandhi's shape, one finds a gradual change overcoming him. Understanding the interplay of both internal and external circumstances and their impact on him is important (Singh: 2002).

Gandhiji was one of the greatest champions of women's rights and equality. To him, women are the incarnation of Ahinsa, to call women a weaker sex is libel, it is man's injustice to women. If I were born a woman I would rise in rebellion against man's cruelty to women. I have mentally become a woman to steal into her heart. I could not steal into my wife's heart until I decided to treat her differently than I used to do, and so, I restored to her all her rights, by dispossessing myself of all my so-called rights as her husband. Gandhi, in a way, started the first feminist movement in India.

Gandhi's Eighteen Point Constructive Programme in which the upliftment of women occupied an important place was an agenda for social revolution and like his various struggles was intended to awaken the dormant spirit of woman and man. He ended the era of 'estrangement' between social reforms and political revolutions. For him they were interchangeable terms. One was incomplete without the other.

A feminist par excellence Gandhi firmly believed that women possessed trust and endurance as innate qualities. These were to be harnessed and channelised for the unleashing of truth that was the essence of *Satyagraha.* The idea of refounding woman's being as a pre-condition to her different roles comes in for vivid exposition in Gandhi's programme of *Satyagraha.* By giving a call to the women to join the non-violent *satyagraha* and shoulder the responsibilities of the Constructive Programme. Gandhi aimed at an inner awakening in the women. In a point of departure from the past unlike the reformers before him, Gandhi believed that only women should head organisations devoted to the cause of empowerment in society. At one of his earliest public pronouncements, Gandhiji makes his stand clear. The Bhagini Samaj, a leading social organisation working towards the upliftment of woman was headed by Bhain Karsandas Chitalia. Addressing the women present at its annual meeting in 1918 Gandhi said, "Your President, I really feel, should be a woman, though you may seek man's help or advice.... The Samaj is dedicated to the noble aim of women's regeneration but in the same way that another's *Tapascharya* does not help one to ascend to heaven, men cannot bring out the regeneration of women, it is only through self-help that an individual or a race can rise." He was also quick to remark that "this is not a new principle, but we often forget to act upon it."

Gandhi destiny, as man has, Gandhi was in fact far ahead of his time. He was sensitive to their sufferings and consciousness of the women's problem, which confined to their status within the traditional family structure. No social reformer before Gandhi had expressed the concern at the fundamental inequality and looked at women as an entity in her own rights capable to shape her own social injustice that were women's lot socially, economically and politically indepth.

To Gandhi, women were not only muted and anonymous mass of womanpower to be energized but symbolised higher human values like compassion and sacrifice. He did not expect woman to be either mere dolls or domestic drudges. Gandhi explained, "To me this domestic slavery of the kitchen is remnant of barbarism mainly. It is high time that our womankind was freed from this incubus. Domestic work ought not to take the whole of women's time."

For Gandhi, it was not enough that the women of India should just achieve political freedom like their male counterparts, but that they should also be socially liberated from the web of superstition and rigid ancient customs and economically self-sufficient. To those who argued that the political struggle ought to have primacy over everything else, Gandhi said, "To postpone social reform till after the attainment of *Swaraj,* is not to know the meaning of *Swaraj. Swaraj* was a continuous process of inward growth."

Hence, the first reform for the women should be "to understand the important idea of freedom and cherish it as part of dharma. The woman who has understood this should enlighten her sisters. Women alone can work and achieve great results among women. There is a limit to what a man can do. He can never understand their deepest feelings."

Gandhi was a great advocate of economic independence of women and articulated his views on this matter with great force and clarity. He firmly believed that a woman by staying at home contributes to the income of the home by cooking and managing the household. But he was not averse to women venturing out of her home if the situation so demanded. When asked would not economic independence lead to immorality among women, Gandhi said, "I would answer the question by a counter-question: has not independence of man and his holding property led to the spread of immorality among men? If your answer is 'Yes' then let it be so also with women. And when women have rights of ownership and the rest like men, it will be found that the enjoyment of such rights is not responsible for their vices or their virtues. Morality, which depends upon the helplessness of a man or woman has not much to recommend it. Morality is rooted in the purity of our hearts."

Gandhi was never regarded as an economist by the intelligentsia though his basics of economics was more than most. On the issue of economic independence of women, he was far ahead of his time. He advocated equal wages for women when the attention of others was yet to be drawn to this glaring disparity.

For Gandhi, the question of the empowerment of women was a social issue and her concern as human rights issue. He worked relentlessly to better the lot of the depressed and the deprived and women were the biggest block in this segment. He held that the need of the day is to change the mindset of the society. He raised his voice condemning discrimination against the girl child, female foeticide, infanticide, domestic violence against women and sexual harassment of women in the work place. All these accumulated ills led him to only one conclusion that something is radically wrong with us and against which the society should be sensitized and changed. Empowerment of women must also entail rights over property and access to credit. Land rights do not mean just control over a piece of property, it accords status to a women as well as strengthens her economic position and social security.

Gandhi's unfinished agenda is the biggest challenge before humanity. He wanted men to realize that the empowerment of women is not a threat but a way to improve families and societies. His holistic approach to social problems, his stress on harmony with self and society as against the fragmented approach to problems, were small steps in the journey towards the more just and humane world of equal.

Gandhi was clear in his mind that the empowerment of women is not only a moral imperative but a pre-requisite for strengthening democratic traditions and fighting against injustice and oppression. Feminism in Gandhi's world view did not mean achievement sans men. But he was also absolutely clear that feminism should not be treated as philosophy marginalised when something else catches the world's fancy. It is a state of being in which gender is secondary, if not insignificant. Feminism is a matter of attitude—an attitude that need not be inherent in every woman or absent in man. Small steps in the journey towards the more just and humane world of equal rights, equal opportunity and equal participation is what the Mahatma had envisioned. For when a woman thrives, her family thrives, when family thrives communities flourish and the nation reaps the benefits.

IV

It is widely acknowledged today that Gandhian philosophy, particularly Gandhi's Doctrine of Trusteeship played a pivotal role in the shaping of the contours of modern corporate ethics. What is the contribution of Mahatma Gandhi to the evolution and growth of modern corporate ethics? How did Gandhiji look at the *inter-se* relationship between the business and the society? What responsibilities did he assign to the business in relation to the cross sections of the society? Does Gandhian philosophy still hold the key for unfolding the new vistas in corporate ethics, as observed by many Management Gurus? This section attempts to examine the above issues at length. The purpose is to bring the relevance of Gandhi to a sharp focus in the post-globalisation corporate scenario.

The Doctrine of trusteeship advocated by Gandhiji, is based on and has its origin in the Bhagavad Gita—in the principles of 'aparigraha' (non-possession) and 'sambhawa' (equalism) which were ardently followed by Mahatma Gandhi. These two principles of the Bhagavad Gita took a strong root in Gandhiji's mind. Gandhiji believed that according to these principles, in reality, all men are trustees, for every man is required to use wealth for the welfare of all the community. Trusteeship involves a code of ethical behaviour as well as a principle of accountability.

According to Gandhian scheme of things, each capitalist and industrialist should consider himself to be a trustee of the wealth that he possesses. He should consider himself to be a custodian of the industry, resources, labour and wealth that he uses for his business purposes. If all capitalists and industrialists begin to believe themselves as such custodians of their own wealth, then collectively, they would become the custodian of wealth of the society. And that would transform the capitalist order of society into an egalitarian one, where the 'greatest good of all' could be achieved.

Gandhiji's doctrine of trusteeship does not recognize the right to individual ownership. The right to individual or private ownership is abolished and permitted only to the extent that it is needed for one's own welfare, as also for the welfare of the society. To quote Gandhiji:

> "Supposing, I have come by fair amount of wealth either by way of legacy, or by means of trade and

industry—I must know that all the wealth does not belong to me; what belongs to me is the right to an honourable livelihood, no better than that enjoyed by millions of others. The rest of my wealth belongs to the community and must be used for the welfare of the community."

Likewise, "It (trusteeship) does not recognize any right of private ownership of property except so far as it may be permitted by the society for its own welfare."

People-Friendly Business

In order to come up to the expectations of the society, business in modern times envisages to bridge the gap between what the society wants and what the business makes it available. Gandhiji while working out a formula for trusteeship advocated for exactly the same model of behaviour on the part of the business. "What they produce in their industries and release to the society should be determined by social necessity with the optimum utilisation of the scarce resources of the society. What they produce should not be determined by personal whim or personal greed." Likewise, he observes elsewhere, "During the process of production and later, management is expected to hold the industry as a trust for the society and the community and not as an instrument to generate unreasonable profit at the cost of the community."

Peaceful Co-existence of Capital and Labour

Gandhiji dreamt of an economic order where labour and management were to live in a co-existence, supporting and supplementing each other. In his own words, "My ideal is that capital and labour should be supplement and help each other. They should be a great family living in unity and harmony; capital not only looking to the material welfare of the labourers, but their moral welfare also, capitalists being trustees of the welfare of the labouring classes under them." Thus Gandhiji tended to assign a paternalist role to management in their dealings with labour.

Mutual Trusteeship

Gandhiji, while talking about the mutual duties and responsibilities of labour and capital also enunciated a relatively new concept of 'mutual trusteeship.' Gandhiji suggests: "The owners should look after the workers and the workers should look after the institution's productivity and profit. Both the owners and the workers should work for the true benefit of consumers."

The Gandhian dream of mutual trusteeship appears to have literally come true in the contemporary world. There are no or fewer labourers today. In the drastically changed global scenario, we have no labourers but knowledge professionals. Power has already shifted from capital to knowledge. This is what Peter Drucker, and Alvin Toffler have shown in their master-piece work on power shift. Today's capitalists like Microsoft of Infosys are nothing more than knowledge professionals. And all over the globe they are turning as trustees suggested by Gandhiji some fifty-five years ago.

Formation of Trade Union

Gandhiji considered trade unions as a means of workmen's material and moral development, and hence encouraged workers to form trade unions and actively participate in them. Referring to trade unions he says:

> "It is not anti-capitalist. The idea is to take from capital, labour's due share and no more, and this, not by paralyzing capital but by reform among labourers from within and by their own self-consciousness, not again through the cleverness of non-labour leaders, but by educating labour to evolve its own leadership and its own self-restraint, self-existing organisation. Its direct aim is not in the least degree political. Its aim is internal reform and evolution of internal strength. The direct result of this evolution when and if, it ever becomes complete, will naturally be tremendously political." He insisted that: "the working class would never feel secure to develop a sense of self-assurance and strength unless its members are armed with unfailing subsidiary means of subsistence to serve as a second string to their bow in crisis."

However, while emphasizing upon the worker's right to form the trade union, Gandhiji was not oblivious of the duties of the workers "... while it is quite proper to insist upon (workers') rights and principles, it is imperative that they should recognize the obligation that every right carries with it.... The workers should treat the business of their employers as if it were their own business and give it their honest and undivided attention", Observed Gandhiji.

Thus, Gandhiji wanted the working class to be organized and united amongst themselves. Gandhiji wanted there to be an awakening among the workers of their own strength and confidence on their own abilities and capacities. Gandhiji wanted moral growth and spiritual development on the part of the workers, so that they do not remain ignorant, unenlightened and immature. Her wanted workers to realize and utilize their moral strength and develop their conscience about righteousness and ethical means of behaviour as also the consciousness about their existence and their just position in the industry. Gandhiji wanted workers to develop a sense of pride in their own strength so that the question of exploitation of labour by the management does not raise.

Right to Strike

Gandhiji also dwelt upon the right to strike, an issue being hotly debated today in the light of the recent judgment of the Supreme Court. He considered the right to strike as the inherent right of the workingman for the purpose of securing justice, but they must be considered to be a crime once the industrialists accept the principle of arbitration. Gandhiji, in fact, meticulously worked out the 'ethical rules' to be observed by the working class while taking resort to the strikes. Given below are the various components of this rule:

1. Workers should seek redressal of reasonable demand only through collective action;
2. If they have to organize a strike, trade unions should seek by ballot authority from all workers to do so, remain peaceful and use non-violent methods;

3. Workers should avoid strikes as far as possible in the industries of essential services;
4. Workers should avoid formation of unions in philanthropical organisations;
5. Strikes should be resorted to only as a last resort after all other legitimate measures have failed; and
6. As far as possible, workers should take recourse to voluntary arbitration where direct settlement has not succeeded.

Gandhiji believed that only with these preconditions, it was possible to avoid bitterness between labour and management, even when they are in conflict. Even though there may be some differences between management and labour on day-to-day matters and routine issues, there should never be any doubt that the interest of management and labour as far as the welfare of organisation was concerned, is totally convergent. Ethical behaviour on the part of both labour and management can be expected in such a state of affairs only (Singh: 2003).

RELEVANCE OF GANDHIAN ECONOMIC PHILOSOPHY IN 21ST CENTURY

In the fast changing modern world equipped with scientific and technological advancements we may find people putting questionmark on the relevance of Gandhian thought in 21st century. One may also ask how can a person who has not seen 'Gandhiji' relate oneself with the vision he nurtured, followed and envisaged as the guiding force of the people of India? Mahatma, as a mortal being, may not be present among us, but he has been constantly guiding as an inspiration, an illuminated light on almost all the diversified issues that an individual, a society or the state may come across. Mahatma Gandhi need not be seen as an individual, but as a movement, a phenomenon and a light removing darkness from each and every walk of life. Wherever there is a struggle for survival, wherever there is injustice, poverty, hunger, illiteracy, inequality and darkness, Gandhiji showed a road to light.

Gandhiji's economic vision and his interest for spinning, hand weaving, handicrafts and cottage industries were directed to provide employment and livelihood to the millions of Indians which big industries could never been able to provide. His ardent followers and the first Prime Minister of India, Pt. Jawaharlal Nehru adopted the course of mixed economy for India. But gradually support for the State owned industries and cottage and small scale industries was reduced due to globalisation, competitiveness and economic feasibility. The larger purpose of providing employment to the millions of India was ignored.

It is difficult to understand how Gandhi is seen as an opponent of machines and modernity—a person who can not really coexist with progress. Quotations from his first book Hind Swaraj are often brandished to prove the Mahatma as anti-modern. It is true that Gandhi has used harsh words with reference to railways, doctors, lawyers and factories. It is also true that Gandhi had at times engaged in heated debate with Rabindranath Tagore and Jawaharlal Nehru about modernity and progress. Gurudev was initiated by Gandhi's 'obsession' with spinning and Nehru, Subhash and at times Jaya Prakash Narayan were concerned with their mentor's lack of enthusiasm about emerging trends. The fact is that Gandhi was not against machines but dehumanizing mechanisation. He said that he welcomed every machine that reduces painful human labour and drudgery. His concern, entirely justified, was that enthusiasm about labour saving machines should not aggravate the problem of unemployment in India. Nor should it be forgotten that Gandhi made these comments at a time when India was under foreign rule and all decisions were taken by the British in their own interest. Industrialisation and urbanisation during this period benefited the natives only accidentally. Modern meant most of the time denigration of everything Indian equating it with traditional/out of date.

Today all this has changed. It is not only the workers but also doctors and engineers in the USA who are worried about being rendered jobless by far more efficient and cost effective Indians. Proliferation of computers and the web of telecommunication have brought about a paradigm shift even in capitalist thinking. The potential of machines to empower the hitherto handicapped is clear. What is required is the political will to harness their power. At the same time the risks have increased manifold. The gulf between the rich and the poor, the cities and the villages threatens to deepen dangerously. In a democratic polity, elites with vested interests can subvert the will of the people. Considerations of caste, community and religion can easily distort the priorities of planning and throw development of the rails. We can save ourselves only if we heed to the warning sounded out by Gandhi.

Gandhi tells us that nature has enough to fulfil every ones need but not to satiate anyone's greed. The obsession with mega projects has at times resulted in disastrous degradation of environment, destruction of a way of life and painful displacement of thousands. Gandhi constantly emphasized integrated development. Environmental conservation, guaranteed employment and empowerment of the weaker section of society, women, the dalits, minorities and abjectly poor must remain our priority. There can be no question of dispensing with or suspending the Gandhian agenda. Gandhi realised that imbalanced development benefiting only a small section of society carries in its womb seeds of strife. His emphasis on equity and ethics has acquired even greater urgency at present.

CONCLUSION

Without falling in the trap of the jargon of welfare economics one may assert without hesitation that Gandhian economic philosophy remains extremely relevant in the context of development in the 21st century.

References

Chakrabati, Mohan (2004): "Recalling Mahatma Gandhi", *Employment News*, Vol. XXIX, No. 27, 2-8 October, New Delhi.

Gandhi, M.K.: "Village Swaraj", Navajeevan Pub. House, Ahmedabad, p. 63.

Gandhi, M.K. (1940): *"Harijan"*, Se[illegible]ember 2[illegible]

Gandhi, M.K., Rebuilding our Village—All Round Village Development, p. 19.

Indireson, P.V. (1994): "National Reconstruction: A Gandhian Approach", *Kurukshetra*, Vol. XLIII, p. 30.

Pant, Pushpesh (2005): "Gandhi and Development", *Employment News*, Vol. XXX, No. 27, 1-7 October, Ministry of I and B, Govt. of India, New Delhi.

Singh, Dr. L.P. (2004): "Quality of Life: The Gandhian Scheme of Things", *Employment News Weekly*, Vol. XXIX, No. 27, October 2-8, Ministry of I and B, Govt. of India, New Delhi.

——— (2003): "Gandhi and Corporate Ethics", *Employment News Weekly*, Vol XXVIII, No 26, 27 September-3 October, Ministry of I and B, Government of India, New Delhi.

Singh, Dr. Savita (2002): "Gandhi and Women's Empowerment", *Employment News, Weekly*, Vol. XXVII, No. 26, 28 September-4 October, Ministry of I and B, Government of India, New Delhi.

•

9

Gandhi's Views on Industralisation and its Relevance

S. RAMACHANDRAN

I. INTRODUCTION

Gandhiji was basically trained as a lawyer. He was not an intellectual in the academic sense of the term. He was not a scholar or a philosopher. He was not a theoretician. His thinking had the quality of creative genius and not that of a student.[1] His thoughts, correspond to various facets of life.[2] Despite the appreciation of the fact that Gandhiji's views on economics are well imbedded in moral grounds, professional economists do not refrain from delineating Gandhiji's economic views and moral aspects and make their appraisal. In simple terms, his economics originates from his moral sentiments.[3] In a sense, one can find a parallel in him to Adam Smith in this regard. Of course, it is obvious that the comparison should not be stretched too far. His economics centered on solving the twin problems of poverty and unemployment of the masses. Gandhiji was for village economies as he thought at the time of British Raj. India was predominantly agricultural economy with few industries.

Most of the small and tiny industries were based on village resources, and labour was predominantly unskilled. Therefore, developing such village and cottage industries, Gandhiji thought, would alleviate poverty and unemployment in rural areas. Gandhiji's economic ideas can, therefore, be best understood in the light of the physical and social conditions prevailed at his times.[4] This paper evaluate the Government's efforts to develop the Gandhiji's vision on industries after independence and its relevance in the present Globlalisation era.

2. SEMINAL IDEAS OF GANDHIJI ON INDUSTRIALISATION

Gandhiji said that the economic activity of man is concerned with the production of material goods and their distribution and consumption. These activities are necessary not only for the existence of man but also for his happiness and progress. Man lives in society and all these activities concern not only the individual in isolation but they create social relations. As a matter of fact if we think of it, all wealth is socially produced.[5] He supported the decentralisation of industries[6] and also he was against the labour migration from rural to urban areas.[7] Therefore, Khadi was Gandhiji's main work for economic reforms in India. He thought that agriculture alone could not provide adequate employment for the growing India's population so he urged the need for the creation of household industries.[8] It is also wrong to believe that Gandhiji was against technology. He had no objection to the use of mechanised power to increase production and diminish the drudgery of workers. The only condition was that such mechanical power must be available to every villager who wanted to use it. But he did not want science and machinery to produce goods and starve men.[9] Gandhiji had no objection to the use of large scale machinery for work of public utility if such public works could not be undertaken by human labour. Under such conditions, it is necessary that some key industries have to be in the public sector.[10]

Gandhiji suggested that the immediate adoption of all those technologies which gave people full employment and met their basic consumption needs.[11] He opposed the imported technologies from the developed countries.[12] He emphasized that the modern large-scale technologies for mass production is inherently violent, ecologically damaging[13] and self-defeating interms of non-renewable resources. Apart from the environmental degradation, which is the by-product of a runway technology, there is the social fragmentation which breaks up families and communities[14] fosters crime and corruption, creates a vaccum in all forms of authority, and promotes a manipulative form of authorianism, rooted not only in the transitional processes of production, but in a closer integration between Big Business and Big Government. Hence Gandhiji insisted that any industry that was conducted in India was Indian industry.[15] From this one can observed that the father of the nation anticipated the evils of globalisation fifty years before the beginning of the modern globalisation era.

3.1. Industrialistion after Independence

Independent India under Nehru did not adopt the Gandhian model of economic development, as he fully supported industrialisation as the decisive prerequisite for independence and progress: "It can hardly be challenged that, in the context of the modern world, no country can be politically and economically independent, even within the frame work of international interdependence, unless it is highly industrialised and has developed its power resources to the utmost. Nor can it achieve or maintain high standards of living and liquidate poverty without the aid of modern technology in almost every sphere of life. An industrially backward country will continually upset the world equilibrium and encourage the aggressive tendencies of more developed countries. Even if it retains its political independence, this will be nominal only, and economic control will tend to pass to others. This control will inevitably upset its own small-scale economy which it has sought to preserve in pursuit of its own view of life. Thus an attempt to build up a country's economy largely on the basis of cottage and small-scale industries is doomed to failure. It will not solve the basic problems of the country or maintain freedom, nor will it fit the world frame work, except as a colonial appendage."[16]

Further, Nehru firmly believed that the Indian economy could be developed on sound lines only by the adoption of a process of intelligent, imaginative and integrated planning and democratic principles. Therefore, India entered into the era of planned economic development, within the framework of a democratic constitution. It was certainly the vision and wisdom of Nehru that had been responsible for firmly laying the foundation of modern planned economic development of the country.[17] The main objective of planning has been to eliminate poverty and transform the stagnant levels of life into a dynamic phase of economic activities, which will assure self-accelerated and regular growth. In this scheme of planning, the first and critical operation objective is rapid industrialisation without which living standards of the masses could not be improved. Therefore, the strategy of planning aimed at building up of an industrial base through heavy industries to be followed up subsequently by a spread of ancillary consumer goods industries.[18] The emergence of the public sector is another major contribution of Nehru to the Modernisation of the economy and the attainment of the goals of socialism. Of course it has been one of the Gandhian ideologies on industries. He believed that in view of the vastness of the country and the magnitude of the tasks confronting it rapid progress would be possible only by creating, expanding and strengthening public sector.[19] But at the same time, Nehru was realistic enough to accord equally important role to the private sector in developing the economy. He therefore felt that the country needed a mixed economy, in which both the public and private sectors closely co-operate each other in speeding up the country's economic progress. Accordingly the government decided to reserve the strategic industries and those require huge financial and technical resource for the public sector, while the others be left open to the private sector.[20]

In the year 1956 Jawaharlal Nehru launched the Second Five-Year Plan based on the Mahalanobis model,[21] which developed the growth parameters in two distinct sectors viz., investment goods and consumption goods. Starting from the initial two-sector model covering labour and capital inputs, the Mahalanobis model provided the basic strategy for the plan.[22] The objectives of the second plan are to substantially increase industrialisation, employment and national income and reduce inequality of income and wealth and it laid heavy emphasis on public investment and rapid industrialisation. Not only, was the basic pattern of investment thus shifted from agronomy to industry, but within the industrial sector itself the focus was on spectacular capital intensive heavy industries highlighted by an emphasis on steel. The plan thus envisaged a setting up of three steel plants in the public sector, expansion of two private sector plants; a seventy percent rise in production of coal; trebling cement production and extensive development of the capacity and infrastructure of the Indian railways.

Though there has been a significant growth in the industrial sector in the Second Plan period it could not achieve its targets.[23] It was mainly due to the continuous absorption of a substantial percentage of working force in the agriculture and allied sectors. This would mean that our planned effort has not been able to make a significant impression in shifting the population to secondary and tertiary sectors rapidly enough to make an impact on the primary sector. Nor primary sector has thrown up surplus to create conditions favourable for expansion elsewhere. With the addition to work force on the normal rate of increase in population, the backlog of unemployment continues to remain at over ten million. This is a very important factor in considering the nature of industrial revolution, which we want to bring about in our economy from the depth of poverty and low income.[24] During the seventeen years of Nehru's premiership, Indian economy achieved spectacular progress towards self-reliance in many crucial areas. Although Nehru did not achieve much success in making the administration development-oriented, he certainly rendered splendid service to the country's economic progress by giving it a modern progressive outlook and by inspiring the people with high ideals.[25]

Indira Gandhi's contribution to India's economic development has been even more substantial than that of her father. She continued most of the major policies initiated by Nehru; but what is more significant, she also displayed considerable originality introducing new ideas to accelerate the growth of the economy. Indira Gandhi nationalised the coal industry and the commercial banks enlarged, the public sector gave many incentives to the private sector so that it might play a more active role, facilitated a large inflow of foreign capital and technology and brought about closer economic relations between India and the rest of world. Indira Gandhi paid special attention to the improvement of agriculture, and her imaginative policies were, to no small extent, responsible for the spread of the green revolution which greatly helped to reduce the country's heavy dependence on imports.

Indira Gandhi was keen on alleviating poverty in the country. She took many bold steps in this direction, the most remarkable one amongst them was the nationalisation of fourteen commercial banks on July 19, 1969. In 1980, six more commercial banks were nationalised and banking was brought into the fold of the public sector. This has given a new turn to the working of the banking system in the country. Gradually, the public sector banks (i.e. 20 nationalised banks and the state bank of India group) transformed the concept of banking from "class" banking to "mass" banking. The banks now developed a social perspective in the business approach and functioning. Their credit policy has been moulded in favour of the priority sector advances.

The country launched upon the Sixth Five Year Plan for the period 1980-85 which coincided with the beginning of a new decade. The major goal of the Sixth Plan has been spelt out in the plan document as 'the realisation of economic and social order based on the principles of socialism and self-reliance'. In general, the Sixth Plan successfully restored economic stability and put the economy on a sound track of rapid growth and development, giving a new hope for the country's future. It has been rightly felt that the sound base of infrastructure established over the last forty years should enable the Indian economy to face the challenges that may emerge in the years to come. Like Nehru, Indira Gandhi did not achieve much success in the economic development as

Indira Gandhi's tenure as Prime Minister showed the weaknesses in the implementation of the various programmes. For example, the number of large sick units without standing bank credit up to rupees one crores or more had increased to 513 at the end of June 1984 from 435 these units went up to Rs. 2,112 crores at the end of June 1984 from Rs. 1,729 crores at the end of June 1982.[26]

Rajiv Gandhi also had firm faith in socialism.[27] Rajiv Gandhi expressed his views thus "our aim is higher productivity, rapid advancement of social justice and continuous modernisation."[28] From this one can reasonably conclude that Nehru played a pioneering role laying a strong foundation for the public sector as a catalyst of planned economic development. Indira Gandhi gave necessary stimulus to nurture and strengthen it. With the liberalisation of industrial policy, Rajiv Gandhi has added a new dimension to the public sector with a view to improving its efficiency. Arjun Sengupta committee which was set-up in September 1984, to evaluate the performance of the public sector, to identify the constraints, and to suggest measures to improve their working felt that on the whole the public sector had failed to achieve its objectives for which it has been set-up.

During 1980, improving the efficiency of the public sector is a problem, which has been exercising the minds of governments in many developed and developing countries. Some of them have tried to tackle it by adopting the policy of privatisation. It was the British government headed by Margaret Thatcher that first initiated in 1979 a bold programme for reducing the role of the state in the economic activity. Some companies have been privatised. The British experiment in privatisation has created enormous interest in many countries and attracted several foreign delegations to make and in depth study of its techniques. The US Government has also introduced a programme of privatisation as an important element in its strategy for accelerating economic growth. Some of the privatisation proposals were carried out in 1987 and in the subsequent years. Similar programmes have been implemented in Canada, France, West Germany, Turkey, Pakistan and Bangladesh. It is not surprising therefore, that in India also some economists and industrialists have urged the government to initiate privatisation.[29]

As it is, privatisation has become a global phenomenon in the 1980s. Gorbachov's policy reforms—Perestroika (restructuring) and Glasnost (openness) have aroused world-wide interest in the issue of privatistion and liberalisation.

This is evident from the fact that during the Seventh Plan the share of private sector has increased to 48 percent from 43 percent from the Sixth Plan. The move towards privatisation has been made because corruption, nepotism, inefficiency have been devilled the management of public sector undertakings. If corruption and delays are eliminated, and state enterprises are managed more efficiently and made more productive, the tendency to privatisation may well curtailed if not reversed. Socialism demands this for and unchecked growth of private sector often generates distortions in the economy.

3.2. Industrialisation in the Era of Globalisation

In the midst of 1991, when the Narashimha Rao's government took over power, Indian economy was facing a serious crisis. The new government announced a series of measures, one after the other, to restore balance in economy. All these measures have been grouped under 'New Economic policy' and broadly they have been classified into stabilisation measures, and structural adjustment or economic reforms. As part of the marketisation of the economy the new policies also aimed at the globalisation of the Indian economy. Globalisation is considered as an important element in the reform structure and several interrelated sets of measures have been taken to achieve this object such as: (1) doing away with the licensing of major part of import and export; (2) private sector is also being expanded by permitting the foreign companies to set-up their establishments within the country independently or in collaboration with the Indian company, and so on. This issue is of great importance in the post-WTO scenario undoubtedly global markets offer opportunities for all, but opportunities do not guarantee the desired.[30]

The process of global integration and the effects of the

WTO agreement were expected to cause increases in India's export of agricultural goods, textiles and garments, leather and gems and jewellery. However, all of these categories have actually declined in share of exports. Instead, chemicals and engineering goods showed substantial increase in export shares.[31] It is observed from this the labour categories' share in exports has been declining.

New economic reforms have by-passed the agriculture which is the mainstay of any programme of economic stabilisation has shown a very low rate of growth. Even the large manufacturing sector, growth rate during the last three years has been very sluggish. The capital goods sector has suffered a sharp decline and thus weakened the fundamentals of the economy. Besides this, the entire process of new economic reforms has initiated a process of jobless growth. The silent implementation of exit policy has led to voluntary retirement on a massive scale. It has led to casualisation of labour that enjoyed better security earlier. The capital-intensive path of development whether with the help of Indian private sector or foreign direct investment through multinationals, is responsible for the phenomenon of jobless growth.[32] Therefore, a genuine fear is being expressed everywhere that the new moves will adversely affect our economic self-efficiency, generate unemployment and will make the country to dependent upon the multinationals.

4. CONCLUSION

From the above discussion one can conclude that the recent trend in our economy has been completely deviated from the path shown by Gandhiji. Foreign Direct Investments may help in the process diversification of production structure, modernisation of the economy, but their overall developmental impact is not of a catalytic nature and is generally felt much more within the urban sector. Gandhiji's views on industrialisation and full employment, did not materialise much in practice due to the fact the policies of various governments took a deviant route. It may be stated here that under new economic reforms regime agriculture and household industries have become neglected the growth rates of employment in the orgnised sector (both public and private) witnessed a declining trend from 1.44 per cent in 1991 to 0.04 per cent in 1999. The decline was more sharp in the public sector (from 1.52 per cent in 1991 to –0.19 per cent in 1996 and zero growth in 1999) than the private sector (form 2.21 per cent in 1992 to 0.11 per cent in 1999).[33] Therefore, Gandhiji's views on industrialisation, should receive due attention of policy-makers leading to appropriate policy changes in the positive direction.

Notes and References

1. He was pre-eminently a man of action. He has written a great deal but his writings are designed as a guide to action and not for the acquisition of knowledge. They are generally concerned with the solution of his actual problems, arising out of the many-sided and complex situations of his time. The discussion of theory is always brief and sketchy.....

   Whatever their external form of presentation and expression, Gandhiji's ideas are new and revolutionary. They arise out of the creative mind of an individual to whose reforming zeal the social situation and the difficulties of those times are a challenge. For him historical precedents and examples are no barrier to fresh thinking and discovery. Gandhiji did not acquire his ideas and knowledge merely from books. He did not pass his time in libraries and museums poring over musty volumes. Much of his knowledge was the result of direct contact with life and the practical experience it offered. He, therefore, placed his ideas before the public not in the language of the learned but in that of the average intelligent man and women. In explaining them he did not use the philosophic and technical language of the schools. He was a man of the masses and spoke to them in their own simple language, which they understood. He addressed them not about what he had read and studied in books but what he had seen, sensed, experienced and thought about. He described his own observations and his reactions to them. This the method that has characterized great religious reformers and prophets. Also, his method is more suited to the intellectual capacity of the common man than that of the learned. It readily appeals to the former and carries conviction. Often, however, it leaves the intellectual and academic mind unconvinced and cold. Also Gandhiji was no great student of history. Like the prophets of old he created history. His practical schemes of work and his explanations, therefore, created his philosophy. See, J.B. Kripalani, *Gandhi: His Life and Thought,* New Delhi: Publications Division, Ministry of Information and Broad Casting, Government of India, (1997), pp. 307-08.

2. Gandhiji's thoughts although corresponds to various facets of life, religious, moral, political, economic, social, individual and collective, one can perceive in them an unified and well integrated philosophy. These are folds of thought that reinforce one another and are inextricably intertwined. See, J.B. Kripalani, *op. cit.*, p. 305. You can not divide social, economic, political and purely religious work into watertight compartments. I do not know any religion apart from human activity. in, Shriman Narayan, (ed.), *The Selected Works of Mahatma Gandhi*, Vol. 5, Ahmedabad: Navajivan Publishing House, p. 275.
3. However, Gandhiji supported them on moral and spiritual grounds. He was not concerned with percapita income or meeting the minimum requirements of a decent life. He always stood for a simpler and ascetic life. See, S.L.Verma, *On Grounds of Gandhian Polity*, Jaipur: RBSA Publishers, (1990), p. 30.
4. J.B. Kripalani, *op. cit.*, pp. 369-70
5. J.B. Kripalani, *op. cit.*, pp. 367- 68.
6. Gandhiji advocated village-oriented economy which is free from violence and exploitation. When the means of production are owned by the millions of people, there is no scope for exploitation of the masses. Decentralised economic system does not lead to violence. The centralised economic system can be sustained and defended with huge defence forces. The People cannot build non-violence on a factory civilisation. See, M.K. Gandhi, *My Religion*, Ahmedabad: Navajivan Publishing House, (1955), p. 86.
7. Gandhi wanted the transformation of society with the centre of gravity shifting to the villages, at least until such times as every one was employed, had enough to meet his elementary needs, and to some extent was self reliant, both individually and collectively. See, J.D.Sethi., *Gandhi Today*, New Delhi: Vikas Publishing House Pvt. Ltd., (1978), p. 89. Gandhiji only did not want the worker to be separated from his village home and work under factory conditions in congested urban areas. He wanted every home to be a factory. See, J.B. Kripalani, *op. cit.*, p. 378.
8. In England the Industrial Revolution began in the latter part of the 18th century. This was made possible not only by the invention of steam power applied to industry, but by the fact that England through its political power had been progressively destroying Indian industries in favour of its own manufacturers. All the raw material was taken from India and products finished in England were shipped to India and found and ready market here.

   One by one our industries were destroyed by the political power that England had acquired here. It is held that our industries were destroyed because England used steam power. This is not altogether true. It England had not destroyed our industries and created a vast market for its own goods, even the application of steam power would have not enabled is to build and economic emplre.

   Deprived of their industry, progressively more and more of the growing population of India had to rely for all its requirements on their income from land. Nearly 75 percent of them were engaged in agriculture. The size of the farm holdings went on diminishing, till most of them became uneconomic. The question before Gandhiji was how to find useful and remunerative work for this vast rural population. The agriculturist in India was without work for atleast three months in the year. The landless labourers whose number was even on the increase could find work only in the sowing and reaping seasons. This unemployment and under employment was the cause of Indian poverty, with span of life, ignorance, squalor and disease. It was this grinding poverty of our masses which first drew the attention of our reformers and public men...

Gandhiji had to take into consideration all these factors devise a method by which the grinding poverty of the Indian masses could be mitigated, if not altogether removed. The only way was to revive the swadeshi movement. The new movement had not only to solve the problem of consumption but also that of production. After all, it is production which would increase the quantum of employment. See, J.B. Kripalani, *op. cit.*, pp. 372-4.

9. J.B. Kripalani, *op. cit.*, p. 377.
10. M.K. Gandhi, *Non-Violence in Peace and War, Volume Two.* Ahmedabad: Navajivan Publishing House, (1955), p. 24.
11. Gandhiji welcomed the prospect of rural electrification and the introduction of tools and instruments in village crafts which could lighten the burden of work and fatigue. He did not, however, support technological innovation for its own sake; mechanisation was acceptable to him only if is did not displace useful labour, and did not lead to the concentration of production and distribution in a few hands. Where machinery was essential, he was all for establishment of factories in which workers were assured not only of a living wage, but of a task which was not mere drudgery. See, B.R. Nanda, *Gandhi and His Critics,* Delhi: Oxford University Press, (1985), p. 124.
12. The main contradiction in the world to day is that whereas the economic and technological interdependence of countries is increasing, neither economic nor technological resources are yet global. They are strictly within the control of the nation-states and each nation maximizes the gain for itself. Therefore, not only is the technological gap between nations widening but transfer of technology has become a source of exploitation of poor nations and, ironically, for perpetuating the technological gap. This implication was not clear two decades ago when the newly independent and developing countries allowed all kinds of technological inroads to be made into their economics from the developed world. These countries have now realised that what has come in the name of technological transfer is designed to (i) exploit the resources of poor countries for the benefit of the developed countries, both communist and capitalist; (ii) Create a dualism by isolating the sectors depending upon Western technology from those dependent on and emerging from endowment of national resources; (iii) Widen the

already wide technological gap; (iv) Stunt the very process of growth by creating a new consumer-oriented industry and a class which consumes valuable resources; and (v) Create a kind of technological imperialism which demoralizes developing countries and marks them accept the superiority of western civilisation. See, J.D. Sethi, *op. cit.*, pp. 111-12.

13. Gandhiji noted that nature was being destroyed by unlimited industrialisation and massive urbanisation which were thought necessary for development. These processes were creating problems of ecological balance. Man's continuous contact with nature as part of his daily life, Gandhi argued, prevented the pollution of air and water, destruction of animal and vegetable life, and above all it pre-empted the large urban conglomerations which lead to all such problems. See, J.D. Sethi, *op. cit.*, pp. 78-9.

14. When Gandhi spoke against technology-oriented mass production, he was talking in the context of consumerism. Any attempt to introduce mass production when structural unemployment is endemic, is self-defeating. More than that, it creates the most terrible problems of highly unequal distribution. Besides the problems created by the separation of production and distribution, there are other organisational problems connected with housing, urban renewals, mass transport, highways, air and water pollution, sewage systems, public facilities, etc., which show that each day the problems of mass society and mass production are becoming too complicated. They have, indeed, reached the point of near breakdown of social systems. It is in this context that Gandhi warned against growing urbanisation, villages, etc. See, J.D.Sethi, *op. cit.*, p. 101.

15. He was quite sure in his definition, an industry to be Indian must be demonstrably in the interest of the masses. It must be manned by Indians both skilled and unskilled. Its capital and machinery should be Indian and the labour engaged in this kind of venture should have a living wage and be comfortably housed while the while the welfare of the children of the labourers should be guaranteed by the employers. See, S.R.Bakshi, *Gandhi and the Mass Movements*, New Delhi: Atlantic Publishers and Distributors, (1988), p. 55.

16. Jawaharlal Nehru, *The Discovery of India*, New Delhi: Oxford University Press (2003), p. 301.

17. R.J.Venkateswaran, D.M. Mithani, *Rajiv Gandhi: Economic Perspective Towards 21st Century*, Bombay: Himalaya Publishing House, (1989), p. 2.

18. Oleg Malyarov, *Nehru on India's Social and Economic Development*, Institute of Oriental Studies, USSR Academy of Sciences (ed.), New Delhi: Sterling Publishers Private Limited, (1989), p. 100.

19. R.J. Venkateswaran, D.M. Mithani, *op. cit.*, p. 3.

20. Nehru was aware of the fact that Indian industrialists had, during the British Period, achieved considerable success in promoting the growth of the economy by starting such major industries as ship building, steel, cement, cotton textiles, jute and chemicals, as a result

of which exports had been stepped up to some extent and imports had been correspondingly reduced. They had also acquired extensive experience and expertise in various other fields of industry, commerce and finance. He, therefore, felt that what the country needed was a mixed economy in which both the public sector and the private sector would not merely Co-exist but closely and sincerely co operate with each other in speeding up the country's economic progress. See, R.J. Venkateswaran, D.N. Mithani, *op. cit.*, p. 3. R.C. Dutt, *Socialism of Jawaharlal Nehru*, New Delhi: Abhinav Publications, (1981), pp. 200-1. *op. cit.*, pp. 200-01.

21. Prof. Mahalanobis has probably been the most profound influence on Nehru's economic thinking since the autmun of 1954, He be came a member of the British Royal Society in 1923 and later held the post of Honorary Statistical Adviser to the Government of India. Prof. Mahalanobis had been greatly influenced and impressed by the planning procedures adopted in Russia. He wanted a similar approach to be made in India. He played a major role in shapping the Second Five-Year Plan with its emphasis on heavy industry and expansion of the public sector. See, R.J. Venkateswaran, D.M. Mithani, *op. cit.*, p. 175.

22. Mohalanobis prepared his well known Plan-Frame, the object of which was to activate the Indian economy by providing for sophisticated machine, building, plants, as well as high technology industrial products, while reserving the less sophisticated consumer goods for the decentralised sector. Agriculture and irrigation were not neglected., and while the allocations for these two items fell in percentage terms both in the Plan Frame as well as in the final draft of the Second Plan, compared to the allocations made in the First Plan in absolute terms the funds allotted rose from Rs. 785 crores to 950 crores in the Plan Frame and to Rs. 1054 crores in the final draft of the Second Plan. It was for Industry and Mining, however, that the Plan Frame made a strong bid, and sought an allocation of Rs. 1100 crores, constituting 25.6 per cent at the total plan outlay against Rs. 173 crores or 8.4 percent of the outlay in the First Plan, and it was here that the private industrialists sensed danger. They succeeded in reducing the allocation to Rs. 890 crores or 18.5 percent of the total outlay in the final draft of the Second Plan. On the other hand, the private industrialists were in favour of higher allocation to Transport and Communication which benefited them and succeeded in raising it from Rs. 950 crores to 1,385 crores. See, R.C. Dutt, *op. cit.*, p. 217.

23. R.C. Dutt, *Socialism of Jawaharlal Nehru*, New Delhi: Abhinav Publications, (1981), pp. 223-4. Babubhai M. Chinai, *India's March Towards Democratic Socialism*, Bombay: Shri Brihad Bharatiya Samaj, (1972), pp. 138-40.

24. See, R.C. Dutt, *op. cit.*, p. 239.

25. P. Thirayan, *India the Critical Decade After Nehru*, New Delhi: Sterling Publishers Pvt. Ltd., (1974), pp. 95-7.

26. R.J. Venkateswaran, D.M. Mithani, *op. cit.*, p. 20.

27. R.J. Venkateswaran, D.M. Mithani, *op. cit.*, p. 54.
28. R.J. Venkateswaran, D.M. Mithani, *op. cit.*, pp. 55-61.
29. R.J. Venkateswaran, D.M. Mithani, *op. cit.*, pp. 14-20.
30. Nirmal Bindra, "Impact of Economic Reforms on Indian Economy," in J.L. Singh, K.D. Gaur, (eds.), *Human Resources and Economic Development*, Delhi: Sunrise Publications, (2004), pp. 443-4.
31. Jayatai Gosh, The export growth Story, *Deecan Chronicle*, 1: 327, Chennai: (20 Feb., 2006), p. 6.
32. Ashu Pasricha, *WTO, Self-Reliance and Globalisation*, New Delhi: Deep & Deep Publications Pvt. Ltd., (2005), p. 183.
33. Government of India, *Economic Suruey*, New Delhi: Ministry of Finance, Economic Division, (2000-01), p. 139.

10

Gandhian Economic Thought and its Contemporary Relevance

R.S. Bawa

Shri Mohan Dass Karam Chand Gandhi popularly known as Mahatma Gandhi and given the title of the Father of the Nation was a philosopher and a practical thinker. He had made tremendous contribution to the general philosophy of life by his actions and directions. He had made significant contribution in shaping the social and political structure of India. His contribution in the freedom struggle and his principle of *Ahinsa* are to well known to need any explanation. Alongwith his contribution to social and political structure of India, Gandhiji made significant impact and contribution to the economy of India at that time, as also has contributed to the basic economic thought. Gandhian Economics as preached by Gandhiji is a part of the way we live. He was influenced and inspired by the philosophy of Tolstoy and Ruskin. Thus he propagated the Philosophy based on equality, simplicity and asceticism. He propounded that economic activities should not be separated from basic ethics and morality otherwise the economic activities and economic growth based on such activities will not be of much help in the welfare of the mankind.

Gandhian economic ideas were a product of the socio economic conditions that Indians were facing during his time under the British Rule. Therefore, his basic economic thought was devoted to solving the basic problems of poverty and unemployment. He has expressed his views and has contributed to various sectors of the economy. The basis of Gandhian thought has been in utilisation of natural resources of the country. He wanted economic change to be brought about through non-violent methods and which should promote general welfare and peace in the society.

Gandhian thought divided the resources of a country into two groups: one set of resources he referred to as current economy resources and the second as reservoir economy resources. The current economy resources were generally those which were readily available like local labour, etc. and which he assumed were unlimited in supply; whereas the reservoir economy resources were the one which were limited and which were not native to a particular country. For example, Gandhian considered *Charkha* (The spinning wheel) as a current economy resource whereas textile mills at that time belonged to the reservoir economy. According to Gandhiji any economy based on current economy resources would have less violence whereas the introduction of more and more reservoir economy resources will lead to more and more violence. This was the reason why he propagated vehemently the use of *Charkha*.

Gandhian economic thought and its use changed alongwith his experience over the years and in different working conditions. Upto 1919 this thought can be termed as anti materialistic and to some extent negative. Between 1919 to 1934 his thought was basically influenced by Swadeshi Movement. However, his thought after 1934 was a marked deviation from his earlier approaches and it was based on practical approach. It was during this phase that Gandhiji evolved the ideal of Sarvodaya and talked about rural reconstruction.

Gandhian economics has a peculiar characteristic that it gives more importance to the man than wealth associated with man, i.e. his emphasis was on the human capital and its development rather than on money capital or wealth. He considered a country with better human capital as more likely to grow and lead to a happy nation rather than a nation with more wealth and unhappiness. His economics can, therefore, be termed as normative in character. He preached the idea of self-discipline alongwith economic development. According to Gandhiji we cannot have a nation of happy citizens unless we learn to discipline ourselves and observe a restraint on our wants. He stressed the fact that a nation without ethics and basic human values cannot provide a non-violent and peaceful life to its citizens. Gandhiji's views on various sectors of the economy can be summed up as follows:

(1) AGRICULTURE

Gandhiji propagated the idea of a self-sufficient nation on the basic needs front like food, clothing and shelter. According to him, a nation first must achieve self-sufficiency on food front before it embarks upon achieving growth in other areas. He propagated agriculture with such methods of production which do not affect the basic qualities of the soil. At that time when electricity and hydro-electric project were a thing of the future, he propagated wider use of wells and rivers waters because this kind of irrigation could be made available to the poorest of the farmers. He was to some extent influenced by communism and socialism and propagated the idea of land-ownership not to the individuals but to the community as a whole. He preached the idea of crop-planning. He also advocated fair distribution of agriculture output based on social justice. Gandhiji's vision of agriculture was the one which should be devoted to production for home-consumption only after the self-sufficiency is achieved and food for all is ensured, should the agricultural produce be sold or exchange.

(2) RURAL DEVELOPMENT

Mahatma Gandhi's views regarding rural development were very realistic. He very much appreciated that real India lived in villages and, therefore, the foremost task before any Government should be rural development. He referred to rural development at that time as rural reconstruction. His idea of rural reconstruction envisaged the emergence of village swaraj, i.e. creation of ideal villages which should be more or less self-reliant complete with good roads, hospitals, educational institutions, a democratic administrative set-up and above all cooperation and unity amongst the residents. He advocated universalisation of cottage industries alongwith good agriculture for the upliftment of rural population. In fact it was in this context that Gandhiji propagated the extensive use of khadi to be produced by using charkhas and handlooms. This also meant self-reliance and use of Swadeshi goods. Although not explicitly mentioned but Gandhiji appreciated the fact that the size of holding with the farmers was low and in majority of cases it was likely to fall further. Thus leading to lot of idle time for the farmers which he felt should be utilised in doing some household or cottage industry so as to augment the meagre income of the farmers. His ideas of 'swaraj' through spinning meant that if each one contributes something to the national output and income it will take the economy towards development and in the process generate some income for each one. This concept of spinning also had in-built appreciation for dignity labour. His opposition to large scale spinning mills and automatic weaving machinery or textile mills was based on the fact that it will lead to less opportunity to the people to do their own spinning and weaving. His emphasis on cotton and textile was due to the fact that India in general and Gujarat in particular were known for producing high quality cotton and handmade cotton clothes during the British days, and he wanted this legacy to continue in the interest of the people as well as for the nation.

(3) INDUSTRY

Gandhiji's views on industry are important from two angles. The first was that he advocated small and village industries against large industries as also he advocated decentralisation of industry rather than concentration of industry only in the urban centres. The second was in respect of the rights of the workers or labourers engaged in industry.

In respect of the decentralisation of industry, Gandhiji wished to encourage production by the masses instead of mass production because in his views mass production can be done by large scale centralised units which were not suitable to India at that time because the gains in terms of wages as also in terms of availability of such produce are not likely to reach the masses. He, therefore, envisaged production by the masses meaning thereby that as many people as possible should be involved in the production process. They may produce for themselves first and if possible, may share, exchange or sell their surplus produce with other fellow countrymen. Although most of this was in the context of textile industry but his views were valid in respect of other industries also. To ensure production by the masses Gandhiji suggested a number of steps in respect of the production of cotton textile by the masses which can be listed as follows:

- Teaching of spinning in schools,
- Cultivation of cotton in new areas,
- Weaving through co-operative societies to be encouraged,
- Price controls over yarn and cloth produced by textile mills, and
- Restriction on the establishment of textile mills, etc.

He further felt that all large industries should be under the trade control, and heavy machinery should be allowed only in selected sectors where small and village industries cannot meet the requirements. He also felt that the trusteeship of all industry should be in the hands of the Government and private ownership should be restricted. According to Gandhiji, the character of production should be determined by social necessities and not by the level of profit or personal whims of the producers.

In respect of the interest of labour, Gandhiji's view was that the interest of workers and labour must be protected and they must share the fruits of their labour which led to huge profits for the mill owners. At the same time, he urged the labourers/workers to put in their very best and treat the unit their working inn as their sacred place and do their work very honestly. He also gave the idea of 'satyagrah' or 'non-violent' non-cooperative later on called as strike by the workers in case their genuine demands were not met by the owners of the industry units. But it is interesting to know that his concept and pre-conditions for going on a strike were such that if they were met it would prove genuinely of their grievances. According to Gandhiji a strike is justified and is likely to succeed only when:

(i) the cause is just,
(ii) there should be a practical unanimity among all the workers,
(iii) there should be no coercion or violence against non-strikers,
(iv) strikers should be able to find some alternative productive temporary occupation to maintain themselves,
(v) there should be no substitute workers to the strikers available, and
(vi) all efforts must be made in the direction of welfare of the country.

These above conditions merely show that most of the strikes held these days in the name of Satyagrah may not be justified.

Apart from these major areas, Gandhiji expressed his views on almost all aspects of economics, including international trade, urbanisation, etc. But these ideas emerged from his basic views regarding agriculture and rural development.

CONTEMPORARY RELEVANCE

Gandhian economics, which has contemporary relevance, remarkable orginality and the attributes of an analytical contribution of a high order has great relevance. Under the Gandhian scheme, reduction of inequalities, provisions of full employment and the eradication of poverty would be the dominant goals, and economic growth would not be a separate growth objective. As can be easily made out from the above discussion regarding Gandhian views on economics, most of his views are relevant today, rather their relevance might have increased with respect to a few aspects of economic development.

Gandhian thought in respect of the propagation of small and village industry was very relevant at that time because the main emphasis for the economists in those days was poverty and unemployment and to meet these challenges his views based on dignity of labour were of great importance. Even today the importance of self-employment generation programmes cannot be over-stressed. Further, the concept of rural industry and rural infra-structure is more relevant today than it was some seventy years ago. It may not be out of place to mention that it is the absence of proper vision regarding rural development and rural industrialisation that the country in general and the state of Punjab in particular have faced tremendous socio-political problems. Furthermore, the concept of production by masses is relevant even today because it implies mass worker participation in the production process. This in turn means decentralisation of industry and other economic activities from already developed centres to less developed urban centres and rural areas. It is also well known that industry generates its own infra-structure, therefore, the Gandhian view that we must provide rural infra-structure and for that rural industrialisation is a pre-condition is very much relevant today. There seems to be an urgent need for re-visiting the Gandhian thought so that the Gandhian economic views can be seen in the proper perspective and they are translated and projected *vis-a-vis* the present day conditions. This is especially so in the context of frequent strikes in the name of Gandhian type Satyagrah engineered by disgruntled politicians or other motivated labour leaders. In Gandhian economics, economic activity is informed by ethical considerations. At the heart of Gandhian thinking is the small man, the man with his individual skill, capital and initiative. It is local production for local use with local resources. It is an economics of decentralisation of independent workers. Not that it rules out large scale production altogether, but it moves in the direction of small scale production and decentralisation. This shows that Gandhi was a great supporter of decentralised development which has been propagated and implemented in its true spirit now a days by many of the states of India. Similarly, how true was the Gandhian economics when it laid emphasis on the concept of sustainable development when he talks about that "we should not pollute the motherland. We should not use up our soil and destroy our forest and foul our waters and exhaust in a few centuries, wealth accumulated by nature over millennium." Gandhian economics says that we should work with renewable resources in a way that what we receive with one hand we give back with the other. The basic hypothesis of the Gandhian system is "Earth provides us enough to satisfy every man's needs but not far everyman's greed."

Another great contributions of Mahatma Gandhi was that he laid more emphasis on improving the quality of human resources. He talks about development and strongly advocated that it should have some relation with human values and human qualities. It was said that human quality does not improve as long as poverty and misery remain. He says, "Development does not start with goods, it starts with people..." Gandhian paradigm of development was based upon this principle. The Gandhian model was basically aimed at building self - reliance and self-respect in a villager and poverty alleviation of India's teeming millions which has steeped in penury.

His model was primarily based on enhanced Biomass production, processing and utilisation. Gandhi was not an economic theorist but an economic reformer. He was great environmentalist too. His entire life and work was an enviornmental legacy for all humanity. In 1920, in *Young India* he wrote, "we want to organise our national power not by adopting the best methods of production only, but by the best method of both the production and distribution." Gandhiji was not against Industrialisation *per-se* but he wanted industrialisation minus its negative impact e.g. labour displacement, exploitation, environmental degradation, etc. He felt that nothing should be produced in cities that villages can produce so that migration of villagers as "Ecological Refugees" is halted. The impact of Gandhiji can be seen from the deliberation and declarations of a plethora of conferences and meetings under the aegis of United Nations and other international and national bodies on the problems of population, women, children, labour, human rights, tolerance, environment together with the associated social, economic, environmental and political dimension. The impact of Gandhian ideas is seen everywhere though not with us physically, today his silence speaks louder than his words; and initially his wisdom constituted philosophy, but now it has become common sense.

The Gandhian economic thought should be interpreted after viewing it from the present day independent India. In the context of the globalisation of all economies and in the light of the present day aspirations of the people we should try to find ways and means to develop economically but keeping in mind the basic conditions laid down in the Gandhian thought. These conditions may be mentioned as:

- (i) dignity of manual labour;
- (ii) welfare of the masses;
- (iii) non-violent change/transition from one level to a higher level;
- (iv) the mass-participation in production process;
- (v) maximum use of swadesi goods and services
- (vi) following the model of all inclusive development; and
- (vii) emphasis on people participation in total process of Planning and Economic development.

I am sure these guidelines provided by the Gandhian thought can give us reasonable ground from which to raise our economic policies and to build up the economic super-structure.

References

Chaudhuri, Ranjit (2007), "Towards Understanding Gandhian Economics", *Essays on Gandhian Thought from Institute of Gandhian Studies*, Wardha downloaded from website www: mkgandhi.org

Das, Rattan (2002), *Gandhi in Twenty-First Century*, Sarup, New Delhi.

Dayal, Parmeshwari (2006), *Gandhian Theory of Social Reconstruction*, Atlantic, New Delhi.

Gangal, S.C. and Anurag Gangal (1995), *Contemporary Global Reforms: A Gandhian Perspective*, Vinod, Jammu.

Khoshoo, T.N. (1997), "Gandhian Environmentalism: An Unfinished Task", *IASSI Quarterly*, Vol. 16, No. 1, July-September downloaded from website www: mkgandhi.org

Koilpillai J. Charles (2007), "Five Myths About Gandhian Economics" downloaded from website www.transnational-perspectives.org.

Kumar, S.B. (2002), *Environmental Problems and Gandhian Solutions: The Only Ray of Hope to the Present Ailing World*, Deep & Deep, New Delhi.

Maharajan, M. (2001), *Mahatma Gandhi and the New Millennium*, Discovery Publishing, New Delhi.

Mishra, Anil Dutta (2003), *Challenges of 21st Century: Gandhian Alternatives*, Mittal Publications, New Delhi.

Narayan, Shriman (1970), *Relevance of Gandhian Economics*, Navajivan Publishing House.

Pani, Narendar (2002), *Inclusive Economics: Gandhian Method and Contemporary Policy*, Sage Publications Pvt. Ltd.

Prasad, Gopal Lala (2004), *Relevance of Mahatma Gandhi in the Twenty-first Century*, Classical, New Delhi.

Sharma, A.K. (1996), *Gandhian Perspectives on Pollution and Development*, Concept, New Delhi

Sharma, R. (1997), *Gandhian Economics*, Deep and Deep Publications Pvt. Ltd.

Sharma, R.C. (2003), *Gandhi Environmentalism*, Global Vision, Delhi.

Singh, Ram Binod (2006), *Gandhian Approach to Development Planning*, Concept, New Delhi.

Singh, Ramjee (2000), *Gandhi and the New Millennium*, Commonwealth, Delhi.

Sharma, Rashmi (1997), *Gandhian Economics: A Humane Approach*, Deep & Deep, New Delhi

Swarup, Ram(1980), "Frontiers Gandhian Economics", MANAS Reprint, Vol. XXXIII, No. 53, downloaded from website www. manasjournal.org.

Tiwari Sanjeev Kumar, Singh Renu Kumari and Anil Dutta Mishra (2004), *Gandhian Alternative to Contemporary Problems*, Abhijeet, Delhi.

Websites Consulted:

www.environmental-expert.com

11

Economics of Mahatma Gandhi

Challenges and Development

BISHWANATH SINGH AND R.P. SINGH

Countries profoundly vary in economic and social conditions. Consequently there may not be any given path to economic development and social upliftment. The choice of route is an applied one, and in Indian conditions where socio-economic revolution is aimed without violence, Gandhian thinking can be effectively useful in deciding the future course of development. U.N. Dhebar rightly remarked (1969):

> "Gandhian orientation needs to be preserved and if possible, continuously strengthened, if that be the right word in every direction."

As a meditator, the Great faquir of India dived deeper and deeper, and the pearls of his thought have glittering beyond time limit. G. Ramchandran (1969) can be appreciated for his opinion that "Gandhian Economics will be studied more and more as the decades pass because he thought and planned not only in terms of the present but even more of the future."

I. ECONOMIC IDEAS OF GANDHIJI

Peculiarity of Gandhian ideology is marked through wideness of his vision, normativism of his approach, emphasis on unskewed pattern of growth based on mass-orientation, etc. So far as his vision is concerned, Sethi (1978) correctly remarks that Gandhi's vision was too wide to concentrate exclusively on economics and too comprehensive to reject it. What Gandhiji rejected is 'theoretical separatism'. His economic thought developed not in the isolation of ideas unrelated to the problem of life but as their effective solution. Gandhian economics has come to be regarded at least in our country as a distinct original and exclusive development in Indian economic thought. Now, to quote Diwan and Gidwani (1979).

There are six basic concepts that are essential in Gandhian economics. They are:

(i) Swadeshi,
(ii) bread labour,
(iii) aparigrah or non-possession,
(iv) trusteeship,
(v) non-exploitation, and
(vi) equality.

"The idea of Swadeshi reflects an urge for use of own goods. According to Mahatma Gandhi, the law of each country's progress demands on the part of its inhabitants, preference for their own products and manufactures. And in case of Swadeshi, the 'bedrock' of efficiency is created by producer-consumer co-operation. Coming to the concept of 'bread labour', it may be mentioned that it favours creation of value-in-use instead of value in exchange. Gandhian concept of 'Aparigrah' bears a clear imprint of vedantic philosophy which prohibits greed for wealth. To quote Ishawasyopanishad—

Ten Tyakten Bhunjithah
Ma Gridhah Kasyaswid Dhanam.

तेन त्यक्तेन भुञ्जीथा ।
मा गृधः कस्यविद् धनम् ।।

—Ishawasyopanishad-I

Aparigrah is supposed to condition and develop social balance. Gandhian 'Trusteeship' ideology is more prescription based than deeply rooted in realism. Rieger's observation at this point is worth notice. According to Rieger (1970):

"Gandhian economics reveals itself to be a set of prescriptions of the way in which economic institutions should be organised and of the way in which the individual in the system ought to behave." Through the concept of trusteeship, Gandhiji prescribed that property (in excess of that needed to enable the owner a reasonable standard of life) must be held as a trust on behalf of the society and especially those who are poor and have no private property of their own. Gandhiji says in 'Socialism of my Conception', "What belongs to me is the right to an honourable livelihood, no better than enjoyed by millions of others. The rest of my wealth belongs to the community and must be used for the welfare of the commuity."

Non-exploitation involves the reduction and eventual elimination of priviledge. In this context, Diwan (1985) referes to three types of privileges: (i) privilege of non-accountability, (ii) privilege of easy opportunities, and (iii) economic privilege. To quote Diwan, "These three privileges though analytically distinct are not independent of each other. On the contrary, these are highly interrelated, one promoting the other. The basis of elite mass contradiction lies in the concept of exploitation. Non-exploitation thus involves the reduction in the elite-mass contradiction."

The concept of equality involves a redistribution of assets in favour of the poor and away from the rich. The effect of such a redistribution is to change prices. Lowering the prices of necessities, consumed and needed by both the elite and mass society and raising those of luxuries, consumed only by the elite society of course.

Besides these basic concepts, if one looks from microscopic lens, it would be vividly clear that Gandhiji aspired for formation of a happy, peaceful and dynamic society in its entirety. Gandhiji (1946) believed that a "Socialistic state is bound to come in being in India", and he further hoped (1947) that "Indian socialism would not be an arm-chair but a practical socialism. The goal must be clear and perfect or else we would be sailing on an unchartered sea and might founder." In his approach he lays emphasis on the principles of social harmoney, peace and non-violence and this is in contrast to the thesis of Karl Marx which lays down the inevitability of class-war and the final victory of the proletariat. On the other hand, non-violence is the bed-rock of Gandhian thinking. Gandhiji (1937) held the view that, "if communism came without any violence, it would be welcome."

Now, it is high time to find out whether the Gandhian thoughts are competent to canalise the up-to-date currents of challenges and development strategy in a fruitful way.

II. GROWTH, EMPLOYMENT, POVERTY REMOVAL AND THE GANDHIAN MARG (GANDHIAN ROUTE)

During the last more than five decades, India in her serpantine movement on the road to planned development (i.e. from command to market based economy and *vice-versa*) has been led to creation of kinky pattern of growth. The two Asian bigs—India and China resemble in the sense of starting development efforts since early 1950s and faced 'Jerks' in the process of development, but even in the 'zig-zag' course the Chinese economy rolls towards 'a set of balances' whereas the forces of development in India are largely exhausted in building enclaves of higher magnitude. Mao directed but Gandhiji appealed, and such appeal being ignored, Gandhian prescription being not effectively into a broader programme of economic development, what one gets today is growth of a few to the neglect of the masses, resultant social tension and classconflict, high incident of unemployment and poverty, growing consumerism on the one side and food deficiency for a large part of population lying below the poverty line. So, India today, has 'Alpodaya' and not 'Sarvodaya'. An MNC/TNC concern on Indian land, like beauty, is to be seen not touched, by incapable ones. So, under current scenario, to heal up the wound of the common man, one will have to look into Gandhian way either for development or employment generation or poverty eradication. Notably in context of India, rather the new problems of the world economy, i.e. the problems arising from globalised system have reinforced interest in Gandhian thoughts. Everyone knows that Gandhiji was not a growth-model-builder like Harrod, Domar and Mahalanobis, etc. but a model can be built on the basis of his economic ideas available in his numerous writings and such model may command more relevance for developing countries, where growth must not be 'job-less' and only for the haves. V.C. Sinha (1985) explains how the Gandhian model of economic growth shows that the remedies of poverty and unemployment in India lie in:

(a) Creating a self-propelling and self-sustaining process of production in villages,
(b) Decentralising the production system, wealth and economic power, and
(c) Practising the principle of trusteeship for social ends.

To Gandhiji village is the basic consideration. He aspired that every village be a republic. Gandhiji (1942) said, "My idea of village Swaraj is that it is a complete republic, independent of its neighbours for its vital wants and yet interdependent for many others in which dependence is a necessity." And at this unit level from the point of view of production, first concern should be for food crop and cloth. In case of availability of more land, useful money crops may be raised. If such view about the use of one major factor of production, i.e. land is backed by political determination, the odds of market on the poor segment of the society as well 'erosion of real wages' can be significantly controlled. Similarly, the emphasis that Gandhiji lays on bread labour conforms to the goal of self-sustained village life. Of course, for this idea of bread labour, Gandhiji acknowledges debt to Ruskin's 'Unto this Last' and to a Rusian writer T.M. Bondaref. Fascinated by the idea of bread labour, he argues that physical labour is an obligation for all and that if all laboured for their daily bread, there would be enough food and enough leisure for all. To quote Gandhji (1935), "There will be no rich and poor, none high and none low." The very concept of 'bread labour' if operationalised even today with states will power and critical 'intervener role'—may culminate into creation of exploitationless rural life assembling 'pyramid-less oceanic circle'. And Gandhiji assumed that in this structure composed of innumerable villages, there will be ever widening and never ascending circles. Life will not be a pyramid with apex sustained by the bottom. Through such notion, Gandhiji virutally recommended a Sarvodaya social order, that reflects as Mathur (1962) explained, "a system of total and integrated progress of all." But such thinking may belong to a great soul, its roots lie in Sarvabhuthitwad philosophy of Geeta.

> सर्वभूत हिते रता: ।
> *(Sarva Bhut hite ratah)*
>
> —Srimad Bhagwad Geeta, 5/25

But practically, it is slaughtered by the materialist self-seekers. Again, the state can have a role, it can impose income ceiling, legalise trusteeship, what Gandhiji also dreamt; and support small ones to grow. Mao has reaped benefit of Gandhian thought and the Maoist strategy of taking industry as a leading factor has not fallen into the error of 'Soviet Giantism', but in India the 'Mahalanobis model' biased in favour of heavy industries, having growing appetite for capital-intensive mode of production has driven the country off the Gandhian route that favours labour-intensive technology. The result is that growth-led employment could not be sufficient nor the 'trickle down' mechanism has functioned effectively. Gandhiji (1934) cautioned that machines are evil where there are more hands than required for the work as in case of India. He also visualised machine-led growth with less employment content will benefit only a few. He said far back in 1924 that "today machinery merely helps a few to ride at the back of millions." To control the growing gap in socio-economic status as well as to boost-up employment effect, some thinkers argue today for re-direction of investment flows towards the more labour-intensive sectors of activity.

An important development related issue is poverty. The problem of mass poverty has become more intricate and less easily soluable. Neither 'trickle down' nor schematic efforts have yielded what may be regarded as satisfactory results on the yard-stick of poverty amelioration, and in this respect major impediment springs forth from structural dualism and lack of necessary changes in structure of property power. And it would not be unwise if one turns to 'Gandhian remedial complex'. Even at the present stage when millions are in high drive for accumulation of wealth, in a competitive race under globalised world order with a motivation to have greater command over the market *vis-a-vis* the means of production. Following measures based on Gandhian economics, may be quite supportive to attack on poverty:

(i) Transforming the Poor into an Agent of Growth

To have a concrete shape, such type of recommendation requires 'capability-generation', job creation and motivation chagnes. If Gandhiji emphasized growth of cottage industries, it is even relevant today from the point of view of economy in converting population into an 'input', because one will not have to incur huge cost for learning the mode of operation as it happens in case of high-tech industries. Likewise, his favour for decentralised industries and development of ancillaries in the cottage sector would be helpful in stabilising the demand side of the labour market. The Charkha and Khadi are symbols, symbols of dignity for small works. From Gandhian Philosophy of 'bread labour'—a lesson can be imparted to the citizens that any job that supports life is valuable. If under Gandhian imprint, status of job (specially its social status) is ignored, and if available work is welcomed as God—poverty will have to enshrink. Without making distinction about jobs, rather for any types of job, Gandhiji remarked (1921), "to a people famishing and idle, the only acceptable form in which God can dare appear work and promise of food as wages."

(ii) Proper Standard of Wages

Phenomenon of poverty is linked up with the style of distribution. If wage income is optimised, poverty should decline. On 'Wages and profits Gandhiji wrote (1921), "A time is certainly coming when there will be no unconciousable dividends. The profits of big concern must bear relation to wages of the workers." Further, according to Gandhiji, as Nayak (1953) observes, a worker must be paid enough to support a family of 4 to 6 members to see to their proper housing, sanitation, to provide them with a balanced diet, in a word, to help them to live a human life. 'Fair standard of wages' that Gandhi intends to have are bound to improve the fortune of the poor segment of the society, depending mainly on wage income.

(iii) Income Ceiling

Despite formulating the idea of trusteeship, Gandhiji wanted to translate it into institutional form. Pyarelal (1952) writes that on December 12, 1942, Gandhiji advanced the thesis that when power would come into people's hand, trusteeship would be embodied in the law of the land. A formula was drafted based on following principles:

(i) State regulated trusteeship, and
(ii) Limit on maximum income.

State regulation of trusteeship emboldens interventionist's role of state and puts curb on individual freedom to hold wealth and to use it for selfish satisfaction. And limit on maximum income or income ceiling should check the tall one from becoming taller and making weak weaker. This formula could not be concretised; but the very idea of ceiling on maximum income is quite relevant under present situtation, to reduce the incidences under present and situation reduce the incidence of deprivation.

III. GANDHISM IN THE WHIRLPOOL OF GLOBALISATION

What would be the fate of Gandhian type of Growth model under the situation of globalisation resting on free flow of capital and technology and removal of trade barriers and consequent competitive environment, in which for survival and growth, refinements are being continuously made for technology and mode of production, distribution and sales? How can cottage and tiny industries face the TNCs/MNCs? Is Gandhian Economics loosing its ground? Such questions are bound to arise. But it be admitted that Gandhian thoughts are neither utopian nor perishable. The three-lane growth path including globalisation is a fast lane for competent ones, ignoring bypass and crossing for poor. Gandhian economics stands for common class, not the elite class, and even under the whirlpool of globalisation, it would provide way of development who have been thrown away by machine based fast style of growth. Pro-poor growth model of Gandhiji is too practical to loose its vitality. Gandhiji realised incapability of poor to follow the luxurious life-pattern of the rich ones; but stood on their side for ordinary amenities of life. He declared (1931).

"The Swaraj of my dream is poor man's Swaraj. The necessaries of life should be enjoyed by you in common with those enjoyed by the princes and monied men. But that does not mean that you should have palaces like theirs. They are not necessary for happiness. You or I would be lost in them. But you ought to get all the ordinary amenities of life that a rich man enjoys."

Now, fast growth-minded critics of Gandhiji disliking 'slow moving' results of Gandhian model, should honestly brood over not about the relevance of Gandhian ideology, but of the MNC's and TNC's from a humanitarian angle of support to masses—the poor ones. In developed countries, employment creation potentiality of large scale industries has reached rather saturity point. To quote Prof. Meghanad Desai (2002), "American 500 largest industrial companies failed to create a single new job between 1975 and 1990, their share of civilian labour force dropping from 17 per cent to less than 10 per cent. "In India too, under current exit policy, for cost-effectiveness and efficiency gains, job-cuts are welcomed by many big enterprises, both in the public as well as the private sector. So, the race run under 'globalisation' has some what ugly shape due to negligence to human factor, but Gandhian model is humanitarian and even in the storm of globalisation, it would be surviving. Planners would have to welcome its basic elements once they lean towards social goal of employment generation, mass welfare and maximum social benefit.

References

Desai, Meghnad (2002), Marx's Revenge The Resurgence of Capitalism and Dealth of Stalinist Socialism, Verso, London.

Dhebar, U.N. (1969), "Gandhiji, India and Democratic Socialism", *AICC Economic Review*, Vol. XXI, Nos. 6-7.

Diwan, Romesh and Gidwani, S., "Elements in Gandhian Economics", *Gandhi Marg*, July, 1, (4), pp. 248-58.

Diwan, Romesh (1985), 'On the Relevance of Gandhian Economics', *Indian Economic Journal*, Conference Volume.

Gandhi, M.K. (1921), *Young India*, June 8 and Oct. 13.

Gandhi, M.K. (1924), *Young India*, Nov. 13.

Gandhi, M.K. (1931), *Young India*, March 26.

Gandhi, M.K. (1934), *Harijan*, 16 November.

Gandhi, M.K. (1935), *Harijan*, June 19.

Gandhi, M.K. (1937), *Harijan*, Feb. 13.

Gandhi, M.K. (1946), *Harijan*, March 31.

Gandhi, M.K. (1947), *Harijan*, May 18.

Gandhi, Mahatma (1966 ed.), Socialism of my Conception, Bombay, Bhartiya Vidya Bhawan.

Ishavasyopanishad (2005 Ed.), Gita Press, Gorakhpur.

Mathur, J.S. (1962), Essays on Gandhian Economics, Chaitanya Publishing House, Allahabad.

Nayak, T. (1953), 'Gandhi on the Dignity of the Human being, *Gandhi Marg*.

Pyare Lal (1952), *Harijan*, Oct. 25.

Ram Chandran, G. (1969), "The Core of Gandhian Economics", *AICC Economic Review*, Vol. XXI, Nos. 6-7.

Rieger, H.C. (1970), 'Gandhi and Economics', *Gandhi Marg*, June 2-3.

Sethi, J.D. (1978), *Gandhi Today*, Vikas, New Delhi.

Shrimadbhagwadgeeta (2006 ed.), Geeta Press, Gorakhpur.

Sinha, V.C. (1985), "Relevance of Gandhian thought in Context of Indian Planning", *Indian Economic Journal*, Conference volume.

12

PMGSY

An Entry Point for Gandhian Vision

With Reference to Bhopal District of Madhya Pradesh

Urmila Vijayvargiya and Sharad Tiwari

I. INTRODUCTION

Mahatma Gandhi's vision for our country was that our villages should have every facility which a city has. Every village should be connected with good road, should have electricity, Hospital and School and other modern amenities. Pradhan Mantri Gram Sadak Yojna (PMGSY) aims to connect villages with black topped all weather roads. India is a vast country, consists of villages scattered all over in an area 3.29 million sq.kms. More than 75 per cent of its population lives in villages. Indian villages are highly backward and lacking in all type of amenities. Village people are poor, illiterate and deprived with basic facilities. This condition is still prevailing, even after 60 years of independence.

Mahatma Gandhi had a vision of villages as self-sufficient units, which would be a complete entity not depending on others for their needs. This concept is not achieved in spite of several five year plans and many schemes of rural development (Ministry of G.O.I.). One of the constraints in making villages an independent unit is absence of well knit road network, which is causing lack of basic facilities.

Function of road network in a country is like function of artilleries in a human body. Blood is circulated in all parts of the human body through these veins and artilleries, keeping all functions intact and in good condition. Similarly, good road network connects all parts of the country and provide all types of facilities in far and near corners of the country. This is basic requirement for all types of developments in a country. Education, medical assistance, banking, employment potentials, livestock, inward transport of agriculture inputs and consumer goods, outward flow of agriculture and forestry products all are dependent on road network. In spite of several schemes for rural development, no stress was given for construction of roads. Some kutcha fair weather roads were constructed under various schemes viz. NREP, RLEGP, JRY, IJRY, BMS, EAS, etc. But no sincere effort was made in this direction.

There is ample evidence—both national and international that provision of Rural road infrastructure holds the key to accelerated poverty reduction, socio-economic transformation, national integration and breaking the isolation of village communities, holistic rural development and achievements of millennium development goals. Absence of connectivity increased rural poverty. Large sections of rural population including tribal are living under BPL and are away from the mainstream of national development. Absence of basic facilities in villages resulted in large scale migration with consequential socio-stresses and law and order problems in urban area.

II. RELEVANCE OF RURAL CONNECTIVITY

Due to lack of rural connectivity lakhs of Indian villages and crores of villagers are suffering prolonged deprivation and tragic isolation. Deprive them of chance of sustainability and development. Some of the eloquent symptoms of such deprivation are given below:

Rural children can not reach the school during rainy season. Pregnant women can not reach health care centre in time from their villages and suffer loss of life, about 300 women per day. In rainy season large number of cattle dies in veterinary epidemics because timely help can not reach them. Agriculture produce can not reach the markets in time leading to heavy losses malnutrition and infant mortality occur as the public distribution system fails to reach the villages. Villagers are deprived of equality of opportunity as compared to urban population due to inaccessibility. Illiteracy, unemployment and poverty are prevailing due to poor connectivity. Water tankers can not reach in drought prone villages.

III. BACKGROUND AND MAGNITUDE

In pursuance of nationally significant cause of 100 per cent rural road connectivity by all weather roads to set the villages free from the handicap of isolation and deprivation of accessibility, the G.O.I. constituted National Rural Road Development Committee (NRRDC) on 6th January, 2000 under the chairmanship of Shri Nitin Gadkari, an engineer politician and leader of opposition in Maharashtra legislative council. In his address on 15th August 2000 the Prime Minister of India, announced Prime Minister Gram Sadak Yojna (PMGSY) as a 100 per cent centrally sponsored scheme, with the target of connecting every habitation with population of 1000 and more, with all weather roads in the next 3 years and every habitation having population more than 500 by the year 2007. Officially this programme was launched on 25th December 2000 and Rs. 2500 crores were released as additional central assistance for rural roads construction programme during 2000-01. The programme seeks to provide connectivity to all unconnected villages in the rural areas with a population of 500 and above with all weather roads by the end of 10th plan period. In respect of hill states (North East, H.P., Uttranchal, J. & K.) desert areas and tribal areas, the object is to connect villages of 250 and above population.

IV.. CONNECTIVITY STATUS

According to NRRDC report, connectivity status of our country is as under: (Table 1)

TABLE I

Population Range	No. of Villages in India		No. of Villages in Madhya Pradesh		No. of Villages in Bhopal District	
	Total	Un-connected	Total	Un-connected	Total	Un-connected
1000 and above	129652	13825	14285	5804	65	23
Below 1000	459462	276628	41434	12688	446	395
Total	589114	290480	55719	18492	511	418

The present study is carried out to test two hypotheses:

1. There is significant improvement in the lifestyle of people of the villages after they are connected with road.
2. People of these villages have been benefited in terms of medical facilities, schooling of their children, greater mobility, opening of new avenues of economic growth, etc.

V. OBJECTIVE OF THE STUDY

The objectives of the present study are as follows:

1. The objective of the study is to assess social and economic changes in villages, connected by all weather roads under PMGSY.
2. To find out the improvements in the lives of village people at the household level and also at village level.
3. The specific objective of the study is to assess the impact of the road.
4. Connectivity, in terms of the following indicators:

(a) Agriculture and allied activities
(b) Employment
(c) Income Level
(d) Transport facilities
(e) Education
(f) Health Services
(g) Saving in Time
(h) Social factors
(i) Environment

VI. SCOPE AND COVERAGE OF THE STUDY

To assess impact of PMGSY, centrally situated state Madhya Pradesh is selected as it in the heart of the country. In selection of the district, Bhopal district is preferred because it is the capital of the state. After selection of Bhopal district, I have selected 11 villages connected in first phase of the programme because those roads are completed in the year 2002 and by this time fruits of developmental activities are ripped. Thus 11 villages connected by 11 completed black topped roads under phase I programme of PMGSY are selected for study. Their names are given in Table 2.

TABLE 2

Sl. No.	*Name of the Block*	*Name of the Village under study*
1.	Fanda	Teelakhedi
2.	Fanda	Pura Chhindwara
3.	Fanda	Khamkheda
4.	Fanda	Barkheda Salam
5.	Fanda	Barkheda Bondar
6.	Fanda	Kolukhedi
7.	Berasiya	Nalkheda
8.	Berasiya	Garhakalan
9.	Berasiya	Kalara
10.	Berasiya	Rampura Balan
11.	Berasiya	Damkheda

VII. METHODOLOGY

In the present study social research method has been used. The advantage that a social research holds over physical research is that in this method researcher can talk to his subjects, know their feelings, ideas, etc. In present study I have visited all 11 villages and collected Data's from 50 households from each village.

For the present study secondary data are obtained from:

1. M.P. Rural road development authority, Vindhyachal Bhawan, Bhopal.
2. Project implementation units, PMGSY, Bhopal.
3. National Rural Road Development Agency, New Delhi.
4. Web site—www.pmgsy.org.in
5. Publications of Ministry of Rural Development, Government of India, New Delhi.
6. Data from Census report of India, 2001.

VIII. IMPACT ASSESSMENT OF RURAL CONNECTIVITY IN BHOPAL DISTRICT

1. Impact on Agriculture

The construction of PMGSY roads has greatly benefited the farmers. Prior to the construction of PMGSY roads, farmers found it difficult to sell agriculture goods in bigger markets that are located at a distance from their villages. Due to lack of transport, the farmers had to often physically carry the baskets of agriculture goods on their heads and thus could transport only a small amount of agriculture produce to the market. Also a lot of travel time was lost. So the isolated village community may be producing just the quantity needed for its consumption. Thus the whole process was not profitable. However the construction of the PMGSY roads has resulted in increased and easier movement of farmers and their produce and has thus increased agriculture profit.

TABLE 3

Sl. No	Name of the Village	Increase in use of chemical fertilizer/ pesticides	Change in cropping pattern	Increase in motorized agriculture vehicles and equipments	Increase in use of high breed seeds
1.	Gadakala	0	10	8	20
2.	Rampura Balan	2	16	6	26
3.	Nalkheda	6	12	16	28
4.	Damkheda	2	20	10	20
5.	Kalara	2	10	14	26
6.	Kolukhedi	0	14	10	30
7.	Pura Chhindawara	0	26	16	28
8.	Khamkhera	0	42	10	22
9.	Barkeda Bondar	2	24	14	26
10.	Barkheda Salam	2	26	10	24
11.	Tilakhedi	0	50	20	20

The key indicators which have been used for assessing the impact of completed PMGSY roads on agriculture and allied activities are:

- increase in usage of chemical fertilizers,
- pesticides and high breed seeds, and
- change in cropping pattern.

The Table below summarizes the responses of 50 respondents at household and habitation level—village-wise.

It has been observed that due to connectivity under PMGSY, Impact on Agriculture is on positive side. Trend of use of chemical fertilizer is increased. Out of 11 villages under study 6 have used it in spite of difficulty in its availability.

Cropping pattern has been changed in all the villages. Average change is 23 per cent. This indicates that nearly one fourth farmers have followed the new track. Increase in use of motorized agricultural vehicles and equipments is also found in every village. Its average is 12 per cent. Use of high breed seeds increase production. Its average is nearly 25 per cent. No doubt this will bring prosperity soon.

2. Impact on Employment

After connectivity an improvement in the employment situation in terms of more job opportunities, more avenues for self-employment, etc. are observed. A lot of housewives mentioned that they have started small-scale industries like making pickles, papads, baris (lentil cakes), etc. non-farm employment opportunities have increased due to shift from grains to cash crops and also multiple cropping. More people are going to nearby towns and villages for odd jobs like selling wood, vegetables, dairy products and locally made items like pickles, papad, chatai, jhadu, etc. Non-farm opportunities like opening of shops, small business, cottage industries has increased. Besides, road connectivity has led to expansion of local industries, which in turn has generated employment opportunities.

TABLE 4

Sl. No.	*Name of the Village*	*% Increase in Non-farm employment*	*% Increase in Off-farm employment*
1.	Garhakalan	10	60
2.	Rampura	14	44
3.	Nalkheda	20	58
4.	Damkheda	16	56
5.	Kalara	20	42
6.	Kalukhedi	20	48
7.	Pura Chhindwara	16	36
8.	Khamkheda	24	38
9.	Barkheda Bondar	30	42
10.	Barkheda Salam	34	48
11.	Tilakhedi	40	44

The Key indicators that have been used for assessing the impact of completed PMGSY roads on employment are increase in off-farm employment opportunities and increase in non-farm employment opportunities. The Table above summarizes the per cent affirmative responses of respondents of the villages under study.

The respondents stated that at the time of construction of road, they got employment on the road construction work, but since work is complete, no cognizance has been taken. Due to construction of Black-top road they can go to nearby town or village daily in less time, on cycle or on feet, for off-farm employment. They can do up and down conveniently.

There has been significant rise in Off-farm employment in all the villages under study average increase is 47 per cent. Due to change in cropping pattern chances of employment are increased in non-farm activities, its average increase is 22 per cent only.

3. Impact on Health

There has been an overall improvement in access to the health facilities like PHCs, sub-health centers and district hospitals. Positive impact is observed with regard to increase in accessibility to preventive and curative health care facilities; better management of infectious diseases and attending to emergencies due to faster access to health facilities and increase in frequency of visits by health workers.

Improvement in ante-natal and post-natal care thereby decreasing obstetrics emergencies is also become possible due to PMGSY road construction. Road connectivity and an improved transport system have enabled families to opt for institutional deliveries in hospitals outside the village resulting decrease in infant and child mortality rate.

The impact on Health is assessed by using following indicators:

1. Access to District Hospitals/PHC/sub-Centers,
2. Mode of Transport to Hospitals/PHC/sub-Centers,
3. Increase in visits of Doctors/Health workers,
4. Increase in deliveries in hospitals,
5. Decrease in incidences of major illness/diseases like Malaria, Diarrheas, etc.

It is observed that overall impact on health is very positive. Respondents have accepted that access to hospitals/ PHC/sub-Centers is increased by 80 per cent as an average of

TABLE 5

Sl. No.	Name of the Village	Improved Access to PHC	Increase in visits of health workers	Decrease in incidences of major diseases	Greater availability of transport to hospitals	Increase in child births in hospitals
1.	Garhakalan	80	0	82	78	90
2.	Rampura	84	6	86	86	80
3.	Nalkheda	90	24	70	96	70
4.	Damkheda	80	20	74	90	64
5.	Kalara	72	0	78	50	74
6.	Kolukhedi	72	20	80	60	68
7.	Pura Chhindwara	70	10	74	80	74
8.	Khamkheda	74	16	86	90	76
9.	Barkheda Bondar	90	24	90	94	86
10.	Barkheda Salam	84	20	96	80	84
11.	Tilakhedi	82	0	100	70	94

Note: The figures in the table indicate % of affirmative responses of the respondents.

all answers. Increase in visits of Doctors/Health workers are only 13 per cent. Its reason is that most of the posts are vacant. When posts are filled, it is expected that no. of visits will be increased. 83 per cent respondents agreed that no. of major diseases occurrence is reduced. Greater availability of transport is confirmed by affirmative answers of 80 per cent people. Child birth rate in Hospitals is accepted by 78 per cent respondents.

4. Impact of Education

With the construction of PMGSY roads, there has been improvement in the accessibility to education facility. This has resulted in increased school enrolment and school attendances. Beneficiaries reported that the road connectivity has lead to an increase in the number of girls going to schools. Most parents mentioned that they were more confident about sending their daughters to school unescorted.

Biggest impact is this that now Middle schools have been opened in every village. Another noteworthy impact has been in terms of regular attendance of the teachers throughout the year and greater inclination of parents to send boys and girls for higher studies and college education.

The indicators, which have been used to assess the status of Primary education are as per following:

Increase in the number of boys going to school for Primary and Middle School Education.

Increase in the number of girls going to school for Primary and Middle School Education.

Increase in the availability and number of Teachers in school.

TABLE 6

Sl. No.	Name of the Village	No. of students	% Increase in No. of boys going to school	% Increase in No. of girls going to school	No. of teachers at. present	% Increase in availability and No. of teachers in schools
1.	Garhakalan	291	15	83	7	15
2.	Rampura	268	20	70	6	12
3.	Nalkheda	417	16	75	8	14
4.	Kalara	646	17	50	12	13
5.	Kolukhedi	284	20	50	6	12
6.	Pura Chhindwara	308	14	69	6	17
7.	Khamkheda	319	20	74	6	15
8.	Barkheda Bondar	520	14	82	7	13
9.	Barkheda Salam	323	15	72	7	11
10.	Tilakhedi	448	12	60	11	12

Major impact of PMGSY roads is that all 11 villages Primary schools are upgraded to Middle schools. Due to increase in number of students posting of Teachers are also increased. It has been observed that increase in number of boy student is less than that of girl student. Increase in boys is 16.5 per cent whereas increase in girls is 69.5 per cent. Obvious reason for this is that people were sending boys to schools even when there were no roads. Now after construction of PMGSY roads, people have started sending their daughters to schools. This is a good change in social and cultural life of village people. So far as attendance of teachers is concerned, it is increased by 13.6 per cent. Now due to Transport facility, Teachers residing in nearby towns can do up and down to attend the job regularly.

In these villages Primary schools were existing in every village and middle schools were in 50 per cent villages. For villages not having Middle school, it was in nearby another village. Hence, education up to middle standard is easy and economical. For education in higher secondary/high school or in college they have to send their boy or girl to nearby town.

Hence, we have combined study of higher secondary/ High school education and College education together and termed as Higher education.

TABLE 7

Sl. No	*Name of the Village*	*No. of boys going to nearby town for study*	*No. of girls going to nearby town for study*
1.	Garhakalan	10	10
2.	Rampura	16	4
3.	Nalkheda	20	6
4.	Damkheda	16	2
5.	Kalara	10	4
6.	Kalukhedi	12	4
7.	Pura Chhindwara	10	2
8.	Khamkheda	12	4
9.	Barkheda Bondar	20	8
10.	Barkheda Salam	16	2
11.	Tilakhedi	10	2

Note: The figures in the tables indicate percentages of affirmative responses of respondents.

For this survey also we have fixed following indicators:

- No. of boys going to other town for Higher Education, and
- No. of Girls going to other town for Higher Education.

It is noted that in case of Higher education average no. of boys going out for education is 13.9 per cent where as no. of girls is only 4.4 per cent. This position reveals that even today long journeys in public transport by girls are not liked by Indian society. Girls of villages, which are nearer to towns, are allowed to go to college/High school, say within 15 km. distance. Boys are permitted to travel any distance subject to financial condition of the family.

With rural connectivity, there is a definite trend of a gradually increasing level of adult literacy in the villages and gradually declining rate of growth of population.

5. Impact on Transport Facility

The benefit of PMGSY road construction is much felt by the villages which are at distant places and are in difficult terrain. Road construction brought an increase in ownership of bicycles and two-wheelers. It has brought an improvement in public as well as private transport system. Some villagers have purchased Jeeps or wagons by obtaining loan under S.G.S.Y. and providing public transport along with self-employment. Transport system contributed to mobility of villagers to access markets, medical facilities, and other avenues of employment available in and around towns and villages. It has been observed that cultivators are now confident about selling their produce to other markets and they have tended to hold and stock grains and other non-perishable food items for selling the same during off-season. This is a remarkable contribution of PMGSY roads and connectivity these roads have established.

Following indicators have been selected to assess the impact-increase in the numbers of Cycles, Motor cycles, Scooters, etc. in the village; Improvement in public transport services; Increase in commercial vehicles or share Jeeps or

TABLE 8

Sl.. No	Name of the Village	Increase in the no. of cycles/ scooters/ two-wheelers	Improvement in public transport services	Increase in commercial vehicles or share jeeps or Taxies
1.	Garhakalan	78	96	74
2.	Rampura	70	50	46
3.	Nalkheda	60	30	66
4.	Damkheda	50	40	78
5.	Kalara	56	10	56
6.	Kalukhedi	18	4	04
7.	Pura Chhindwara	66	34	64
8.	Khamkheda	72	64	50
9.	Barkheda Bondar	68	78	48
10.	Barkheda Salam	75	68	46
11.	Tilakhedi	80	80	48

Note: The figures in the tables indicate percentages of affirmative responses of respondents.

Taxies PMGSY roads have provided all-weather connectivity, facilitated induction of public and private vehicles and contributed to mobility of villagers to access markets, medical facilities and other avenues of employment available in and around towns and villages. Average increase in number of cycles and two-wheelers in these 11 villages under study is 63 per cent. Improvement in public transport system is 52 per cent. Increase of commercial vehicle, Taxies and shared Jeeps is 53 per cent.

6. Impact on Income Level

The economies of these villages were depended mainly on agriculture and allied activities. Due to absence of connectivity with all weather roads to the market centers, there were limited business opportunities available to the inhabitants. It was very difficult in rainy season (almost 4 months) for them to earn even for their livelihood.

A spin-off benefit of PMGSY roads has been on the income level of the habitants benefiting from these roads. The roads directly or indirectly have provided opportunity for farm and non-farm employment as well as self-employment. With the improvement in farm and non-farm employment beneficiaries have reported increase in their average household income.

In villages more than 50 per cent population is below poverty line. They formed Self Help Groups (SHG) and under SGSY got assistance and loans from Banks and credit societies and started some activity for earning. Main activity which is found in almost all villages is "Diary Industry." Under this people use to purchase Cows and Buffalo for milk. Now with black topped road, they can take it to nearby Town and get good price. Another advantage of road connectivity is that farmers can sell their produce to Mandies directly, thus getting more money.

The Key indicators used to assess impact on income level are the following Increases in number of families selling Milk; Increase in selling price of Milk; Increase in number of

TABLE 9

Sl. No.	*Name of the Village*	*Increase in no. of households*	*% increase in price of Milk*	*Increase in no. of households selling food grain and vegetables in town*	*% increase in price of food grain and vegetables*
1.	Garhakalan	26	78	20	30
2.	Rampura	40	76	36	24
3.	Nalkheda	50	50	44	10
4.	Damkheda	34	60	30	26
5.	Kalara	20	78	20	30
6.	Kolukhedi	28	78	20	30
7.	Pura Chhindwara	26	70	30	24
8.	Khamkheda	56	75	40	20
9.	Barkheda Bondar	54	50	20	10
10.	Barkheda Salam	50	50	24	16
11.	Tilakhedi	30	74	30	24

Note: The figures in the tables indicate percentages of affirmative responses of respondents.

households selling Foodgrain or Vegetables directly to Mandi/co-opretive society; Increase in selling price of Food grain/Vegetables. It is observed that after construction of PMGSY roads, many persons have adopted selling of milk as business. Rate of milk was Rs. 9 per litre before construction of road, is being sold at the rate of Rs. 16 per litre in the town, thus giving increase of 78 per cent.

Village-wise findings reveal that selling rate of milk is increased from 50 per cent to 78 per cent. On enquiry it was informed that distant villages got higher increase than nearer villages. Reason is this that nearer villages were, already, selling milk at an higher rate. Thus average rise in rate of milk comes to 67 per cent. Similarly, villages situated at longer distance from Town got higher price for food grain and vegetables. Average rise in price of these commodities is 22 per cent only.

The average income effectively hides the inter-house differences in income but even with this limitation, it can be observed that the average income of common family is increased by 20 to 25 per cent. Significantly persons having agriculture land have realised higher increase in income say 25 to 40 per cent by changing cropping pattern and access to market through PMGSY road.

Those who succeeded in getting jobs (on or off farm jobs) obviously earned additional income. Again those cultivators who experimented with cash crop and vegetables, other than traditional grains, apparently realised higher incomes by selling these products at a higher price in a wider market than hitherto.

7. Impact on Land Prices

PMGSY roads have contributed to increase in Land prices in varying degrees depending upon the location of the Lands along these roads. Naturally lands located by the side of these roads have commanded higher prices. The Table 10 shows the change in the land prices over the period of one to one and a half year.

In Kalukhedi there is no increase in land price as there is a nallah in-between road and the village. Until a bridge is constructed on that nallah no effect on land price is possible.

TABLE 10

Si.. No	Name of the Village	Agriculture Land price earlier (Rs. in '000 per acre)	Agriculture Land price at present (Rs. in '000 per acre)
1.	Garhakalan	40-45	50-55
2.	Rampura	45-50	60-70
3.	Nalkheda	45-50	60-70
4.	Damkheda	40-45	50-55
5.	Kalara	30-35	35-40
6.	Kolukhedi	35-40	35-40
7.	Pura Chhindwara	40-45	50-55
8.	Khamkheda	35-40	40-45
9.	Barkheda Bondar	50-55	60-70
10.	Barkheda Salam	40-45	50-55
11.	Tilakhedi	40-45	60-75

However on other villages there is an average rise of 10 to 30 per cent.

8. Impact on Industry

At the time of Survey, an attempt was made to assess Impact of PMGSY road construction on industry. In small villages we can not imagine for big industry, but possibility of Small and Cottage industry can not be over ruled. But these are also yet to be started. It seems government's scheme of TRYSEM; SGSY, etc. relating to industry are not fruitful in these villages. As a matter of fact, roads can establish connectivity but growth of industry including village industry depends on other factors notably investments, markets and availability of inputs. Hence, it was felt that it is too early to expect growth of industry in villages covered by PMGSY. However, the roads have facilitated the induction of Buses and Vehicles which in turn has encouraged the setting up of small shops/establishments by relatively better villagers who are located near the road. In a way, opportunity for setting-up shops, diaries, repair workshops, etc. have been presented by the PMGSY roads. Also small shops of tea, Pan Bidi, etc. have come-up.

9. Impact on Time Saving

Earlier considerable time and energy were wasted by villagers in going from one place to another. Cultivators used to take more time to reach markets, students had to spend more time in traveling to school and back home, sick persons used to take time to reach Doctor. Villagers narrated that previous to construction of road, a sick person used to lie on a *khat* in four persons used to carry that khat on their shoulders, traveling on their foot. This process was laborious and time consuming. In cases of emergencies patient could die in the way. With the coming of roads now, everyone is able to save travel time and conserve energy for constructive work and accessing health and medical care, schools and colleges, etc. The opportunity benefit is substantial.

10. Impact on Social Aspects

The construction of PMGSY roads has brought a great change in social aspects of the villages. Following are a few:

(i) Neon Light Attraction Effect

Impressionistic youth, who were not able to access easily various types of entertainments available in the nearby towns, are now being increasingly attracted to these, due to new transport facilities. Now they go to watch movies, circus, fairs, etc. to towns like Bhopal, Berasia, etc. Even some youths, as reported by female respondents, go frequently to towns and other villages to while away their time and not necessarily for job hunting. This has made life more pleasant.

(ii) Decline in Gender Discrimination

Earlier for higher schooling, children used to walk down for some kms. and then to catch a bus for the schools and this traveling used to take at least 3-4 hours a day. This was the major factor which discouraged the parents to send their daughters for higher schooling. After passing Vth or VIIIth standards, from the village school, girls used to sit at home and parents would get them married at an early age of 15-18 years. Now with the construction of PMGSY roads and plying private buses and jeeps, girls have got opportunity to go for higher classes even when these schools are far flung.

The parents are also not apprehensive in sending their daughters to these schools. Thus the gap in educational level of girls and boys has started bridging up and the girl-child is no longer discriminated against in regard to higher education.

(iii) Maternity Care

Previously, when there was no roads, the pregnant woman, even in complicated cases very rarely could get quality medical attention, as there was no proper means of transportation on kutcha footway. Thus many pregnant women and newly born child have died because of delay in medical treatment. Now private jeeps and cars may be hired in the case of emergencies and these women can be taken to the hospitals for safer child birth and better maternity care.

(iv) Women Empowerment

Earlier in the absence of roads, men and women had to walk down for visiting relatives and going to work places. The roads were not only bad but also descreted in many places so that every time a female would venture out to go other places including their work places, a male companion was required. Now with the availability of buses and private jeeps women have started going alone to the markets and also to visit their relatives. Now they no longer depend upon the men to take them to these places. This independence has boosted the confidence of all and particularly those who are working, like Aanganwadi workers, Village teachers, Nurses, etc. Now they reach on time in meetings, can attend till late and come back safely and in lesser time. Their mobility, independence and efficiency have thus increased. A new sense of awakening among women has emerged.

(v) Social Integration

Because of kutcha roads and lack of means of transportation, people used to face difficulties in communication. So generally, relatives staying outside the unconnected villages used to avoid coming to these villages. Even people were quite apprehensive in making new relationships. Thus people were not ready to marry their daughters to the boys of these villages, as it would have restricted their visits as well as their daughters sit to parent's houses after the marriage. Now with improved connectivity, mobility has been made easier and parents are no longer hesitant to give their daughters in marriages to boys of distant villages.

(vi) Visit of Officials

The construction of PMGSY roads has led to an increase in frequency of visits by government officials. This is likely to result in better implementation of various government schemes and programmes. This will affect the social life of villagers indirectly.

(vii) Visit of Health Workers

There has been an increase in the visits of grassroots level functionaries like health workers/Auxiliary Nurses and Midwives (ANMs.), Village Level Workers (VLW) and Village Aaganwadi Workers (VAW) in the villages. All these have indirect effect on the lifestyle of villagers.

(viii) Better Law and Order

Road connectivity has enabled a quicker access to police services. This has ensured an improved law and order situation in all the villages.

(ix) Urbanisation of Lifestyle

Trend towards urbanisation of an area as an immediate and direct impact of providing rural road connectivity is observed in course of study. There have been some rapid changes from traditional to modern ways of life. There has been an increased use of Television, Radio, Electric Fans, Electric Press, Room Heaters and Washing Machines, etc. in the houses of above middle class families.

(x) Poverty Alleviation

PMGSY roads have played major role in poverty alleviation. It has increased the income level, changed cropping pattern, and provided avenues for employment. Thus it have played great role in bringing people above poverty line. Roads have made lives of people happier.

11. Impact on Environment

Generally people criticize that Environment is badly affected by the construction of roads. Cultivable land is taken for construction of road. Trees are cut and vehicles plying on the roads make noise and fumes coming out of silencer makes atmosphere smoky.

Sometime land of vulnerable group is taken for road construction. In some cases community resources viz. Wells, Tube-wells, Hand pumps or religious structures are affected adversely by road construction.

But in all 11 roads under study, no such case is encountered. In guidelines of PMGSY road, it is clearly mentioned that no acquisition of private land would be done for the construction of road. Hence question of taking land of vulnerable group do not arise. Road alignment is to be taken from government land. If some piece of private land is required, it will be taken with good will of that party.

For PMGSY road construction, Right of Way (RoW) required is only 15 meters. This much government land is available every where for the cart track. Similarly, none of the community resources have been affected by the road construction.

Cutting of trees is totally prohibited by GOI. However if cutting of some tree is essential, permission of forest department is essential. That permission is given with some conditions. One of the important conditions is that you have to plant as much new trees as much you are going to cut. Thus number of trees is not going to be reduced.

So far as noise and smoke is concerned, only a few vehicles will reach the villages. It is not a National Highway so high number of trucks and buses will not ply. Hence this disturbance is negligible.

Thus there is no adverse effect on the environment due to these roads.

IX. SUGGESTIONS

Although PMGSY connectivity opens door for enhancement of the quality of rural life and has a positive impact on them, but it is not enough. In our opinion, to have immediate benefit of the scheme, planners should explore natural resources in and around the village, as soon as road construction work is started, so their benefit may be availed on road completion.

Similarly, the action should also be taken to know the skill, proficiency and professionalism of the villagers so concerning activity may be started, just after connectivity.

Simultaneously to the programmes of rural connectivity, other agencies must initiated the rural development programme.

There should be co-ordination among all government departments and providers of essential services, viz. telephone, electricity, etc. This will lead towards Economy of the village.

There should be proper linkages between the old and new roads. Construction of Major bridges should also be sanctioned for complete connectivity.

X. CONCLUSION

There are very effective impacts over the life of villagers due to rural connectivity. Roads are affecting the lifestyle of the people and bringing them prosperity. Their social status is improving and income and education is increasing. Medical care chances are enhanced. These roads have exhibited manifold results. Thus it can be truly said that PMGSY is an entry point for Gandhian vision.

References

Indian Highways, June 2006.

Report of Gadkari Committee.

Proposals submitted by Department of Rural Development in M.P. Government of India for Prioritisation of Rural Roads in M.P.

Report on Impact Assessment of PMGSY, M.P. by NRRDA.

Summary of Findings of Impact Assessment of PMGSY by MORD, New Delhi.

Evaluation Report of LEA International.

Publication and C.D. of the Department of Census India.

M.P. Rural Roads Development Authority.

13

Gandhian Views on Sustainable Economic Development

R.S. GADAGE

Gandhi's spiritual beliefs provided the foundations for economic thoughts. His ideas were inspired by the ideas of in the book 'Unto this Last' by Ruskin. Gandhian views on economic thoughts are relevant even today. Had we adopted indigenous model of Gandhian thought right from the beginning, socio-economic problems could have been avoided. Now past is past, let us see that, such mistakes should not be committed again. The non-Gandhian model of economic development has failed because model was un-Indian, elitist and pushed more people into poverty line. The technology adopted by the model did not satisfy the objectives of the Gandhian polity of the economy, such as full employment, non-alienation, non-exploitation, ecological balance, rural-urban equality, etc. According to Gandhiji, the economics, that hurts the moral well-being of individual or society was considered as sin. True economics never ignore the moral values. Gandhiji was against the multiplicity of wants. Hence there should be deliberate limitations of wants. More we get, more we want and still remain unsatisfied.

Multiplication of wants and industrialisation of mass scale production will lead to exploitation, competition and problem of marketing. Gandhiji was not opposed the large scale production with the machine if it does not reduces the employment. His objection was for rural textile, which was facing competition from mill made clothes. In his economic thought man is more important than wealth. Indians should have faith in their eastern tradition, which helps us to escape from their vicious circle of violence and exploitation. Gandhiji emphasized establishment of ideal village where people could pursue the simple living and high thinking. Man is a part of nature and he must grow within the parameters of the natural surroundings. Human body is meant for service and not for indulgence. We should eat to live, not live to eat. Gandhiji insisted on an ethical framework for the practice of trade and industry as other occupations. It is duty of industrial enterprises to offer maximum satisfaction to the customers. Rural development is not mere economic prosperity for a few at the cost of many. It is participation of an entire population in production and consumption. Gandhiji emphasized the development of village industry. For this purpose people should live in cooperation and work for common good. Tolstoy's Bread Theory of Labour had great influence on economic philosophy of Gandhiji. All labour is dignified. Mental labour is for the satisfaction of soul, while manual labour for existence of the body. It is the responsibility of management to win the cooperation of the labour by creating favorable atmosphere for accelerating the production. In the production process, Gandhi's approach towards machinery was pragmatic and practical. Mechanisation is good when the hands are few. Use of machinery for large-scale production should not hurt the social objectives. The public utility service with capital-intensive techniques of production should be owned by the state because it benefits entire people, but India need to adopt labour-intensive techniques of production for the absorption of abundant labour supply. The village industrialisation will prevent the migration, congestion and slums of the big cities. Hence it is imperative to return Gandhian indigenous model of economic development.

INTRODUCTION

Mahatma Gandhi's spiritual beliefs provided the foundations for economic thoughts. His ideas were inspired by the ideas of in the book 'Unto this Last' by Ruskin. He was outstanding social and economic reformer in the world. He was a multi-dimensional man. His position in the public life was unique. He was called as father of the nation. Gandhij provided valuable contribution to the science of economics, which constitutes the foundation of the economics. The various aspects are relevant even today. Let us begin with his eight-fold vow that everyone should consider truthfulness, non-violence, celibacy, control of the palate, non-stealing, non-possession, Swadeshi, and fearlessness. Had we adopted indigenous model of Gandhian thought right from the beginning, many of the socio-economic problems could have been avoided. Now past is past, let us not make such mistake again. It is imperative to return Gandhian model of economic development despite liberalist and Marxist have dismissed Gandhiji in their arrogance. The Gandhian economic thoughts are essential for the sustainable development. The non-Gandhian model of economic development has failed, as a result; frustration in our country has increased. Our country has grown under the strong influence of Nehru, which was based on Marxian thoughts. Gandhian views of economic development had neglected after independence. Gandhian model of economic development was based on indigenous model, which can meet the challenges of the modern world. It can also make use of the best aspect of the Indian tradition through which the mass of the people can be involved in the political and economic development. But unfortunately intellectuals in India failed in applying the Gandhian model of sustainable economic development. After failure of the non-Gandhian model, now mass of the people in India and abroad seriously concern to the Gandhian thought of economic development. The model adopted earlier was un-Indian, elitist and pushed more people into poverty line. It created cynical elite class. As a result, corruption and immorality in public life has increased with leafs and bounds. The non-Gandhian model of economic development has created many problems and liabilities. The polity and its institutions have been seriously eroded. The economy is passing through a prolonged phase of stagnation and inflation. The technology adopted by the model did not satisfy the objectives of the Gandhiji's polity of the economy, such as full employment, non-alienation, non-exploitation, ecological balance, rural-urban equality, etc.

ECONOMICS AND ETHICS

According to Gandhiji there is no difference between economics and ethics. The economics that hurts the moral well-being of individual or society was considered as sin. True economics never ignores the moral values. An economics that inculcates mammon worship, and enables the strong to amass wealth at the expense of the weak, is a false and dismal science. Economics always stands for social justice; it promotes the good of all equally, including the weak for decent life. Gandhiji was against the multiplicity of wants. More we get, more we want and still remain unsatisfied. Even the economic laws of diminishing utility and insatiable wants clearly indicate that, lower the consumption and higher the satisfaction. Further, it is necessary to stop the consumption at a point, i.e. Mux=Px. Satisfaction of a unlimited wants seems to be delusion and snare. Hence, civilisation is not multiplication, but deliberate and voluntary reduction of wants. Gandhiji opposed multiplication of wants and industrialisation of mass scale, because it leads to exploitation, competition and problem of marketing.

The earnings of individual or income were fixed at Rs. 500 a month. Extra income should be used for a public cause. Generally rich people will not own kinship with poor people. The rich loose interest in their relatives and others who are needy. Gandhiji was not opposed the large scale industries. His objection was for rural textile, which was facing competition from the mill-made clothes. Some industrialists like Jamunalal Bajaj, on the advice of Gandhiji have helped the social activities of the country like village industries, untouchables, basic education, etc.

MAN AND WEALTH

According to Gandhiji that economics is untrue which disregards the moral values. In his economic thought man is important than wealth. Indian should not be obsessed with catchwords and seductive slogans of imported from the west. Indian should have faith in their distinct eastern tradition, which will help us to escape from the vicious circle of violence and exploitation. Craze for multiplicity of goods is destructive of contentment, peace and tranquility. Gandhiji emphasized establishment of ideal villages where people could pursue the simple living and high thinking. The less you possess, the less you want, and the better you are. Gandhian philosophy is integrated with the development of man because the man is part of nature and he must grow within the parameters of the natural surroundings. Human activity is a kind of discipline to improve the quality of life, which involves ethical and spiritual values of existence. Again he added that the human body is meant for solely for service, never for indulgence. The secret of happy life lies in renunciation. Renunciation is a life. Indulgence spells death. God created a man to work and those who eat without work are thieves. If everybody lives by the sweat of his brow, the earth would become paradise. Everyone should do some sort of manual labour to earn his bread. We should eat to live not live to eat. Gandhiji appealed for simple living, i.e. superabundance of wealth does not bring peace or happiness. Minimum standard of living should be ensured. The deliberate and voluntary restriction of wants promotes happiness and contentment and increases the capacity for service. For promoting better living, voluntary poverty is essential to serve the god and humanity. Compulsory obedience is slavery and willing obedience is a glory.

BUSINESS AND ETHICS

The basic elements in his philosophy were the deliberate limitations of human wants. Business is to be conducted with scrupulous, honesty and truthfulness. Gandhiji insisted on an ethical framework for the practice of trade and industry as other occupations. The business chosen by the family should be free from debt, no business credit, no business forbidden of goods and must not engage in a business to get rich quickly. According to Gandhiji whatever capital invested in a professional business for greed, competitiveness and exploitation of human beings was considered as sin. Legal and medical services are unobtainable by the poor, hence lawyers and doctors be paid a fixed sum by the State, and public to receive their service free of charge. Gandhiji appealed to industrialists to conduct their business for national rather than on commercial lines. It is duty of industrial enterprises to offer maximum satisfaction to the customers. Businessmen should avoid the publication of misleading advertisement, and invoice export and import at correct prices. Correct weights and measures is to be ensured. There should not be artificial scarcity, i.e. the economy of shortages should be replaced by economy of abundance. According to Gandhiji, economic progress is to be measured in terms of the moral character and social integrity of its citizens. Truth and non-violence is a powerful means to achieve goal of life. Orthodox economics unnecessarily gave undue importance to money and material wealth and excluded moral and human values.

ECONOMIC PROTECTION OF A COUNTRY

August 1920 non-cooperation movement gave birth to the economic protection of the country. If British Government refuses to an autonomous Government, without the empire, then India had a right to set-up an internal national policy of its own. The boycott of foreign goods and tariff to protect our own native industries. The boycott method was followed because of non-legislative function to the Indians. So that she would not be dependent upon any foreign nation. In order to protect the country from machine clothes, Gandhiji's Swadeshi Movement was started. He advocated that Khadi is to be made by hand-spun yarn. Development of hand-spinning is a key solution of India's poverty. Swadeshi must permeate every particle of our blood. It was considered as sin if someone touches foreign clothe. For perfect peace, removal of poverty, employ the people whole-heartedly, Gandhiji emphasized the Khaddar production. So Gandhiji himself changed his dress and took only loincloth. Preserving the foreign clothes means just like a sign of our slavery. Hence Swadesi is beneficial to crores of people. It is a sign of union of hearts between Hindu and Muslims and compassion towards the poor. In order to win the Swaraj Gandhiji emphasized peace in the society, relieving suffering of the poor and Hindu-Muslim unity.

RURAL DEVELOPMENT

Rural development is not a mere economic prosperity for a few at a cost of many. It is a participation of an entire population in production and consumption. Village Swaraj should be complete republic, independent of its neighbor for its wants. Everybody must have to grow its own food crops. The village must have school, public hall, water supply, recreation and playground. Every activity should be conducted on cooperative basis. The Government of a village will be conducted by village panchayat based on democracy. The rural development considers use of Khadi, promotion of village industry, education, rural sanitation, uplift of backward classes, welfare of women, education in public health, hygiene and prohibition. Gandhiji advocated purely indigenous solutions for different problems of rural India without external assistance. He stressed on schemes of short gestation period like, minor irrigation, dairying and handloom. Charkha was used because of simplicity, low cost, cultural acceptance, love for manual work, etc. Gandhiji pleaded for village industries because of limited capital, local raw material, short gestation period and easy marketing. Gandhiji was not totally opposed the large-scale industries for large and quality product, but he was concerned to mass production through large-scale industry results into concentration of economic power. So he emphasized decentralised sector, rural industrialisation is panacea for India's growing pauperism. As stated earlier Gandhiji was not against the large-scale industries. He advocated few industries. But such industries need to be centralised and nationalised. He opposed key industries to be left in the hand of private selfish individual entrepreneurs. Cost involved in centralised production is higher compared to decentralised production. Centralisation of economic function creates difficulties and irregularities. Centralisation could not continue without adequate force. When production is carried on large-scale basis distribution is not regulated automatically. There is also scope for speculation and fraud. The consumer goods industries should be decentralised. Economic efficiency is higher in decentralised production. But after liberalisation, the reverse trend is found in India. Now-a-days the accelerated growth of multinational business is controlling the poor countries. Such economic imperialism is dangerous to poor countries.

COOPERATION

For sustainable development of the villages, men should live in cooperation and work for the common good. Cooperation should be based on non-violence. Members must be honest and know the merits of cooperation. The success of the cooperatives can be measured in terms of moral condition of cooperatives. Gandhiji emphasized cooperative form, which can remove poverty and idleness. The success of this is possible if people becomes friends of one another and live as one family. Economic exploitation and class conflict can be eschewed by following the bold policy of decentralisation through the organisation of self-sufficient village communities, which are based on cooperation.

BREAD LABOUR

Tolstoy's Bread Theory of labour had great influence on economic philosophy of Gandhiji. All labour is dignified. Physical work done by a man is entitled to his daily bread. Mental labour is for the satisfaction of soul, while manual labour is for the satisfaction and existence of body. This was revolutionary aspect for caste-structured society. This paved the way for establishment of genuine equality of India. Gandhiji raised the dignity of labour. Even now manual labour is looked down. He believed that relative equality of wages of all kinds of labour. If there is the disparity that has to be in the ratio of one to twelve. It is the responsibility of management to win the cooperation of labour by creating favorable conditions for accelerating the production. Worker should be trained in terms of leadership in management. Gandhiji emphasized the constant stress on the performance of duties along with the rights. As trusties, the managers ought to treat the workers with sympathy and understanding and try to make co-partners.

EMPLOYMENT AND TECHNOLOGY

Gandhian approach towards machinery was essentially pragmatic and practical. Mechanisation is good when the hands are few. Simple tools and machinery, which save the individual labour of cottagers, can be welcomed. Use of machinery for large-scale production should not hurt the social justice. Sometimes use of machinery will result into exploitation of many for the benefit of few. Hence, India needs to adopt labour-intensive techniques of production for the absorption of abundant labour supply. Simultaneously it is possible to harmonise cottage and big industries if later are so planned as to help the villagers. The heavy machinery is to be used for the public utility purposes. The public utility should be owned by the state because it benefits the entire people. The heavy machinery should not deprive the people from their employment exploit village craft, i.e. atrophied the limbs of man.

According to Gandhiji every able-bodied citizen must have to secure gainful work for his livelihood. Our constitution also guaranteed the fundamental right to work. The aim of economic planning is to provide full employment. He strongly pleaded village industries to provide the work. Gandhiji opposed use of machines if people remain unemployed. If Government provides full employment to the people without village industries, then Gandhiji was ready to wind up village programs. Large-scale industries in developing countries like India have failed to achieve the full employment. So village industries are essential and we know that small is beautiful. To go for gigantisms is to go for self-destruction. In order to provide employment Government of India has started so many rural employment programs. Robert McNamara, president, World Bank urged to encourage the small industries in developing countries. The employment in villages will also prevent the migration, congestion, slums that have, became herculean problem to big cities of all over the world.

CONCLUSION

Gandhiji was multi-dimensional man. He was father of nation. He occupied important position in public life of the world. Gandhian model of sustainable economic development is quite simple. Had we adopted indigenous model of Gandhian right from the beginning many of the socio-economic problems could have been easily avoided not only in India but also in the world. Gandhian model of development was based on indigenous modèl of development, which can meet any challenges in the world. The non-Gandhian model pushed more people into poverty and created cynical elite class. As a result corruption and immorality in public life has increased. According to Gandhiji there is no difference between economics and ethics. The economic hurts the morality was considered as sin. Ethics always stands for social justice. Gandhiji opposed multiplication of want and industrialisation of mass scale, because it leads to exploitation, competition and marketing. In his economic thought man is important than wealth. Indians should have the faith on eastern tradition, which will help us to escape from the vicious circle of violence and exploitations. He emphasized the establishment of ideal village where people could pursue the simple living and high thinking. For promoting better living and life voluntary poverty is essential to serve the god and humanity. According to Gandhiji business is to be conducted with scrupulous, honesty and truthfulness. Lawyers and doctors should provide their service at free of cost since the poor are unobtainable. The economic progress is to be measured in terms of moral characters and social integrity of its citizens.

In order to protect trade and business, it is need to boycott the foreign goods and impose the tariffs. It was considered as sin if someone touches foreign cloth/goods. Gandhiji advocated purely indigenous solutions for rural India without external assistance. He stressed the schemes of short gestation period. Gandhiji was not totally opposed large-scale industry, but he was much concern to concentration of economic power. Hence emphasis was given to bold policy of decentralisation through the organisation of self-sufficient village communities, which is based on mutual cooperation. Gandhiji gave much importance to manual labour for happy life. Mechanisation is good when the hands are few. Thus, Gandhiji economic thoughts are relevant even today.

References

Nanda, B.R. (1990), In Gandhiji's Footsteps, The Life and Times of Jamunalal Bajaj, Oxford University Press, New Delhi.

The Collected Works of Mahatma Gandhi (1957), The Publication Division, GoI, New Delhi.

Profile of Gandhi (1969), Edited by Norman Cousins, Indian Book Co., New Delhi.

Mohan, Radhey (1982), Gandhian Economic System, *Vichar*, New Delhi.

Bharati, K.S. (1989), Socio-religious thoughts of Mahatma Gandhi, Dattsons Publishers and Distributors, Nagpur.

Reddy, K. Venkata (2001), Agricultural and Rural Development (A Gandhian Prospective), Himalaya Publishing House, Bombay.

Sethi, J.D. (1978), Gandhi Today, Vikas Publishing House, Bombay.

Jha, Shiva Chandra (1990), Indian Economic Thought: Mahatma Gandhi to Indira Gandhi, Deep and Deep Publication, New Delhi.

14

Gandhian Industrial Development Model and its Relevance Today

M.G. Basava Raja and K.S. Rajashekar

I. INTRODUCTION

In the Gandhian Industrial Development Model, central place is accorded to the development of Khadi and Village Industries (KVIs) since they can act as efficacious tools for galvanizing and developing rural and backward regions of India. At the time of India become independent and even to this day, considerable sections of rural people remain poverty stricken; and consequently, educationally, socially and economically very backward. Most of the rural persons have neither adequate financial resources nor the requisite technological and managerial skills and expertise to establish industries even on a small scale along modern lines. It is precisely to remedy this pathetic situation that Gandhi along with his ardent disciple Joseph C. Kumarappa advocated a very simple industrial development (ID) model based on the establishment of KVIs in rural and backward regions of the country.

II. OBJECTIVES OF GANDHIAN INDUSTRIAL DEVELOPMENT MODEL

The principal objective of Gandhian ID Model is to make the people productively employed and self-reliant. The main concern is elimination of mass poverty by providing employment and improving the quality of life of the people. Gandhi in many of his speeches and writings suspected, as has been proved today that indiscriminate technological modernisation in industries, may make the reduction of poverty more difficult. Excessive modernisation and use of inappropriate technology lead to rapid urbanisation imposing big burden on the existing infrastructural facilities and natural resources. Much of this sort of industrial development lies beyond the means of less developed countries. Gandhi, hence warned his countrymen to give up the craze for too much of modernity, mechanisation, industrialisation, and urbanisation which cannot solve our major problems such as unemployment, poverty and pollutions. On the other hand, they create lots of hardships by creating economic, social, political, ecological and many other problems in the country.

III. ADVANTAGES OF KVIs

Gandhian ID Model rightly enumerates various advantages of KVIs. Accordingly, the KVIs are small in size, simple in organisation, capital saving, non-violent and non-exploitative. Definitely, they are not anti-theoretical to useful large scale industries. They use locally available resources and ensure economic price for them. They do not create noise pollution, water pollution and air pollution. They are eco-friendly and human-friendly with an added advantage of the shortest gestation period. They involve the use of natural resources, no adulteration and are hygienic. The KVI products come out from a healthy blend of earthly resources, skills of hand and appropriate technology devised indigenously. They are not a burden on the national exchequer as in the case of various large scale public and private sector industries, which have borrowed heavy amount of funds from the public financial institutions and responsible for the growth of non-performing assets.

In the opinion of Gandhi, Spinning Wheel (SW) has various advantages in the context of rural development and they are enumerated as given below:[1]

1. The SW provides work to those people who have leisure.
2. The operation of SW can be easily learnt.
3. It requires practically no outlay of capital.
4. It fights drought.
5. It spells equitable distribution of wealth.
6. It solves the problem of unemployment and underemployment.
7. It supports other village industries.
8. People have no repugnance to SW.

IV. HISTORICAL BACKGROUND OF KVIs

Khadi became symbol of country's freedom movement under the stewardship of Gandhiji. During the pre-independence period, constructive workers undertook the Khadi programme in a decentralised manner. In the year 1925, Gandhiji as an independent institution set-up All India Spinners' Association by joining together Khadi associations formed by constructive workers. Establishment of All India Village Industries' Association in 1934 was another land mark in the history of develoment of KVIs in the country. J.C. Kumarappa took keen interest and much pain for the development of KVIs in the country. After the independence of the country, Akhil Bharat Sarva Seva Sangh took over the activities of All India Spinners' Association and All India Village Industries' Association. While formulating First Five Year Plan, the planners decided to promote KVI Programme on a national level with proper policy support. In 1953, All India Khadi and Village Industries Board was set-up to work in collaboration with Akhil Bharath Seva Sangh. However, the Board was by and large advisory in character. Therefore, Government felt the need of a national level institution for administering different programmes of KVIs development in the country. In this background, the parliament enacted an Act known as Khadi and Village Industries Commission

(KVIC) Act 1956 and thus the Khadi and Village Industries Commission came into existence. KVIC is a statutory organisation. It plays a very important role in strengthening the rural economy by promoting and developing KVIs in rural areas. KVIC has the social objective of providing employment to unemployed persons, economic objective of producing saleable articles and wider objective of creating self-reliance amongst rural people and constructing of a strong rural community spirit.[2]

V. GANDHIAN ID MODEL: EMPLOYMENT, FOOD AND FREEDOM

Gandhian ID Model prescribes KVIs not only as a best remedy for the country's problems such as unemployment, poverty and pollutions, but also as the best means for industrial development in the rural and backward regions. In the opinion of Gandhiji, the spinning wheel would spell equitable distribution of wealth of the world and the product of the spinning wheel—Khadi was the symbol of unity of Indian humanity, of its economic freedom and equality.[3] In this context, he quotes Jawaharlal Nehru's Poetic expression of 'Khadi is the livery of India's Freedom."[4] Gandhiji firmly believed that Khadi Programme would help to alleviate country's wretchedness and misery. As the Khadi Programme developed he discovered that without the revival of other village industries, Khadi could not make further progress. In his constructive programme manual he opined that rural economy cannot be complete without the essential village industries such as hand grinding, hand pounding, soap-making, paper-making, match-making, tanning, oil-pressing, bee-keeping, pottery, carpentry, etc. Gandhiji said that the revival of village industries was but an extension of the Khadi effort. He claimed for spinning wheel the honour of being able to solve the problem of unemployment and economic distress in a simple way.

In Gandhian ID Model of industrial development, employment to all is a key factor. The human resources, the wealth of the country should not go waste and it should be efficiently utilised. Any programme which neglects human resources as lop-sided.[5] In the Gandhian ID Model the basic tenet is how to create employment opportunities for the increasing population of country. In *Young India*, Gandhiji wrote, "Everybody should be able to get sufficient work to enable him to make the two ends meet."[6] Gandhiji's desire was to provide jobs to every able bodied individual he did not believe in the utilitarian principle of the greatest good of the greatest number.[7]

Gandhian ID Model gives importance to food, freedom and employment to all. According to Gandhiji, food and freedom are inseparable concepts. He was very much concerned about the problem of food and freedom for the people. He said that Almighty God has created man to work for his food.[8] Indeed, to Gandhiji, food was superior even to freedom. To the idle persons, the form in which God appears was employment. He was not in favour of reducing the working hours because he thought that working for several hours everyday was necessary for the moral progress of people. Gandhiji advocated the use of spinning wheel not because he had any psychological prejudice against large scale industries but because of practical considerations. He suggested home-spinning as the ready means of driving away penury and making famine of work and wealth impossible.[9]

VI. GANDHIAN ID MODEL: LARGE SCALE INDUSTRIES, USE OF MACHINERY AND SPINNING WHEEL

Western type of large scale indusrialisation, in total, was not acceptable to Gandhiji. That type of industrialisation was not calculated to remove mass poverty and unemployment. He regarded the spinning wheel and other village industries as counter poise against machinery. He considered hand-spinning, hand-weaving and other village industries as the means for the creation of employment opportunities to disguised unemployed persons of our villages. He did not argue that under all conditions, mechanisation or industrialisation was necessarily bad. His major concerns were to give jobs to our unemployed persons and protecting our environment. Regarding mechanisation, he said that mechanisation is good when the hands are too few for the work intended to be accomplished. It is an evil when there are more hands needed for the work, as is the case in Indian economy.[10] Gandhiji studied his bar-at-law in England and he understood that labour saving devices which have some relevance in under-populated countries, were out of place in over populated countries.

There is much publicity that Gandhi opposed the use of machinery, but this was not correct. He was ready to favour the use of machines if thereby country's pauperism and idleness could be avoided. He did not mind using electricity or even atomic energy for the spinning wheel. His only stipulation was that the use of such energy should not lead to unemployment. Acharya Vinoba said that if the government or industrialists were able to demonstrate to him that it was possible to provide full employment to the people through the method of large scale industrialisation he would unhesitatingly burn his SW and use it for cooking one of his meals.

Gandhian ID Model discards large-scale industrialisation as the solution of Indian unemployment. Unemployment being structural in character many of the prescriptions of Gandhian ID Model are sound. Most of the farmers of the country could not maintain a minimum level of subsistence, unless there was supplementary employment. Hand spinning, hand weaving and other village industries could create employment and make a visible dent on the poverty of the people. Machinery and equipment cannot help those who are rendered unemployed as a result of mechanisation. The essence of Gandhian ID Model is properly analysed by BN Ganguli like this—modernisation, industrialisation and mass production were not calculated to remove mass poverty and unemployment, rather they tended to create pockets of prosperity that merely accentuated the surrounding poverty and privation. According to Gandhiji this was not socialism and the socialism that India can assimilate is the socialism of the spinning wheel.[11]

Gandhiji characterized SW as the symbol of village and small industries and he felt that it encourages and sustains many other village industries. Khadi is the sun of village system.[12] When the demand for Khadi increases the demand for SW also increases. As the demand is increasing, rural carpenters and blacksmiths produce more SWs. This will also be followed by increased demand for dyeing and printing business and other village industries. These industries will in their turn support Khadi. Without Khadi, other village industries cannot grow and without the revival of other village industries, Khadi cannot grow. In this way, there will be inter-dependence between Khadi and other Village industries.

VII. GANDHIAN ID MODEL: SWADESHI, QUALITY AND METHOD OF PRODUCTION

Gandhiji considered Khadi as the symbol of Swadeshi. He defined it as that spirit in us which restricts us to the use and service of our immediate surroundings to the exclusion of the more remote.[13] People need to use only goods that are produced by their immediate neighbours and serve those industries by making them efficient. Swadeshi fulfils two important economic objectives and they are economic—self-reliance and employment for the people. Swadeshi through Khadi removes poverty, unemployment, idleness and dependence on others.

While Gandhiji emphasized the effect of KVIs on employment, he did not neglect the importance of quality and efficiency in production. He suggested to the KVI entrepreneurs to give importance for the improvement of quality and efficiency in production. Also, he announced a cash prize of Rs. One Lakh to the inventor who improve the spinning wheel that was more productive. He was aware of the waste of production of Khadi. He thought that since there was a limit to the improvement in technology, there had to be utmost cost reduction in other ways.

Gandhian ID Model is based on the preference for labour intensive method of production as opposed to capital-intensive method of production involved in large-scale industries. Labour intensive method is suitable in the labour abundant rural India. Leading Economists like Arthur Lewis have supported labour intensive method of production for countries like India. Also, growth models have been developed on this line of thinking."[14] According to G.D.H. Cole, the advocacy of homemade cloth by Gandhiji is no more fad of a romantic eager to revive the past, but a practical attempt to relieve the poverty and uplift the standard of the rural areas.[15]

VIII. RELEVANCE GANDHIAN INDUSTRIAL DEVELOPMENT MODEL

Though Gandhiji was not aware of the pure economics and the economic tools; in the words of EF Schumacher, he was a greater economist than J.M. Keynes and the greatest economist of the people.[16] The relevance of Gandhian economic thought to the country is unbelievable. The relevance of Gandhian economic thought is felt to the economists when they think that the Indian planning and policy measures are not able to solve the problems like poverty, unemployment and pollutions in an expected manner. On employment, Gandhiji favoured rural industrial development through the development of KVIs.

There are various KVIs even now they can play a very important role in the development of our villages. Khadi is considered as one of the village industries and its distinct feature of universality of employment. In other village industries, local processing of local raw materials by using simple technology would not create any environmental pollution problem and the problem of degradation of natural resources.

Many of village industries' products are useful from the point of view of: (i) Nutrition (Honey, Gur and Khandsari, Oil, Neera, Gulkhan, Coconut and Groundnut Sweets, Palm Gur), (ii) Use of non-exhaustible resources (Biogas, Solar Energy, Wind Mills), (iii) Use of non-conventional raw materials (Handmade paper, soaps of different kinds, etc.), (iv) Recycling of waste on conversion of waste into wealth (Palm Gur and fiber), (v) Supporting agriculture such as bee-keeping which can increase agricultural productivity by cross- pollination, (vi) use of locally available resources such as lime stones for lime products, clay for pottery, leather for making leather products, (vii) Avoiding waste such as fruits preservation and making fruits products.

It is very well realised by the planners that in order to provide employment opportunities to rural people, it is necessary to encourage to establish large number of KVIs in the rural and backward areas in such a manner that the people of these areas are able to organize industrial activity side by side with agriculture. With a view to checking the migration of people from the villages to cities seeking jobs, it is convenient to provide jobs to the village people in their own places.

IX. EMPLOYMENT SUPPORTING AND EMPLOYMENT GENERATING KVIs

Even in the regime of globalisation, there are large number of KVI units which have economic relevance.[17] Hence, (1) Efforts should be made to strengthen following traditional KVI units which are being practiced since ages in the rural sector: Carpentry, blacksmithy, leather work, weaving, goldsmithy, bamboo work, pottery, tailoring, mason, oil units, braziery, stone work, fibre and rope-making, metal work, forest produce collections, etc., (2) All efforts should be made to increase the production base of these KVIs by introducing appropriate technical up-gradation, introduction of new production tools in the production system, product diversification, (3) There is greater need for introducing new systems of production in the rural sector like: food-processing, medicinal herb-processing, fibre and fibre products-making, hand-made paper and board-making, bakery and dairy products, scientific collection and processing of non-timbers forest products like gum, honey, lackshilak, tubers, etc., charcoal, briquettes-making, printing, herbal pesticide, bio-fertilizer, compost-making, alternative energy systems in production processes.

X. CONCLUDING REMARKS

Gandhian ID Model represents an Indian mode of economic development. It is implied in the Model that KVIs are for supplementing agriculture, providing job opportunities for the rural unemployed poor and for development of rural and background areas. But there are people doubting the economic relevance of KVIs in the regime of globalisation. They think that the KVIs will put the hands of the clock back and reverse the engines of economic development.[18] But this way of thinking is not correct. Gandhiji did not ask the technologically trained persons to take up the KVIs and live in the villages. His concern was to provide jobs to the rural people. He called upon the urban people to render unto the villages that were due to them. In order to provide job opportunities to the rural unemployed, it is essential to establish useful and helpful KVIs throughout the countryside in such a manner that the villagers are able to organize industrial activity side by side with agricultural work. Instead of encouraging migration of people from the rural areas to urban areas seeking jobs, it is easier to provide jobs to the rural people in their living places. In many countries of Asia and Africa, the problems of poverty, unemployment, and pollutions have become grave; Gandhian ID Model has relevance for these countries. The more we think about the problems of unemployment, poverty and pollutions facing developing countries, the more we feel convinced that Gandhian ID Model alone will be able to solve them.

Notes and References

1. *Young India*, 28.10.1926.
2. KVIC (2003), Khadi India—National Convention on Rural Industrialisation (Mumbai: Director (Publicity), Khadi and Village Industries Commission), pp. 10-11.
3. *Young India*, 21st October 1921.
4. Reprinted in *Kurukshethra*, "Gandhiji on Village Industries" (*Harijan*, 29.08.1936), p. 2.
5. *Ibid.*
6. *Young India*, 15 November 1928.
7. Gandhi, M.K. (1957), Socialism of My Conception, Ed. Hingorani, A.T. (1957), (Mumbai: Bharathiya Vidyabhavan), p. 34.
8. *Harijan*, 16.05.1934.
9. *Young India*, 3.11.1924.
10. *Harijan*, 16.11.1934.

11. Ganguli, B.N. (1973), Gandhiji's Social Philosophy (New Delhi: Vikas Publishing House Pvt. Ltd.), p. 311.
12. *Harijan*, 16.11.1934.
13. Tendulkar, D.G. (1960), Mahatma: Life of Mohandas Karamchand Gandhi (New Delhi: Publications Division, Government of India), p. 202.
14. Lewis, Arthur (1963), "Economic Development with Unlimited Supplies of Labour" in Eds. Agarwal, A.N., and Singh, S.P., *The Economics of Underdevelopment* (New York: Oxford University Press), p. 110.
15. Cited in Nehru, Jawaharlal (1946), Discovery of India (Kolkata: The Signet Press), p. 347.
16. Hoda, M.M. (1978), Ed. Future is Manageable, E.F. Schumpachers Lectures (New Delhi: Implex India), pp. IX-X.
17. Raju, K.V., Somaiah, Malathi, Kedere, Shireesh (2002), Development Reforms for Resurgent India—A Nodal Strategy (New Delhi: Ministry of Culture and Tourism, Government of India), p. 127.
18. Vepa, Ram K. (1975), New Technology: A Gandhian Concept (New Delhi: Gandhian Book House), p. 174.

15

Relevence of Gandhian Economic Thought in the Era of the Globalisation

Rethinking National Economic Planning, Priorities, Policies and Programmes

MAHESH V. JOSHI AND MOHAN BHAI PATEL

India is basically agriculture and rural-oriented country. Therefore the overall development is depending upon the rural and farm development. Mahatma Gandhi had given top most importance to the same for economic and social development of the country. During the planning era Government has formatted and implemented many schemes and programs for the same. But still it would required more attention for rural and farm development. The problem of poverty, unemployment, inequality, exploitation, hunger, and concentration of economic and industrial ownership, etc. problems can be solved by agricultural and rural development. Continuous flows of migrant's people can be stopped by rural industrialisation and non-farm development in rural areas. This would require rural reforms with farm and allied sectors development and rural industrialisation.

But unfortunately we put more stress on non-farm and non-rural sectors in our new economic reforms started from 1991. We adopted and implemented the concept of Globalisation and become a member of W.T.O. The process of globalisation is very harmful to us. It is created the serious problems of poverty and unemployment in the country.

Poverty has risen during the reform time due to increasing in unemployment. There are several studies and expert's opinions which show that unemployment has increased during time of economic reforms. Agriculture is a backbone of our economy. Still farm sector provides employment to the major portion of population. Farm reforms are needed for increase agricultural production with employment generation. But we totally neglect this crucial sector in reforming process. There is no effects of green revolution in the many parts in the country and similarly too in the many crops. Steps have been taken to boost agriculture production, income and employment. The Indian economy is burdened with foreign domination, industrial expansion and the Indian farming and farmers are decapitating the village's dedication.

For higher employment generation it is needed to identify the sectors of high employment elasticity. Employment elasticity shows the employment capability and potentiality of the sector. Higher employment elasticity means higher employment capability.

It shows that the investment in this particular sector would lead increase in employment. B.B. Bhattacharya and Arup Mitra[1] have calculated employment elasticity in different economic sectors. They said that employment elasticity measured as the ratio of employment growth rate to income growth rate.

The World Bank-IMF instructed economic reforms are not suit with our economy, society and our political and cultural system. We need Indianisation instead of Globalisation. Indianisation means implementation of plans and policies which are suit with Indian economy, society, politics and culture. The economic thought of Mahatma Gandhi is suit with Indian system. Because he carefully observed Indian situation, problems and prospects at a time of introduction of his very valuable and very relevant economic thought. He gave top most importance to agricultural and rural development with the rural and cottage industries. But unfortunately we forgot his valuable and very useful thought. Gandhiji says, "Village is a heart of India....India is in a villages. If villages perish, India perishes."

According to Gandhiji rural industry and agriculture is a backbone of the country. All should use the goods, produce by rural industries. He says, "All should make it a point of honor to use only village articles, whenever and wherever available. Given the demand, there is no doubt that most of our wants can be supplied by the villages. When we become village minded, we shall not want imitations from the west of machine-made products."[2]

According to a study of NCAER top class of 10 per cent people have a 33.6 per cent rural and 42.4 per cent of urban total income. Disparity of income and wealth is serious in our country. Imbalanced and unequal centralised industrial development is responsible for this. According to NSSO study, 71 per cent of farmers have only 17 per cent of land and 6 per cent have 30 per cent of land. 60 per cent of rural poor have 14 per cent animals and 10 per cent farm primary tools. According to Dr. G.M Mansukha, 51 per cent people have only 8 per cent of wealth, 15 per cent possesses 61 per cent of total wealth and only 4 per cent top people are owner of 31 per cent of wealth. This high disparity can be reduced by rural development. We can achieve balanced, equal, sustainable and just decentralised growth by rural industrialisation. There is an urgent need of Indianisation for tearless, fearless and sustainable Development. The problem of poverty and unemployment is very serious and dangerous one. We can not even image about the effect of this problem. Poverty is a result of unemployment. Militants and other destructive and anti-Nation activity is result of this crucial problem. Therefore we should solve this problem by hook or by crook. We should develop village and cottage industries in rural areas and link agriculture with industries. For this we should developed rural entrepreneurship in villages. We should suggest some measures for this type of Rural industries based Indianisation.

The membership of the WTO is not benefited to us. because developed countries are obtained their targets by hook or by crook and India and other developing countries are victimized by these countries. According to Article 25 of the WTO, there should be agreements of the agricultural matter upto establishment of WTO. It means there should be agricultural agreements among the member countries upto 1999, but till 2005 it is not possible. The main agenda of the forthcoming Hong Kong ministerial level summit of December, 2005, would be agricultural agreements among nations about 5 subsidies and tariffs and trade of agricultural products. This was not possible in last Doha summit and too difficult for Hong Kong summit. India and other developing countries should sound presentation with unity and co-ordinations.

The membership of WTO to India is not benefited in the context of agricultural in specific and economic sectors in general. Hong Kong summit would be our last summit. Because either we should be represent our case soundly with the help of other developing countries. Or we should leave the WTO with the six months advance notice. Because developed countries are able to give subsidies of billions of dollars to their farm sectors by blue box or green box and having a heavy protection to farm sectors. What is the meaning to live in WTO?

In this context we should give top most priority to agriculture, rural development, rural industries, small scale and tiny industries, etc. labour-oriented sectors. Labour is huge in our country and capital is scarce. In this context, there is an urgent needs of encouraging labour intensive sectors, factors, trade and technology and production methods and systems. We should development and would materialize true, balanced and overall "Green Revolution. We should also develop rural industries for achieving equal, balanced, sustainable, tearless and fearless just economic development. The other sub-sectors, viz. Dairy and animal husbandry, forestry, aquaculture and fisheries, bee-keeping and horticulture, mushroom farming should also develop. All the facilities, finance, market, managerial skill, technology, etc. should be provided to these sectors. Rural and town entrepreneurship should also develop for encouraging more and more self-employment opportunities. The structure of education should be employment, occupation and economic sector-oriented.

There must be higher import tariff and quotas, permits and licenses for protecting our agriculture and rural sectors. We shall remain free to exit from the WTO, if not accepted. Our own national interest and well-being of the countrymen is first than the rules of WTO. There should be direct people involvement in each stage of policy and plan formation and implementation. We should develop panchayati raj and cooperative institutions. There is an urgent need of reforms in political system and administrative machinery and removing corruption from all level.

I. INTRODUCTION

India is basically agriculture and rural-oriented country. Therefore, the overall development is depending upon the rural and farm development. Mahatma Gandhi had given top most importance to the same for economic and social development of the country. During the planning era Government has formatted and implemented many schemes and programs for the same. But still it would require more attention for rural and farm development. The problem of poverty, unemployment, unequality, exploitation, hunger, and concentration of economic and industrial ownership, etc. problems can be solved by agricultural and rural development. Continuous flows of migrant's people can be stopped by rural industrialisation and non-farm development in rural areas. This would require rural reforms with farm and allied sectors development and rural industrialisation. But unfortunately we put more stress on non-farm and non-rural sectors in our new economic reforms started from 1991. We adopted and implemented the concept of Globalisation and became a member of W.T.O. The process of globalisation is very harmful to us. It is created the serious problems of poverty and unemployment in the country. The time has unorganised labourers. Second generation reform is for the upliftment of poor, unorganized labourers, etc. Here in this paper the effort has been made for thrown the light on effect of new economic policy of 1991, on employment and the necessitate for labour reforms for employment generation.

II. IMPACT OF ECONOMIC REFORMS ON EMPLOYMENT

Economic reforms have started from 1991. It stresses on the use of capital intensive autonomous technology, modernisation and the use of automation. This lead to increase in unemployment. World Bank, IMF instructed this so-called new economic reforms increases unemployment and poverty in the country. The center's main anti-income to rethink about whole system and process of economic reforms. The target of average annual employment generation 2.6 per cent to 2.8 per cent during 1992 to 1995. But it was increased 2.03 per cent actually. Open unemployment was 170 lakh in 1992, which was rose by 187 lakh in 1995.

The achievement in employment is far less than target in eighth plan. Poverty has risen during the reform time due to increasing in unemployment. There are several studies and expert's opinions which show that unemployment has increased during time of economic reforms. Agriculture is a backbone of our economy. Still farm sector provides employment to the major portion of population. Farm reforms are needed for increase agricultural production with employment generation.

But we totally neglect this crucial sector in reforming process. There is no effects of green revolution in the many parts in the country and similarly too in the many crops. Steps have been taken to boost agriculture production, income and employment. The Indian economy is burdened with foreign domination, industrial expansion and the Indian farming and farmers are decapitating the village's dedication.

The membership of labour organisations is on the decline after 1982. The trade union membership in Sweden is 84 per cent, and in Germany 32 per cent. It is only 15 per cent in U.S.A. and 10 per cent in France of the total work force is affiliated to the unions. According to the report of the

I.L.O. (1993), the reduced memberships of the trade unions are the result of unemployment and a inability to pay a membership fees.

The national regional labour organisations in India have adopted a conciliatory attitude as labour problems have grown. 40 to 45 trade unions of Indian Drugs and Pharmaceuticals have agreed to postpone wage increase demand towards off financial losses in these sick companies. There has been a decline a membership of trade unions in India also. The labour movement in India is weakened by numerable trade unions attached to it.

This so-called new economic reforms are unemployment-oriented. Because it encourages capital intensive modern labour saving technology which increases unemployment in the country. It puts stress on mega giant industries instead of small scale industries. It totally neglects farm sector which is employment-oriented. Due to huge entry of multinational companies, Indian companies have only two alternatives, either surrender before them or shut down. Due to economic reforms thousands of companies are victimized by closures. Sick, small-scale industries, marginal industries and many other industries are not able to work with these multinationals and giant industries due to their incompetitiveness and inefficiency.

Thousands of hundreds labourers became unemployed due to closures of these industries. New economic reforms damaged badly to farm and rural sector. We have not attempted reforms in the sectors where they are necessary. The main problem is that of unemployment. We should develop labour-oriented economic and industrial sector instead of capital and automation-oriented sectors. We are cutting over our feet. The economic development of China is labour-oriented. We should adopt the employment-oriented new economic reforms. New economic reform is stress on modern technology and foreign trade. These both are unemployment-oriented. One of the main objective of economic reform is to accelerate modern technology and trade.

Due to competition in foreign trade many units surrendered against foreign companies. Trade acts as a medium of encouraging unemployment in the country.

Because technology is transmitted from external sources is resulting in unemployment. They are purely capital intensive and labour saving. Due to trade-oriented reforms our import is increasing at very level then export. There is no proper import substitution. Reform is purely pro-import. This also encourages unemployment in the country. We are victimized by WTO and western countries through the ban of our export in the name of social clause.

WTO formulations are anti-employment for our country. Labour organisations have opposed unemployment-oriented new economic reforms and observed national level "BANDH" in many times. The Spanish labour had organized violent demonstrations against layoff and factory closures. The labourers had expressed their anger through burning tires and grappling with the police in a demonstrations against the discharge of 4000 employees in Air France. In Italy the Government managed Italian chemicals faced the wrath of its labour against disbandment. The labour fears its very existence following the economic reforms and consequently is giving greater weight age to issues of employment rather than wages. The drive to privatize and liberalize raises issues relating to the very existence of lakh of labourers. The market must be friend of a society sets people. The interests of the masses must be their prime objective. In a developing country like India, where the public sector is very extensive, it is important that social and economic security is achieved through friendly market and competent management.

III. EMPLOYMENT ELASTICITY AND EMPLOYMENT POTENTIALITY

For higher employment generation it is needed to identify the sectors of high employment elasticity. Employment elasticity shows the employment capability and potentiality of the sector. Higher employment elasticity means higher employment capability. It shows that the investment in this particular sector would lead increase in employment. B.B. Bhattacharya and Arup Mitra[3] have calculated employment elasticity in different economic sectors. They said that employment elasticity measured as the ratio of employment growth rate to income growth rate.

They calculated employment elasticity in following sectors.

Sector	*Employment Elasticity*
Whole economy	0.45
Construction	1.12
Primary sectors	0.74
Service sector	0.65
Manufacturing sector	0.19
Storage and communication	0.34
Trade and commerce	0.37

This table shows higher employment elasticity in construction and primary sectors and lower in manufacturing sector. After 1991, we give top most importance to this sector. Therefore the reduction in work force in this sector. Unemployment has increased after 1990 in organized sector.

This can be seen from the following table.

Year	*Unemployment (in million)*	*Rate of Unemployment*
1990-91	11	3.1
1991-92	17	4.7
1992-93	19	5.1
1993-94	21	5.5

Here we can observe that the rate of unemployment is continuously increased during the time of new economic reform. This means there is adverse effect on labour of structural adjustment programme. This led to retrenchment in organized sector.

In economic survey of 1993-94, it was stated that special employment programs can play only supplementary role in short-term period. Lasting solution of the problem of unemployment and poverty lies in faster generation of productive employment in the employment-oriented growth sectors. During the NEP period there is a higher growth in capital intensive sector.

IV. RURAL ENTREPRENEURSHIP FOR EMPLOYMENT-ORIENTED SUSTAINABLE, TEARLESS AND FEARLESS ECONOMIC DEVELOPMENT

The World Bank-IMF instructed economic reforms are not suit with our economy, society and our political and cultural system. We need Indianisation instead of Globalisation. Indianisation means implementation of plans and policies which are suit with Indian economy, society, politics and culture. The economic thought of Mahatma Gandhi is suit with Indian system. Because he carefully observed Indian situation, problems and prospects at a time of introduction of his very valuable and very relevant economic thought. He gave top most importance to agricultural and rural development with the rural and cottage industries. But unfortunately we forgot his valuable and very useful thought. Gandhiji says, "Village is a heart of India.... India is in villages. If villages perish, India perishes." Gandhiji have a dream of an ideal village. This can be put in his own words, a village in which, and "perfect sanitation of the traditional kind, based on local recycling of human and animal manure. The cottages built of materials found within a five miles radius would be well lighted and well ventilated. They would have courtyards where the householders could plant vegetables and house for their cattle. The lanes and streets would be clean and free of dust. There would be adequate wells accessible to every one. There would be places of worship, a common meeting place, a village common for grazing, a co-operative dairy, primary and secondary schools, where the main subject would be practical crafts and village industries. It would have its own panchayat (local disputes) for setting disputes. Finally, it would produce its own milks, grains, vegetables, fruits and khadi, cotton cloth."[4] According to Gandhiji rural industry and agriculture is a backbone of the country. All should use the goods, produced by rural industries. He says, "All should make it a point of honor to use only village articles, whenever and wherever available.

Given the demand, there is no doubt that most of our wants can be supplied by the villages. When we become village minded, we shall not want imitations from the west of machine-made products."[5] The freedom movement was linked with "swadeshi." The time has come for second time movement for the swadeshi for true economic freedom. We want independent and self-sufficient sovereign India. We put this in the words of our Father of Nation", Independence must begin at the bottom... It follows therefore, that every village has to be self sustained and capable for managing its affairs... The Government of the village is conducted by the Panchayat."[6] He said in 1944, that, economic equality is the master key of non-violent freedom. This means avoidance of conflicts between labour and capital. It also means reduce economic and industrial concentration. Therefore, he gave equal importance to both production and distribution.

He wrote in *Young India* in 1920, "We want organize our national power not by adopting best methods of production only, but by the best method of both, the production and distribution." He strongly believed that this can be materialised by development of rural industries. He dreamed India as a country in which there will be no unemployment and poverty. We put his golden dream in his own words, "I have not pictured a poverty stricken India, containing ignorant millions. I have pictured to myself an India continually progressing along the lines best suited to her genius. I do not, however picture it as a third class or even a first class copy of the dying civilisation of the west."

He had expected about the Indians and India before a year he leafed this earth, "Independent India, as conceived by me, will have all Indians belonging to different religions, living in a perfect friendship. There need be no millionaires and no paupers, all would belong to the state and for the state belonged to them. I will die in the act of realizing this dream."

He believed that rural industries are very helpful in more and more employment and income generation and in achieving development with equity, stability and justice. He believed that there should be production for mass, and not mass production. The problems of competition and market with the big industries. This would be resulted in exploitation of rural mass directly or indirectly. Therefore, we have to concentrate in independent and self-sufficient rural system. He had no objection to use modern tools and techniques that prepared and applied by rural people.[7]

He believed that India is not living in few big cities and towns, but in 7.5 lakh villages. He worried about villages and human status compared with cities and machines. He wanted to link village with town. He worried from the exploitation of villages by cities.[8] He opposed only those machines and techniques that increased unemployment in the country. Machine can not replace living man, he says. Machine should help the man in his work and should make easy and smooth his work by the use of machine, he believed. Machine can not help only few capitalists for increasing their wealth, power and ease.[9] He believed that the approach of rural industrialisation is creative and constructive and not destructive. Big industries are not able to provide employment to crores of unemployers of the country.

Their main purpose is only to earn to few capitalist owners. Their main aim is never remain for provide employment to the crores of people.[10] More than 17-18 lakh people obtaining employment from Khadi work. With the investment of only Rs. 500 to Rs. 600 a person is able to earn daily of Rs. 20-25. If everybody in the country consume only one meter of khadi, then the production of 60-70 crore meter of khadi will provide employment to more than 18 lakh people.

The centrally mill section produced about 15000 lakh kilogram of "sutras" and provide employment to (lakh people in a year). Where in charkha sector producing a 200 lakh kg and provide employment to more than 15 lakh people. According to a study of NCAER top class of 10 per cent people have a 33.6 per cent rural and 42.4 per cent of urban total income. Disparity of income and wealth is serious in our country. Imbalanced and unequal centralised industrial development is responsible for this. According to NSSO study, 71 per cent of farmers have only 17 per cent of land and 6 per cent have 30 per cent of land. 60 per cent of rural poor have 14 per cent animals and 10 per cent farm primary tools.

According to Dr. G.M. Mansukha, 51 per cent people have only 8 per cent of wealth, 15 per cent possesses 61 per cent of total wealth and only 4 per cent top people are owner of 31 per cent of wealth. This high disparity can be reduced by rural development. We can achieve balanced, equal, sustainable and just decentralised growth by rural industrialisation. There is an urgent need of Indianisation for tearless, fearless and sustainable Development. The problem of poverty and unemployment is very serious and dangerous one. We can not even image about the effect of this problem. Poverty is a result of unemployment. Militants and other destructive and anti-Nation activity is result of this crucial problem. Therefore, we should solve this problem by hook or by crook. We should develop village and cottage industries in rural areas and link agriculture with industries. For this we should developed rural entrepreneurship in villages. We should suggest some measures for this type of Rural industries-based Indianisation.

1. Top most priority would be given to the farm and rural development. There is an urgent need for true over-all "Green-Revolution" in the country.
2. We should link rural with the urban and agriculture with the industry.
3. We should develop modern rural industrial sector with competitiveness and efficient but purely labour-oriented. We should adopt labour-oriented modernisation and technological up-gradation in rural industries.
4. We should also developed farm connected sectors just like, animal husbandry and dairy, forestry, fisheries, mining, agro-industries, food processing industries, etc.
5. In small towns and cities we should develop tiny and small scale industries, self-employment sectors, artisans, etc.
6. Our education structure should be directly linked with the employment, professions, agriculture,

trade and industry, transportation and communications, and services. There should be very practical training and extension which can be applicable directly in economic sectors.

7. There should be control on globalisation and foreign companies working in our country. No permission would be given to them in opposite circumstances for us. We should stop globalisation and multinationalisation of our economy.
8. Because from this the problems of poverty and unemployment, culture and society, economy and politics are considerably increased.
9. There is an urgent need to protect our industries in general and small scale industries in specific against multinationals.
10. There must be higher import tariff and quotas, permits and licenses for protecting our industries. We shall remain free to exit from the WTO, if not accepted. Our own national interest and well-being of the countrymen is first than the rules of WTO.
11. There should be direct people involvement in each stage of policy and plan formation and implementation. We should develop panchayati raj and cooperative institutions.
12. There is an urgent need of reforms in political system and administrative machinery and removing corruption from all level.

V. CONCLUSION

The objectives of the economic planning and policy in India are very wide and broad. They aimed overall economic and social development of the country by development of agriculture, industry and service sectors. During planning period, there is economic growth, but less absorption of labour force. This is resulted in increasing in unemployment and poverty. The recent economic reforms can not reverse the present trends of increasing unemployment or decreasing employment opportunities. In this context we have to rethink about our policy, reforms, strategy of development and priority of the same. We should adopt labour-oriented development strategy, planning, programs, reforms and policy.

In this context we should give top most priority to agriculture, rural development, rural industries, small scale and tiny industries, etc. labour-oriented sectors. Labour is huge in our country and capital is scarce. In this context, there is an urgent needs of encouraging labour intensive sectors, factors, trade and technology and production methods and systems. We should development and would materialize true, balanced and overall "Green-Revolution."

We should also develop rural industries for achieving equal, balanced, sustainable, tearless and fearless just economic development. The other sub-sectors, viz. Dairy and animal husbandry, forestry, aquaculture and fisheries, bee-keeping and horticulture, mushroom farming should also develop. All the facilities, finance, market, managerial skill, technology, etc. should be provided to these sectors. Rural and town entrepreneurship should also develop for encouraging more and more self-employment opportunities. The structure of education should be employment, occupation and economic sector-oriented.

Similarly social and service sectors should develop for huge employment generation in short and long-run. In short, second generation economic reforms and all the development efforts. India is basically agriculture and rural-oriented country. Therefore, the overall development is depending upon the rural and farm development. Mahatma Gandhi had given top most importance to the same for economic and social development of the country. During the planning era Government has formatted and implemented many schemes and programmes for the same. But still it would require more attention for rural and farm development.

The problem of poverty, unemployment, unequality, exploitation, hunger, and concentration of economic and industrial ownership, etc. problems can be solved by agricultural and rural development. Continuous flows of migrant's people can be stopped by rural industrialisation and non-farm development in rural areas. This would require rural reforms with farm and allied sectors development and rural industrialisation. But unfortunately we put more stress on non-farm and non-rural sectors in our new economic reforms started from 1991. We adopted and implemented the concept of globalisation and became a member of W.T.O. The process of globalisation is very harmful to us. It created the serious problems of poverty and unemployment in the country. The time has unorganized labourers. Second generation reform is for the upliftment of poor, unorganized labourers, etc. Here in this paper the effort has been made for thrown the light on effect of new economic policy of 1991, on employment and the necessitate for labour reforms for employment generation.

There is an urgent need of rural entrepreneurship development for tearless, fearless and sustainable Development. The problem of poverty and unemployment is very serious and dangerous one. We can not even image about the effect of this problem. Poverty is a result of unemployment. Militants and other destructive and anti-Nation activity is result of this crucial problem. Therefore we should solve this problem by hook or by crook. There is an urgent need for true over-all "Green-Revolution" in the country. We should link rural with the urban and agriculture with the industry. We should develop modern rural industrial sector with competitiveness and efficient but purely labour-oriented. We should adopt labour-oriented modernisation and technological up-gradation in rural industries. We should also developed farm connected sectors just like, animal husbandry and dairy, forestry, fisheries, mining, agro-industries, food processing industries, etc. In small towns and cities we should develop tiny and small scale industries, self-employment sectors, artisans, etc. Our education structure should be directly linked with the employment, professions, agriculture, trade and industry, transportation and communications, and services.

There should be very practical training and extension which can be applicable directly in economic sectors. There should be control on globalisation and foreign companies working in our country. No permission would be given to them in opposite circumstances for us. We should stop globalisation and multinationalisation of our economy. Because from this the problems of poverty and unemployment, culture and society, economy and politics are considerably increased. There is an urgent need to protect our industries in general and small scale industries in specific against multinationals. There must be higher import tariff and quotas, permits and licenses for protecting our industries. We shall remain free to exit from the WTO, if not accepted. Our own national interest and well-being of the countrymen is first than the rules of WTO. There should be direct people involvement in each stage of policy and plan formation and implementation. We should develop panchayati raj and cooperative institutions. There is an urgent need of reforms in political system and administrative machinery and removing corruption from all levels. The objectives of the economic planning and policy in India are very wide and broad. They aimed overall economic and social development of the country by development of agriculture, industry and service sectors. During planning period, there is economic growth, but less absorption of labour force. This is resulted in increasing in unemployment and poverty.

The recent economic reforms can not reverse the present trends of increasing unemployment or decreasing employment opportunities. In this context we have to rethink about our policy, reforms, strategy of development and priority of the same. We should adopt labour-oriented development strategy, planning, programmes, reforms and policy. In this context we should give top most priority to agriculture, rural development, rural industries, small scale and tiny industries and labour-oriented sectors. Labour is huge in our country and capital is scarce. In this context, there is an urgent needs of encouraging labour intensive sectors, factors, trade and technology and production methods and systems. We should develop and would materialize true, balanced and overall "Green-Revolution." We should also develop rural industries for achieving equal, balanced, sustainable, tearless and fearless just economic development. The other sub-sectors, viz. Dairy and animal husbandry, forestry, aquaculture and fisheries, bee keeping and horticulture, mushroom farming should also develop.

All the facilities, finance, market, managerial skill, technology, etc. should be provided to these sectors. Rural and town entrepreneurship should also develop for encouraging more and more self-employment opportunities. The structure of education should be employment, occupation and economic sector-oriented.

Notes and References

1. Alagh, Yogendra, K. (1999), "From Employment Planning to Employment Policies", *The Indian Journal of Labour Economics*, Vol. 42.
2. Anant, T.C.A., K. Sundaram and S. Tendulkar (1999), Employment and Labour in South Asia, SAAT, *International Labour Organisation*, New Delhi.
3. Chaddha, G.K. (1994), Employment, Earning and Poverty: A Study of Rural India and Indonesia, Sage Publication, New Delhi.
4. Chaddha, G.K. and Alakh, N.A. Sharma (1997), (ed.) Growth, Employment and Poverty in Rural India, Vikas Publishing House, New Delhi.
5. Datt, Rudra (1997), Organising the UN Organised Workers, Vikas Publishers, New Delhi.
6. Ghose, Ajit (1999), "Current Issues in Employment Policy in India," *Economic and Political Weekly*, Vol. XXXIV, No. 36.
7. Gupta, S.P. (1999), Globalisation, Economic Reforms and the Role of Labour, Mimeographed paper.
8. Hashim, S.R. (1999), "Employment and Poverty: Some Emerging Policy Issues," *Indian Journal of Labour Economics*, Vol. 41, No. 2.
9. ILO (1993), India: Employment, Poverty and Economic Policies, ILO-ARTEP.
10. Joshi, Mahesh V. (1999), Women Rural Labourers, APH Publications, New Delhi.

    Joshi, Mahesh V. (1997), Economic Reforms in India, APH Publications, New Delhi.

    Joshi, Mahesh V. (2000), Impact of Green Revolution, APH Publications, New Delhi.

    Joshi, Mahesh V. (2002), Basic Elements of Entrepreneurship, Anada Prakashna, Ahmedabad.

    Joshi, Mahesh V. (2004), Towards Success: Basic Elements of Entrepreneurship, Adhyayan Publication, New Delhi.

    Joshi, Mahesh V. (2004), Advanced Managerial Economics, Adhyayan Publication, New Delhi.

    Joshi, Mahesh V. (2004), In Search in New Economics, Adhyayan Publication, New Delhi.

16

Gandhian Views on Economics of Khadi and Perpetual Unemployment

RAJESH PAL

India is the second fastest growing economy in the world, and its growth has brought more jobs and helped bolster the income of its bourgeoning middle class, which is now demand more vehicles, durables and services such as communications and entertainment than ever before. The rising demand has manufacturing companies running at full steam. For example, petroleum refiners are reporting 96 per cent capacity utilisation and car-makers and cement manufacturers are running their plant at 85 per cent capacity. Agricultural production is not growing fast enough to satiate the increasing appetite of a billion plus population.

In Indian villages more than 80 per cent of labourers are engaged in agricultural activities. Most of the rural labours engaged in non-form sector work as iron-smith, carpenter, etc. and in different types of services. Mahatma Gandhi has emphasised on development of agricultural activities and cottage industries. It is estimated that more than two third of rural workers are self-employed. Just one-third of the workers work for other. Problem of involuntary unemployment is not much in rural areas. In rural areas of India, the problem is of disguised unemployment and of seasonal unemployment. During the last 20 years in India, labour force has increased at the rate of 2.5 per cent per annum whereas employment has increased at the rate of 2.2 per cent. Consequently, the number of people remaining unemployed has tended to soar overtime. The palpable fact is nearly 10 million people are estimated to be unemployed.

A Gall-up poll taken in 1987 in U.S.A. illustrates this concern. When asked what the country's most momentous problem was, half of the population cited unemployment, government spending, budget deficit, inflation or the other economic concerns. Even more remarkable is the response to a Gall-up poll taken in October 1943. That poll asked people what they thought the greatest problem facing the country would be in the year ahead. Although the nation was deeply involved in World War-II, most American thought job and economic readjustment would be our greatest problems. Little concern was expressed for the prospects of peace. Even Mahatma Gandhi was very much concerned for unemployment. His economics of Khadi emphasised on employment. He himself said that Khadi will cease to have any value in my eyes, if it does not usefully employ the millions.

Open unemployment refers to that situation wherein although the worker is willing to work and he has the necessary ability to work yet he does not get work. He remained unemployed for full time. This type of unemployment is usually found among agricultural labourers, educated persons and those who come from villages to urban in search of the job but fail to get any work.

It implies that the process of economic growth in the country is not hijacked by only a handful of oppulent sections of the society. Instead, there must be a high rate of participation by the masses in the process of economic growth. Mahatma Gandhi's economics of Khadi is such an industry, which has capacity to absorb masses. The ideas at the back of khadi is that it is an industry supplementary to agriculture and co-existence with it, that it is the life breath of millions of destitute weavers who derive sustenance from it. The spinning wheel cannot be said to have been established in its own proper place in our life, until we can banish idleness from our villages and make home a busy live. Unemployment and idleness of millions must lead to a bloody strife. Khadi is the only alternative to this and not the so-called socialism, which presupposes industrialism. The socialism that India can assimilate is the socialism of the spinning wheel. Let the village workers; therefore, make the wheel the central point of their activities.

Our compulsory or voluntary idleness has to go. If it does not go, no panacea will be of any avail and semi-starvation will remain the eternal problem. He who eats two grains must produce four. Unless the law is accepted as universal, no amount of reduction in population would serve to solve the problem. If the law is accepted and observed, we have room enough to accommodate millions more to come.

The principles of economics are not, like the principles of mathematics for instance, immutable and for all times and climes. England will not accept the economics of France, nor France that of Germany, Nor Germany that of America and they would be wrong if they did so. A country which produces no foodstuffs and produces only mineral must have different economic from that which produce foodstuffs but has no mineral resources. India, therefore, cannot afford to go by the economics of France, England, America or Germany. India was once the land of gold. Not that it produced much gold, but it has such treasurers of art, it produced cloth of rich quality, and spices of such value that other lands paid for them in treasurer of gold. We have lost that proud position today and have become mere hewers of wood and drawers of water. But even now we can regain that proud position for our natural resources are unique and no other country in the world, excepting China, can boast of the crores of living machines. We can't afford to have a machine, which will displace the labour of crores of living machines. It would spell their unemployment and their ruin. We have to employ all these crores of human machines that are idle.

To employ these living machines, it is essential that

labour intensive technology is encouraged in place of capital intensive technology in production. Technique of production ought to be suited the needs and means of the country. We are guilty of a grievous wrong against the villagers, and the only way in which we can expiate it is by encouraging them to revive their lost industries and arts by assuring them of a ready market. We have to be rural minded and think of our necessities and the necessities of our household in the terms of rural mindness. The task does not involve much expenditure either. Volunteers are needed to go to the nearest villages to assure them that all their produce would find a ready market in the towns and cities. This is a task, which can be undertaken by men and women of all castes and creeds, of all parties and faiths. It is in consonance with the marching towards the matured economy of our country.

To solve the problem of unemployment, Gandhi devised the cottage and village industries programme. Apart from the sociological advantages of the decentralised industry he wanted to utilise the leisure of the masses or as he used to say to utilise the waste of the nation. One wonders what fundamental law of economics is violated in creating wealth from waste and thus adding to happiness.

After independence, it is heard that the Gandhi's concrete schemes of the production of wealth through decentralised industry have no validity. This will be true only if the conditions under which Gandhi formulated his economic schemes, which the Congress and the nation had accepted, were radically changed. This is not so, even former President of the Congress in an open session was constrained to admit that after Swaraj, "the rich are getting richer and the poor poorer." So to say, the economic ideas of Gandhi hold good and are valid even today not only for our nation but also for the entire developing countries.

Is India living in her 10 or 20 cities or is she living in villages? What is then is the programme that can weld together million of people scattered in villages? What is it that every villagers, man, woman and child, Hindu and Musalman can do with profit and at the same time uplift the whole of India. The one and unequivocal answer is to encourage small-scale industries and cottage industries.

The message of cottage industries can perpetrate to remotest village if we only will that it shall be so. The cottage industries can be taken by millions of the villagers of India who have been reduced to pauperism, who have been ground down to dust, not merely under the foreigner's heels but under your heels, under my heels.

The economic idea of Gandhi is some what similar to the Ricardo's comparative cost theory. A country should produce that good which require relatively less cost. India's millions require full meals in order to sustain their energy, therefore, the congress has passed the resolution making it necessary for the congressmen to wear Khaddar habitually and not merely on ceremonious occasions as production of Khadi requires comparatively less cost and it will generate employment to millions if it is worn habitually.

The time has changed, we have come a long way, but the thought of Gandhi will remain static. The then spinning wheel and Khaddar was the only answer for uplifting India and to do away with unemployment as no other industry was existing then which can provide employment on large scale. Under the altered conditions and now that we have some breathing time to put our heads together and to collect our thought, we shall do well to hark back to the original conception and think of our future work in its terms. Now, the one and unequivocal answer is to change in educational patterns. From the very beginning emphasis should be laid on vocational education. Educated persons must inculcate the spirit of serving in villages in the capacity of teacher, doctors, etc. Qualified engineers should be given financial assistance to set-up their own small units in villages. Institutions providing employment information and guidance should be strengthened and their activities should be properly coordinated with employment agencies.

Gandhi himself considered that besides spinning wheel, there is enough room for agricultural improvement. But that is a matter of time and education, whereas the ever-growing poverty demands, immediate remedy. Standing on the cross-road of India's diamond jubilee of independence. It is not only annoying but also disgraceful that every village does not have a pucca road, electricity, telecom, a functioning school and health centre. Had these been developed by government, it would have generated employment to poor and rural people and have uplifted India. Instead of providing these basics, which would have converted, many villages into prosperous towns' successive governments have spent 14 per cent of GNP on subsidies, most of which benefit the non-poor. To do away with immediate poverty Gandhi has emphasised on cooperative industries. On cooperative basis the Government of Kerala set-up a textile mill in Cochin covering 600 unemployed people, every employed person contributed Rs. 500 and rest of the capital was provided by the government. This indeed is a novel approach to the problem of unemployment. Different state governments should initiate necessary steps in this direction. Quick yielding industries should be given preference.

No organisation is as capable as SSI and cottage of industries giving employment to an almost unlimited number of youths, who will be context with an honourable livelihood and who will be content to pass their lives in the closest touch with the villages and share their food, their sorrows and joys. I want you to give me what you can and what you have for the sake of paupers, for the sake of those who do not even get one square meal a day. If you are satisfied that this organisation is being worked well, and with ability and self-sacrifice and if you are convinced that it is not sinful to buy product produced by your starving poor countrymen and that is right and proper and necessary to do so, you will give your copper and silver, gold whatever you have, such type of statement was made by Gandhi regarding Khaddar.

Do any minister making such statement like Gandhi for indigenous organisation, instead they are taking disinvestment policy, which is not all the time right. Government is expected to encourage and protect SSI and cottage industries where masses are employed. Gandhi has always favoured indigenous organisation, as he knew that business may come to loss. In this case wealth would not be drained, it will exist in its own country. Moreover, it is not the drain that matter so much as poverty and it is not even poverty that matters so much as idleness which was at first enforced, and has now become a habit that matters. The drain may be stopped and poverty is merely a symptom, but idleness is the great cause, the root of all evil and if that can be destroyed most of the evils can be remedied without further effort. Gandhi has gone a step ahead on doing away with unemployment. He has seen idleness as the great cause of unemployment, which government and our planners have never thought of. Gandhi's social philosophy incorporating with employment generation theory can be explained through diagram 1.

DIAGRAM I

Gandhian Social Philosophy Incorporating with Employment Generating Theory

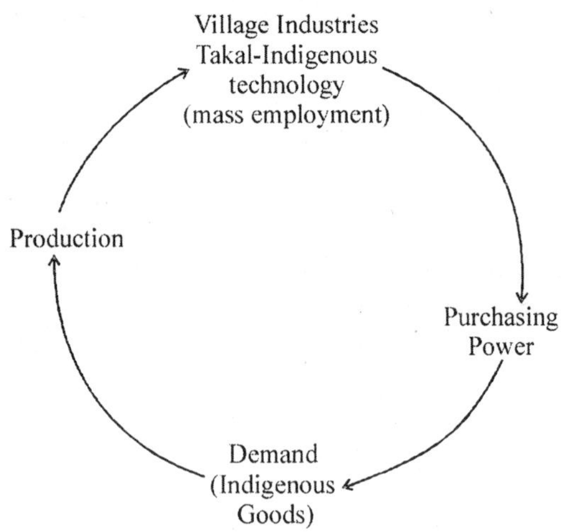

In the said diagram Takali is representing indigenous technology. By using this technology, demand for indigenous good, i.e. Khadi cloth representing indigenous product can be increased, which ultimately generate employment for masses. Mahatma Gandhi has always emphasis on ready market for those goods produced by indigenous technology and poor people, as he believes that ready market for indigenous goods will encourage production and thereby help in increasing employment. This can be explained through diagram 2.

DIAGRAM 2

Gandhian Social Philosophy Incorporating with Employment Generating Theory

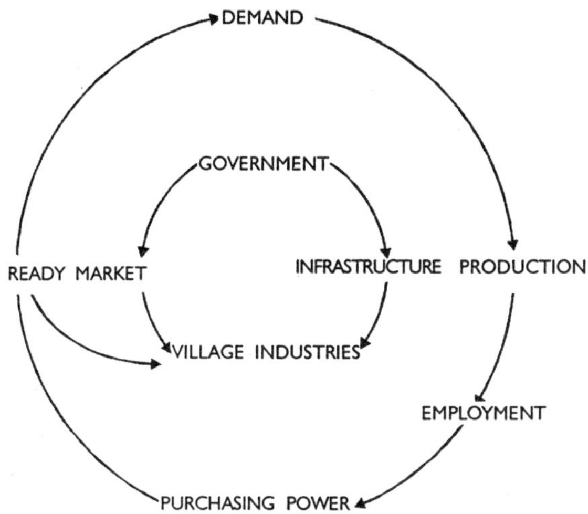

Gandhi has always asked government to develop basic infrastructure and provide ready market, which is shown in the above diagram. Ready market will find demand for the product produced by village industries. Increasing demand for the product help in increasing production and thereby generating employment, this will help in increasing purchasing power of masses. Increased purchasing power will boost demand for the product. This will encourage farmer and poor people to increase production, which will ultimately solve the problem of unemployment. Infrastructure is not only a important prerequisite to economic growth; it is direct benefit to large numbers of semi-skilled and unskilled workers. Construction is the second economic activity generator in this country after agriculture and accounts for 11 per cent of our GDP. However, the greatest challenges faced by this sector are the lack of quality human resources. Opportunities for training are limited, with just a few scattered initiatives like the school for masons established by

L&T in Chennai. The government's proposal to ensure the certification of labourers in the construction sector is a move towards Gandhian theory of employment. If enough initiatives can be undertaken to upgrade their skills, Naysayers who claim that economic growth can only happen by placing extra burden on the poor will be effectively debunked.

Khadi lovers ought to know that economics of Khadi are different from and often contrary to the ordinary economics of the competitive system, which is not governed by the principle of the greatest good of all, i.e. of the least among the downtrodden. The economics of Khadi is to a great extent contrary to those of mill cloth. Cloth manufactured in Manchester is meant for use not in Manchester or England or Europe, but to be exported to Asia or Africa for the use of the people there. On the contrary Khadi is meant to be made for the millions by the millions living in villages. Mills use cotton imported from parts of the world. Cotton for Khadi should be produced where it is turned into Khadi. The economics of Khadi require that from cultivation of cotton to the manufacture of Khadi and its disposal all the process should, as far as possible, be gone through in the same village or centre. Thus, it is wrong to spin yarn in Punjab, weave it in Bombay, and sell it in Malabar. Khadi is the central sun round which the other village industries resolve like so many planets. They have no independent existence. Nor will Khadi exits without other industries. Gandhian thought encourages those industries which all process from manufacturing to ultimate buyer must take place at a single place, as it generate employment to rural and urban youth of the country.

The consumer with the most money has the greatest pull in the market. As a result, resources may be devoted to produce luxuries for the rich to the exclusion of the necessities for the poor. While this is really brought about by the unequal distribution of wealth and income rather than by the market system, the fact is that the latter tends to produce, and even to increase unemployment as demand for luxuries goods comes from the rich, which constitute small section of the total population. Production of these luxuries will not provide employment to masses but to a few people, but production of necessities' goods will generate employment on large scale.

Gandhi has always favoured for decentralisation of production and distribution of the necessaries of life. Therefore, the formula so far evolved is, every village to produce and use all its necessaries and in addition, produce a certain per centage as its contribution to the requirements of the cities. Heavy industries will necessarily be centralised and nationalised. But they will occupy the least part of the vast national activities in the villages. Gandhi's vision was growth with equity. The vision of growth with equity is commendable, more so for China as there is no other country (forget India) in history that has pulled as many people out of destitution in the last three decades. It is just because of this that in the last 30 years, China came from nowhere to become the epicentre of global economy. She has made herself completely indispensable by making almost everything affordable to the middle and lower middle class populace of the world through the gigantic production machinery of the SEZs (who make these products in a huge scale leading to a drastic reduction in cost price). The huge influx of foreign direct investment created a huge increase in employment opportunity and gave rise to an affluent Chinese middle class. In terms of purchasing power, the Chinese economy is among the top three in the world and has been able to consistently maintain a hitherto unheard, unseen 10 per cent GDP growth rate for nearly a decade. This growth rate is trickling down to the poor and generating employment for these poor people and thereby bridging the gap between the rich and the so-called deprived mass. In India it is fashion to always speak about the so-called deprived mass while the polity rarely takes any constructive steps to empower them. Likewise this year, our Honourable Finance Minister in his Budget speech proudly claimed that another 55,512 habitations have been provided with drinking water, another 19758 villages have been electrified and 15,054 more villages have been given telephone connections. In a country of 6,00,000 plus villages, at this rate no doubt, the government would be able to provide basic infrastructure to all Indian villages in the next 300 years for sure spending on education and health stand at a pittance of Rs. 32,352.00 crore and Rs. 15,291.00 crore, and the allocation for school expenditure of Rs. 17,133 crore. Keeping aside the revenue expenditure (the expenditure on paying salaries of lakhs of government employees in these departments which must be more than 50 per cent of the allocation, and then keeping aside the wastage in terms of leakage, imagine how much is left for each village when divided by 6,00,000 villages. After 60 years of independence unemployment and poverty still exists, villagers are not self-sufficient to produce foodstuff for their own consumption. What type of industry should be developed to make villagers self-sufficient and provide them employment? Mahatma Gandhi has advocated spinning why? Let draw attention towards striking figures.

"Taking an industry like the textile that is open to both methods we shall be able to compare the figures satisfactorily. An average cotton spinning and weaving mill uses about Rs. 13 lakhs of capital and employs about 1400 men. This works out to about Rs. 900 per person employed. The production per rupee invested works out to 2.5 lbs of yarn and 1.5 lbs of cloth. (The figures are for the year 1932-33). A cottage unit of one loom, ten Charkhas and with Rs. 60 as working capital works out to an investment of about Rs. 9 per person employed and the production per rupees invested is about 10 times as much as in a mill. Computed from this we would need Rs. 300 crores of capital employing 33 lakhs of people. If we supplied all our requirements by mill production, while we would require about Rs. 72 crores of investment employing of 800 lakhs of people if our supply were to come from cottage units. The two methods have their undoubted advantages, which no one will deny. The question before us is to choose that method which will fit into the conditions that prevail in our country. We are poor but we have an ocean of labour wealth. Therefore, an intelligent plan will find the cottage method fit into the scheme for our country. An engineer who is planning the buildings in a country abounding in good clay and wood will plan on building with bricks and timber, but one who is planning for a country abounding in cement and iron will recommend reinforced concrete. It will be foolish if the recommendations were the other way round. There is no single-patented road to progress. Planning has to coordinate the available factors of production to produce the best possible outcome, not only material, but social and cultural. Any development planning in our country that ignores the absorption of labour wealth will be misplaced. Our analysis has shown that centralised method of production, whatever may be its capacity to produce is incapable of finding employment for a large number of persons. Therefore, it stands condemned in this country." That is why Gandhi has always advocated village production as against factory production.

Without a doubt that SSI and cottage industries or indigenous industries cannot compete with the large-scale industries, it is never meant too. If the people will not understand or appreciate the law governing SSI and cottage industries or village industries it will never be universal. Village industries has a big mission it provided dignified labour to the millions who are otherwise idle for nearly four months in a year. Even apart from the remuneration the work brings, it is its own reward. We Indian must know that buying of foreign product will lead us nowhere except widening gap between the rich and the poor. We must encourage buying cloth produced by cottage industries or indigenous organisation as it provides employment to masses.

Life is more than money indeed. It is cheaper to kill our aged parents who can do work and are a drag on our slender resources. It is also cheaper to kill our children whom we do not need for our material comfort and whom we have to maintain without getting anything in return. But we neither kill our parents nor or children, but consider it privilege to maintain them no matter what their maintenance costs us. Likewise, one must maintain SSI and cottage industries products to the exclusion of all other product. It is the force of habit, which makes us think of cottage industries, in terms of price. We must revise our notion of SSI and cottage industries services. And when one has studied them from the point of view of the national well-being we shall find that SSI and cottage industries product is never dear.

Thus the government can encourage using product produced by SSI and cottage industries, guarantee loss in sales of these products. It is the primary duty of the state to guarantee employment of its choice to everyone in need of it.

It ought to be born in mind that the possibilities of village industries have not yet been explored by any Government. Government must investigate the employment generating capacity of village industries. I am of opinion that such investigation will yield startly encouraging results. No industry, indigenous or foreign, can be allowed to increase unemployment and thus harm the true interest of the community as a whole.

Under plan such programmes should be given more importance as to raise the level of employment. The programmes that can best serve this end are: irrigation, roads, flood control, power, agriculture, forestry, rural electrification, soil conservation, development of cottage and small industries and construction work. Crash employment programmes should not be encouraged, as these cause more wastage of resources without any corresponding increase in employment on permanent basis.

"We stand today in danger of forgetting the use of our own hands", concluded Gandhi "To forget how to dig the earth and tend the soil is to forget ourselves. To think that your occupation of the Ministerial Chair will be vindicated if you serve the cities only, would be to forget that India really resides in her 6,00,000 village units. What would it profit a man if he gained the world but lost his soul into the bargain?

References

Mathur, J.A. and A.S. (1962), "Economic Thought of Mahatma Gandhi, Chaitanya Publishing Houses, 5-A, University Road, Allahabad (India), pp. 269-76.

Harvey, Jack (1994), "Mastering Economics", The Macmillan Press Ltd., Houndmills, Basingstoke, Hampshire, RG21 ZXS and London, pp. 203-07.

Ohri, V.K., *et. al.* (2006-07), "Indian Economic Development", V.K. Publications, 4323/3, Ansari Road, Darya Ganj, New Delhi-2, pp. 21, 191.

Schiller, Bradley R. (1989), "The Economic Today", Random House, Business Division, New York, p. 5.

Ankleshwar Swaminathan S., "Reducing Poverty Unwittingly", *The Times of India*, 5-4-2007, Lucknow.

Chaudhary, Arindam, "China has a lot to Teach, Provided We are Ready to Learn", *The Times of India*, 16-4-07, Lucknow.

Kamerschen, *et. al.* (1989), "Economics", Houghton Mifflin Company, Boston Dallas Geneva Illinois Pal Alto Princeton, New Jersey, p. 21.

Baumol, J. William *et. al.* (1982), "Economics: Principles and Policy", Harcourt Brace Jovanovicsh, Inc., New York, p. 37.

Mehta, J.K. (1984), "Gandhian Thought—An Analytical Study", Ashish Publishing House, 8/8, Punjabi Bagh, New Delhi, p. 68.

Andrews, C.F. (1987), "Mahatma Gandhi's Life and Ideas", Anmol Publications (India), p. 190.

The Times of India, April 23, 2007, Lucknow, p. 5.

17

Relevance of Gandhian Economics for Meeting the Challenges Culminating in the Present Day Global Era

Birendra Kumar Jha and Arun Kumar Thakur

Mahatma Gandhi was neither a student of economics nor trained in applied economic apparatus. He did not have a well-defined economic theory but he had a very clear economic philosophy that was certainly the domain of economics. Gandhism, like Marxism, is a complex whole in the making of which multiple and multi-dimensional factors are involved, due to which it is not always easy to categorise his thinking in terms of traditional school of thought but that does not matter really. He had a first hand understanding of Indian economy, and he not only diagnosed India's economic ills but also prescribed far reaching solutions to these ills although the academic economists had kept the Gandhian economic ideas outside their ambit on the ground that they were unrealistic and inadequate for the modern world whereas a few decade ago, it was the fashion to regard Gandhi as well intentioned but somewhat eccentric individual unsuited to modern times, it is now being realised that there is no alternative but to adopt a new development strategy which is both indigenous and workable to solve our basic problems and this new development strategy will have to blend Gandhi's vision with new techno-economic realities of the 21st century.

GANDHIAN ECONOMICS

Gandhi's economic ideas are based on four cardinal principles—truth, non-violence, dignity of labour and simplicity. He built a system of decentralised non-violent economy whereas Marx built a system of violent socialist economy. Unlike Adam Smith who had championed the case of *laissez-faire,* Gandhi dreamed of Ramraj for the upliftment of the masses. Of course, his approach to economic development of the country is a practical proposition and not merely a theoretical orthodox doctrine and it is based on Indian philosophy of ethics framed in a socialistic system of mixed economy and composed with the economic factors of unbalanced growth, rural development, employment orientation and self-reliance under labour intensive technique. He was adhering to one of the two streams from which economics has flowed and grown—the ethical on the one hand and the engineering on the other—as one of the recent treatises reminds us. The ethical tradition as pointed out is in ancient one Indian way of approaching any human problem a tradition which includes Kautilya and Valluvar and more recently Vivekananda and Tagore in India, and Mill, Marx and Marshall outside India. The engineering tradition is more recent and goes back to the French Physiocrat Quesnay and our own Dadabhai Naoroji, and more recently to Leon Walras and the mathematical economists who have followed him. Gandhi belonged to the ethical tradition and affirmed his belief that economics is related to metaphysics and other human sciences with the responding words. "I must confess that I do not draw a sharp or any distinction between economic and ethics." (As quoted by Adiseshaia, M.S., 1993). No doubt, he wanted modernisation and reconstruction but he was of the opinion that side by side with economic development and progress proper emphasis needs to be laid on promoting ethical and spiritual values in life. For him real progress was moral progress and true economics should stand for social justice and moral values. He was of the opinion that real planning consisted in the best of utilisation of entire manpower of India. He wanted purity of means. He was not in favour of mass production but production by the masses. Thus, so-called Gandhian model relates to an ideal economic order where his vision of Swaraj was not merely an instrument of achieving political liberation from the British colonial rule but the symbol of achieving self-reliance and self-respect. He made a case for Khadi as a device to counter the exploitation of colonial resources for growth of British mills. He formulated an entirely new approach to socio-economic development in which man would be at the central stage and he was extremely opposed to the accumulations of wealth earned by profit. He was in favour of simple living and high thinking, which may prove instrumental in solving most of the ills of modern civilisation. His economic ideas on self-sufficiency, self-reliance, employment, decentralised development, equality, trusteeship, capital-labour relations, technology, machinery, role of the state and so on have systematically integrated to construct what may be called Gandhian Economics. And the basic principles of the Gandhian economic progamme are the following: first, avoidance of mechanisation and encouragement of cottage industries, as specially spinning and weaving; second, improvement of rural small scale agriculture; third, making the village community as much self-sufficient and self-reliant as practicable; fourth, decentralisation of the administrative and economic structure; fifth, reducing income inequalities by raising the income level among the poor and changing the attitude and motivation of the rich; and sixth, ensuring that the capitalists and big businessmen trustees for the whole community" (Datta, Bhabatosh, 1978). Thus, Gandhi's model of growth is basically an ideological alternative to formulate a strategy of rural development in the context of socio-cultural heritage of rural India and there are six basic concepts essential to Gandhian economics, i.e. (i) swadeshi,

(ii) bread labour, (iii) aparigrah or non-possession, (iv) trusteeship, (v) non-exploitation, and (vi) equality. For Gandhi true economics stands for social justice, it promotes good of all equally, including the weakest and indispensable for a decent life (Gandhi, 1937, *Harijan*, p. 292) and thus, Gandhian economics is life-oriented and servant of humanity at large, which is conducive to social justice and human welfare.

NEGLECT AND REVIVAL

Gandhi who is more widely known and applauded for his contribution in the field of spiritualism and humanitarian outlook rather than his contribution to the science of dynamics of people's material conditions of living and so there is no surprise if Gandhian economics has remained neglected for a long time in this materialistic era. Two major schools of thought stand out clearly. While the Nehru-Mahalanobis model favoured a strategy of building basic and key industries with the expectation of maximizing growth rates over the long-run. Gandhi did not think that large factories would be able to solve either the problem of un- and under-employment or that of providing the Indian masses with their basic requisites (Chakravarty, 1987). Although the merit of Gandhian philosophy was not completely lost to the Nehru-Mahalanobis school of thought, as is well known, ultimately the Nehru-Mahalanobis strategy prevailed over the Gandhian approach. According to Gurley the Maoist government in China, as it followed the Gandhian path was able to feed, educate and provide minimum health care to all of its people in China whereas India, which adopted the economic model borrowed from the westerners, possesses a vast number of homeless and shelterless people living on streets, Malnourished Children, beggars, prostitutes, etc. (Gurley, 1976). Perhaps we feel pride in following faithfully and blindly the western model. We are remembering Aristotle and his philosophical writings as an original source of economic ideas and have forgotten Kautilya and his Arthashastra, which contains in it several economic ideas. We are recalling the Industrial Revolution of England

and have forgotten the fact that upto the 15th century India was regarded as an industrialsed country. Then, there is no wonder in forgetting Gandhian model for economic development. J.D. Sethi goes to the extent of saying that the socio-economic failures of Indian planning can be attributed to Nehru's abandonment of the Gandhian philosophy (J.D. Sethi, 1978) although economist like Raj Krishna found no basic differences in Gandhi and Nehru except that Gandhi had a strong religion orientation and Nehru had a strong Fabian orientation (Raj Krishna, 1979). Whatever may be, there is no denying the fact that there were many who accepted Gandhian political tenets, but at the same time were convinced that economic salvation of the country lay in a process of development which should largely follow the line of evolution in the western countries. Gandhian economic ideas need not be taken as entirely an antithetical to what the economists and planners have believed in up till the recent past. There is no need for neglecting Gandhian model particularly when there is an evidence that economic growth of Japan is primarily and largely dependent on small scale and cottage industry and so far our economic development there is no need for following western model which remained unable to secure the desired magnitude and pattern of development.

For more than last one hundred years or so, there were many experiments with the development strategies with different variations of both capitalism and socialism, but none of them could reach their targets in a satisfactory and sustainable manner as in the present globalised and inter-connected world system, any development strategy which leads to growing inequality among countries and within country and unable to remove poverty, hunger and malnutrition from the society is clearly unsustainable as well as undesirable. The provision of food security, employment and education for all is likely to be a greater problem even in the 21st century than ever before, in view of the expected rise in population by nearly 3 billion people or 50 per cent in the next three decades to come. Evan now economists raise four-fold question, whether growth has trickled down, inequality widened, poverty deepened and unemployment increased.

The answer is in the affirmative. About 25 per cent of the world population lives in poverty and one-fifth of the people share hardly 1.4 per cent world's income. The problem of unemployment particularly almost all the developing countries appears to be uncurable. Besides, environment deteriorates causing growing damage to the basic support systems of soil, water, flora and fauna and the atmosphere. Whatever the model of economic development adopted till now, results in widening the gap between rich and poor and converts the world into developed and developing economies. The global era witnesses the fact that the development effort gets tilted in favour of the elitist sections in society and the poor are becoming poorer. Doubt about adopted model of economic development till now arises, which is but natural particularly when the fruits of economic development fall only in the lap of the privileged sections in society. Moreover, out of the total population of the world, hardly 10 per cent lives in urban areas and so the model of developmental growth visualised and suggested by Gandhi fits humanity at large not only for India but for the world.

India, as a compromise solution to the debate on the relative superiority of the two major systems of economic development, viz. market capitalism and socialism, adopted mixed economy with a hope to enjoy the virtues of both capitalism and socialism with a target to gradually expand the public sector further from the commanding heights of the economy that it occupied gradually it was felt by an increasing share of the population that perhaps in the name of a mixed economy we have created a mixed up economy by courting the vices of both the systems. (R.K. Sen, 2004). This realisation led to the revision of the development paradigm in India and ultimately in 1991 the economic reform policy was adopted and it was supposed to remove the existing deformities of the economy like slow rate of income growth (the so-called Hindu rate), to reduce the fiscal deficit, which was described as unsustainable, to control the inflation rate, to solve the foreign exchange crisis, and above all to uncage the economy so that it can progress towards an all-round prosperity but our experience of nearly 17 years under this new paradigm, i.e. LPG has led us to search for an appropriate development paradigm as we are gradually realizing that perhaps we are not following the correct development path appropriate for India which may find out a meaningful solution to poverty, unemployment, inequality and so on. The strategies of development that we have followed so far have given us at best only moderate successes, and none has helped so far to address the fundamental problems of poverty, unemployment, inequality, etc. and it is in this context that there has been a greater awareness of the relevance of Gandhain model of development. Even when the success of the LPG strategy of the global era is measured only in terms of an increase in the rate of growth of national income only, an analysis of experiences of these countries reveal the fact that there has been success for only a few, mixed for a few others like India, and failure for a large number of countries, resulting in raising inter-regional disparity to a great extent and when we adopt parameters suggested by Dudley Seers about the stage of development of an economy, viz. what has happened to poverty, unemployment and inequality in that particular economy, it is needless to say that the ongoing development paradigm of the LPG strategy needs to be changed in favour of a truly people centric developmental model. Instead of dwelling on the many alternative models that are available we might hardly do better than reconsider Mahatma Gandhi's profoundly original formulations on this matter that are contained in his Hind Swaraj almost a hundred years back in 1907. In this Gandhiji advocated what he called Swadeshi, a decentralised, village-based self-sufficient economic order, with rural small scale agriculture and village-based small industries which would absorb the vast labour force of this country (Pulin B. Nayak, 2006). The planners who went in a direction almost exactly opposite to the Gandhian way have now in favour of Gandhian model. If the large and widespread problem of poverty, unemployment and inequality are to be solved and for protecting and conserving environment along with the development process we need to follow the path visualised and suggested by Gandhi. Modern economists like Gadgil, Vakil and Brahmananda have accepted Gandhian ideas of decentralised structure of planning to be optimally suited to Indian economy. Even if we admit that to some extent the need of development which occurred in the Nehru and post Nehru periods was inevitable since the first phase of building up of the industrial base has been completed, now the present state of economy is ripe for the adoption of Gandhian model in which greater emphasis should be given to rural development and the creation of employment to eradicate poverty from the country (S. Sen Gupta and Vinod N. Singh, 1987). Even our Hon'ble President Abdul Kalam also appears to be in support of Gandhian model when he has suggested PURA and home-grown model of development for realizing his vision of a developed India by 2020.

TRACING RELEVANCE OF GANDHIAN ECONOMICS FOR MEETING CHALLENGES CULMINATING IN THE GLOBAL ERA

We have cultivated the habit to look to the western developed world for answers to many of our problems although some these answers may lie right at home (B.K. Jha, 2005). The most worrisome fact is that we are not ready to take a lesson from our past experiences and are committing blunder one by one. As is well known we have adopted the Nehru-Mahalanobis strategy in the past and Gandhian approach to economic development could not attract the attention of Indian planners. As a result the second Five Year Plan embarked upon an ambitious programme of building a network of basic and key industries whose gestation period was long, whose investment requirements are too heavy and whose growth propelling effects were to follow after big time gap (G.K. Chadha and P.P. Sahu, 2005). But the Nehru-Mahalanobis strategy could not succeed in solving our problems and even after a long period of nearly 60 years after Independence India is a developing country. Once again in the last decade of the last century we have adopted the new LPG strategy for economic development but we forget the fact that proper diagnosis is highly desirable for curing particular disease. A mistake has been committed when globalisation has been deemed the panacea for solving all problems. With present phase of globalisation, which cannot be stopped India needs to look into the evils effects of globalisation. It is neither permissible nor desirable to allow Indians to starve, to lose their employment and to become destitute in the global era. Is it not true that Indian farmers have committed suicide in this era for which directly or indirectly globalisation is not less responsible? And so we need to change our outlook towards Gandhian ideas, which were considered misfit in the present century by many critics. Very few agreed with him during his lifetime when he warned us against the evils of centralised economy and technology without a human face. But with environmental crisis, widening of the hole in the ozone layer that protects the earth and pollution of various kinds, the world over finds much sense in what Gandhi said (Nirmala Desh Pandey, 2002). The thinking community finds sense in one of the basic and profound tenets of his environmentalism. The earth provides enough to satisfy everyone's need, but not for anyone's greed. His belief lies in this fact that non-violence and compassion are not to be practiced only towards living beings, but also towards inanimate materials. Overuse of the latter motivated by greed and the desire to make undue profits at the expense of biosphere is also violence, since it deprives others of the use of such materials. Such statement makes him, not only a prophet of the past but also of the future. Srikanta K. Panigrahi in his article Gandhi and Environment published in *Yojana*, Vol. 46, Oct. 2002 quoted the statement of former executive director (UNEP), Mustafa Jolba, "unless we begin to use our natural resources rationally and fairly the world would face an environmental catastrophe as complete and irreversible as any nuclear holocaust." Unfortunately, globalisation adds fuel to the fire through making human community more greedy and commercial in outlook. In the global era the situations has been further worsened "Where market is the temple and money is God" (R.K. Sen, 2004). And if we let the present trend continue, it is all too clear that we will be loser in all fronts in general. In this scenario Gandhian model of economic development appears to be only alternative and more relevant which places people before government, men before machines, villages before cities, welfare before growth, craftsmanship before expertise, decentralisation before centralisation and above all truth, non-violance, simplicity as well as equality before all. Is it not meaningful in this global game when he has clarified the fact in these words. "I do not want my house to be walled from all sides and windows to be stuffed. I want the cultures of all lands to blow freely in my house but I refuse to be blown-off my feet by any." Whatever Gandhi said regarding cultures, is also a warning for our economic fields with the same force particularly when we accepted to be blown-off our feet by western model of economic development.

Globalisation, which denotes an economic process of integrating the country's economy with the world economy has raised apprehensions and expectations, more often the former than the latter and the global and the Indian experience so far, has produced the negative impact more often than the positive impact. Ultimately, challenges, which India is facing from very beginning, has culminated in the global era and emerged in very ugly form. These challenges are unemployment, poverty and inequality and it is needless to say that these are inter-linked. In the global era unemployment has increased and where employment has increased it is mostly in the informal sector and in its more flexible such as casual, contract and temporary forms. Gandhi gave us on unfailing test to judge the validity of any strategy or policy and that test is to recall the face of the poorest and the most helpless person and ask whether it will make any difference to his lot. Globalisation has remained failure in passing this Gandhian test. For Gandhi, political freedom is meaningless if we cannot achieve economic independence but unfortunately instead of attaining economic independence after political freedom we are loosing political freedom through economic dependence and in the global era we are compelled to follow the path dictated by different international institutions which may be WTO or IMF or World Bank or these all. The LPG strategy adopted in India has failed in generating employment opportunities and so resulted in jobless economic growth, which cannot be desirable in a populous country like India. Moreover, the strategy which is capitalistic in character, proves to be an instrumental in widening the gap between rich and poor and raising the disparity between developing and developed regions on the one hand and on the other works as an incentive for expansion of imperialism in new form. In this scenario Gandhian approach to economic development is only hope in this sense it was he who was completely aware of Indian problems and gave solution to these problems in his own way. He was well aware of the darker side of the western technology, which is neither labour intensive nor friendly to nature, and so he had cautioned his countrymen about these perils of western technology. Recognizing unemployment as the most serious challenge confirming the Indian economy, he held that the method of doing or manufacturing a thing by machinery was harmful when the same thing could be done or manufactured easily by millions of hands not otherwise occupied" (Gandhi, 1931). He further stressed, "With crores of human beings going idle India cannot afford to have large machinery which will displace their labour. It would spell their unemployment and their ruin. Our problem is how to find employment for all the crores of our people not how to save their labour. Continuous unemployment has already induced in them a kind of laziness or listlessness which is most depressing" (Gandhi, 1937). Gandhi, the torch bearer of village industries and handicrafts had a clear mind that a technology which increases output per worker through increase in capital investment per worker but saves labour, suits developed countries which enjoy high incomes and, therefore possess a high capacity to save but it is out of tune in a populous country like India having labour force in abundance and scarce capital. He was in favour of such production methods or techniques, which would economies capital and labour intensive in character. The industrial and corresponding technological development of over a century has increased the gap with adverse consequences for India and this gap can be reduced only through adoption of Gandhian model of economic development. He was aware of the fact that large-scale industrialisation, generally, would add to the profits of capitalists unless coupled with proper distribution, and so it has not solved any of the problems which industrial growth was expected to do in the developing countries like India. Our past experience reveals the fact that the Second Five Year Plan embarked upon an ambitious programme of building a network of basic and key industries, whose gestation period was long, whose investment requirements were too heavy, and whose a growth propelling effects were to flow after big time gaps whereas tiny and small industries were to play a significant role on the employment and consumer goods fronts. Thus, he was opposed to modern machine-based industrial development not because he was against machines *per se*, but because they displace labour. They deprive men of their employment and render them jobless. The other reason why he was against machin—based production on large scale was because it would concentrate production and distribution in the hands of the few and would therefore sharpen inequalities. Thus, he was aware of the role of human capital in the process of economic development and so his model is truly people centric in character. A point that needs to be clarified is that a major scientific and technological effort must be devoted largely to the utilisation of resources that are available in the country, and not geared to the resource pattern of western developed countries. Of course, the use of labour saving machinery which the west had to take-up because of its lack of manpower is not relevant in India where manpower is available in abundance and unemployment has become chronic disease which appears to be uncurable particularly in the global era. Gandhi made it clear that he was not against machinery as such but only on their indiscrimate use. He was aiming not at the eradication of all machines but only on their limitation. Of course, what is needed is an man-machine mix. It is desirable to devise a technology, which would make small operations viable in themselves and not necessarily depend upon mass production devices, which the west has so far developed to suit its own requirements. He intended to develop a technology which would satisfy both the criteria namely, that of decentralised production on a small scale as well as economic efficiency. In his vision the utilisation of existing resources is an important parameter for making any technology successful. Our experience outside our country supports Gandhian approach and shows its relevancy in Indian context. The example of post-war Germany and Japan can be quoted. Prosperity in modern countries is based not on the accumulation of capital but on the people—the labour force, in the broad sense of the term. The experience of Germany and Japan after World War II illustrates this point. Their cities, ports, rail roads, bridges, factories and power stations, all the riches accumulated by half a century of hard work, were reduced to heaps of rubble and ashes. Half naked people were living among ruins. All they had left was their hands and their brains trained for collective, creative work and determination. With these assets they started rebuilding. A decade later they came back as greater economic powers than before the war (W.S. Woytinsky, 1987). Better results would probably be achieved if Gandhian model were preferred in the process of economic development. Of course, India own vast resource is human power and fuller utilisation of this resource can be only best strategy for its development (B.K. Jha, 2005). Heavy industry and specially heavy-machine making industry, says W.S. Woutinskey, has never been the root and base of economic growth. The basis of economic growth in early phase of industrialisation was agriculture, trade and handicrafts. In all the great industrial power except USSR and Japan, heavy industry grew on the basis of consumer goods industries, responding to their demand and adjusting it to their needs. This refers not only to the United States, Great Britain and Germany but also to France, Itlay, Canada and so on. The opposite course of development in Russia and Japan was due to historical conditons. . . . In both countries heavy industry was pushed ahead as the basis of military power rather than the foundation of further industrialisation (W.S. Woytinsky, 1957). And thus, there is relevancy behind his advocacy for small and cottage industries for economic development of the country. There is no doubt about the recent performance of the Indian economy as the GDP growth rate is appreciably at 8.1 per cent during 2005-06 and is expected to be in double digit but at the same time a perusal of the scenario of poverty tell a real tale. Around the beginning of this millennium the percentage of the population below the poverty line was still around 28.6 per cent. After more than a half century of planned economic development to have this level of poverty is a correct indication for something wrong in the planning process but even now we seem to be ready for adopting most advanced technologies of developed countries which are capital intensive and labour saving. What would be the result of neglecting Gandhian approach even now? The technological growth was increasingly associated with increasing capital labour ratio and increasing joblessness in the capitalistic world. Even the most advanced capitalist nation finds itself unable to eradicate unemployment and social degradation associated with it. After the mid-twentieth century this process witnessed significant and increasing environmental degradation and growing threat to world pace. (Pradhan H. Prasad, 2000). It is hereby needless to say that, "If we are to eradicate poverty, we must first do away with this widespread unemployment" (Nehru, 1929). Of course, Gandhi was aware of this reality and so it was natural for him to lay emphasis on providing employment to all. The reality lies in this fact that with the traditional industrial sector thrown in crisis, unemployment problem has turned grave making poor more poor and rich richer and unfortunately, with the present policy of liberalisation of Indian economy to fit into the process of globalisation to push through the exit policy to further worsen the terrible problem of joblessness causing poverty and inequality in the country. Relevancy of Gandhian model is easily visible when we come to know that with less than 1 per cent of the plan allocation for the entire Khadi and Village Industries sector, it has been able to provide part time and full time employment to 53.25 lakhs of the poorest section of our people in over two lakh villages in India. These vast numbers who would otherwise have remained idle have been able to earn Rs. 1140.65 crores during the period 1993-94. It is not beyond doubt that ecologically and economically inappropriate technology adopted so far can become cause of, not solution to underdevelopment of our country. Gunnar Myrdal in his *Asian Drama* has fully supported Gandhian approach to economic development through protection and promotion of cottage industries in the village and has also advocated decentralised industry as best suited for India (Gunnar Myrdal, 1972). Gandhi was an advocate of appropriate technology that is technology with human face and wanted to build up a new Indian in terms of Gram Swaraj. He said, "My idea of village swaraj is that it is a complete republic, independent of neighbours for its own vital wants and yet interdependent for many others in which dependence is a necessity." (Gandhi, 1958) and in order to build village republics his scheme envisaged maximum decentralisation of political and economic powers to the villages. His strategy of rural reconstruction was based on his programmes of village swaraj and swadeshi movement in which he introduced many apparently very simple activities like Charkha, revival of household/cottage industries and village handicrafts, village sanitation and hygiene, basic education for harmonious development of the whole personality, etc. Of course, his plan of the self-sufficient village swaraj and swadeshi was to provide full employment and thus, this plan resulted in eradication of poverty as well as lessening the inequality prevailing in the society. In his vision economic "equality is the master key to non-violent independence. It means the leveling down of a few rich in whose hands is concentrated the bulk of the nation's wealth on the one hand and a leveling up of the semi-starved naked millions on the other. A non-violent system of government is clearly impossibility so long as the wide gulf between the rich and hungry million persists." His advocacy for trusteeship was to reduce inequality and so poverty, in his own words "what belongs to me is the right to an honourable livelihood, no better than enjoyed by millions of others. The rest of my wealth belongs to the community and be used for the welfare of the community" (Gandhi, 1966) and thus, it provides a means of transforming present capitalist order of society into an egalitarian one. Jan Tinbergen, the Nobel Prize winning Dutch economist, endorses the Gandhian approach to planning in these words. "It will have to be realised that India's problems can only be solved by certain types of idealism on the side of its leading personalities to be under stood in a wide sense an idealism based perhaps on the Gandhian principles of simplicity and austerity" (Quoted by Ram K. Vepa, 1977). Jan Tinbergen was not alone the noted British economist GDH Cole remarked, "Gandhiji's campaign for the development of hand-made cloth industry is no mere fad of romantic eager to revive the past but a practical attempt to relive the poverty and uplift the standard of the Indian village." More surprisingly, Henry Ford, whose Model T car revolutionised the automobile industry also believed in decentralised village units: pragmatically, he found it costs less to produce in small units: "Wherever it is possible, a policy of decentralisation ought to be adopted. We would need instead of mammoth flour mills, a multitude of smaller units distributed through all the sections where grains is grown—our communities ought to be more complete in themselves. They ought not to be unnecessarily dependent on railway transportation out of what they produce, they should supply their own needs and ship the surplus" (Ram K. Vepa, 1977). He advocated limitation of wants which may yet be the single most important economic postulate that may be consistent with sustainable ecology in the millennia to come. This is precisely the obverse of what the mainstream economic thinking associated with Smith, Ricardo, Mill and Marshall which regards the ever expansion of the goods space as a natural goal. More than two and a half centuries after the onset of the industrial revolution and the untold plunder of ecological system it is now imperative for human species to consider this Gandhian view with great importance (Pullin B. Nayak, 2006).

CONCLUDING REMARKS

Gandhian Plan of village based democracy and his concept of decentralisation of powers to panchayats to enable them to become self-sufficient village republics along with all other economic development policies and programmes were considered very difficult to work out in practice. Indian planners and policy-makers didnot share. Gandhian belief in the urgency of adopting a pro-poor growth strategy and restructuring Indian rural economy. Unfortunately, the picture of development which our policy-makers had in mind was that of Europe and America which were highly industrialised and urbanized and they succumbed to the wiles of industrialisation, forgetting the traditional Indian masses living in villages as Gandhi himself repeated times without number that "India is to be found not in its few cities but in it 70,000 villages" (Gandhi, 1936) and "If the village perishes India will perish too. It will be no more India" (Gandhi, 1936). Having observed the fast growth of Soviet System, India opted soft corner for soviet model of planning and control, not fully realizing its limitations in a democratic polity. In order to enjoy the virtues of both capitalism and socialism India officially adopted mixed economy as it development paradigm almost since its Independence and later on in 1991 the new development paradigm suddenly emerged. Thus, we have traveled a long way from mixed economy and so-called a socialist economy to finally the economic liberalisation of today but the net result of development paradigms adopted so far is that we have more poverty, more unemployment more inequality and more frustration. Even in the global era we find that challenges which we have to face, were culminated and becoming worse-off. The way globalisation is working it must almost automatically lead to an 80/20 society in which 80 per cent will be looser and only 20 per cent gainner. Gunnar Myrdal has gone to the extent of saying that we have created petty islands of highly organized western type industries surrounded by a sea of stagnation taking "work and bread away from millions with no immediate alternative source of employment and income" (Gunnar Myrdal, 1972). He clearly admitted the reality and said, "If Indian planning has not been more successful than it has actually been, the main explanation is that they have not kept so close as they should, to the fundamentals of the teachings of the father of the Nation."

Of course, Gandhi never enunciated any economic theory but his knowledge, his analysis of Indian economic problems and their solution was so clear and relevant that impresses not only Indian economists but also economists outside of India. No other problem worries our policy-makers from the very beginning as the explosive one of finding suitable employment to their growing population, which can only a reliable means for eradication of poverty and lessening inequality between, rich and poor as well as disparity between rural and urban regions. It is this aspect, more than anything else that bothered Gandhi in relation to large-scale production based on heavy machine on the western pattern. He was in favour of certain type of machines to be used those which did not deprive men the opportunity to labour, but which helped the individual and added to his efficiency and which men could handle at will without being its slave. Even so confirmed a believer in industrialisation as Jawaharlal Nehru was conscious of the intrinsic logic of Gandhi's viewpoint in the Indian context and he held a clear-cut concept in this concern when he wrote in his book *Discovery of India*, "Foolish comparisons are made between man power and machine power. Of course, a big machine can do the work of thousand or ten thousand persons. But if those ten thousand sit idly by or starve, the introduction of that machine is not a social gain (Nehru). However in our planning process Gandhian labour intensive technology was not preferred up to now, and as a result India is problem ridden country in this global era. There was no reason for neglecting Gandhian model on the basis of considering it far from reality and very difficult to work out. It is well known that India got Independence under the leadership of Gandhi and his unique and complete unwitting, unthinkable and non-traditional weapons like non-violence and non-cooperation were used for winning a war and winned. Then, why not, Gandhian diagnosis and his prescription were believed to cure economic ills of the country. Of course, when neither capitalism nor socialism has succeeded in curing these ills, when neither neo-liberal policy of today nor mixed economy strategy of the past becomes successful in its mission, Gandhian model of economic development which is pro-poor growth model appears to be more relevant for the developing populous country like India. Undoubtedly, none can contradict the fact that advanced technology improves labour productivity, quality of product and rate of surplus and so far socio-economic development it is absolutely necessary but we should take a lesson from Japan, Korea and Taiwan which are some of the shinning examples where tremendous techno-industrial development has been achieved along with heavy reliance on small units household production at the lower level and so what is desirable is to establish and strengthen small scale industries based on intermediate technology and household cottage system of production and handicrafts. Thus, the challenges like the ecological and environment imbalance and the acute economic distress suffered by the people in the form of poverty, unemployment, inequality, exhaustation of non-renewable resources, exploitation, etc. make Gandhian economics more relevant. Moreover, his preaching of non-possession and non-accumulation and current consumption implies the surest way of tackling the life-threatening problem of environment denudation and destruction and the relevancy of his approach is beyond doubt. There is no scope of doubt about relevancy of Gandhian economics when the modernisation-industrialisation-growth-trickle down model of development has been found woefully inadequate to challenges culminating in the global era. There is no other way out than that of rebuilding the economic system suggested by Gandhi. Above all, what makes Gandhian model more relevant is the prevailing scenario of the country. "The prevalence of corruption raises strong obstacles and inhibitions to development" (Gunnar Myrdal, 1972) and India has broken all the past records of corruption. India's moral standard has deteriorated to a damaging degree. The usual way to make money by corrupt practices has become general rule. In this scenario any development programme, even if it is targeted towards the weaker sections, would automatically bring more benefits to those who have resources than to those who have none, and so Gandhian model of growth based on spirituality, morality and ethical background appears to be more relevant. Charan Singh, the former Prime Minister has rightly observed, "If we have good of the people as a whole of heart by and large in a capital poor and labour rich country like India, there is no escape from an economy Mahatma Gandhi advocated. His kind of economy will, not in the present context produce greater wealth in the total, but will also serve all our other aims, that is it will provide maximum employment, ensure equitable distribution of national product and promote a democratic way of life (Singh, Charan, 1981). It is heartening to take down that the Neo-Gandhian approach to economic development conceptualised by our Hon'ble president Abdul Kalam called PURA or Providing Urban Amenities to Rural Areas which has been considered as the lever of economic upliftment of the villages is more or less similar to Gandhi's gram swaraj. "Though the government has adopted this new approach in Principle, yet it is not clear how it can co-exit with the ongoing strategy of economic reforms, which has a clear elitist anti-rural. It is also true that there are attempts to adorn the globalisation processed with a human face, but it is obvious that a policy dependent on the market is strictly based on exchange and price mechanism and there cannot be any place in it for the human face." (R.K. Sen, 2004). Thus, there is need for honest acceptance of Gandhian pro-poor growth model, which was relevant, is relevant and will be relevant in Indian context in the near future.

References

Chadha, G.K. and Sahu, P.P. (2005), Rural Industrialisation in India: A Critical Assessment of Policy Perspective in Rural Transformation in Indian Institute for Human Development, New Delhi.

Chakravarty, Sukhmoy (1987), Development Planning: The Indian Experience, Clarendon Press, Oxford, Chapter 2.

Datt, Bhabatosh (1978), Gandhian Economics in Indian Economic thought, Tata McGraw Hill Publishing Company Ltd., pp. 150-58.

Deshpande, Nirmala (2002), Gandhi More Relevant Today, *Yojana*, Vol. 47. Oct.

Gandhi (1931), *Young India*, 2 July.

Gandhi (1936), *Harijan*, 20 July.

Gandhi (1936), *Harijan*, 4 April.

Gandhi (1937), *Harijan*, 2 January.

Gandhi (1937), *Harijan*.

Gandhi (1947), *Harijan*, 23 March.

Gunnar Myrdal (1972), *Asian Drama*, Vintage Books.

Gupta, S. Sen and Singh, Vinod (1987), Gandhian Economics: Its Relevance, *Today Khadi Gramodyog*, Vol. XXXIII, No. 12, Sept.

Gurley (1978), China's Economy and the Maoist Strategy, New York, Monthly Review Press, p. 33.

Jha, B.K. (2005), "Gandhian Economics *versus* Globalisation", in *Globalisation and Contemporary Economic Scenario,* Abhijeet Pub., Delhi.

Nayak, Pulin B. (2006), The Economic Scenario: Need for Purposive Intervention, Memorial Lecture in the 9th Conf. EAB.

Nehru, Jawaharlal, *Discovery of India.*

Pradhan, H. Prasad (2000), India: Dilemma of Development, Mittal Pub., New Delhi.

Raj Krishna (1979), The Nehru-Gandhi Polarity and Economic Policy in Gandhi and Nehru, OUP, Delhi.

Sen, R.K. (2004), Development Alternatives for India in the Next Decades, Memorial Lecture in the 8th Conf. EAB.

Singh, Charan (1981), Economic Nightmare of India, National Publishing House, Delhi.

Vepa, Ram K. (1977), Development of Backward Economy—Relevance of Gandhian Technology in *IJPA,* Vol. XIII, No. 3.

Woytinsky (1957), India: The Awakening Giant, Harper and Brothers, New York.

18

Globalisation Laying Development Path of Village Economy

Relevance of Gandhian Economics in 21st Century

K.M. Naidu, L.K. Mohan Rao, K. Srinivasulu Naidu and
K. Mahesh Naidu

"India lives in villages. The villages should grow to make India global power in the world as it is a leader in spiritual Sphere"

–*M.K. Gandhi*

Globalisation is a buzzword in the World, making people to think in new ways and work on new methods. World has become a global village in the sense that whatever happens in a village is easily known all over the World. Globalisation means many things so many people. Positive thinkers view it as an opportunity to grow to higher level and negative persons picturise it as a devil pregnant with destructive and exploitative qualities, particularly undermining the developing economies. Whether M.K. Gandhi (hear in after referred as Gandhi) is a global man or local man representing only a village man? The answer lies according to the interpretation given to Gandhian ideas. The paper presents only positive picture of Gandhi as a global man, mainly interested in the prosperous development of villages in India. The first section explains the difference between Pandit Jawaharlal Nehru—the builder of modern India and great global thinker and Mahatma Gandhi—father of the Nation, in their approaches to development in India, Section II deals about present position of India; growth of villages is analysed in Section III and Section IV provides suggestions for prosperous growth of villages.

SECTION I

NEHRUJI AND GANDHIJI

Gandhiji as a peerless leader of prominence led India to gain Independence to India in August 1947. He fulfilled his task and the mandate of God to achieve political liberty to India. Moreover he advocated valuable views on the economic development of India as well as the strategy to be followed by government to make India a great Nation in the World. Gandhiji is basically village-oriented man as he roped in (influenced) the country's village population to join the independence movement. For this purpose donning farmer's dress he travelled as a villager throughout India and understood the living conditions of villagers and their views. Based on this understanding he stated his views popularly known as Gandhian economic philosophy or called as village development model, the base being the farmer. Gandhiji in this model advocated production for masses and not mass production to make the village as a self-sufficient economic unit.

There is wide difference between the approach of Pandit Nehru and Mahatma Gandhi on the planning for economic development of India. Nehruji was a Fabian socialist from the beginning as he was influenced by that philosophy while he studied in London (U.K). Later he very much appreciated the development model of Russia (former USSR) under the leadership of Lenin who operationalised Marxian ideas of development in that country. In 1950s USSR was a giant in may respects competing with U.S.A. Hence

Nehru introduced certralised planning, giving priority to public sector which was implemented by his advisor on planning, Sri P.C. Mahalonobis. Nehru leap-frogged many stages of growth to accelerate India's development. Hence he chose socialistic pattern of society way to give a predominant role to public sector. In other words, Nehru's way of development was the socialistic pattern with state playing the prime role. In a way Nehru became urban in character associated with the growth, though slow and slovenly; in due course it led to consumerism with its attributes of opulence and wasteful expenditure. Nehru's followers and admirers, slowly getting reduced every day, still talk radical and remind the times from Karl Mark to Harold Laski. Nehru's priorities were industry, rapid growth, urbanisation, etc., some criticise even now his view's as being wrong and term them as failure. But others view them even now as correct and useful for India. Let us see Nehru's ideas. The First and Second Five Year Plans formulated under his direction, wanted to industrialise the country in order to lessen its dependence on land which is a victim of whimsical monsoons. It may be a scientific approach (for some), but it has been left half way. Nehru initiated land reforms and amended the Constitution, the first Constitutional Amendment after independence, to implement them. But he could not give land to the tiller free; he only introduced ceiling on the individual holding at 8 acres per family. Nehru no doubt constructed the large irrigation dams during his period like Bhakra Nangal and Nagarjuna Sagar projects, but they benefited only a few areas and some land owning classes leaving the small and marginal farmers high and dry. Villages as a whole could not be rejuvenated and put on the prosperous path. Agriculture as a sector was neglected with low public investment in infrastructure that could enhance prosperity of people depending on agriculture. Even to-day the situation has not very much improved in the rural areas, what with the neglect of agriculture and allied activities.

Mahatma Gandhi on the other hand wanted village economy to be prosperous and progressive as majority of people live on agriculture and its future decides the prosperity or otherwise of people, particularly rural population. Hence he popularised the concept of self-sufficient country side, from the beginning without interference by the State. In a way his approach was primarily rural and village-centred, emphasizing values and idealism as the sheet anchor of village life influenced by Sanatana Dharma, Vedas, Puranas, etc. He saw the entire countryside during Padayatras and understood their feelings and living status and hence admired their simple and contended living avoiding excessive wealth and wasteful expenditure: Gandhi experienced the adverse fall out of opulence and wasteful expenditure like poverty and neglect. Therefore, he wanted to remove them through dynamising village economy, using the available skills, resources and opportunities to the maximum. Gandhi and his followers were close to the ground; have become sceptical of foreign ideologies not suitable to India.

Gandhi was against large scale industrialisation, as it would by-pass rural people and areas, neglect villagers, marginalised sections and lead to poverty and exploitation, which is a reality now in India. On the other hand wanted encouragement of agriculture and allied activities, related to agriculture. He was favourable to the development of small scale industry using local resources, skills, like handlooms, dye Industry, sugarcane and paper industries on a small scale. His idea was that all these activities would promote more employment, lessen poverty and help people live a simple and dignified life earning at the place of living. However, Gandhiji's ideas were given least importance in planned era and the government neglected his approach to development, largely called as simple is beautiful, sanguine and salutary and sustainable for a peaceful and happy living by the farmer, villagers and even the ordinary worker. Village life to Gandhiji is a wholesome life. He believed in the truth. "If villages are prosperous, India is prosperous."

Gandhi and Globalisation

Mahatma Gandhi is definitely a global man, universal thinker, world leader committed to the philosophy of Ahimsa which he popularized through intense practice. His entire life is transparent and truthful in implementing what he preached. Hence he is a global thinker for the up-liftment of common man. He advised people to keep all the windows of the house (life) open so that noble thoughts would fill them and inspire to make individuals grow and glow prosperous with new, innovative and prosperous, ideas. Gandhi at the same time cautioned people not to be blown-off the ground (where he is living). He wanted villagers to gain modern knowledge and skills to obtain higher productivity and production from cultivation (agriculture) or any occupation being practised by them. In other words he encouraged positive aspects of globalisation, privatisation and liberalisation and advocated and addressed governments to protect the farmer and villagers including craftsman from the ill effects of globalisation policies like market exploitation, trade malpractices, illegal competition and excessive subsidisation and tariff barriers being practiced by developed countries. His firm view was that in the absence of protection of farmers and craftsman by government, from the ill and evil effects of globalisation (practised now by developed countries) to selfishly protect their client citizens interests at the cost of developing countries farmers; the Indian village system will collapse having deleterious effect on the Indian economy as the back bone (village economy) weakness and loses shine. The same is happening in India due to World Trade Organisation policies of heavy protection of developed economies, particularly farmers and their produce.

The same situation is experienced by small scale and tiny industries whose growth was emphasized by Gandhi as they provide major share of employment to semi-skilled persons from villages. These industries policies are also closely linked to the prosperity of the villagers and rural areas. Gandhiji's economic philosophy encouraged the idea of 'small is beautiful' that would make the village economy beautiful, life of rural people sustainable and equitable. Thus Gandhiji's global philosophy is relevant in 21st century for both developing and developed countries as well as to WTO.

Globalisation and World Trade

Globalisation resulted in the innovative creation of global institute called World Trade Organisation to promote world trade benefiting mostly developing countries with the cooperation of developed countries. In trade matters it is the apex organisation to solve disputes, disagreements and bring about consensus between members. Gandhiji's ideas are enshrined in the aims of World Trade Organisation—like protecting the small and medium farmer from the ill-effects of globalisation as explained above. But in actual practice WTO is unable to do so what with stubborn attitude of developed countries—not to reduce heavy subsidies to its farmers but at the same time to ensure market access to developing countries without reciprocal action from developed countries. Hence it led to Doha Round of Trade talks. Begun in 2001, the Doha Round was supposed to be about trade-level and trade facilitated development of world's poor countries—a Gandhian idea indeed. After five years of negotiations, the talks collapsed because of non-resolution of differences among the EU, the US and developing countries led by India, Brazil and China. Each group defends its position and each has its favourite argument. In this intransigent position of developed countries (to protect their farmer's interest with high subsidies and wanting access to the markets of developing countries), developing countries have decided to protect the livelihood of their farmers and rural (agricultural) development on the lines of Grandhian ideology. This is essential for social stability and economic progress of poor farmers particularly in India as wanted Gandhiji. The talks failed mostly due to US insistence that developing countries are free to export jet engines and super computers to the US, but not textiles, agricultural products or processed foods—Gandhiji cautioned against this tendency in his writings related to Economics. Developing countries require implementation of market-friendly incentives and regulatory regimes, increase their farmers' productivity, which needs technical assistance from international donors to achieve this (productivity) through investment in training, infrastructure and research. They also require additional social safety nets, like for example, to protect them against price and market volatility for their products. Hence Doha talks on Trade should succeed to the benefit of small and marginal farmers in developing countries as advocated by

Gandhiji. In agriculture, as in other sectors, problems without passports require solutions without borders.[1]

India Abandoned Gandhi

Gandhi through his economic ideas attempted to build credible India, but the present behaviour and acts of higher-ups in administration loses Gandhi; he must be restored and respected by adopting his sane advice. Wrong means will not lead to right results. The government should employ non-violence instrument to solve even economic problems, e.g. SEZ problems and house site problems for the poor are being solved by government applying non-violent means by police force to suppress unwilling small farmers to handover land to SEZs; similarly police force is violently chasing away poor when they occupy government open land and demand house-sites. Gandhiji's fear after four months independence has become a reality when he said, "Today politics has became corrupt. Anybody who gets into politics gets contaminated. But in general there is too much corruption today that it frightens me." Gandhiji aimed and promised that the Nation (people) should have food, employment and shelter after independence, but the development methods followed by the government benefited a few (rich) at the expense of millions of poor, e.g. Special Economic Zones which make farmers loose their lands with government force (without their consent) have not been his aim and idea. The greedy industrialists and speculating builders have destroyed the agricultural economy, and the urban scene. Gandhi might have gone on 'satyagraha' experiencing shock to find that on an average ten farmers are committing suicide every day as they are unable to clear their debts or survive if their crop is destroyed by drought.

Gandhiji wanted last person first. But the government policies follow the reverse and give preference to first person first, e.g. Government supports the organized sector, the five per cent, first against the unorganized sector 95 per cent. The poor, the last person, is getting learner and learner and the first person fatter and fatter. It means poor are becoming poorer and the rich, richer, which Gandhiji opposed. Gandhiji's country, inspite of government's hype, should feel sorry for more poverty, disease and crime, low trickling down effect of development benefits to the poor and marginalised sections of society. Gandhiji's values, according to Kuldip Nayar, the renowned and reputed journalist, has been lost in incredible India, where survival of the fittest is actively promoted and at the same where the poor are knowingly being pushed to the wall and under development.[2]

Gandhiji's economic ideas frankly disapproved of unbelievable, unexpected India promoting rich, neglecting the poor as well as creating dichotomy in development policies, entailing rich urban areas and declining and poor rural landscape with low preference for agricultural and rural development and lower allocation of resources in budgets for total development of agriculture and its allied activities, inspite of the entire agricultural sector is suffering from unbelievable and forced crisis. The persons depending on agriculture are experiencing distress though government intervenes by way of high tariffs, price support and direct input subsidies. This is a cause for concern for the government and the World Trade Organisation. The WTO clearly stated the reasons[3] for the continued slow and erratic growth of the countries primary sector. They are: low labour productivity in this sector, fragmented land holdings, poor mechanisation, inadequate public investment in infrastructure and research, dependence on rainfall, etc. These problems could be solved by the Government, both at the Centre and the States, to rejuvenate and reactivate agriculture so as to realize the Gandhiji's goal of prosperous rural India for achieving wealthy India with happily living rural people and rural areas.

Section II

PRESENT POSITION OF INDIA

India has travelled a long period of fifty-eight years after Gandhi left to heavenly abode after gaining Independence. We are in the Eleventh Five Year Plan and is likely to initiate steps soon to formulate XIth Five Year Plan. India's economic development has seen many ups and downs, the latest being economic crisis suffered by the

Country in 1990s. India has overcome the crisis through Economic Reforms since June 1991. Luckily the architect of these Reforms Dr. Man Mohan Singh is now the Prime Minister of India. Under the able Presidentship of the reputed Scientist Dr. A.P.J. Kalam, the economic Scientist and his successor from 25th July 2007, Smt. Pratiba Patil, equally respected and experienced politician, Dr. Manmohan Singh, is all set to make India a great economic Power by 2020. Dr. Kalam's dream would succeed provided the entire India moves forward as one Nation. Mrs. Pratibha Patil also, it is hoped, will help Dr. Singh to promote India as a member of highly developed G-19 Group of Nations by 2009.

We are in the age of Globalisation, Privatisation and Liberalisation. India is a part and parcel of this Globalisation process. It has both positive and negative impacts on the emerging and developing economies. India has the capacity to convert negative characteristics into positive force. This has been proved by extra ordinary growth path India has entered into since the economic reforms implemented in the country. This success is elaborated below.

With the cooperation of Confederation of Indian Industry (CII), Price Water House Coopers undertook a key initiative (a survey) in 2005 to map the current state of affairs in the emerging modern India relating to agriculture, Industry, service and other sectors and came out with telling facts on Indian economy. India is a rising elephant and is definitely poised for rapid growth. The Indian economy is on a bull run. During the last decade, Indian Gross Domestic Product (GDP) registered an average growth of 6 per cent per capita income rose at the same rate for the last five years. According to World Bank survey, India ranks fourth in terms of purchasing power parity (PPP) next only to the U.S.A., China and Japan. In 2004-05, the economy recorded a growth rate of 6.9 per cent mostly due to developments in the service sector and trade. The economy today is strong and vibrant due to many factors including government policies.

Nearly 72 per cent of the Indian population lives in villages and mostly dependent on rural areas. Despite such high predominance, the share of agriculture and allied activities in India's GDP is only about 25 per cent. India is among top producers of milk, fruits and vegetables in the world. Considerable portion of fresh fruits and vegetables is lost because of inadequate post harvest handling, cold storage, processing facilities and convenient marketing channels. Huge quantities of grams are also wasted due to improper handling and storage, pest infestation and poor logistics management. The result is that intermediaries are eating up a large portion of the earnings that rightly belong to the farmer.

The average holding of a typical Indian farmer is less than five acres. Lack of information and pressure of consolidators force the Indian farmer to make inefficient decisions on crop selection and pricing. This results in huge wastage upto 40 per cent and poor quality produce. The farmer is unable to realise better value as his produce varies in size, shape and quality. Smaller harvest lots do not bring economies of scale in transportation and earn lower net gains. Pilferage also eats into his earnings. A simple farmer faces many difficulties in obtaining required credit, technical benefits, extension help, storage facilities, etc. The market yard, meant to benefit the farmers, does not provide him the needed help to obtain the correct price for his produce.[4] Recently TPRB of WTO stated that the share of agriculture and allied activities in India's GDP declined from 23 per cent in 2000-01 to 18 per cent in 2005-06,[5] though 59 per cent of rural people depend on agriculture for their livelihood. This resulted in distress among small and marginal farmers.

Government of India's Official View

The latest Economic Survey, 2006-07, of Government of India, presented to Parliament on February 27th, 2007 unveils the current status of the India economy. The survey printed a picture of shining India and rising economy experiencing the Robust growth. It demonstrated the nascent strengths of the Indian economy. After growing at 8.5 per cent in 2003-04, 7.5 per cent in 2004-05, 9 per cent in 2005-06 is projected to grow at 9.2 per cent in 2006-07. The growth trend particularly for the last four years (2003-07) indicate the start of a new phase of cyclical upswing in the economy from 2003-04.

According to Dr. C. Rangarajan, Chairman, Prime Minister's Economic Advisory Council, the economy was witnessing "cyclical overheating" but expected the inflation to come down between (June-Dec. 2007) due to good monsoon during 2007-08. Cycling heating takes place when the existing capacity was fully utilised and the demand was still increasing. He says that the government should see "that cyclical overheating does not get translated into structural overheating, that means there are no structural imbalances in the economy." The hope to avoid this depends on good monsoon and agricultural season, even better than last year, then the expectations (chasing demand) will have dampening effect.[6]

However, the growth of agriculture is not sharing such up-trend. After dipping to a low level of 0.7 per cent in 2004-05, due to erratic rainfall, its growth reached to 6 per cent in 2005-06 is projected at 2.7 per cent in 2006-07; however in 2002-03 its growth rate was (minus) –7.2 per cent, but surprisingly rose to 10 per cent in 2003-04 which definitely influenced the overall growth of the economy (at 8.5% the highest plateau). The only point of high concern is decline in the share of its (agriculture's) capital formation in GDP; it fell from 2.2 per cent in the 1999-00 to 1.9 per cent during 2003-04 to 2005-06 (three years) which is due to the stagnation or fall in public investment in irrigation, particularly since mid-1990's. The other cause for concern is fall in the share of agricultural sector in the overall economy from 38 per cent in 1990's to 18.5 per cent in 2006-07 indicating its weak position in the economy though 72 per cent of population depend on this sector for their livelihood.[7]

Some Unfovourable Facts

Inspite of exuberant growth of the economy poverty and unemployment is increasing, prosperity and gains from growth are reaching only to 30 per cent of India's population, making them richer and richer. Nearly 400 million or 50 per cent of population live below poverty line, unemployment rate is reaching to a level of 10 per cent. The sufferers are rural people and villages where these two drawbacks—unemployment and poverty are quite visible. Unless village economies are made prosperous with proper distribution of the growth in judicial and equitable way, the rural economy and people will crumble and violence will rise throwing up law and order problem in the country. If villages and rural economy grow benefiting small and marginal farmers as well as workers depending on agriculture, as visualised by Gandhiji, his contribution to globalisation would be substantial and sustainable.

The National Development Council (NDC) meeting held on May 29, 2007 deliberated on the strategy for agriculture in XIth Five Year Plan decided to reorient the agricultural development strategy to meet the needs of farmers and recommitted to achieve 4 per cent annual growth rate in this sector; the government believes that this would almost solve all the problems of this sector. But given the ground realities the government may not achieve this aim. The fact of technology fatigue, degradation of natural resources, especially land and water during the last two decades and declining interest in farming—all point to the non-achievement of targeted growth in XIth Five Year Plan. Moreover, this growth rate on high side, may put heavy pressure on the already burdened natural resources. There is a large yield gap, i.e. difference between the yields on farmers' fields using the existing technology and the yields that can be attained with improved and available technology. The prime reason for this yield gap across crops is (found to be) lack of knowledge with farmers about improved technology—the failure of extension services is identified as the underlying factor. The additional factors that would reduce the yield gap and increase production are greater availability of quality seeds, tailoring of technology for adoption on a wider scale, better supply of fertilizers, increased credit flow and above all a remunerative price environment (markets-friendly to farmers). But NDC gave importance only to seeds, being silent on other aspects.

Decline in per capita food production is another area of concern and due to this, we witnessed food price inflation and the import of wheat. To meet India's seeds for foodgrain supply, government has to raise supply by 2 per cent every year which is not possible with the present growth of less than half per cent. Other areas of serious concern have not been touched by NDC.

However much emphasis has been laid on investments to increase irrigated area. In the words of Deputy Chairman, Planning Commission Dr. Montek Singh Ahluwalia, "While expenditure on irrigation exceed the target, the addition to potential irrigated area, was only 50 per cent of the target and the actual area under irrigation did not increase at all." It means new investments are only helping to cheek a decline in the area under irrigation. The reasons are: a decline in water table in many parts of the country, a reduced flow of rivers and streams and a shrinking size and number of water resources. Hence solution is to ensure a judicious use of water, afforestation in catchments, water harvesting and conservation. NDC also avoided decisions on the sensitive issues of pricing of irrigation and power subsidies, which entail over exploitation and unsustainable use of water resources. Such avoidance of hard decision may be politically wise to gain power, but will make the economy (people) pay a heavy price. NDA also paid inadequate attention and emphasis on rain water harvesting and conservation, watershed, and improvement in soil fertility—may help reduce the quality of natural resources, essential to raise and sustain agricultural production.[8] Non-fulfilment of gaps in the development of agriculture will result in increase in the yield gap in crop production and low income to farmers through low market prices.

Section III

GROWTH OF VILLAGES

Government of India appears to have been influenced by Gandhiji's ideas in that they have begun to show concern for village development and agricultural growth. Globalisation process has picked up speed particularly from second generation of economic reforms introduced by government of India since 2001. These reforms are to be taken-up by the States and the Central Government is only a facilitator and the Catalyst, the latter is the full supporter for the programmes of the Union Schemes being implemented by the state governments. Government of India is very particular to develop village roads, install telephones, provide computer facilities, health centres, clean drinking water facilities, schools, housing programmes, employment generation schemes, agricultural facilities linked with processing of agricultural produce, value addition to crops, insurance to crops, market yards, warehousing facilities for storage of agricultural produce, information technology facilities so as to help villagers, that is farmers, sell produce at profitable price. Moreover, government is also concentrating on connecting all villages to global facilities so that trading benefits would reach farmers. It is global scenario that influenced government to implement National Rural Employment Guarantee Scheme (NREGS) through state governments so as to provide employment for one person in a village for 100 days in a year for those who are below poverty line. Central government has allotted nearly Rs. 14,300 crores for this scheme in 2006-07 budget which includes Rs. 3000 crores to be spent on the Sampoorna Grameen Rojgar Yojana. Moreover an amount of Rs. 3750 crores fund has been created for programmes and policies (jointly by State and Central Governments) that would remove barriers to growth in rural areas and accelerate the development process. The health sector was given the second highest hike in allocation of Rs. 12,546 crores for health and family welfare during 2006-07, of which Rs. 8207 crores will be spent on the National Rural Health Mission.

Major boost was given to Bharat Nirman with a provision of Rs. 18,696 crores, an increase of 54 per cent. This programme will be executed in the mission mode. This approach to governance is a paradigm shift that would enable our country to use the resources thrown up by the engine of growth for building infrastructure and bringing basic amenities to rural India. This programme has six components with fixed targets to be achieved by 2009: accelerated irrigation development programme with a target of 6 lakh hectres of irrigation potential, accelerated rural water supply project, rural housing programme, rural electrification programme, rural health scheme and Pradhan Mantri Gram Sadak Yojana. These programmes are expected to rejuvenate the village economy many fold and place the farmer and the villager on a stable and strong economic base. Primary education was also given a big boost with more incentives like mid-day meal scheme, free education to girls upto 10th class, etc. All these programmes are expected to transform rural economy into dynamic state so as to help reduce poverty, improve education, health, employment, skills on a sustainable basis.

Andhra Pradesh government has provided lion's share of Rs. 10 thousand crores in 2006-07 budget for irrigation,[9] unmatched by any other state in this country, with an ultimate aim of spending Rs. 65 thousand crores during five years, to provide irrigation facilities for an additional one lakh hectares. Electricity is provided free to farmers for agriculture purpose; education and health were also given substantial importance in the budget to help the growth of rural people. The neglected agriculture during the last five years has been given due importance by the present government since June, 2004 so that village economy regains all the strength and the farmers would regain the status of the back bone of the State's economy by retaining the popular name of Andhra Pradesh (A.P.) as the *"Granary of India."* Globalisation and Gandhiji's ideas have definitely coincided in this shift in approach to development of both Central and State Government.

More than India, China gave appropriate importance to Gandhiji ideal of village growth. When agriculture is turning out to be weak and losing its importance in the economy, Chinese leaders have innovated schemes like rural small industries, closely linked to agriculture and encouraged non-farm activities by encouraging village entrepreneurs.

The government of China even encouraged ownership of farms upto five to ten acres and permitted starting of small scale industries, with government support, by the rural entrepreneurs.

Similar is the trend in many developing countries in the world. It means Gandhiji's village prone development has become global programme and the World Bank is also helping village development programmes by sanctioning liberal grants and loans.

SECTION IV

SOME SUGGESTIONS

Gandhiji has become relevant in the globalisation trend of 21st century that has spread to all parts of the world. He has become more relevant to developing economies like India who has initiated paradigm shift in the development approach, giving required importance to village-prone and farmer-centred growth, emphasizing promotion of employment and removal of poverty and elevating the life of small and marginal farmers and poorer sections in society depending on agriculture.

Providing Urban Facilities in Rural Areas (PURA) is very essential as popularized by president of India Dr. A.P.J. Kalam. This scheme if implemented properly would rejuvenate villages through reform strategy and make them regain old glory as independent, self-sufficient economic units, enjoying all modern facilities. It would discourage migration of rural people in search of employment, education, health care, etc. to urban areas.

In the context of agriculture slowly losing its prime importance, gradually declining its share in G.D.P. (from 50 per cent in 1950 to 18 per cent in 2006-07), becoming a losing occupation and failing profession, government has to search for new ideas to make it a profitable venture. Apart from providing more irrigation facilities by adding to the existing acreage through construction of dams, as is being done by A.P. farmer requires Total Factor Support (TFS) for soil, seeds, credit, technical help, processing and marketing, etc. so as to gain value for his produce.

Non-farm activities should be promoted in villages, clubbing and uniting them into clusters. China's example with appropriate adoption to Indian conditions is suggested so that with government support by way of supply of seeds, fertilizers, credit, technical facility and reasonable price (for his produce) would help rise income from his occupation; this may act as a sufficient income incentive to the farmer to stay in rural areas and village unit. It means that profitability of agriculture should be seen by the farmer and the government has to ensure this profitability as is being done by developed countries like USA, Japan, etc.

In the context of unprofitable agriculture at the time of globalisation process accepted by government, it would be better that Contract Farming is encouraged, without the farmer losing ownership of land accrued to him as a family property. He should be given employment by the corporate firm using his land for farming on contract basis for a few years. This would ensure stable income to the family and the surplus members may seek other avenues of living.

NREGS, SGRY, etc. are only palliatives and not permanent schemes; moreover leakages and wrong targeting may lead to their failure as in the case of PDS. Hence on a permanent basis, the farmers should be encouraged to become independent earners of living in the family.

India has the advantage of being home to the youngest population in the world, where 50 per cent are under the age of 25 and 85 per cent below that of 50, the median age of population is 24 years.

During 2005-06, about 100 million Indians come under age group of 17-21 years. This growing working population in India, 70 per cent of whom reside in villages, is providing fire-power to the demand of modern type. These advantages are to be turned into positive events to develop the villages and rural India to a very high level to fulfil the dream of Gandhiji.

Retail business and trade has enormous potential in India with rising demand from young people. Globalisation encourages trade and the retail outlets should be linked to trade at the all India level and through it to the world. If this is done, Indian villages would also be linked to world trade, through Indian business and Corporate firms, resulting in prosperous villages and rejuvenated farmers and rural areas.

Agriculture should be given the status of industry by the government of India as in the case of USA, Japan, France, etc. This would enable the farmer to obtain all facilities and exemptions from the Government which is very generous by extending to industry. The processing industry based on agricultural produce would receive a boost and farmers can easily secure employment nearer home.

SUM-UP

Mahatma Gandhi and his economic ideas are relevant to globalisation and in 21st century. His vision to make Indian villages prosperous and progressive is possible through globalisation. In a positive sense, there are enormous possibilities and ways to make agriculture, village economy, farmers life and rural areas prosperous if global trends of trade is spread to villages. PURA facilities should be spread to Villages. Corporate farming be introduced, keeping the ownership of land in the hands of the farmer. However the farmer should be given preference in employment in contract farming. Government of India has to treat agriculture as industry so that all the facilities and exemptions provided to industry be equally extended to agriculture. Trade and markets with reasonable price are the only way to make agriculture profitable. Globalisation has this capacity to make rural trade profitable through retail outlets. Gandhiji's dream of making villages self-sufficient and independent economic units could be realised through globalisation, provided positive strategy is followed by government retaining full freedom and land ownership with the farmer. Indian villages have better prosperous future through globalisation.

The positive effects of globalisation should be identified by government of India, so that when Doha talks relating to WTO succeed, major concessions have to be obtained for Indian agriculture and the trade in agricultural goods. Gandhiji's forecast of Indian farmer being global man and global trader could be realised if WTO follows and makes developed countries provide trade facilities to Indian farmers to obtain maximum income for their produce through world trade. Favourable trade with and not compassionate grant to the farmer and agriculture of developing countries from developed countries would make agriculture prosperous and the Indian small and marginal farmer happy and contended in his profession aid hence make Indian agriculture a sustainable sector for the benefit and alround growth of India.

Notes and References

1. Government of India: Economic Survey, 2006-07, pp. 1 to 3 and 159 and 171.
2. Govt. of Andhra Pradesh, Budget Speech of Minister for Finance, 2006-07, p. 9.
3. Kuldip Nayar, "Incredible India Loses Gandhi" in *Deccan Chronicle,* Monday, 5 February, 2007, p. 4 (Nellore Edition).
4. Review by the Trade Policy Review Body (TPRB) of World Trade Organisation, May 23-25, 2007. Discussion by Moana Bhagabati in *The Hindu,* June 24, 2007. p. 15 (A.P. Edition, Chennai).
5. See Confederation of Indian Industry (2005), "The Rising Elephant: Benefits of Modern Trade to Indian Economy", pp. 5-21.
6. See *Economic and Political Weekly,* June 16, 2007, pp. 2231-32.
7. See Ramesh Thakur, "Globalisation and Trade for Development" in *The Hindu,* dated January 12, 2007, p. 10 (A.P. Chennai edition).
8. *The Hindu,* dated June 7, 2007, Business, p. 17 (A.P. Edition, Chennai).
9. TPRB of WTO, *op. cit.,* p. 15.

19

Relevance of Gandhian Economic Thoughts in 21st Century

M.M. Goel

The adoption of October 2—the birthday of Mahatma Gandhi by the United Nations on June 15, 2007 as the "International Non-violence Day" for the whole world has certainly justified the relevance of the Gandhian economic thoughts in all times to come.

Although, there are more writers on the Gandhian Philosophy than there are readers, Gandhian values have faded but most recently Gandhigiri of different kinds has appeared in bollywood in feature film "Laga Raho Munna Bhai."

With "Lokasangraha" (spiritualize society for the well-being of everybody) of the Bhagavadgita—a major focus of the Mahatma's teachings—as its "Guiding Light", we are convinced that everybody from India should turn the "International Non-violence Day" into a grand celebration of Gandhi Jayanti all over the world. However, it is also the time to recognize that India has apparently moved away too far from the teachings of Mahatma Gandhi. By forsaking the principle of "Trusteeship" in Gandhian economics, greed has been accepted as the driving force in Indian economics today. Mahatma Gandhi's emphasis on simple but free life, symbolised by Khadi and Charkha, is now-a-days openly ridiculed by top intellectuals like Nobel Laureate Dr. Amartya Sen. To justify his anti-Gandhi propaganda, Dr. Amartya Sen smears the Mahatma in his 2005 book, "The Argumentative Indian" (page 7) with terms like "not entirely with propriety or elegance" which are more piercing than Nathuram's bullets.

Young people who want to follow the "The Path to Peace" will be very confused by Dr. Amartya Sen's anti-Gandhi propaganda. In fact, the Internet today is full of anti-Gandhi propaganda based on lies and illogical analysis. No amount of dance-drama will persuade people to understand the Mahatma unless the anti-Gandhi lies and illogical analysis are refuted.

In my humble opinion, Gandhiji is immortal and being followed by South African Indians more than Indian in India as they have removed caste system and dowry, a unique reality of its own kind which will be confirmed orally by a delegation of South African Indians visiting India in September 2007 at the instance of Antarjyoti to which I am personally associated as its Vice-President.

In the present socio-economic scenario, it is most appropriate and desirable to investigate and market the economic thoughts of Mahatma Gandhi. There are certainly some lessons to be followed from the father of the nation for 21st century, which are under investigation in this paper.

Mahatma Gandhi is the greatest people's economist as observed by Dr. E.F. Schumacher, was not a professional economist and had not developed a formal model of economic growth. Gandhi was a practical man, a fighter and reformer, and saw intuitively and instinctively. Engaged in the freedom struggle of India, he had no time or inclination to engage in the elaboration of utopian lines of thought. All the same, in an endless stream of articles and speeches, all designed to deal with actual problems and situations he did produce arguments in the language of the people.

The basic principles of the Gandhian economic programme are six:

1. Avoidance of mechanisation and encouragement of cottage industries, especially spinning and weaving.
2. Improvement of rural small scale agriculture.
3. Making the village community as much self-sufficient and self-reliant as practicable.
4. Decentralisation of the administrative and economic structure.
5. Reducing income in equalities by raising the income level among the poor and by changing the attitude and motivation of the rich.
6. Ensuring that the capitalists and big businessmen serve as 'trustees' for the whole community.

Three remedies for the maladies of the modern society, namely, smallness, simplicity and non-violence. In the language of contemporary social science (economics) Gandhi was a pioneer analyst of the phenomenon of growth with increasing poverty. Gandhi correctly diagnosed the phenomenon as the result of an inappropriate technological mix of investments in a situation of quasi-insufficient investible resources. The Gandhian solution (which involves the maximum feasible stress on the traditional labour-intensive techniques and efforts to improve the technology and organisation of the traditional sector 'the kernel of Gandhian economic thought') being explained here in detail and interpreted in the context of modern planning theory. We need to note that how Gandhian framework can be filled into a theory of investment allocations in a framework of development planning. The Gandhian logic of investment planning compares very favourably with conventional (capitalist and socialist) formulations of the problem. In particular attention is drawn to the following features:

1. Gandhi poses the planning choice as between more employment and more accumulation in the current period. This avoids the unrealistic attempts of conventional development economics to pose the problem as a choice between present and future levels of per capita consumption (capitalist

subjective value version) or a choice between present output and future output (socialist version). Such attempts are unrealistic because we can never know with certainty what conventional economics treats as already known.

2. A second point of analytical superiority is that the problem of making adequate provision for the future is posed on an objective basis; in the form of the condition that the rate of capital accumulation must exceed or equal the rate of growth of the labour force. This clarifies that the concept of 'adequate provision for the future' is one of a lower-limit constraint, and not a matter of time preference either of the planner or of the consumers and savers. This develops the correct context for discussing the problem and puts an end to the interminable wrangling about what constitutes the 'proper' rate of time preference—a question to which there can in principle be no answer.
3. By posing the employment target both concretely and objectively as a certain minimum increase to be attained in the current period; it brings employment planning to a relevant and practical level. Employment policy is something which needs to achieve a determinable result, now, in terms of helping the poor. It is not something that relates to a vague goal of full employment (with an unspecified technology) in the unspecified future.
4. By posing the planner's decision problem as an exercise in satisfying choice, it rejects the conventional superstition that the planner has the duty of determining a social intertemporal optimum. The framework of satisfying choice indicates a feasible and reasonable task for the planner: to ensure that society does not bias its decisions too for in the direction of neglecting either the future or the present. Further, objective criteria against both types of errors are provided.

5. Finally, the approach directs attention to the importance of 'balance' in investment allocations and develops it into a trenchant critique of the ideology of rapid growth via investment imbalance. At the same time it provides a corrective to the danger of encouraging labour-intensive industries and activities to non-viable extremes.

These important gains in analytical clarity about the logic of investment planning also result in developing a total rather than partial approach to the problem of encouraging labour-intensive activities.

The Gandhian approach makes it absolutely clear what barriers stand in our way when we attempt to increase the labour-intensity of the investment mix. The barriers involved are three fold:

(a) Low reinvestment rates per unit of capital invested in the labour-intensive sector.
(b) The problem of capital goods and intermediate goods shortages.
(c) The problem of deviation from a 'balanced' set of allocations.

The low rate of reinvestment in the labour-intensive activities can be increased by three types of changes. First, the rates of reinvestment actually prevailing in the labour-intensive sector can be improved by: (a) better arrangement for marketing of its products, (b) better organized and less exploitative modes of credit and input supply, and (c) building into the credit and marketing cycle institutionalised processes of 'retention and reinvestment' of savings. These are infect the critical functions which Gandhiji set as the prime targets for the associations of constructive workers he formed to revitalize village industry.

The second way the reinvestment rate of the labour-intensive sector can be improved is by the widespread introduction of 'small' improvements in traditional techniques. Such innovations, while they raise the capital-intensity of labour-intensive traditional techniques only marginally, can have unexpectedly strong impact in raising the rate of reinvestible surplus in such technologies. This kind of effort was also recognized by Gandhiji as one of the important forms of constructive work.

As far as the problem of capital and intermediate goods shortages were concerned, Gandhi's conception was to apply a version of what would now be called as 'basic goods' strategy of development. A 'basic good' is defined as a good which enters into the consumption of workers or a good (capital or intermediate) which enters into the production of such goods. Gandhi's version of the basic good strategy was the following:

(a) Capital-intensive methods of consumption goods production will be discouraged (and to the extent possible eliminated).
(b) The labour-intensive sector entrusted with producing the consumption goods needed by workers.
(c) Modern (capital-intensive) industry should be limited to the production of intermediates and capital goods needed by the growing sector of labour-intensive industries.

Finally, the pattern of 'balanced' allocations was expected to be solved in the following way: Rural industry and rural agriculture was to be balanced within groups of small communities involving the maximum mutual balance between (a) local 'needs' and local 'resources', and (b) local 'output' and local 'consumption'. The balancing between rural industry/rural agriculture and urban industry was to be achieved in terms of the basic goods strategy. Through the modus of state ownership/planning of most large scale plants, a minority of privately-owned large scale units being subjected to a Gandhian form of social control known as 'trusteeship'. Thus, around the 'kernel idea' is organized the structure of Gandhian theory of elimination of mass poverty in the backward nations.

The root cause of the chaos that is facing us today is

the current economic growth of a handful of successful investors in complete disregard of millions of common people represented by the 500,000 villages. The successful investors are developing a terrible mental attitude that common people just create over-population, that the common people are incompetent, foolish and ordinary. To my mind, we need to debate and discuss the following: "*What is the value of their soul? Do they have any money? What is the value of their self-respect? What is the value of their skill? Do they have any money? What is the value of their pride?*"

Mahatma Gandhi's main concern was the common people of India. They plough their own land and produce food. Under British rule, at some point in time, they were not allowed to cultivate crop of their own choice, and Gandhi fought for their cause in Champaran. The common people could not compete with the modern spinning and weaving tools invented in England, and all their cloth were forced to be imported from England, aggravating terrible poverty in India. Following Tilak's idea of Swadeshi goods, Gandhi asked people to boycott foreign cloth, to spin with a Charkha and to wear homespun Khaddar, an action that closed down the cloth mills in England. Self-confidence soared high in India, and the mass people started to become ready for independence from foreign rule in an absolutely non-violent way. Charkha, the spinning wheel, became the symbol of a "non-violent weapon" in the struggle for India's independence.

It is the need of the day to draw lessons from the wise words of wisdom (www) the real world wide web of life long learning from Gandhian thoughts in general and Khadi in particular. Gandhi talked of Khadi for more than clothing—a way of life in swadashi strategy of survival, subsistence and self-sufficiency (an objective of a closed economy where there is no international trade) best suited to the needs of that time. But if Gandhi would have survived and seen the present times of post-reform era he would have certainly talked of Khadi for self-reliance, the present objective of Indian economy with international trade and of course, Khadi. In my well considered opinion, India can fit into the framework of World Trade Organisation (WTO) by converting Khadi and Village Industries Commission (KVIC) into a Multi-National Corporation (MNC) and possess the potential of solving the twin problems poverty and unemployment. Indian economy including Khadi have to be internationalised at all costs for fetching the fortunes under mantra of Globalisation. This certainly calls for extrication of purest thread of Khadi as perceived by Ms. Tara Gandhi, the grand daughter of the father of the nation.

In view of its increasing ideological, philosophical and environmental appeal, Khadi can be internationalised as a triumph of human beings over oil-guzzling machinery. What was a "freedom struggle against the British Rule" for Mahatma Gandhi will expand to a "freedom struggle of human beings against super-mechanisation" all over the world. The "charkha" once again will become the symbol of "non-violent weapon" to fight against the slavery of blind economic growth of endless greed that is crushing the downtrodden all over the world.

Endless greed is the real menace facing the world today. Low-life entertainers are exploiting the situation by creating "Who will become a Millionaire" shows in the TV in the western world. Indian TV mercenaries have shamelessly copied these exploits as "Kaun Banega Crorepati" to eulogize greed as an acceptable behaviour. Bhagavadgita identifies greed as one of the three doors to hell (verse 21, chapter 16) leading to the ruin of the soul.

It is unfortunate that leading economists of the world promote greed as the basis of economic growth, turning it into a "greedonomics." Economics should be based on need, not on greed. It should be a "needonomics", and not a "greedonomics." In the Kaun Benega Crorepati (KBC) programme telecasted in India by the Star Plus TV, the host talks the language of money devoid of any moral responsibility which will cause terrible behavioral pollution in the mind of the viewers. Such a language will convince the population that money is the greatest reality of life. The KBC Programme may engender terrible crimes of multi-dimensional nature.

The charisma of the great personality of Mahatma Gandhi who not only stood for non-violence and secularism but real ethics in economics. To me, true Gandhism symbolizes simplicity, equanimity and love for the suffering humanity for which Mahatma toiled in his lifetime.

Gandhi will continue to stay on for its mass appeal since it is the ultimate savior of the suffering humanity. The maladies of the modern society can be cured with the Mahatma's principle of smallness, simplicity, non-violence and production by the masses. "The earth can produce enough to satisfy everyone's need, but not everyone's greed is the immortal sermon of Gandhiji for economists of all generations to come. My only submission to our countrymen is, let's follow the great Mahatma's ideals in our life.

References

Das, Amritananda (1979), 'Foundations of Gandhian Economics', Allied Publications Private Ltd., Bombay.

Datta, Bhabatosh (1978), Indian Economic Thought, Tata McGraw-Hill Publishing Co. Ltd., New Delhi.

Goel, M.M. (2007), An Introduction of the Drama "The Portrait of Mahatma Gandhi" by Er. Himendra Thakur, Founder President Antarjyoti under publication.

Goel, M.M. (2002), Gandhian Model of Growth, *Economic Dateline,* Volume II, No. 4, April 2002.

Hoda, M.M. (1978), 'Future is Manageable', Schumacher's lectures (edited) Impex India, New Delhi.

Mathur, J.S. and Mathur, A.K. (1994), 'Economic Thought of Mahatma Gandhi' Arihant Publishing House, edited book in three volume, Jaipur.

Sen, Amrtiya (2005), The Argumentative Indian, published by Penguin Allen Lane.

20

Gandhian View of Sustainable Development: Some Issues

SACHINANDAN SAU

The Gandhian perspective of sustainable development is non-materialistic, non-violent, harmonistic, egalitarian and value-driven. These values highlight the virtue of simplicity, of social and inner peace, the sanctity, necessity and dignity of manual labour, and the valuation of the spiritual and the moral over the sensual and the material planes. The central unit is the eternal village and villagers who are deemed to be reservoirs of what is intrinsically valuable in society. Village-level self-sufficiency is an objective. Production for wider markets and market exchange processes are frowned upon. If material needs could be contained surpluses would not be necessary. Combining these dimensions of no exchange and no surplus, Gandhi argues that distribution can be equalised when production is localised, in other words, when distribution is simultaneous with production, and thus sustainable development occurs.

Village industries, especially Khadi, which are seen as employment-friendly, environment-friendly and hinterland-friendly, occupy an important place in such a scheme.

Swadeshi becomes an aggregation of the principle of self-reliance and self-sufficiency.

Several issues, however, concern Gandhian view of sustainable development. The first one is technical. The individual construction of a good and virtuous life can be transformed into a social one on the basis of the assumption of the homogeneity of perceptions of individuals about that life. Is there a scope of the diversity of these individual perceptions in the Gandhian 'model'? Given the diversity of perceptions of individuals about a good and virtuous life, it is to be accepted that there can be no linear transformation of the individual construction of the said life into a social one to form the macro (aggregate) concept of sustainable development.

The second one is institutional. That is, there is the problem of conversion of the wholesome Gandhian principles into a set of rules on which economic life could be rationally ordered, and which could be expected to overcome poverty and illiteracy.

Third, there is the issue of extreme inequality in the ownership of land and assets, or power structures, of caste oppression and social exclusion. The Gandhian answer to all these lay in the unrealistic principle of trusteeship with respect to property, or voluntary renunciation on the basis of self-realisation.

Fourth, the Gandhian view of sustainable development presents a static equilibrium based on the assumption of a changeless society free from all external influences or global environment.

Fifth, the Gandhian view of sustainable development (both quantitative and qualitative) mainly relies on the quality of man assuming that quality will necessarily change quantity. But quality may also be affected by quantity.

Lastly, neither growth nor development in the sense of change is well accommodated and established in the Gandhian model. Not only external but also intra-national or inter-regional exchange is precluded in this model of village sufficiency, and thus it ignores conditions for changes in the society. Thus sustainable development is bereft of development in the true sense of the term, though arguably the conditions may prove to be sustainable in a static framework.

I. INTRODUCTION

Sustainable development is the key word in the modern development literature. It has acquired an important dimension in the context of gradually depleting exhaustible resources which are limited and finite, destruction of forests, ecological imbalances, pollution of air and water, environmental disaster, spread of terrible diseases affecting plant and animal life and colossal waste (Singh, 1998: 168, Kedia, 1997: 244) and thus usually high costs of development which a rational society can not bear for long for its sustenance and development. There has been a recent surge of interest in sustainable development.

Against this brief backdrop it is pertinent to look into Gandhian view on sustainable development.

II. GANDHIAN VIEW OF SUSTAINABLE DEVELOPMENT

Gandhi is regarded as an apostle of humanism and of what is good and virtuous in man and he is among those eminent thinkers and philosophers who could foresee the social and ecological consequences of economic development. He noted that nature was being destroyed by unlimited industrialisation and massive urbanisation which were thought necessary for development. These processes were creating problems of ecological balance. He was highly critical of modern civilisation (Misra, 1997: 122).

To him, the so-called modern civilisation of the West was 'satanic' or representation of a 'black age' (*Hind Swaraj*). His indictment of western civilisation was based on his objection to the dehumanising aspect of modern civilisation (Unnithan, 1997: 217). He had profound concern for human development and human progress and out of this concern he articulated many thoughts on the subject (Haq, 1997: 86).

Instead of high speed production as an impact of modern industrialisation resulting in destruction of human dignity and individuality and making human-being a mere cog in the machine and contaminating environment with prisons of many kinds, thus inviting unforeseen natural disasters, humankind should, Gandhi said, decentralise and simplify production in such a way which will help promote human creativity and develop individual personality which alone can achieve harmony between man and his environment. The Gandhian model of development has potentialities for offering remarkable opportunities for social reconstruction for perennial social and human progress locally, nationally and globally (Unnithan, 1997:220). Unnithan observes, 'the Gandhian model of development ...will help the world to protect its environment and obtain sustainable development...'.

Sustainable development is a macro (aggregate) concept, which qualifies the sustained and perennial nature of development of the country, region or society. It is defined as one, which can be sustained over a long period of time keeping the value of assets of the society intact. It is held that Gandhiji's 'model' of non-violent development satisfies the requisites of sustainable development.

Some of the central planks of the Gandhian model of sustainable development are the following. The Gandhian perspective is non-materialistic, non-violent, harmonistic, egalitarian and value-driven. These values highlight the virtue of simplicity, of social and inner peace, the sanctity, necessity and dignity of manual labour, and the valuation of the spiritual and the moral over the sensual and the material planes. The central unit is the eternal village and villagers, who are deemed to be reservoirs of what is intrinsically valuable in society. Village-level self-sufficiency is an objective.

His development model addresses the issue of sustainable development, which requires resource management and control over the pace of development and the rate of resource consumption, and restraint over insatiable demands for goods and services. The Gandhian model is sensitive to this critical issue. In this model, the guiding principle is not maximisation of utility and economic gains but minimisation of wants. It only means control over the insatiable propensity to consume, great sensitivity to needs. In the Gandhian model, over-exploitation of resources, disruption of ecological balance and deterioration of the environment are forms of 'violence' inconsistent with the Gandhian model of development and progress. The principle of Non-violence rules out violence against nature and violence against man the same way (Misra, 1997:122). Gandhi was the advocate of sustainable development in the world and he was against the massive industrialisation (mechanisation) for the existing world precisely because of its undue exploitation. Gandhi was an absolutist (Leary, 1998:133). Satya or truth is derived from Sat which means being as 'abiding, actual, right, wise, self-existent essence, as anything really is, as anything ought to be'. As a Truth seeker, he could not ignore the desperate poverty of most of India's population (Leary, 1998:134-5). He saw all things in the light of good. He will strive for 'the greatest good of all'. 'It is the good of all that we are to promote'.

As long as the hunger, malnutrition, and exploitation of the poor continued in any part of the world there could be no economic stability, social justice and ecological sustainability (Awasthi, 1997:20). He was of the view that as long as the greed prevailed and the natural resources and the fruits of economic development were not shared equitably among the masses of the world, poverty and hunger would persist.

Man's continuous contact with nature as part of his daily life, Gandhi argued, prevented the pollution of air and water, destruction of animal and vegetable life and above all it pre-empted the large urban conglomerations which lead to all such problems (Sethi, 1978:212).

Gandhi was in search of individual as well as social development, particularly of the rural areas, which will be lasting. Sustainable development really refers to human development and not to economic development *per se*. The latter is the means, not the end; at best, it is a component, not the whole. Besides, it is participatory in nature, that is, it is achieved, not given. It is again based on equity and justice (Misra, 1997:112). Gandhian model of social development rests essentially on the values of Truth and Non-violence and the goal of Sarvodaya.

If development is accepted as human centred process of change it includes not only the economic aspects of human life but also the blossoming of the cultural, intellectual, spiritual and other non-material aspects of it. In Gandhiji's 'grand model' of human development and human progress, economic development and progress appears as an important sub-model (Haq, 1997:91).

Gandhi did not want to divorce Economics from Ethics (Gokhale, 1961:72). The philosophy of 'Savodaya, Non-violence and Truth' is the foundation of the Gandhian model of economic development. 'Sarvodaya' implies the welfare of all and welfare, in the Gandhian model, is a composite of material, moral and spiritual welfare. Gandhi was thinking of basic needs of man (Datta, 1997:66). In his model economic development which makes provision for basic needs like food, shelter, clothing and shelter is a means to achieve the moral and spiritual development of man. The primary micro-unit of development in the Gandhian model is the individual. Development of the individual—economically, morally and spiritually—is the essence of development from the Gandhian perspective. Sarvodaya, Non-violence, Non-Possession, Trusteeship, Swadeshi, Bread labour and Decentralisation—all these Gandhian doctrines are designed to mould the process of growth of the individual, and the growth of the village economy. Trusteeship means all money and property belongs to society and those who are possessing it are only the trustees of the society whose duty is to increase the earning and value of the trust property. He should charge only that much from the trust property as is absolutely essential for his subsistence and honourable living. Excess of one's income over and above one's living is a social surplus to be employed for the benefit of the society.

Gandhi believed that the economic good of all lay in adopting the principle of swadeshi or self-sufficiency. His belief that India lived in villages led him to propound the concept of village swaraj which, among others, envisaged village sufficiency. In extreme form, village sufficiency not merely meant non-dependence of the village on other villages for its needs but also meant self-sufficiency among households. This meant that each household would produce its own requirements – food, clothing and other things – and never depend on others for its economic needs (Maharajan, 1997: 19).

Village self-sufficiency serves as a basis of economic development. To him, the concept of village sufficiency implies that production and consumption should be as proximate as possible, and based on the proper use of local resources. He emphasised time and again that 'the first concern of every village will be to grow its own food-crop and clothes' (Jain, 1988:311).

Rural industrialisation forms a central plank in the Gandhian model of non-violent development, which is itself drawn from a holistic prescription for the social and individual construction of the good and virtuous life (Saith, 2001:88).

Village and cottage industries support the villages, self-sufficiency and improvement in the level of living. Gandhi repeatedly expressed the view that such industries should be in the hands of the masses (Desai, 1989:15). Decentralisation of production would lead to decentralisation of economic as well as political power. According to Gandhi decentralisation is one of the means to create classless, unexploited and egalitarian society. The word decentralised sector in economics is used to refer to the cottage industries located in the rural areas (Maharajan, 1997: 62).

He opposed to modern industry because it tends to create unequal distribution of money and exploitation of the persons who worked for their masters, and it would create unemployment in a very populated country. He welcomed tools and instruments, which lightened the burden of the millions of cottages, such factories should not work for profit but for the benefit of humanity, love taking the place of greed as motive. More than any other evil, it brought about displacement of labour and it was followed by social evils. On the contrary to it, decentralisation of production in the form of cottage industries in the village, was linked with the decentralisation of political power that was basic to Gandhi's ideal of non-violent society. A non-violent society could be organised where inequalities and tensions were removed by a just distribution of things and money (Sharma, 1997:97). Gandhiji's saying that "the earth provides enough for every man's need but not for every man's greed" has proved to be true in the fast growing consumeristic culture throughout the world. Corruption goes with consumerism.

Village industries, especially Khadi, which are seen as employment-friendly, environment–friendly and hinterland-friendly, occupy an important place in such a scheme. Large-scale mechanised production methods producing for distant markets, an extensive division of labour, modern industrialisation, are all viewed as conflicting with the essential Gandhian perspective. Swadeshi becomes an aggregation of the principle of self-reliance and self-sufficiency. All basic needs deserve to be satisfied (Datta, 1997: 67).

Gandhiji's Khadi stands for humanity. His Khadi was based on philanthropic ideals, rather than pure economics in modern terms. He introduced it to find work and wages for millions of villagers who were fast losing the will to work to think and even to live. It gave them hope, money to live and removed their blank despair of long past years. Khadi economics is based on patriotism, purity, sacrifice, non-violence, justice, and love for the poor, truth, purity of soul and body and humanity (Sharma, 1997:148). There is a provision for ecological balance—a balance between resource consumption and conservation in an appropriate pattern of development of small-scale rural industries.

Gandhi clearly comprehended that production alone does not ensure its proper distribution. To this effect the production model would have to be so structured or organised as to absorb all the working people. His famous statement "not (only) mass production but production by the mass" also shows the concern for just distribution (Singh, 1997:193).

To him, the concept of 'village self-sufficiency' implies that production and consumption should be as proximate as possible, and based on the proper use of local resources.

III. ISSUES CONCERNING GANDHIAN VIEW OF SUSTAINABLE DEVELOPMENT

Several issues, however, concern the Gandhian view of sustainable development through rural industrialisation. The first one is technical. As noted earlier, his model of non-violent development is drawn from a holistic prescription for the individual and social construction of the good and virtuous life. How can this social construction be made? The individual construction of a good and virtuous life can be transformed into a social one on the basis of the assumption of the homogeneity of perceptions of individuals about that life. Is there a scope of the diversity of these individual perceptions in the Gandhian 'model'? Given the diversity of perceptions of individuals about a good and virtuous life, it is to be accepted that there can be no linear transformation of the individual construction of the said life into a social one to form the macro (aggregate) concept of sustainable development. It may be mentioned, given the Paretian framework, the derivation of the social welfare function based on individual freedom and preferences is impossible, which is referred to in welfare economics as Arrow's Impossibility.

The *second* one is institutional. That is, there is the problem of conversion of the wholesome Gandhian principles into a set of rules on which economic life could be rationally ordered, and which could be expected to overcome the poverty and illiteracy in which Gandhi's supremely wise and cultured villager was mired (Saith, 2001:90).

Third, there is the issue of extreme inequality in the ownership of land and assets, or power structures, of caste oppression and social exclusion. The Gandhian answer to all these lay in the equally unrealistic principle of trusteeship with respect to property, or voluntary renunciation on the basis of self-realisation. Trusteeship means that surplus wealth and income must be distributed to those who do not have enough to satisfy their needs. It is apparent that this Gandhian approach is romantic and idiosyncratic, which relies on the preservation, revival or reconstruction of pre-industrial egalitarian systems. (Saith, 2001:89). Gandhi was also aware that trusteeship is difficult to reach and so is non-violence difficult to attain.

Fourth, the Gandhian view of sustainable development through rural industrialisation presents a static equilibrium based on the assumption of a changeless society free from all external influences or global environment, which appears to be highly unrealistic (within the then imperialistic framework of India) and also unscientific (precluding the scope of interaction).

Fifth, sustainable development and rural industrialisation defined as processes of some quantitative as well as qualitative transformation involves an interaction of both quantitative and qualitative variables. But the Gandhian perspective mainly relies on the quality of man assuming that quality will necessarily change quantity. But quantity may also be affected by quantity, namely wages paid and conditions of work and structure of employment may affect volume of work and output, and the process of determination of quantitative values has not been fully worked out in the Gandhian model of rural industrialisation and sustainable development and thus his model is not complete.

Sixth, rural industrialisation carried on a small scale using local resources and labour-intensive technology is seen as a virtuous process while modern industrialisation a vice on the ground that it leads to exploitation of nature and workers. But rural entrepreneurs whether small or petty may also be seen to exploit labour and pollute environment because all small is not pretty or beautiful (Banerjee, 1981: 277-295, Saith, 2001:88-98).

Lastly, on conceptual basis, it may be argued that neither growth (in the sense of increase in quantitative variables like per capita output and income) nor development (in the sense of quantitative growth as well as change in the structure of the economy or society) is well accommodated and established in the Gandhian model. From the supply side it may be argued that surplus or profit as well as saving which is necessary for investment in rural industries and thus for their development is not accepted as a virtue in Gandhi's model. From the demand side it is seen that low production and low consumption are projected in this model as a good and virtuous quality of life, which may, however, lead to a vicious circle of low demand, low production and low employment. Then how would the massive problems of unemployment and poverty among the rural people, particularly the rural artisans be solved? Moreover, not only external[1] but also intra-national or inter-regional exchange[2] is precluded in this model of village sufficiency, and thus it ignores conditions for positive and optimal growth and structural changes of the local or regional or national economy. Thus sustainable development is bereft of development[3] in the true sense of the term, though arguably the conditions prescribed by Gandhi may prove to be sustainable in a static framework. Gandhi, it may be noted, was not a professional economist in the true sense of the term (Maharajan, 1997: 61).

IV. SUMMARY AND CONCLUSIONS

The Gandhian perspective of sustainable development is non-materialistic, non-violent, harmonistic, egalitarian and value-driven. The central unit is the eternal village and villagers, who are deemed to be reservoirs of what is intrinsically valuable in society. Village-level self-sufficiency is an objective. Production for wider markets and market exchange processes are frowned upon. If material needs could be contained surpluses would not be necessary. Combining these dimensions of no exchange and no surplus, Gandhi argues that distribution can be equalised when production is localised, in other words, when distribution is simultaneous with production. Village industries, especially Khadi, which are seen as employment-friendly, environment-friendly and hinterland-friendly, occupy an important place in such a scheme. Swadeshi becomes an aggregation of the principle of self-reliance and self-sufficiency.

Several issues, however, concern the Gandhian perspective of sustainable development. *First*, the individual construction of a good and virtuous life can be transformed into a social one on the basis of the assumption of the homogeneity of perceptions of individuals about that life. Given the diversity of perceptions of individuals about a good and virtuous life, it is to be accepted that there can be no linear transformation of the individual construction of the said life into a social one to form the macro (aggregate) concept of sustainable development. *Second,* there is the problem of conversion of the wholesome Gandhian principles into a set of rules on which economic life could be rationally ordered, and which could be expected to overcome the poverty and illiteracy. *Third,* there is the issue of extreme inequality in the ownership of land and assets, or power structures, of caste oppression and social exclusion. The Gandhian answer to all these lay in the equally unrealistic principle of trusteeship with respect to property, or voluntary renunciation on the basis of self-realisation. *Fourth,* the Gandhian perspective of sustainable development presents a static equilibrium based on the assumption of a changeless society free from all external influences or global environment, which appears to be highly unrealistic (within the then imperialistic framework of India) and also unscientific (precluding the scope of interaction). *Fifth,* sustainable development is defined as processes of some quantitative as well as qualitative transformation involves an interaction of both quantitative and qualitative variables. But the Gandhian view mainly relies on the quality of man assuming that quality will necessarily change quantity. But quality may also be affected by quantity. *Lastly,* on conceptual basis, it may be argued that neither growth (in the sense of increase in quantitative variables like per capita output and income) nor development (in the sense of both quantitative and qualitative change) is well accommodated and established in the Gandhian model. Not only external but also intra-national or inter-regional exchange is precluded in this model of village sufficiency, and thus it ignores conditions for changes in the society. Thus, sustainable development is bereft of development in the true sense of the term, though arguably the conditions may prove to be sustainable in a static framework.

Notes and References

1. Datta (1997) observes, the Gandhian model is, to a large extent, both anti-market and anti-state. The model is anti-market in sc far as it recommends production to be organised, as far as practicable, with

locally available labour and resources for the satisfaction of local needs. Maharajan (1998; 27) also observes, 'it is doubtful whether Gandhi ever envisaged a growth path which made use of foreign trade either as an engine or as an instrument of employment promotion. He was a staunch follower of the principle of Swadeshi, which shunned even inter-village trade not to speak of international trade. As a matter of fact Gandhi was against foreign trade not because he hated foreign political domination but because he thought that foreign trade was responsible for the decline of the flourishing cottage and small-scale industries'.

2. The pattern of investment preferred by Gandhi was such that it not merely produced essential consumer goods but also attained simultaneity in production and distribution. The latter condition was achievable only where the production and consumption centers were not divorced from each other. In other words, in Gandhi's system each household produced its own requirements with simple tools and implements and never, perhaps, thought of exchange as that would bring in possibilities of exploitation (Maharajan, 1998; 27).
3. Leary (1998: 128) observes, 'Gandhi had no economic theory nor did he concern himself with economic development though many of his specific proposals can be found in contemporary theory'.

References

Awasti, R.K. (1997), 'Environmental Challenges and Gandhi's Vision', in Singh, R. (ed.), *Gandhi and the Future of Humanity*, Gandhian Institute of Studies, Rajghat.

Banerjee, N. (1981), 'Is Small Beautiful?' in Bagchi, A.K. and Banerjee, N. (eds), *Change and Choice in Indian Industry*, Centre for Studies in Social Sciences and K.P. Bagchi and Co., Kolkata.

Datta, A. (1997), 'Radical Decentralisation', in Singh, R. (ed.) *op. cit.*

Dantawala, M.L. (1978), 'Some Issues of Employment Planning', *Economic and Political Weekly.*

Desai, M. (1989), In (Introduction to) *Hind Swaraj*: by Gandhi, Sarva Seva Sangh Prakashan, Rajghat, Baranasi, p. 57.

Jain, L.C. (1988), 'Poverty, Environment and Development', *Economic and Political Weekly*, 13 February, p. 321.

Gandhi, M.K., *Harijan*, 23 March 1947, p. 79.

——, *Collected Works.*

Gokhale, B.G. (1961), *Indian Thought Throughout the Ages*, Asia Publishing House, Bombay.

Haq, A.M. (1998), 'Welfare Criteria in Gandhian Economics', in Mukherjee, S. and Ramaswamy, S. (eds.), *Economic and Social Principles of Mahatma Gandhi*, Deep & Deep Publications, New Delhi.

Kedia, K. (1997), 'The Development Model and the Challenge of Development', in Singh, R. (ed), *op. cit.*

Leary, B.O. (1998), 'An Approach to Gandhian Economics' in Mukherjee, S. and Ramaswamy, S. (eds.), *op. cit.*

Misra, R.P. (1997), 'Development without Destruction: The Gandhian Alternative', S. and Ramaswamy, S. (eds.), *op. cit.*

Misra, R.P. (1997), 'Development without Destruction: The Gandhian Alternative', in Singh, R. (ed.), *op.cit.*

Maharajan, M. (1998), *Economic Thought of Mahatma Gandhi,* Discovery Publishing House, New Delhi.

Saith, A. (2001), 'From Village Artisans to Industrial Clusters: Agendas and Policy Gaps in Indian Rural Industrialisation', *Journal of Agrarian Change*, Vol. 1, Jannuary 2001, pp. 81-123.

Sethi, J.D. (1978), *Gandhi Today*, Vikas Publishing House, New Delhi.

Sharma, K.D. (1997), *Impact of Gandhiji on Rural Development and Social Change*, Mohit Publications, New Delhi.

Singh, R.P. (1997), 'Trickle Down Theory *vs.* Gandhiji's Village Self-sufficiency', in Singh, R. (ed), *op. cit.*, pp. 193-94.

Unnithan, T.K.N. (1997), 'A Gandhian Approach to Environmental, Human Ecological and Developmental Challenges', in Singh, R. (ed), *op. cit.*

21

Modern Relevance of the Gandhian Concept of Swadeshi

RATAN LAL BASU

Globalisation in the form of large-scale industrialisation based on indiscriminate import of foreign capital and technology has taken demonic turn and endangered the economic, environmental and social stability of the less developed countries like India. Under such circumstances the Gandhian concept of Swedeshi has once again come to the fore as devising the correct path of industrialisation catering to the well-being of the masses and generating adequate employment opportunities. In course of planning in India, stress was laid, especially since the Second Five Year Plan, on development of large scale basic and capital goods industries on the basis of Mahalanobis Strategy of industrialisation. Then in the early nineties, India adopted the policy of liberalisation, globalisation and privatisation, opening the doors for import of foreign capital and technology. But the adverse impact of this new economic policy on economic conditions of the majority of the population and on ecology and environment could be felt only a decade after the adoption of the new policy. The large-

industry-biased policies resulted in continuous degeneration of the small and tiny sectors making the unemployment problem grave. Now there has arisen the problem of large scale exodus of the peasants as a consequence of acquisition of agricultural lands for establishment of large scale industries. In brief, industrialisation process in India at present has revealed all its demonic features. Now the matter has drawn attention of the thoughtful persons and the question has arisen if it is possible to endow a human face to the process of industrialisation under the new scenario of globalisation. In this context the Gandhian concept of Swadeshi has once again come to the fore. Underlying the concept of Swadeshi is the spirit of industrial development based on the efforts of the masses and locally available technology and catering to the needs of the majority without at the same time obstructing the establishment of modern industries and import of sophisticated foreign technology wherever they are really essential. The concept of Swadeshi also indirectly takes into account the question of preserving environment and ecology.

SECTION I

INTRODUCTION

One of the central points of Gandhian economic thought was the concept of Swadeshi. After independence, the Nehru group eschewed the Gandhian Path and accepted the Stalinist Path of Industrialisation in modified form and thus the concept of Swadeshi went completely into oblivion. In course of the worldwide awareness as regards the necessity of attaching 'Human Face' to the process of industrialisation, the concept of Swadeshi has once again come to the fore. In course of planning in India, stress was laid, especially since the Second Five Year Plan, on development of large scale basic and capital goods industries on the basis of Mahalanobis Strategy of industrialisation. This was akin to the Socialistic (Stalinist?) pattern of industrialisation. As a result, in course of only a few decades, India could achieve a mention worthy large scale industrial sector. But this sector did not play any trickle down effect to remove the problems of unemployment and poverty.

However, the existence of the state sector could provide some safety net. Then in the early nineties, India adopted the policy of liberalisation, globalisation and privatisation. Doors of import of foreign capital and technology were opened. But the adverse impact of this new economic policy on economic conditions of the majority of the population and on ecology and environment could be felt only a decade after the adoption of the new policy. Worse was the case of the employment situation. Supply of labour force went on increasing because of high rate of growth of population, but the rate of job creation in the organized sector started falling. Agricultural sector has already been over-burdened with the pressure of population, and because of the large-industry-biased policies, there has been continuous degeneration of the small and tiny sectors and thus rate of employment generation in the unorganized sector as a whole is also declining. All these have made the unemployment problem grave.

Now there has arisen the problem of large scale exodus of the peasants as a consequence of acquisition of agricultural lands for establishment of large scale industries. This is a very serious problem and has resulted in social tensions and peasant revolts, especially in West Bengal, where "industrialisation" as such, without considering its adverse impacts on employment, poverty and ecology, has become the basic political slogan of the ruling party. In brief, industrialisation process in India at present has revealed all its demonic features. Now the matter has drawn attention of the thoughtful persons and the question has arisen if it is possible to endow a human face to the process of industrialisation under the new scenario of globalisation. In this context the Gandhian concept of Swadeshi has once again come to the fore. It is true that objective conditions, since Gandhiji devised the concept, have changed significantly. Still the concept in its essence may play an important role in resolving the trade-off between industrialisation and welfare of the majority. Underlying the concept of Swadeshi is the spirit of industrial development based on the efforts of the masses and locally available technology and catering to the needs of the majority without at the same time obstructing the establishment of modern industries and import of sophisticated foreign technology wherever they are really essential. The concept of Swadeshi also indirectly takes into account the question of preserving environment and ecology. To go into these matters in detail and to consider their relevance for the present day problems, we are to define first the concept of Swadeshi as conceived by Mahatma Gandhi. So the rest of the paper is organized in the following manner.

Section 2: Definition of Swadeshi; Section 3: Economic and Ethical Aspects; Section 4: Swadeshi and Large Scale Industries; Section 5: Swadeshi and Foreign Trade; Section 6: Modern relevance.

SECTION II

DEFINITION OF SWADESHI

The common definition of Swadeshi as came out of the works of Gandhiji is use of all home-made products to the exclusion of foreign products which are not beneficial to the people of the country and harmful on the contrary.

To quote: "The broad definition of Swadeshi is the use of all home-made things to the exclusion of foreign things, in so far as such use is necessary for protection of home-industry, more especially those industries without which India will become pauperized. In my opinion, therefore, Swadeshi which excludes the use of everything foreign, because it is foreign, no matter how beneficial it may be, and irrespective of the fact that it impoverishes nobody, is a narrow interpretation of Swadeshi."[1]

Swadeshi, defined in this manner, has far reaching significance as regards removal of poverty and unemployment, upgrading the skills of the masses, encouraging their creative powers, inculcating the spirit of self help and self confidence in them regarding their own powers (without approaching the authorities, begging bowls in hand) to change their own fate and also supply of mass consumption goods. Swadeshi, if practiced properly, would prevent wastage of resources available within the country and frittering away of these resources to the production of goods catering to the needs of the foreigners or luxury needs of the well to do minority within the country at the cost of production of mass consumption goods. Gandhiji rightly emphasized that departure from Swadeshi and blind rush for foreign goods and technology was the basic cause of mass poverty in India.

To quote: "Much of the deep poverty of the masses is due to the ruinous departure from Swadeshi in the economic and industrial life."[2]

Gandhiji suggests that there are still innumerable rural industries, which are capable of catering to the needs of the masses and at the same time creating significant employment opportunities. These industries are at present unable to play their roles properly because of the lack of assistance in terms of organisation, training, supply of quality raw materials, technology up-gradation, etc. and above all, competition from the large industries and imported foreign goods boosted up by the pro-rich policy of the government. To quote: "In that of economics, I should use only things that are produced by my immediate neighbours and serve those industries by making them efficient and complete where they might be found wanting. It is suggested that such Swadeshi, if reduced to practice, will lead to the millennium, because we do not expect quite to reach it within our times, so may we not abandon Swadeshi even though it may not be fully attained for generations to come."[3] "If we follow the Swadeshi doctrine, it would be your duty and mine to find out neighbours who can supply our wants and to teach them to supply them where they do not know how to proceed, assuming that there are neighbours who are in want of healthy occupation."[4]

Gandhiji had already realised that agriculture was under much pressure and considering the number of peasants *vis-à-vis* total available cultivable land, agriculture alone could hardly provide sustenance to the innumerable poor peasants. Here cottage industries are likely to play the role of subsidiary occupation to the small cultivators. To quote: "So, when we find that there are many things that we cannot get in India, we must try to do without them."[5] "Swadeshi, therefore, is the problem of inducing and enabling the farmers to take up the supplementary industry of spinning and weaving."[6]

"Without a cottage industry, the Indian peasant is doomed. He cannot maintain himself from the produce of the land. He needs a supplementary industry. Spinning is the easiest, the cheapest and the best."[7]

"Swadeshi, therefore is a question of finding a subsidiary industry for our farmers."[8] Swadeshi in the form of revival of the cottage and rural industries also has an indirect beneficial effect, besides employment and income generation and supply of mass consumption goods. Works in cottage industries require inculcation of individual skill and therefore small and cottage industries improve mental faculty of the artisans. On the other hand, mechanistic jobs with machines in large scale industries stultify mental and creative faculties of the wage labourers. Development of mental faculties of the masses through the rural industries would enable them to be organized on the basis of self-help, fellow-feeling, self-confidence and self-respect.

To quote: "I swear by Swadeshi as it affords occasion for an ample exercise of all our faculties, and as it tests every one of the millions of men and women, young and old. It can succeed only if India acts as one mind. And if India can do so in Swadeshi, she will have learnt the secret of Swaraj. She will then have mastered the art of destruction and construction in a scientific manner."[9]

Because of age-old suffering and deprivation, rural masses are languishing in the darkness of resignation and fatalism. So it is the duty of the educated and cultured people to instill the spirit of confidence among the masses by themselves directly participating in the practice of Swadeshi. To quote: "We will have experts and chemists who will be prepared to place their knowledge at the disposal of the villagers. We will, through our experts, offer to test the articles manufactured by village handicraftsmen and make them suggestions to improve their wares."[10]

"In other words, we should evoke the artistic talent of the villagers."[11] "It provides limitless work for the creative genius in the country."[12]

"The condition of success is that cultured men and women take up spinning and weaving. The people will follow their example."[13]

Gandhiji opines that the spirit of neither nationalism nor internationalism could be inculcated unless 'charity begins at home', i.e. unless one begins from concern and fellow feeling for the immediate neighbours. This spirit of fellow feeling and service mentality for the neighbours would gradually rise upwards to generate a true feeling of nationalism and internationalism. Talks of internationalism without any concern for the neighbours are sheer falsehood and hypocrisy.

To quote: "If this interpretation of Swadeshi be correct, then it follows that its votary will, as a first duty, dedicate himself to the service of his immediate neighbours. This involves exclusion or even sacrifice of the interests of the rest, but the exclusion or the sacrifice would be only in appearance. Pure service of our neighbours can never, from its very nature, result in disservice to those who are far away, but rather the contrary."[14]

"Therefore, one who serves his neighbour serves all the world."[15] To start with Gandhiji's Swadeshi had its central point Khadi, i.e. cotton textiles of the craft industries. The reason is very simple. The industry which had the widest coverage, in terms of both demand and supply, was Khadi. So Gandhiji attached highest priority to this age-old industry. At the same time he did not fail to emphasize that besides Khadi, other traditional rural industries should also be revived. To quote: "But Khadi is not the only such struggling industry. I, therefore, suggest to you to direct your attention and effort to all the small-scale, minor, unorganized industries that are today in need of public support. They may be wiped out if no effort is made in their behalf. Some of these are being pushed back by large-scale industries which flood the markets with their manufactures. It is these that cry for help."[16]

"We must promote every useful industry that was existent a short while ago, and the extinction of which has now resulted in unemployment."[17] "Our clear duty is, therefore, to investigate the possibility of keeping in existence the village wheel, the village crusher and the village pounder, and, by advertising their products, discovering their qualities, ascertaining the condition of the workers and the number displaced by the power-driven machinery and discovering the methods of improving them, whilst retaining their village character, to enable them to stand the competition of the mills."[18]

"There are numberless other village, and even town, crafts that need public support, if they are to live and thus maintain the thousands of poor artisans depending upon them for their daily bread." [19] Gandhiji had observed with concern that the plans and economic policies of the government were directed at extracting resources from the rural sector to cater to the needs of the foreign industries and well-to-do minority in the cities. He strongly suggested that this process should be discontinued forthwith and Swadeshi is the best means to do so.

To quote: "whereas, at the present moment, we are exploiting the villagers without making any return worth the name."[20]

"This is much more impossible than the one of reviving the village industries and stopping the progressive poverty, which is due as much to enforced unemployment as to any other cause."[21]

"But I heartly endorse the proposition that any plan, which exploits the raw materials of country and neglects the potentially more powerful man-power, is lopsided and can never tend to establish human equality."[22]

"Therefore, real planning consists in the best utilisation of the whole man-power of India, and the distribution of the raw products of India in her numerous villages instead of sending them outside and rebuying finished articles at fabulous prices."[23]

Section III

ECONOMIC AND ETHICAL ASPECTS

Gandhiji's economic thought has the unique characteristics that it is inexorably associated with his ethical and religious norms and is a part of his living. Gandhiji strongly points out that conventional economics based on gratification of selfish ends is highly unethical and immoral and contrary to his own economic thinking based on philanthropy and ethics. Thus while defining Swadeshi Gandhiji does not fail to point out its religious and moral aspects.

To quote: "Swadeshi, as defined here, is a religious discipline to be undergone in utter disregard of the physical discomfort it may cause to individuals."[24] Claiming to serve foreigners in the name of internationalism is highly immoral according to Gandhiji.

To quote: "I cannot starve my neighbour and claim to serve my distant cousin in the North Pole. This is the basic principle of all religions, and we will find it is also of true and humane economics."[25]

Economics that encourages one country to exploit another is also unethical.

To quote: "Economics that hurt the moral well-being of an individual or a nation are immoral and, therefore, sinful. Thus, the economics that permit one country to prey upon another are immoral. It is sinful to buy and use articles made by sweated labour. It is sinful to eat American wheat and let my neighbour, the grain dealer, starve for want of custom."[26]

"That economics is untrue which ignores or disregards moral values."[27]

"The economics that disregard moral and sentimental considerations are like wax works, that, being life-like, still lack the life of the living flesh. At every crucial moment, these new-fangled economic laws have broken down in practice. And nations or individuals who accept them as guiding maxims must perish."[28]

Gandhiji also points out clearly that economic ideas developed under the objective conditions of one country may not be suitable for other countries with different set of objective conditions. Unfortunately economists and policy-makers of our country have failed to realize the essence of this view of Gandhiji even today. Gandhiji specifically mentions the case of free trade in this respect. Unrestricted free trade is beneficial for the developed countries but they are likely to have serious adverse consequences for the developing countries like India. Here lies the seed of economic thinking that flourished later in writings of Neo-Marxists like Raul Prebisch, Singer, etc.

To quote: "The economics of a nation are determined by its climate, geological and temperamental conditions. The Indian conditions are different from the English in all these essentials."[29]

Section IV

SWADESHI AND LARGE SCALE INDUSTRIES

Gandhiji goes into the pros and cons of the operation of the large scale industries and dispels the false belief that use of cloth produced by mills owned by Indians is also Swadeshi. Mills, whatever is the ownership, use mainly imported raw materials and thereby assist employment and income generation in exporter countries, not in India.

To quote: "Thousands of men believe that by using cloth woven in Indian mills, they comply with the requirements of the Swadeshi vow. The fact is that most fine cloth is made out of foreign cotton, spun outside India. Therefore, the only satisfaction to be derived from the use of such cloth is that it is woven in India."[30]

"Even on handlooms for very fine cloth only foreign yarn is used. The use of such cloth does not amount to an observance of Swadeshi. To say so, is simple self-deception."[31]

According to Gandhiji, mills are solely guided by profit motive and not the interest of the well-being of the masses. On the contrary they won't hesitate to exploit the masses if earning of profit warrants so.

To quote: "It is my firm belief that mills, by reason of the limitations under which they must work, will fail us in the end if we rely upon them. Then, they being concerns predominantly for making profits irrespective of national considerations, will not scruple to exploit the public and even to sell foreign cloth as Swadeshi."[32]

"The only thing they reluctantly contribute is to employ cheap labour of the country and make a gullible public believe that these are Swadeshi concerns."[33]

Large scale industries are based on mechanisation and indiscriminate development of such industries would have harmful effect on the Indian economy with a vast body of unemployed. Gandhiji explains how mills generate fewer jobs than they are likely to displace and thereby aggravate the unemployment situation.

To quote: "Mechanisation is good when the hands are too few for the work intended to be accomplished. It is an evil when there are more hands than required for the work, as is the case in India."[34]

Mill-made cloth may be cheaper and the difference of price between mill-made cloth and handloom-cloth may be considered as a social gain. But if looked more closely, it would be found that the social cost of additional unemployment created by the mills would far outweigh this paltry gain derived from lower price. Here Gandhiji dwells upon the concept of Negative Externalities of large scale production.

To quote: "For, if they have displaced thousands of workers, the cheapest mill cloth is dearer than the dearest Khadi woven in the villages."[35]

"Strange as it may appear, every mill generally is a menace to the villagers. I have notworked out the figures, but I am quite safe in saying that every mill-hand does the work of at least ten laborers doing the same work in their villages. In other words, he earns more than he did in his village at the expense of ten fellow-villagers."[36]

Gandhiji did not deny the importance of large scale industries in essential spheres like basic and capital goods. But they are to be developed only as complementary to small scale and cottage industries, not as rivals. Moreover, he opines that these large industries should be centralised in industrial centers alone and should not be permitted to penetrate the rural sector indiscriminately. Probably, he had in mind the ecological question besides the adverse effect on rural economy and culture.

To quote: "Heavy industries will necessarily be centralised and nationalised. But they will occupy the least part of the vast national activity in the villages."[37]

Section V

SWADESHI AND FOREIGN TRADE

It is a commonly held wrong impression that the

concept of Swadeshi is against all foreign goods, capital and technology. This is highly erroneous. Gandhiji was well aware that for an industrially backward country like India, foreign trade, foreign capital and foreign technology may be essential in certain fields. But it is to be seen that they are not resorted to indiscriminately to cater to the needs of foreign business and luxury consumption of the rich minority at the cost of the majority and environment. For a poor country like India, unrestricted free trade would only serve the interests of England and other developed nations, and the luxury requirements of the native rich. The same is the case for foreign capital and technology if permitted without any restriction and consideration of the well-being of the masses. Gandhiji here makes clear that imports of foreign goods, capital and technology should be strictly restricted to areas where they are essential and where they are likely to serve the interests of the majority and future economic prospect of the country.

They should never be permitted to destroy local industries and employment opportunities. Gandhiji points out that free trade was the root cause of economic bondage of India. To quote: "Free trade for India has proved her curse and held her in bondage."[38] "India was enslaved for satisfying the greed of the foreign cloth manufacturer. When the East India Company came in, we were able of manufacture all the cloth we needed and more for export. By processes that need not be described here, India has become practically wholly dependent upon foreign manufacture for her clothing."[39]

"We forget that what may be perfectly good for certain conditions in the West is not necessarily good for certain other, and often diametrically opposite, conditions in the East. Free trade, which may have been good enough for England, would certainly have ruined Germany. Germany prospered only because her thinkers, instead of slavishly following, England took note of the special conditions of their own land, and devised economics suited to them."[40]

He clarifies why free trade which is beneficial for developed countries like England is not so far a poor country like India.

To quote: "The economics of a nation are determined

by its climate, geological and temperamental conditions. The Indian conditions are different from the English in all these essentials."[41]

"A country remains poor in wealth, both material and intellectual, if it does not develop its handicrafts and its industries and lives a lazy parasitic life by importing all the manufactured articles from outside."[42]

"The process is now reversed and we are dependent upon the outside world for most manufactured goods."[43] Gandhiji cites examples how free trade was responsible for destruction of indigenous industries and aggravation of the employment situation in India.

To quote: "The Lancashire cloth, as English historians have shown, was forced upon India, and her own world-famed manufactures were deliberately and systematically ruined." [44] "Many weavers have become sweepers. Some have taken to the profession of hired soldiers. Half the race of artistic weavers has died out, and the other half is weaving imported foreign yarn for want of finer hand-spun yarn." [45]

"But free trade has ruined India's peasantry in that it has all but destroyed her cottage industry. Moreover, no new trade can compete with foreign trade without protection."[46] He strongly dispels the misgiving that he is blindly against all foreign goods. He welcomes import of foreign goods where they are essential for the benefit of the nation and its people.

To quote: "All British goods do not harm us. Some goods, such as English books, we need for our intellectual of spiritual benefit."[47] "In my opinion, therefore, Swadeshi which excludes the use of everything foreign, because it is foreign, no matter how beneficial it may be, and irrespective of the fact that it impoverishes nobody, is a narrow interpretation of Swadeshi."[48]

"Swadeshi admits of and welcomes the introduction of all foreign goods that cannot or need not be manufactured in India and that would benefit her people. Thus Swadeshi admits all foreign books containing pure literature, all foreign watches, foreign needles, foreign sewing machines, foreign pins."[49]

He also opines that guarantee of security of all

beneficial foreign companies and honest foreign citizen is a part of Swadeshi. "I would guarantee the fullest protection for every European living in India and all honest European Enterprises."[50]

"To reject foreign manufactures merely because they are foreign, and to go on wasting national time and money to promote manufactures in one's country for which it is not suited, would be criminal folly and a negation of the Swadeshi spirit. A true votary of Swadeshi will never harbour ill-will towards the foreigner, he will not be actuated by antagonism towards anybody on earth. Swadeshism is not a cult of hatred. It is a doctrine of selfless service, that has its roots in the purest Ahimsa, i.e. love."[51]

"There is no harm in importing raw material when it cannot be found in India."

Section VI

MODERN RELEVANCE

Globalisation in India has at present manifested in the form of blind craze for establishment of large scale industries based on imported and unaltered foreign technology and capital at any cost. The matter has taken a horrible turn in West Bengal revealing all the demonic features of globalisation. There are lengthy processions and street meetings organized by the ruling party and with party toughs clamouring nerve rending slogans: "Industrialisation is a must and anyone opposing it would be crushed ruthlessly." The Nandigram and Singur episodes of successful mass resistance against displacement of poor cultivators by party goons under police coverage has once again brought to the fore the question of assigning human face to the process of globalisation and need to devise methods of industrialisation not to serve the interests of foreign MNCs and luxury needs of native well-to-do minority, but the interest of the nation and well-being of the majority of its population, and preservation of environment and ecology. In this regard the Gandhian concept of Swadeshi as defined above comes to the fore. Establishment of large scale industries with unaltered foreign technology would serve the interests of the foreign

MNCs and their domestic counterparts, and the native well-to-do minority at the cost of the majority by aggravating unemployment situation through takeover of agricultural land displacing poor cultivators and destruction of rural craft industries. They will also have irreparable adverse impact on environment and ecology and the culture in the country side. In general, overall employment elasticity of the highly capital-intensive modern sector is low compared to that of the craft industries and small industries. (Sen, Abhijit, 1996). All the studies reveal clearly that since the adoption of Structural Adjustment Programme (SAP), rate of growth of employment opportunities in the modern large scale sector (organized sector) has been declining steadily and has even become negative in recent years. Rate of growth of employment declined from 2.6 per cent during 1980-81 to 0.4 per cent during 1992-93, to (–) 0.3 per cent in 1997-98 and further to (–) 0.6 per cent in 2000-01 (Tata: Statistical Abstracts, 2003-04). The SAP also adversely affected both output and employment of the conventional unorganized sector (Chakrabarty, 2002). Thus it is highly fallacious that indiscriminate establishment of large scale modern industries on the basis of unaltered foreign technology would generate additional employment (this is the essence of the slogan of the ruling party men in West Bengal). On the contrary, by both its direct and indirect impacts, it would make the unemployment situation more serious. So the sustainable path of industrialisation with employment generation, enhanced supply of mass consumption goods, removal of poverty, preservation of environment, ecology and rural culture and on the whole well-being of the majority, ought to be based on the Gandhian concept of Swadeshi by revitalizing the craft sector, the history, prospects and current problems of which are given below in brief.

Historical Background

A large number of highly efficient crafts flourished in ancient India as early as the 700 B.C. the artisans in those days had acquired remarkable skill in all branches of crafts because of many conducive factors, which had emanated from ancient Indian tradition and socio-economic conditions since the Vedic times (Buch, M.A. 1974, Vol.-I, pp. 116-236). Kautilya, in his Arthashastra mentioned a large number of craft products (Kangle 1986, Chs. 11-13, 17, 18, 25, 33). These crafts were organized under strong guilds, which used to look after all relevant matters like supply of raw materials of appropriate specification and quality, inspection of quality and standard of products, arrangement of marketing facilities, etc. (Panikkar, 1966, p. 36; Mookerjee 1980, pp. 601-02).

Till the early 19th century these crafts evinced great prosperity. East India Company's global trade depended considerably on craft products from India. The native kings and their courts used to generate considerable demand for high-quality and costly craft products. However, these crafts faced a serious crisis since the mid-19th century because of inimical attitude of the British Rulers, degeneration of the kings and the noble class, and above all disintegration of the guilds by deliberate policies of British Administration. This resulted in decline of major crafts industries like cotton, wollen and silk textiles, etc. (Gadgil, 1973, Ch. 3, pp. 33-36). The plight of the artisans of innumerable other crafts was also precarious because of poverty, exploitation by middlemen and moneylenders, and erosion of market for high-quality costly craft products. Many artisans were compelled to leave their hereditary profession and seek employment elsewhere.

In recent decades there was a sign of revival of many crafts mainly through export (Economic Survey, 2000-01, Table 7.3 (A), pp. S-87, 88). But the existing problems coupled with the very recent craze for indiscriminate establishment of large scale industries in rural areas is likely to stultify this growth potential of these crafts unless the policies are reversed.

Employment Potential

The basic problem in analyzing employment potential of the craft industries in India is that it is very difficult to obtain reliable employment data as the crafts are widely scattered over the whole country. Employment data, as available from the 8th and 9th Five Year Plan documents, cover only a few industries like Khadi-cloth, handloom-cloth, raw silk, coir fiber, etc. Total employment in these crafts increased from 18.43 million in 1984-85 to 32.83 million in 1996-97, the average annual rate of growth being 6.51 percent. This is remarkable considering the dismal performance of the organized sector in this regard. In this connection it is worthwhile to have a brief glimpse of the performance of the handloom sector *vis-a-vis* the mill sector in West Bengal. The remarkable performance of the handloom sector in West Bengal (where the slogan for unconditional development of large scale industries is most vociferous and even menacing to peace and security of common people) presents an ironical picture. According to Government of West Bengal, "Handloom industry is the largest cottage industry, which provides widest avenue for employment opportunity. There are about 3,50,994 handlooms in the State providing full time and part time employment to about 6,66,514 handloom weavers." (*Economic Review*, Government of W.B., 2004-05, p. 135). Production of handloom cloth in West Bengal increased from 401 million meters in 1995-96 to 1199.75 million meters in 2003-04 (*Economic Review*, Statistical Appendix, Table 6.19, p. 127). In contrast cloth production in the mill sector was only 2.395 million meters (*Ibid.*, Table 6.3, p. 109).

From the above analysis it becomes clear that the crafts sector in India is expected to play a significant role in employment generation. But realisation of this target is hardly possible if we do not adopt appropriate policies to resolve their existing problems, and on the contrary, choke the growth potential of these industries by our craze for large scale industries. The best way to revitalize these industries in line with the Gandhian Concept of Swadeshi, is to organize the crafts under co-operatives modeled according to the ancient guilds, with the following tasks:

1. Maintenance of skill of the artisans and quality of the products.
2. Arrangement of easy credit facilities for the artisans from banks and other financial institutions.
3. Sales promotion in internal and foreign markets.

4. Technology up-gradation and re-designing.
5. Arrangement for collection of products from the small artisans, provision of storage facilities and export promotion.
6. Arrangements for supplying to the artisans raw materials of appropriate quality.

Formation of co-operatives with these tasks is the most worthwhile method for revival of the numerous conventional and unconventional crafts in India so as to generate adequate employment opportunities, enhance foreign exchange earning through them and initiate the practice of true Swadeshi to endow a human face to the process of globalisation. At the next step Swadeshi may be extended to small and ancillary sector catering to the intermediate and accessories requirements of the large scale assembly sector. Taking a cue from Japan, most of the intermediates and accessories could be produced in small scale even in tiny sector without going through the hazards of large scale industries in all spheres.

Swadeshi does not preclude the import and assimilation of sophisticated foreign technology in case they are essential to keep this small sector technologically efficient and cost effective.

Notes and References

1. *Young India*, June 17, 1926.
2. *Young India*, May 12, 1927.
3. *Speeches and Writings of M.K. Gandhi*, p. 385.
4. *Ibid.*
5. *Ibid.*
6. *Mahatma*, Vol. II, p. 53.
7. *Ibid.*
8. *Ibid.*
9. *Mahatma*, Vol. II, p. 53.
10. *Ibid.*
11. *Harijan*, Nov. 30, 1934.
12. *Harijan*, Aug. 10, 1934.
13. *Mahatma*, Vol. II, p. 53.
14. *Harijan*, Dec. 7, 1934.
15. *Ibid.*

16. *Ibid.*
17. *Ibid.*
18. *Harijan*, Aug. 10, 1934.
19. *Ibid.*
20. *Harijan*, Nov. 30, 1934.
21. *Ibid.*
22. *Harijan*, March 23, 1947.
23. *Ibid.*
24. *Young India*, Oct. 13, 1921.
25. *Ibid.*
26. *Ibid.*
27. *Ibid.*
28. *Ibid.*
29. *Ibid.*
30. *Young India*, May 13, 1919.
31. *Ibid.*
32. *Young India*, Mar. 7, 1929.
33. *Ibid.*
34. *Constructive Programme*, p. 7.
35. *Ibid.*
36. *Ibid.*
37. *Ibid.*
38. *Young India*, July 13, 1921.
39. *Ibid.*
40. *Young India*, Dec. 8, 1921.
41. *Young India*, May 12, 1927.
42. *Young India*, Aug. 20, 1931.
43. *Ibid.*
44. *Young India*, July 13, 1921.
45. *Ibid.*
46. *Young India*, May 15, 1924.
47. *Young India*, Dec. 26, 1924.
48. *Young India*, June 17, 1926.
49. *Young India*, July 1, 1926.
50. *Ibid.*
51. *Young India*, June 18, 1931.
52. *Young India*, Aug. 20, 1931.

References

Buch, M.A. (1979), *Economic Life in Ancient India*, R.S. Publishing House, Allahabad.

Gadgil, D.R. (1973), *Industrial Evolution in India in Recent Times*, Oxford University Press, Delhi.

Government of India, *Economic Survey*, 2000-01.

Government of India, Planning Commission, *8th and 9th Five Year Plans.*

Government of West Bengal, *Economic Review* and *Statistical Abstract,* 2004-05.

Kangle (1986), *Kautiliya Arthashastra* (English Translation), Motilal Banarasi Dass, Delhi.

M.K. Gandhi (1967), *The Gospel of Swadeshi,* Bhartiya Vidya Bhavan, Mumbai.

Mookerji, R.K. (1980), "Economic Conditions" in Majumder (ed.), *The History and Culture of the Indian People,* Bharatiya Vidya Bhawan, Bombay.

Panikkar, K.M. (1966), *A Survey of Indian History,* Asia Publishing House, Bombay.

Sen, Abhijit (1996), "Economic Reforms, Employment and Poverty", *EPW,* Special Number.

Tata Services Limited: *Statistical Outline of India,* 2003-04.

22

Gandhi on Equity and Land Questions in India

D.M. DIWAKAR

I. INTRODUCTION

Inequality in distribution of land and absentee land ownership remained the concerns for policy-makers, development strategist and social scientists to unleash productive forces for growth and eradication of poverty even today (Thorner, 1976; Bagchi, 1988; Joshi, 1982; Dorner, 1972; Mishra and Diwakar, 2005; Mishra, 1996). Agrarian violence and unrests rooted in unequal distribution of land is not new phenomenon but it has been continuing since the British colonial rule. There was growing realisation regarding proper institutional arrangement for land management to initiate a process of egalitarian development in India among national leaders during freedom struggle against the British Rule. Vision of the national leaders during freedom struggle remained crucial and decisive in shaping land relation after independence. Gandhiji remained the most popular and widely accepted leader among the national leaders from late

1920s until his assassination. Needless to mention that Gandhiji prevailed as mass leader and acquired his experiences from and among the masses therefore his insights need close examinations to understand the basics of success and failure of agrarian reforms in India. Therefore, his views on the issues of land questions may, therefore, provide important insight towards understanding the land questions in India. One can hardly escape reading ideas of Gandhiji in this regard. However, not much on land questions, that Gandhiji expressed, has been examined so far. Later of course, after his assassination the Bhoodan-Gramdan Movement was launched by Acharya Vinoba Bhabe, which attracted many scholars (Iyenger, 2007; Nanekar and Khandewale, 1973; Ommen, 1972; Chandra). This exercise is intended to deal with ideas of Gandhiji on the questions of land relations. Besides introduction, this paper is divided into three parts. Part one deals with the idea of Gandhiji on equity, and part two with land relations. Part three discusses its implications and imperatives.

II. QUESTION OF EQUITY

In any agrarian society question of equity is closely connected with land relations. Before going into the question of land it appears cogent to deal with the essence of the idea of Gandhiji on equity. A few important texts may reveal the essence of his writings. He said: "Everybody should be able to get sufficient work to make the two end meet. And this ideal can be universally realised only if the means of production of elementary necessaries of life remain under the control of masses. . . . they should not be made a vehicle of traffic for exploitation of others. Their monopolisation by any country, nation or groups of persons would be unjust" (Gandhi, 1928). Thus achievable ideals of equity starts with basic minimum of square meals articulated in the forms of ownership of masses and goes beyond the national boundaries and dominations. Adding economic dimension to his concept of non-violent social order he emphasised with operational directives: "Economic equality is the master key of non-violent independence, working for economic equality means the levelling down of the few rich in whose hands is concentrated the bulk of the nations wealth on the one hand and levelling up of the semi-starved naked millions on the other" (Gandhi, 1994:20). Gandhiji advocated an ideal of a non-violent social order and outlined the dreams of "India in which the poorest shall feel that it is their country in whose making they have an effective voice; an India in which there shall be no high class and low class of people; an India in which all communities shall live in perfect harmony.... Women will enjoy the same rights as men.... I shall be satisfied with nothing less" (Gandhi, 1931).

He was very much concerned about the decent livelihood and social development of the landless labourers (Gandhi, 1947:90). He suggested a talisman and brought the concept of the last man, which was a hallmark indicator of equity and justice. Running through pages in his *Village Swaraj,* he emphasised on poor man's swaraj (Gandhi, 1931) where 'no one is to be the first and none the last' (Gandhi, 1959:76, 73, 9 and 100) and elsewhere also Gandhi articulated his ideals of just social order in terms of removal of poverty, and unemployment, providing proper food, clothes, education and creative healthy condition of living for every human-being so that common masses can work and earn easily to meet their needs (Gandhi, *CWMG,* Vol. 87, p. 463). Thus, the concept of equity is well grounded in non-violent social order very much focussed on the poorest individuals to bring them into the mainstream with a vision of creating a finest cultured society.

III. LAND RELATIONS

There is hardly any disagreement that agriculture is an advance stage of human civilisation over hunting era. Importance of land since then remained vital for any agrarian society. Land remained one of the important sources of livelihood, means of production, status of powers, and prestige. It has been one of the crucial determinants and bases of transformation and development. Institutional arrangements and pattern of land distribution indicate access to livelihood resources and the level of equity or otherwise that an agrarian society enjoys. Institutional arrangements of land across time and space are reflected in the forms of ownership, control over land and process of surplus appropriation. Therefore, changes in agricultural institutions have far reaching effects on land-based social order. Needless to mention that institutional arrangements have been changing in the process of social transformation in consonance with the changing objective and subjective conditions of a society.

In India, generally tributary mode of surplus appropriation continued predominantly until the Mughal Rule. The Mughal Empire played important role in shaping land relations from tributary to revenue farming. It is argued that imposition of revenue farming as an institutional arrangement was not only the root of inequality and poverty but also the seed of the growth of the Zamindar class (Tandon, *et. al.,* 1936: 2). There were inherent regressive tendencies to aggravate inequality between the rich and poor in the countryside (Raychaudhuri and Habib, 1982, Vol. I, Ch. IX, see also Ch. VII). This mechanism of revenue collection was further reinforced by the Company Government, which entered into agreement with Zamindars (Tandon, *et. al.,* 1936: 2-3). In this process small peasantries were subjected to exploitation, and ejection of large section of small peasantry who lost their rights of ownership on land and forced to the situation of sub-ordination as 'tenants at will' to Zamindars. Rampant exploitation of the peasants during colonial rule resulted into a series of peasant movements during national freedom struggle. Champaran, Bardoli, Khera, Tebhaga, etc. were a few major peasant uprising and unrests in different parts of the British India. This was also a challenge before the national leaders to set agenda and programmes for agrarian reforms and institutional arrangements to address the issues of poverty, inequality and exploitation.

At this backdrop, this exercise is attempted to examine the views of Gandhiji on land issues. If one goes through his writings spread in many volumes of the *Collected Works,* he suggested the moneyed class to behave as trustees of the subjects, without any superiority over poor (*CWMG,* Vol. 48, p. 53). He was expecting all the goodness from a model zamindar to treat his tenants as his wards and discharge the responsibility of a sensitive guardian towards their well-being in all respects. This model he believed necessary without choice to avert forthcoming disaster (*Young India*, 5-12-1929 see also *CWMG*, Vol. 48, pp. 53-54). Therefore he was proposing a harmonious model of existence of tenants and zamindars. Generally he expected the changes in behaviour of zamindars and tenants contrary to existing conflicts between them.

In an interview to S. Hasan Ali Khan on March 6, 1931 Gandhiji replied about the position of zamindars in the forthcoming Constitution: "They will have the same privileges and the same rights as at present. Every justice will be extended both to the zamindars and the tenants, provided they go hand in hand with us. In the course of the recent movement some of the young Congress workers have attempted to set the tenants against the landlords. Further, Pandit Jawaharlal Nehru, in his presidential address at Lahore, explicitly expressed his views against the landlords of the country. No such instruction was sent by the Working Committee. We do not want that the tenants should stand against the zamindars. As a matter of fact, we have every sympathy for the zamindars if they show a fair attitude towards the peasantry. We assure the zamindars that their rights will be given due consideration in a swaraj constitution" (*The Pioneer*, 16-3-1931).

Gandhiji was opposed to proposition of socialist programmes on land relations, which were gaining currency in favour of the abolition of landlordism. On May 29, 1934 Gandhi made observation on M.R. Massni's Socialistic Programme: "The elimination of Landlordism clearly means usurption of the zamindari and Talukdari tracts in clause 13. I am not for elimination but for just regulation of the relations between land lords and tenants" (*CWMG*, Vol. 58, p. 37). He further proposed favourably and categorically: "Zamindars should be compensated if their land to be taken away" (*CWMG*, Vol. 58, p. 251). This can further be buttressed through his writing in 1938, answering to ex-premier of Orissa—Gandhi said: "You are quite right in saying that I do not wish the extinction of old zamindars. All the Congressman do not think so the remedy lies in the hands of zamindar friends" (*CWMG*, Vol. 66, p. 459, March 31, 1938). It is evident that there was pressure from socialist group within Congress and Gandhiji was very much in favour of zamindars with some modifications of an agreeable space for peasants to be created.

Feeling the heat of the peasants and socialist he cautioned zamindars also on April 13, 1938 in Calcutta: "I say zamindari system should be mended, and if it can not be mended, it would end itself" (*CWMG*, Vol. 67, p. 22). However, with the mounting pressure of mobilisation of farmers later he also agreed to the proposition of the abolition of zamindari system in principle and advised to do so non-violently. He expressed his agony on May 7, 1939 when Kisan uprising turned violent: "It pains me to hear the Kisans resorting to violence. They fight with zamindars. If you want to abolish zamindari it is well and good. Do so through non-violence" (*CWMG*, Vol. 69, p. 241). Later he advocated in favour of judicious distribution of land to end the menace of poverty. *"No man should have more land than he needs for dignified sustenance. Who can dispute the fact that the grinding poverty of the masses is due to their having no land that they can call their own?"* (Gandhi, 1940:97). This statement of Gandhiji was in conformity to his concept of equity and social justice.

Gandhiji was of view that tillers of the land should have the first right on land but at the same time he remained consistently in favour of zamindars and therefore, he was not in favour of evicting absentee landlords by force. He said: "the peasant, whether as a landless labourer or a labouring proprietor, comes first. He is the salt of the earth, which rightly belongs or should belong to him, not to the absentee landlord or zamindar. But in the non violent way, the labourer cannot forcibly eject the absentee landlord" (Gandhi: 1947: 89). On October 29, 1944 giving an interview to N.G. Ranga Gandhi turned gradually in favour of strengthening farmers: "I have no doubt that if we have democratic swaraj, as it must be if freedom is own through non-violence, the Kisan must hold power in all its phases including political powers." (*CWMG*, Vol. 78, p. 246). Thus, Gandhiji was although sympathetic to zamindars and he had faith in change of heart of zamindars, he articulated the basic principle of power structure in favour of peasants and the land to the tillers. Writing a letter to Zamindar, on September 3, 1946 Gandhi said: "My opinion, in brief, is that no zamindar or rich man should perish. The greatest need is to bring about a change of heart in them. If every zamindar, every Rajah and every millionaire lives as servant of the people there will be no problem. In the final analysis land belongs to the man who has worked on it. The present system which divides people into capitalists or landlords on the one hand and the have-nots or serfs on the other, should not be tolerated" (cwmgebk: *CWMG*, Vol. 92, p. 117).

Graduating with better understanding of the problems involved in land issues he was trying to repose the confidence of trusteeship and in zamindars. He has strong belief that change of the heart of resourceful person can bring equality and harmony through voluntary austerity. Visualising the compulsions Gandhiji, while talking with a zamindar on April 23, 1946, said: "You will be as free as any scavenger, but whether you will be able to retain all the privileges which you are enjoying under the British Government is a question you can answer for yourself." (*CWMG*, Vol. 84, p. 50, see also *Harijan*, 28-4-1946). He was still not in favour of elimination of zamindars, and were trying to explore possibility of cordial relation between zamindars and tenants. At Patna on April 18, 1947 he said: "Abolition of zamindari is but a small matter. When the zamindars and peasants develop cordial relations the former need not be eliminated." (*CWMG*, Vol. 87, p. 305). This also suggests that in absence of coardial relation, elimination of zamindars would be inevitable. Time and again he was emphasising to unite the opposites of interests and trying to strike balance. On the same day at Patna, i.e. on April 18, 1947, visualising emerging pressure from peasants and talking with zamindars he said: "Zamindars or capitalists will not be able to survive if they continue to suppress peasants and labourers. Now you should behave towards them not as their masters but as partners and friends, and act as their trustees; then alone can you survive. For a long time during the

British regime you have been exploiting the labourers and peasants. Therefore I advise you in your own interest that if you do not see the writing on the wall, it will be difficult for you to adjust" (*CWMG*, Vol. 87, p. 304).

Same day talking with peasant and labour leaders in Patna on April 18, 1947 Gandhi said: "If labourers aim at asserting their rights, they can do so only by co-operating with zamindars, not by harassing or killing them. Abolition of zamindari is not a very difficult task. We have only a handful of zamindars here. But if you take the law into your own hands you will be striking at the root of your own interest. You can place your complaints before the Government but you cannot take the law into your hands and resort to violence... If you work whole-heartedly during your working hours, your employers will have to pay you your proper wages. But if you harass them in any manner you will not earn anybody's sympathy" (cwmgebk: *CWMG*, Vol. 94, p. 331). Thus he always tried to avoid confrontation between zamindars and labourers and in doing so mostly he took the side of zamindars. He was always emphsising the role of government towards removal of misery of the toiling masses. Although he always alerted zamindars to mend their behaviour. In his speech in prayer meeting at Maner on May 23, 1947 Gandhi said: "Take for instance the question of the zamindars. You all know that the century-old reign of the white indigo-planters was brought to an end by the will and concerted action of all the people and their leaders... But I have been told that the tyranny of the white rulers is being continued even today by the Indian zamindars. They exploit their ryots economically, terrorize them through their officials and escape due punishment through collusion with the authorities. If it is true, the zamindars are digging their own graves. They can survive only if they become trustees of their ryots. (cwmgebk: *CWMG*, Vol. 95: p. 129).

Gandhiji had full confidence in non-co-operation as an instrument for struggle against exploitation. On May 25, 1947 expressing his view in Delhi he said: "The present power of zamindars, the capitalists and the rajas can hold sway only so long as the common people do not relies their own strength. If the people non-cooperate, what can a raja, a zamindar or a capitalist do?" (*CWMG*, Vol. 88, p. 2). Explaining the steps of civil disobedience Gandhiji said: Second steps of the peasants will be to snatch away land from zamindars. Violence is possible in such situation but zamindars may cooperate also. Perhaps zamindars will cooperate by fleeing away from the land. Gandhiji was of firm view that they would not have to ask peasants to take away land from zamindars. Peasants would take away land at their own. (CWMG, Hindi, Vol. 76, p. 484). In a response to the question of Luis Fischer regarding compensation now Gandhiji had different stand—contrary to 1934. He was in favour of capturing the land of zamindars without paying any compensation, as it was economically impossible. (*ibid.*, pp. 494-95). Moreover he added that State should play an active role in redistributing land using minimum violence (India of My Dreams, 1995, 7th eds.). In order to resolve contradictions he suggested Satygraha to sharpen their struggle. "To establish the farmer's ownership of the land, there is only one way; and that is to teach him the mantra of satyagraha.... If a farmer could realize that by peacefully resisting injustice his land could be prevented from being seized by anyone, he would never fall a victim to injustice. It would be good if peasants were to join the school of satyagraha. Then intricate question of the ownership of the land would be solved by itself." (*CWMG*, Vol. 43, p. 139).

Thus, it is evident from the views of Gandhiji that have been presented above, that initially he was directly in favour of zamindars becoming trustees but later he agreed to the proposition of the abolition of zamindari system. Gandhiji always remained conscious of abstaining violent resistance against zamindars, which directly and indirectly helped zamindars to retain land in their possession. However, he also suggested non-violent non-cooperation as means and ways for tenants and labourers to resist injustices and oppression. He categorically brought in the role of State to ensure redistribution of land. However, even today, the question of redistribution of land remains unresolved and the root cause of agrarian stagnation and unrest.

IV. IMPLICATIONS AND IMPERATIVES

After transfer of power abolition of zamindari was enacted as one of the most radical steps that Indian government could take towards institutional reforms. However, implementation of this initiative raised many questions and remained unresolved even after more than two generations. Too many loopholes in Acts and delays in implementation provided manipulative spaces for evasion of land especially through provisions of exemptions and benami transfers. Connivance of interests within structure of ruling class made the reform process toothless. Bhoodan Gramdan Movement in the Gandhian framework could not make much difference and remained almost inconclusive. Resultantly agrarian tensions compounded by many folds as apprehended. Government of India is on record that more than 200 districts are in the grip of Naxalite Movement of which land struggle is the core of its issues. Instead of paying heed to inherent dangers of structural violence Government of India has pushed the land reforms at the back seat and opened the door for corporate farming and special economic zones threatening the livelihood of the poverty ridden majority. Insensitive initiatives could results into addition of aggressive resistance at Singur and Nandigram. Inequality in distribution of land needs a fresh look even today. Question of land to the tillers and absentee land ownership, which have been in the realm of institutional puzzles, have now been complicated with reverse reforms and globalisation. Lop sided delivery and transfer of technology with continued neglect of agriculture has aggravated poor peasants further.

There is an imperative need to examine further whether change of guard without changing the system can deliver the goods. It reminds the concerns of Nehru about inefficient bureaucracy and also message from Gandhiji: "Unless the present system of administration is completely changed the oppression of the people will continue unabated even when the reins of government have passed into Indian hands." (*Young India*, 25th July, 1929, see also comments in 30th July 1929 by J'ai Accuse, and also *CWMG*, Vol. 41, pp. 312-13). There is hardly any disagreement that in the era of globalisation, WTO regime, corporate agriculture amidst threat of SEZ, and uncritical diversification, marginalisation and pauperisation has increased. Farmers have been overburdened with debts and committing suicides. Policies have not been able to restore confidence of cultivators and rural labourers. This situation reminds us the speech of Gandhiji at Borsad, on March 18, 1930: "To be loyal to this government, that is to say to wish it well, is as good as wishing ill of the crores of the people of India. To approve the policy of this government is to commit treason against the poor. You should free yourselves from this latter offence. I am commencing it by violating the salt law. Today we are defying the salt law. Tomorrow we shall have to consign other laws to the waste-paper basket" (*CWMG*, Vol. 43, pp. 100-01). The country is celebrating centenary year of Satyagraha. We must recall what Gandhi said: "It is the birth right and the duty of the people to disobey orders which, on mature consideration, they regard as unjust or oppressive." (*CWMG*, Vol. 14, pp. 346-47). Let us deliberate consciously whether land should belong to the tillers and means of production of elementary necessity should be controlled by the masses.

References

Bagchi, A.K. (1988), *Economy, Society and Polity*, Oxford University Press.

Chandra, Nirmal (1997), *Bhumi Samasya aur Bhoodan*, Gandhi Peace Foundation, New Delhi.

Dorner, P. (1972), *Land Reforms and Economic Development*, Penguin, Harmondsworth.

Gandhi, M.K. (1928): Economic Constitution of India, *Young India*, November 15.

Gandhi, M.K., *Young India*, 26.03.1931.

Gandhi, M.K., *The Pioneer*, 16-3-1931.

Gandhi, M.K., (1940): *Harijan*, 20.4.1940.

Gandhi, M.K. (1947), *India of My Dreams*, Navjivan Publishing House, Ahmedabad Revised Edition 1959, see also *The Bombay Chronicle*, 28.10.1944.

Gandhi, M.K: Collected Works of Mahatma Gandhi, Publication Division, Government of India, Vols. 14, 41, 43, 48, 58, 66, 67, 69, 78, 87, 88, 92, 94, 95.

Gandhi, M.K. (1994), Constructive Programmes, Navajivan, Ahmedabad, Reprint.

Iyengar, S. (2007), Bhoodan Movement as a Gandhian Approach to Resource Distribution and Development, *Gandhi Marg*, Vol. 28, No. 4, pp. 402-21.

Joshi, P.C. (1982), *Land Reforms in India*, Allied Publishers, New Delhi.

Mishra, G.P. (1996), *Distribution of Surplus Land and Rural Poor*, APH Publishing Corporation, New Delhi.

Mishra, G.P. and D.M. Diwakar (2005), Land Reforms and Human Development, Manak Publications Pvt. Ltd., New Delhi.

Nanekar, K.R. and Khandwale, S.V. (1973), Bhoodan and the Landless, Popular Prakashan, Bombay.

Oommen, T.K. (1972), Charisma Stability and Change: An Analysis of Bhoodan-Gramdan Movement in India, Thomson Press, New Delhi.

Raychoudhuri, R.C. and I. Habib (1982), *The Cambridge Economic History of India*, Vol. I, Orient Longmans.

Tandon, P.D. *et. al.* (1936), *Congress Agrarian Enquiry Committee Report*, 1936, Prabhu Publications, Gurgaon (Haryana).

Thorner, D. (1976), *The Agrarian Prospects in India*, Allied Publishers Ltd., New Delhi.

23

Gandhian Economics and Consumerism

NIRAJ KUMAR

The history of modern economics is tagged along consumerism. Before the industrial revolution people satisfied their limited and natural wants easily, but science brought about the industrial revolution and gave impetus to the production of luxuries in plenty. Consequently, the affluent states began to create artificial wants in order to make more and more profit. Thus modern economics is inextricably tagged to consumerism. As a result, modern civilisation has thrown many a challenge to humanity.

Gandhiji propounded the theory of humanistic economics to cope with the challenges posed by consumerism and found out a lasting solution to all the fundamental problems facing not merely India but the entire humanity. Though Gandhian economics presents multi-dimensional concepts, our aim in this paper is to highlight the fact that Gandhian economics is entirely opposed to consumerism. (Gandhian economics and consumerism are not only different from but also opposed to each other; for there is no point of agreement between the two.) But it does not mean that Gandhian economics ignores the basic needs of man and is blind to their fulfilment. In fact, it does not ignore reality and favour asceticism.

Today education and health have assumed as much importance as the three basic needs—food, clothes and shelter. Gandhian economics favours the fulfilment of these minimum fundamental wants. It, however, insists on refraining from consumerism in that consumerism cannot ensure real happiness to man.

Consumerism is basically concerned with sensual pleasures or hedonism. It patronises material pleasures and encourages selfish pursuits. Under its influence an individual loses his sense of reasoning and refuses to listen to his conscience and gets directionless. *Yayati's* (a king) desires remained insatiated even after having enjoyed material and sensual pleasures to excess for years. Then he realised that a man's desires could not be satiated even though he was made lord of all the belles and of all the riches of the world. He said that an effort to satisfy the desires by enjoying sensual pleasures was just like adding fuel to fire. Thus consumerism is an aberration of mind born out of hedonism. It has entrapped not only the well-to-do people but also the middle class people. A modern economist *Duesenberry* in his theory "Demonstration effect" has shown how an individual imitates a richer individual, a family a richer family, a society a richer society, a state a richer state and so on. In this rat-race expenses get naturally imbalanced, which begets numberless evils. As a result, people get entrapped into limitless desires and aspirations and cease to make any progress. It adversely affects savings and capital formation and hinders the progress of a developing economy like India. It is clear then that an individual hankering after consumerism spends more than his income, which proves fatal to him from socio-economic viewpoints. Based on self-restraint, Gandhian economics does not favour consumerism in any way. Gandhiji pleaded for limiting one's wants. He believed in simplifying life and minimising needs. His concept of simple life was 'Let me do with the minimum'.

The first President of India, *Dr. Rajendra Prasad* in a

paper presented to Gandhi Darshan Parishad in 1952 said that removal of poverty of the people was Gandhiji's basic programme but so far as we understand he was never in favour of raising the standard of life to an unlimited and infinite extent. Though he wanted that all essential things were availble to us so that our life was not unhappy. He did not want that an individual should amass more than he needed or wished to have more than his needs. Let an individual not even determine even his essential needs according to his wish; let several other factors be taken into consideration for determining them. An individual should above all keep it in mind that what was essential for him might be essential for others as well, so let it be distributed among all. So long as this kind of distribution was not possible, he should think that he had no right to consider it essential for himself. Hence Gandhiji put stress on restricting and restraining one's needs.[1]

Thus Gandhiji favoured humanistic economics. The western economists consider the material acquisitions as the scope of economics. In their economics wants are unlimited but the resources to satisfy them are limited. For Gandhiji economics is a moral science-based wholly on human values. Throwing light on Gandhian economics *J.C. Kumarappa* has said in his book 'Gandhi Artha Vichar', 'The objective of man's earning is not to attain material happiness but to make moral and spiritual progress'.[2] The Indian economist Prof. *J.K. Mehta* too believes that satisfaction lies not in unlimiting the needs but in curbing them. Gandhian economics views man's life in totality, i.e. his economics stands for social justice and ethical values.[3] Gandhiji has himself said, 'The whole gamut of men's activities today constitute an individual whole. You cannot divide social, economic, political and purely religious work into watertight compartments'.[4]

An eminent modern economist *Maurice Dobb* too has supported the Gandhian concept, 'I shall be the first and most vehement in denying that economic factors cannot be separated from their social background and from political implications'.[5]

Thus we find Gandhian economics cannot stand unlimited and unrestrained wants. To quote Gandhiji, 'The less you have, the more cannot you are; the less desire you have, the better you will be'.[6]

It's no good lossing one's rest after accumulating amenities by increasing one's wants. There's no point in grabing the things of others' use. It causes trouble not only to the needy but also to the grabber:

Bhoga Na Mukta Vaymeo Bhukta,
Trishna Na Jirna Vaymeo Jirna.

That is, we don't consume the consumables; we ourselves are consumed instead. If we think that by fulfilling our particular wants, we will satiate our desire, we are in the wrong.

It is a well-known psycho-economic fact that desires and wants never get lessened and satiated. No sooner does one desire or want get fulfilled than another comes up. Desires never die; we die. We have no strength left to consume the things. So one must consume but with restraint. Consuming with restraint is human, consuming without restraint is bestiality.

Modern culture of consumerism lets many socio-politico-economic evils flourish. They include social violence, economic disparity and discontent, unbalanced economic development, misuse of resources, destruction caused by cultural pollution, principleless politics, amassing wealth without labour, trade sans ethics and enjoyment sans conscience. Once trapped into this evil man gets worn out hankering after limitless wants. The western countries which pursue consumerism testify to this fact. In these countries every individual runs after material gains so much so that he does not know even his next door neighbour and suffers from many a physical and mental ailment. Today the number of mental patients and suicides is the largest in America.

Gandhiji was critical of this so-called 'high standard of living' and pleaded for simple life, where one could enjoy real happiness by restricting and satisfying one's wants. He says in clear terms, 'Desire for a thing only for the pride of ownership is a disease of a narrow and uncivilised mind. I don't know why it is so. A man who was close to me said that when he wanted to flee to London, he did not wish to flee from his village but from himself. He sold himself out to unlimited property but because bankrupt from within.[7] This is the consequence of consumerism which Gandhiji has subjected to ridicule. We find that owing to this consumerism the modern age has become an age of obsession. Life has become mechanical so much so that man gets no time for meditation and having lost his man-like faculties, he has himself become machine-like. We know that Gandhiji was greatly influenced by Ruskin's concept of 'Unto the Last'. Ruskin was convinced that a cut-throat competition for amassing wealth was sure to create socio-economic disparity. To quote Ruskin, "Riches are a power like that of electricity acting through inequalites or negation of itself. The force of a guinea you have in your pocket depends wholly on the default of guinea in your neighbour's pocket. If he did not want it, it would be of no use to you. He further said what one person has another cannot have." *Ved Vyas* too writes in the 'Mahabharat' that possessing more wealth than one needs is an act of stealing and one who does so deserves punishment. Shankaracharya calls it an intellectual offence to impose one's ideas and theories upon unwilling individuals, likewise, it is a crime begotten of consumerism to amass more wealth than one needs and lead a luxurious life by exploiting others.

So in order to realise the vision of an exploitation-free society into a reality it is essential to restrict consumerism related to wealth. In Gandhiji's opinion, Nature has given us enough to satisfy our wants. The greatest obstacle in this way is our unlimited greed and unbridled tendency to amass more and more wealth. In this connection he says, "There is enough in this world for everyone's needs, but not enough in this entire universe for one man's greed."

Gandhiji was greatly influenced by Tolstoy. In one of his stories Tolstoy shows how a man kept running from down to dusk in order to possess more and more land and falls down dead in the evening, finally getting a piece of land just enough for his burial. This is the crux of consumerism, which leads man to disaster.

Even after ascending the fifth stage of development,

America is still not rid of economic disparity, unemployment, murder, theft, exploitation and terrorism. This is simply because the people pursue consumeristic culture.

India has pursued planned economic development since 1951, still socio-economic evils like unemployment, poverty, economic disparity, exploitation and decline in moral values afflict it. Had the culture of consumerism not flourished in India, the story would have been different here.

What vision did Gandhiji have of India? He said once, "I shall work for an India in which the poorest shall feel that it is their country in whose making they have an effective voice, an India in which there shall be no rich and no poor class of people, an India in which all communities can live in perfect harmony. This is the India of my dream." Gandhiji's dream of an India 'in which there shall be no rich and no poor class of people' is indicative of his humanistic and idealistic vision. The fulfilment of such a dream is possible only when people restrict their wants and do not resort to amassing wealth by exploiting and starving others. In the India of Gandhiji's dream neither the too rich nor the too poor had any room, i.e. poverty and disparity. Once he said, 'A semi-starved nation can have neither religion nor art nor organisation. Whatever can be useful to starving millions is beautiful to my mind. I want art and literature that can speak to millions. My ambition is to wipe every tear from every eye.'

Swami Vivekanand said that talking of spiritualism to a starving man was just like playing a tune to a buffalo. He sees 'Ram' and 'Krishna' in a loaf. Is there any likelihood of Gandhiji's dream of India come true in this maddening race of consumerism? As things stand today, the country is divided into what we may call 'India' and 'Bharat'. 'India' belongs to the affluent section of the people who live in big cities and are wholly given to western culture and consumerism and its off-shoot luxury and control the larger portion of the resources of the country. On the contrary, 'Bharat' belongs to the villagers who strive hard for food, clothes and shelter.

Outside Gandhiji's cottage at seva-gram there hung a board on which were inscribed seven evils. They were:

(i) Politics sans principle,
(ii) Riches sans labour,
(iii) Trade sans ethics,
(iv) Education sans character,
(v) Happiness sans conscience,
(vi) Science sans humanity, and
(vii) Worship sans sacrifice.

Of these seven evils 'Riches sans labour' and 'Happiness sans conscience' explicitly point to the evil of consumerism which has its roots in amassing of wealth by foul means.

Thus Gandhian economics pleads for minimising one's needs and living a simple life. His economics, like *Chanakya's*, (a great saint, statesman and economist) wants even a minister to live a normal simple life and expects the government to avoid misusing wealth. Like *Mahatma Vidur* (an intelligent and amicable character of Mahabharata) is expected to eat and feed even his guests simple food. His principle of simple life believes in the all-round development of man for which it is essential for an individual to satisfy his basic needs and pursue truth, non-violence and such other human values. The life that does not pursue these values is not perfect and the economics that does not include these values is not economics in the real sense. Gandhian economics is humane, largely based on moral values. Gandhiji says, 'That economics is untrue which ignores or disregards moral values.' 'Humanity today needs to follow Gandhian concept of simple life. If the world today does not understand Gandhian concept of non-violence and simple life, the future will surely be troublesome'.[8]

Notes and References

1. Rajendra Prasad, *'Gandhi Marg'*, p. 10a, 1953.
2. J.C. Kumarappa, 'Gandhi Artha Vichar', p. 94.
3. Harijan, October, 1937.
4. G.V. Tendulkar, 'Mahatma', p. 387.
5. Maurice Dobb; 'Some Aspects of Economic Development', p. 1.
6. G.V. Tendulkar: 'Mahatma', p. 157.
7. *Ibid.*
8. Dr. Rajendra Prasad, *'Gandhi Marg'*, p. 5.

24

Economics of Gandhi's Satyagraha and Development

RAM NARESH THAKUR AND YOGENDRA KUMAR

India has produced great thinkers, social leaders and social reformers who, by their revolutionary and pathbreaking thoughts and actions, have left a lasting impact on not only India, but on the world as a whole. They have developed indigenous ideas and have provided cultural and ethical identity to India. There is a great need to acquaint the people, youths, women, teachers, students and different sections of society with their thinking and their work. In the present era we owe our duty to the nation to know and analyse the thoughts which are pertinent and apply to their ideas in the construction of human society on moral, ethical and spiritual foundations for a non-violent society. In accordance with his rational approach to life, Budha emphasised on the age old concepts for the formation of an equalitarian society. Mahatma Gandhi gave a social dimension to the 'concept of non-violence' and demonstrated, both through his life and work, how it can be used as an instrument for fighting injustice at all levels. Our nation is known for the doctrines of 'truth' (Satya) and 'non-violence' (Ahimsa) in the world only due to Gandhi. Nehru, a great deal to the application of 'non-violence' for resolving conflicts at the national, and more so at the international level, as well as modernisation of society with emphasis on science and rationality. Baba Saheb Ambedkar stressed on the empowerment of the oppressed as a means of their release from exploitation and injustice, which are social forms of violence against the oppressed. The idea of all those thinkers have a framework of interrelated views which are mutually supportive to each other and yield profound insights into the conditions of the individual, his/her personal being, in socio-economic and political life.

Not only Budha, Gandhi, Ambedkar and Nehru, but there remained many greatmen and thinkers who contributed for the society as well as sacrificed their all on the alter of nation as Bhagat Singh, Raj Guru, Sukhdeo, Chandrashekhar Azad, Netaji Subhash Chandra Bose, Pandit Madan Mohan Malviya, Rahul Sankrityayan, Swami Sahjanand Sarswati, Dr. Radha Krishnan, Dr. Rajendra Prasad, Dr. Zakir Hussain, Swami Ram Krishna Paramahans, Swami Vivekanand, Raja Ram Mohan Roy, Swami Daya Nand Sarswati, Pandit Ishwar Chandra Vidyasagar, Rabindra Nath Tagore, Shri Aurovindo, Sardar Vallabh Bhai Patel, Acharya Narendra Dev, Dr. Ram Manohar Lohia and others. It becomes essential to understand and disseminate the concepts relating to those philosophers and fundamental thinkers and the philosophies enunciated by them, related to social justice and equity, conflict resolution, non-violence and non-violent protest movements, empowerment of women, rural development and related ideas for the upliftment of the society.

Mahatma Gandhi was a great philospher, thinker and journalist. He studied Tolstoy's "The Kingdom of God is Within You", Ruskin's "Unto The last," Sir Edwin Arnald's "The Light of Asia," Carlyle's "Hero Worship," Thoreau's "Duty of Civil Disobedience", Karl Marx's "Das Capital" (during his jail period in Aga Khan Palace) and George Benard Shaw's "Plea for vegetarianism" in addition to the Indian authors' works consequently, he developed his ideas on number of matters. Again, Mahatma Gandhi made his mark as protester, social worker, reformer and as liberator. He was religious and the "practical idealist."

How far 'Satyagraha' is concerned, it is a fundamental element of Gandhism or Gandhian philosophy. 'Satyagraha' is Gandhiji's great contribution to the political principle and behaviour. It is a focal point on which all Gandhian thoughts revolves. But there is a contradiction about the invention of the word 'Satyagraha'. Generally, it is known that the word 'Satyagraha' was invented by Mahatma Gandhi. On the contrary an expert diplomate, Mr. Pascal Allan Nazerath tells us that the word 'Satyagraha' was not invented by Gandhiji but by his cousin Magan Lal Gandhi. Mr. Nazerath has revealed this fact in his famous work entitled "Gandhi Abhootpurva Netritwa Mein." In this book, he holds that it was Magan Lal Gandhi who had helped him (Gandhiji) when latter was in search of naming his 'Ahimsa Andolan' (Non-Violence Movement) that was being launched by himself. Actually when Mahatma Gandhi decided to start 'Ahimsa Andolan', he declared to reward that person who might suggest appropriate name to his above movement (Andolan). Mr. Magan Lal Gandhi suggested the word 'Sadagrah' to name 'Ahimsa Andolan' which meant to be firm for good tasks. Although Gandhiji ameliorated (amended) this word 'Sadagraha' as 'Satyagraha' that means 'holding on truth' or "insistence on truth." Any way, it is a universal truth that Satyagraha is associated with Mahatma Gandhi and it became weapon of Ahimsa.

We know very well that Gandhiji believed in moral means. But how to resist and overcome evil and oppression by ethically pure method. For this he evolved the methods of civil resistance, non-co-operation and downing of tools. He had believed that due to our co-operation with injustice the latter might flourished. If we might not co-operate with it, it would not have grown up. Gandhiji told, "Like stream which is a kind of energy, Satyagraha or soul force is more potent and pervasive." He further said, "It is the vindication of truth by bearing witness to it. It is a play for action." In true sense Satyagraha excluded violence but includes active resistance which consists of the active force of love, faith and sacrifice.

Now, it is essential to mention sundary aspects of Satyagraha relating to humanity, struggle and social harmony. These are following as:

1. The Goal of Satyagraha

It is acknowledged that Satyagraha is a dynamic philosophy. It is the opposite of coersion. The goal of Satyagraha, therefore, must be concrete, firm and definite. A Satyagrahi should be held on the truth. He has to make the opponent to realize his wrong and to induce him to change his course of conduct. A Satyagrahi must try to overcome evil by good, anger by love, untruth by truth, himsa by ahimsa. This principle has also been expounded by Lord Budha, Christ and they practised in their lives. Tolstoy, Thoreau and Ruskin also mentioned that in their works. In this process, a Satyagraha should distinguish between the wrong and wrong doer. A satyagrahi must be honest and non-violent. According to Gandhiji, "non-violence is non-killing. It is not the cult of defencelessness, a weapon of the weak, but on the contrary it can be employed only by the strong."

Besides it, as satyagrahi must be disciplined and legal to his immediate commander. In the realisation of his object nothing not even the loss of liberty, possession, family, should deter him. He must accept everything cheerfully as a great Greek philosopher, Socrates who drank a cup of poision for the truth and obeyed the principle of Satyagraha. In addition to him, Meerabai and Prahalad had obeyed Satyagrah by enduring insult by her own Kinsmen and by going against his father respectively. It is a truth.

2. The Codes of Conduct for a Satyagrahi Leader

There are several codes of conduct for a Satyagrahi leader. Anybody who wanted to be sincere Satyagrahi who had to follow the code of conducts.

These are as following:

(i) *Brahamcharya*: It is notable that Gandhiji had followed Brahamacharya when he was 37 only. Gandhiji, however, didnot use the term. 'Brahmacharya' in the popular sense. It does not means that one should not marry or that a married man cannot be Brahmachari. He (Gandhiji) used to emphisis the sex-discipline. "It consists in the fullest control over all the senses in thought, word and deed." It would provide one the power to achieve ones aims. For this, Satyagrahi must observe the Brahmacharya.

(ii) Gandhiji used to say that Satyagrahi must eat to live, not live to eat. It means that they should have fully co-operation between body and mind. Gandhiji has prescribed for a satyagrahi the appropriate strict restrictions coupled with fasting and prayer.

(iii) Satyagrahi must not be frightened at any rate. He should frighten from God only. In the words of Gandhiji, "Let us fear from God and we shall cease to be fearman."

(iv) He must get rid of wordly pleasures. He should not practise stealing and possession/collection.

(v) He should have his surplus property as a trust for the weaker sections of society. He therefore, should use his genius for the sake of society too.

(vi) Satyagrahi leader must abide by the principal of bread-labour, that means caring ones living by physical labour. It includes so needs of food and clothing.

(vii) He should believe in Swadeshi. It implies that the Satyagrahi for his needs should rest on the locally available goods and services. He should boycott the foreigner goods and jobs.

(viii) A Satyagrahi leader should deny any basis of discrimination such as caste or religion between man and man. He must adopt the unity and all life as a fundamental reality.

(ix) He must respect all religions equally.

(x) Humanism must be his way of life. Gandhiji was of opinion, "True humanity means strenuous and constant endeavour entirely directed to the service of humanity." "So long as one does not, of his own free will, put himself last among his fellow creatures." There is no salvation for him. Destruction of 'ego' within is strike for harmony and freedom complex.

3. Do Satyagraha like a Corporate Action

Whether Satyagraha may be individual or corporate, Gandhiji has indicated the following methods of corporate Satyagraha:

(i) Non co-operation with the evil is the foremost method of corporate or individual Satyagraha. All the tasks have been performed by dint of co-operation. Force can not assist the government alone to enforce its desires. Gandhiji said, "The subject ceases to fear the despotic force, its power is gone." Non-cooperation is the weapon that can be used to migrate the evil (as mentioned above).

(ii) *Civil Disobedience:* Law is essential for welfare and better life of the people. But if the law is made in disregard, to this purpose, it would not be moral and just. In this case, disobedience to law is moral. Civil disobedience in the legitimate weapon available to a citizen. To refuse to assist the ruler who misrules in the recognised right of the people since immemorial.

(iii) *Fasting:* It provides moral strength to Satyagrahi. It is means of purification.

(iv) *Hartal (Strikes):* This ceasation business to draw attention of the government and the people to issue the Satyagrahi has taken in hand. To make it effective, it must be voluntary. It must also be infrequent.

(v) *Social Boycott:* It is a social ostracism. It is an old practice to pressurise, the offender to abide by the norms. It must be resorted to in a limited sense against the person who challeges the public opinion. It presupposes a compact social system and a small community.

(vi) *Picketing:* It is resorted to prevent 'a particular preson' in general. The act of preventing should be peaceful, free from coercion, intimidation and discourtesy.

(vii) *Hijrat:* It is an arabic word, means, movement by the people in protest settle at another. Gandhiji advised Hijrat to the Harijans of Kavitha to migrate, as the caste Hindus of place were regularly terrorising over men and this had caused extreme disappointment among the Harijans. It can be resorted to only in extreme cases.

4. Satyagraha and Passive Resistance

Satyagraha is impassive resistance. According to Gandhiji, there is a sharp difference between two. Satyagrah gets involved active resistance to the evil. In active resistance is a misnomer. Satyagraha is non-violent, in active resistance has scope for use of weapons. Satyagraha has its own goal to change ones heart in active resistance has no goal for the ruin of evil but not the evil doer. Inactive resistance has no such distinction.

5. Duragraha (Prejudice)

To keep hatred, ill-feeling and anger towards others, is called Duragraha (Prejudice). Latter is not permissible for a satyagrahi. Mahatma Gandhi said, "It is the acid test of non-violence that in a non-violent conflict, there is no rancour left behind and in the end the enemies are converted into friends. This was my exprience in South Africa with General Smut, who was my bitterest opponent and critic.

Today, he is my "warmest friend." Ending the prejudice (Duragraha) the friendly relationship was set-up between India and Great Britain in post 1947. It resulted that India became a Member of Common Wealth and it is of even today. Similarly, Dr. Nelson Mandela, former President of South Africa became to be called a "Gandhi of South Africa". He made himself had identified to be a true Satyagrahi by forgetting prejudices towards white people whose rule had Jailed him for 28 years. Yet, the white people were included in the government when South Africa got freed by dint of Dr. Mandela. Consequently, Dr. Mandela became President and P.K. Botha (White origin) Vice-President of South Africa. In the same way Martin Luther King (of black origin) of USA sacrifies his life on the alter of Ahimsa and Satyagraha. He also experimented the doctrine of Gandhi in USA.

EXPERIMENT OF SATYAGRAHA BY MAHATMA GANDHI

It is well known that when Mahatma Gandhi was in South Africa, he was very influenced by the ethical ideal of Tolstoy which had been waving the heart of former. Consequently, he abnegated everything and began to live as a saint. He obeyed non-violence in his all tasks. This period of Gandhi was very significant because Gandhiji practised his self-purification and developed the system of Satyagraha. It was synonymised as weapon of Ahimsa. He, first of all, used that weapon in South Africa in his struggle against self-indulgence, political bluff and racial snobbery of the white regime. Later, he established satyagraha Ashram at Ahmedabad (now Gandhi Nagar) to house for eighteen children (all were members of his family) along with Magan Lal (his cousin). There the relatives and associated of those who had joined in the struggle in South Africa. were also housed. Again, due to inadequate accommodation and the outbreak of plague, the Ashram was shifted to the bank of river Sabarmati that was named as Sabarmati Ashram covering 150 acres. Gandhiji and Sardar Ballabh Bhai Patel made the peasantry launch a Satyagrah at Kheda district of Maharashtra (then Bombay). It began with the non-payment of revenue in face of threats of confiscation of land and other property. Finally, the government had to declare that the land revenue should be changed only if a peasant may be in a position to pay. This was the first success of Gandhiji's Satyagraha. Morever, this Satyagraha had the effect of liberating the peasantry from the fear of officialdom. Again, Gandhiji had been using his Satyagraha as a weapon (non-violence) during the whole period of the 'Freedom Movement' of India and he got the country freed only by dint of Satyagraha. We cannot understand the 'theory of Satyagraha' without talking of 'Champaran Movement'. We all know that how the white Sahebs of England used to exploit the poor and innocent peasants of Champaran. The helpless farmers had to grow indigo plants in their land on the order of those white Sahebs (foreign rulers). It is evident that Gandhiji took step to abolish this system with the help and co-operation of the people of Champaran. Champaran

Satyagraha became world-wide famous and it became the first pillar of 'Indian Freedom Movement' by Gandhi after his coming from South Africa. Gandhi expressed his views over Satyagraha and non-violence on broad sense. According to him, "The progress of nations takes place through both ways by evolution and by revolution. But that revolution is better which is non-violent. Revolution does not mean violence always." He uttered that the non-violence is the climax of love. We have no moral right to destroy those things (or beings) what we cannot create. Non-violence is the religion of a brave or bold person, not of a timid or coward ones. But inability/timidity/strengthlessness in response of violence is not non-violence, but it is cowardness. We should not compare non-violence with cowardness. But we cannot find truth (Satya) without non-violence. Non-violence is completely innocenceness (harmlessness). Full non-violence means complete absence of jealousy towards the whole well-beings of the world. But the result of non-violence comes late whereas the result of violence appears quickly. The fundamental condition of non-violence is love and pure selfless (non-vested) love is impossible without spotless purity of heart and body. If our non-violence is not such, our nation will have to face great jeopardy. Gandhi emphasised that satyagraha is not possible without non-violence. A Satyagrahi should have strength of truth (Satya). A Satyagrahi becomes the friend of all and foe of none. It is the just and primary condition of a successful Satyagraha. The root of Satyagraha depends upon to believe in the human nature. A Satyagrahi should not pain to others but he should always suffer from pain himself. This leads to the way of safe guarding Satya (truth). Satyagraha is again impossible without total abandonment of violence. The Satyagraha made for snatching the power and right is not Satyagraha, but 'Duragraha' (Mal-practice of truth). If the Satyagraha is the strongest power of the world, it is essential to have capacity to tolerate the maximum level of pain without having any ill- will or anger in the heart. If the Satyagrahi is defeated, he should not be ashamed to accept it. A Satyagrahi becomes always 'brave', he has not any minute feeling of cowardness in his heart ever.

Gandhi and Economics

Gandhi is known more as the father of Indian Independence movement, a practitioner of the technique of Satyagraha than as a celebrated economist in the conventional use of the term. Gandhi was not a theorist, he was primarily an actionist (activist)—a 'Karmyogi'. The solutions he offered for the alleviation of economic ills did not derive from any rigid approach (Misra, 2007). His solutions rooted in the necessity. His economics emerged primarily in response to the challenge that poverty ridden India faced at that point of time. Gandhi took into account India's most pressing economic problems and offered his own solutions. His economic thought took shape from these solutions and experience. Gandhi pleaded for an ideal economy where there was more truth than gold and greater charity than love of self (self-interest).

The centre of Gandhi's economic thought is 'man' and not the 'material prosperity'. He aimed at the development, upliftment and enrichment of human life rather than the standard of living with scant respect of human and social values. He regarded economics as a 'moral science' and laid tremendous emphasis on ethical aspect of the problem. According to him the pursuit of 'Swaraj' must necessarily involve the acceptance of 'Swadeshi'. Revival of hand spinning, a hopelessly uneconomic craft, signifies Gandhi's revolt against western machines, no less than the British Raj.

Gandhi focussed directly on *'economics'* in a lecture delivered at Allahabad on 22th December, 1916. In the major part of his address, Gandhi argued that *'material advance'* had a strong tendency to lead to *'moral decay'*. Gandhi influenced the various social groups by his charismatic appeal during the years 1915 to 1922. The years began with Gandhi's return from Sourth Africa, dramatic assertion of his leadership in the Indian National Congress and a radical restructuring of political life in India. The social and economic environment in India during the First World War created a congenial context for the emergence of Gandhi as an undisputed leader of Indian nationalism. It was a climate of moral and physical despondency (despair) that greeted Gandhi, arriving in India with his background of successful encounter with the British in Sourth Africa.

ECONOMICS OF SATYAGRAHA AND DEVELOPMENT

The Gandhian experiment concerning 'Satyagraha' was made on small scale first of all in India. In beginning its objective was to alleviate the complains and problems of the specific groups of farmers, peasants and labourers. Its political horizon began to increase and became comprehensive simultaneously. Gandhiji used this tool of 'Satyagraha' in the form of 'nation-wide movement' with two aims, first to unite the different social, lingual and religious groups in one chain and second to press the Britishers that they should leave the dynasty of South Asia, in the broad national interest and for the future course of huge economic devleopment of India.

The nation-wide 'Satyagraha' launched by Gandhi remained one of the biggest movements of collecting the people in the history of human beings. The social background of India is worth investigable for the beginning and success of *Satyagraha* at that time, in its disguise form to bring the scenario of economic development in India. At that time the population of India was 40 crore, out of which more than 75 percent resided in rural areas or in villages. Gandhiji wanted to use those people in the 'nationalist movement' through the 'Satyagrahi programmes'. Really, the colonial government exploited the labourers working in the farms and factories, far more than the middle class of that time. In spite of this, the 'nationalism' of the elite (Prosperous and happy) class was more eloquent, forceful and organised. To the contrary, the 'nationalsim of the poor and resourceless (depressed and down-trodden) class' was neither organised nor it had any modern (up-to-date) ideology. Practically the poor and down-trodden people used to express their voices of sorrows and agonies through spontaneons and local agitations, which were suppressed by the colonial rulers. In the 19th century there became many small-big agitations against the terror of British rulers and their allied Zamindars. Some of which continued for years. There was an unanswerable question in the beginning of 20th century that how to link the sorrows and agonies of poor and resourceless persons and the expectations of the middle class and to co-relate them with the 'public-based nationalism' meaningfully (Rao, 1995). Gandhiji remained successful in this compaign. Thus Gandhi became successful in co-relating and linking about 10 percent population, i.e. about 4 crore people for non-violent struggle against the most powerful imperialist force of that time. This endeavour was meant for people and by the people for the purpose of strong base of economic development in free India further.

Gandhi's early entry into Indian politics occured in 1917 and 1918 by his three localised Satyagraha movements, those were:

(i) Champaran (Bihar),
(ii) Kheda (Maharashtra—then Bombay),
(iii) Ahmedabad (Gujarat—then Bombay).

On every occasion Gandhi was invited to provide leadership where considerable mass mobilisation had already taken place under local initiative (Mishra, 2007). Thus it is evident that Gandhi had a tremendous task to eradicate the bottlenecks in the agararian system which was to be collapsed due to unrest of people. This activity proved as a pre-condition for reforming and systems and problems as well as for prosperous self-reliant farming further (after independence). This encouraged the peasants, farmars and agricultural labourers of that time who were suffering under 'forced farming' by the white sahebs (Bureaucrates of British Rulers).

Dandi Satyagraha

Although the compaigning of all Satyagraha done with cleverness by simple organisations and efficiency as the tokens of future programmes as a part of his vision. In 1930, the Dandi March, a travel of 241 miles was launched initially with his only 79 devoted volunteers including all classes of people throughout India which emerged into very large gathering further. This Satyagraha was launched against the tax (cess) on salt. The poorest and the marginal persons of India were being adversely effected by this act. His Satyagrahi companion travelled from Ahmedabad to Dandi village of Arabean Sea.

These activities of Gandhi as Satyagraha encouraged people, made the people vigilant and it prevailed awareness in the masses.

Non-Co-operation Movement

Gandhi launched non co-operation movement between 1919 to 1922. It was the decisive point of history. It entrusted confidence in the Indians with a view to eradicate the raj of slavery and for launching the self-reliant development path for India. By this movement it was no doubt that British raj would go, but the people were guessing for time (when it will go).

"Our all these towns are not India. India resides in its 7.50 lakh villages and all these towns depend upon these villages for their livelihood and lives. Since 200 years ago foreigners are exploiting India, in that activity those towns are the parties to it" (Upadhyaya, 2005).

The suitable job and employment as well as the grains obtained as the wage of it is actually the God for those unemployed and hungry people (*Ibid.*, 2005). The persons who get their food without doing work of their share are thieves. More that 80 percent people of India spend their lives as thieves, at least six months of the year. Gandhi said that the swaraj has no meaning until the lakhs and crores of our brothers do not learn to lead their lives to do any work instead of remaining idle or unemployed.

The boycott of foreign clothes by Gandhi had two aims, first to prevent the import of foreign goods and second enhancement of works, jobs and employment in Swadesh (own country) (*Ibid.*, 2005).

The cream of Gandhi's political programme was set out in Hind Swaraj (Gandhi, M.K., 1909). Hind Swaraj is the seed from which the tree of Gandhian thought has grown in full stature. Gandhi was anxious to impress upon the Indians that modern civilisation posed a great threat to them than colonialism. He belived that Indians took it for granted that modern civilisation was an unmixed blessing and colonialism an unmixed evil, forgetting that colonialism itself was a product of modern civilisation.

While Gandhi was still in South Africa (1906), he

developed a novel technique of political agitation which he called *'Satyagraha'* or *'moral persuation'*. Through this form of struggle he impressed upon the rulers of that country to extend to the Indian settlers a status of dignity in society. Satyagraha continued to be the ideological basis of Gandhi's political action since his arrival in India. Gandhi believed that the weapen of *Satyagraha* could persuade exploiters and evil doers to undergo a change of heart and redress the wrongs, moral and material, which they were inflicting upon others. Gandhi asserted that *Satyagraha* as a mode of social and political action was particularly relevant to the problem which confronted India in the opening decades of the 20th century. In the opinion of Gandhi, the best suited and judicious form of power is that, which by linking 'expectations of people' and 'life of truth' together, gives birth to the movement of social transformation and ethical upliftment (Rao, 1995).

When the industrialisation and technological progress is on the climax in the country, the Khadi, Swadeshi and Charkha (Spinning machine), etc. of Gandhi seem to be irrelevant today. But Gandhi was not against the industrialisation, machines or technological enhancement. Really Gandhiji was against that system of industrial production which does not make equitable and justiceable distribution of wealth and income (Parekh, 2007). Thus the idea (thought) of Gandhi is as like the learned economists of today. 'The economics of Gandhi' concentrated on the development of villages is any way not different from the concept of those thinkers who advocate about 'allround integrated development'. It is not any way different from the nobel laureate Amartya Sen's concept of 'freedom of choice' (Sen, Amartya 1998). The economic theories of Gandhi may be understood in the light of its inherent meaning or practical sense, not by its 'words' or 'literal meaning'. Gandhi never opposed the use of machines and capital. He never concentrated over only on the employing poors in more number. Gandhiji showed ethical vision for human life (Parekh, 2007). He was of the view that the matter which will have the maximum impact on the human life that will be the quality of his heart and mutual social relationship. Gandhi said that poverty is the curse for humanity and the meaning of development is not only the creation of wealth and assets. This wealth and asset should be equitably distributed instead of its concentration in limited hands. Economic equality means eradication of dispute (controversy) between capital and labour coming from an indefinite period. It means distribution of national income among crores of hungry and semi-nacked persons snatching from the hands of selected prosperous persons of the country. The concept of 'integrated development' also has the same value and supports this very ethos of Gandhi. This concept is based upon agriculture and such development which will have its access over far off villages where majority of India resides. This is the economics of 'Bharat' residing in the lakhs of villages, not only of that 'India' which plays in some hands of big cities or towns. He acted all over his life for "Bharat Mata Gram Vasini (India resides in its villages)." The relationship of development should be with the prosperousness and liberty of human beings. The contribution of income is possible as a constituent element of welfare and liberty but not as the only (sole) elements (Sen, Amartya, 1999).

The real thing Gandhi always meant to say that really the meaning of economics is social justice which encourages the welfare of all people including the most depressed class of society and is evident for a good life (Gandhi, M.K., 1937). It appears that at such time when industrial powers like Britain, U.S.A. and Germany were runnings rapidly towards industrialisation, Gandhiji was advocating of such path of development in which the village would produce all its essential goods. Besides it, the village would produce some more goods so that it might supply the essential food and clothings for the towns when the western powerful industrial sovereignties were communicating the imperialism in the colonies of Asia and Africa, Gandhiji was advocating for a closed and self-reliant economy which had nothing or negligible relationship with the world. It is evident that Gandhi wrote that the big industries would had to be centralised and nationalised. The heavy industries would have least participation in the comprehensive national activities concentrated in the villages (Gandhi, 1945). Gandhi used Charkha (spinning wheel) as the tool or weapon against the big industrial power of Great Britain and saw it as the biggest source of employment for the crores of Indian poors after agriculture. Gandhi said, 'I see God in the each fibre of cotton spoon by the Charkha' (Constructive Programme, 1945). He said that Charkha (spinning wheel) was the only profession which may provide employment to crores of Indians. Gandhi was not the apponent of heavy industries and industrialisation rather than those conditions in which a man is made the passive tools (machines) of that technology. This inhuman activity was as curse for him. He treated a man as an end, not as only a means. He was the follower of the middle path. The then communist and capitalist thinkers both crticised Gandhi.

Gandhi advocated 'trusteeship'. He said the owners of wealth and assets should treat themselves as the trustees of poor persons, which was undigestible for both communist and capitalist thinkers. In that mode he said, 'Sabai Bhumi Gopal Ki (all land belong to the tillers)'.

It reveals the insight or the inner vision of Gandhi towards wealth and man. Gandhiji was always afraid of two things first 'foolish consumeralism' and its explosive fetal (adverse) effects and second 'neglecting environment' in dealing with development. He always advocated for 'sustainable development'. Such systems should be developed which may care of 'social production' as well as 'the protection of environment'. Both these matters are not contradictory to each other, but are complementary to each other. These thoughts of Gandhi reflect practicability as well as feasibility. His economic philosophy shows his intensive inner vision towards the economic development of developing as well as developed countries. Gandhiji remarked that the creation of God (means all natural resources) is adequate for the satisfaction of human wants, but it is not sufficicient for fulfilling man's greed (selfishness or self-interest).

Gandhi advocated sustainable development, but it does not mean that he was uninterested with procedures of development of modern society. He was much interested with the 'market' and 'command systems', etc. because these are the sources for increasing production in the current world. But Gandhi said that if the market is allowed to go in its own way (freely or spontaneously), it may be bottleneck in the way of production in lieu of encouraging it (*Hind Swaraj,* 1990). He was aware of the fact that command systems of social production may bring then unnatural deformities.

Gandhi made us emancipated from fear. It was the pre-condition of development. The Britishes chalked out the path of development from their own point of view. Gandhi wanted to disconnect their system and to establish own channel for our future course of development which was impossible without freedom, and before freedom it was essential to dismantle and destroy their systems. Now India is free. We have launched our own system of planning for economic development. We have emancipated ourselves from famine which is immensable achievment of India. But we have remained unsuccessful in eradicating hunger, disease, illiteracy, mal-nutrition, economic exploitation, worst condition of dalit, injustice, communal biasness (prejudice) towards minorities, negligence and unequal treatment with women, racial and cast discrimination and many other economic and social deformities. We have pride over the role of economic growth. But we forget Gandhi's social justice.

Economic growth is good, but it is meaningless without equality, employment and creating income opportunities. Balanced growth is needed. We need sustainable development and the first condition of sustainable development is equal distribution. Our economists recommend 'trickle-down theory' as a means to alleviate poverty. But how wonderful it is to concentrate the wealth in the hands of wealthy persons and to drop a drop of water in the mouth of those poors whose wombs are empty due to mal-nutrition. Gandhi always pleaded for villages. But the disparity of villages and towns is visible evidently.

Our struggle was started by Gandhi as Satyagraha and other compaigns. He began struggle of independence. But that struggle is not over upto now. It will continue till the last person of the society is not fed and quenched his thirst. The corruption is great challenge for our system now. The cancer of corruption must be extinguished from the development and democracy. Let us think for millions of persons living below poverty line! Let us do something for those down-trodden people of nation!

By all means we can say that Satyagraha of Mahatma Gandhi is more relevant than other principles or theories in this environment of global unrest, i.e. terrorism, corruption, communal rift and for chosing the proper path for economic development of India. Use of power force and legal actions taken by the government are not proving adequate to end these evils. By those means both evil and evil-doers will be ended. Here evils have to be abolished but not evil doers. In this case Satyagraha of Mahatma Gandhi only remains as a final alternative to abolish above evils all over the globe and nothingelse.

> *'Woods are lovely, dark and deep.....*
> *And miles to go before I sleep'.*

References

Chakravarty, Madhumita (2007), 'Vikash Ki Andhi Mein Ab Bhi Chalenge Gandhi', *Hindustan*, Hindi Daily, August, 3.

Chandra, Bipin (1988), *India's Struggle for Independence* (1857-1947), Penguin Books, New Delhi, pp. 172-78.

Gandhi, M.K. 'Gramodyog', Sarva Sewa Sangh Publication, Raj Ghat, Varanasi, June.

Gandhi, M.K. (1909), 'Hind Swaraj', Sarva Sewa Sangh Publication, Raj Ghat, Varanasi, June.

Gandhi, M.K. (1926), '*Young India*', Sarva Sewa Sangh Publication, Raj Ghat, Varanasi, June.

Gandhi, M.K. (1937), 'The Harijan', Sarva Sewa Sangh Publication, Raj Ghat, Varanasi, June.

Gandhi, M.K. (1945), 'Constructive Programme', Sarva Sewa Sangh Publication, Raj Ghat, Varanasi, June.

Grover, B.L. (1993), 'Modern Indian History (From 1707 to the Present Day)', S. Chand and Company Ltd., New Delhi, pp. 424.

Gupta, Vishw Prakash/Gupta, Mohini (2004), "Sardar Bhagat Singh," *Vyakti Aur Vichar*, Radha Publication, New Delhi, Sharma, Shri Ram (2004), 'Gandhi, The Man Among Men,' Radha Publication, New Delhi.

Jain, V. (2004), 'M.K. Gandhi; Leader of the Masses,' Radha Publication, New Delhi.

Kapoor, A.N./Gupta, V.P. (2004), 'Facts of Gandhian Life and Thought,' Radha Publication, New Delhi.

Maiduli, Dr. Ram Dayal (1991), 'Bapu Ne Kaha Tha,' Pubication Department, Ministry of Information and Broadcasting, Government of India, New Delhi.

Misha, J.P. (2007), 'Emergence of Gandhi,' *Yojana* (English), August, pp. 45-46.

Parekh, Bhikhoo (2007), 'Thoughts of Gandhi on Poverty Alleviation and Public Empowerment.

Parekh, Bhikhoo and Prahalad, C.K. (2007), Political Analysis International Conference on 'Peace, Non-Violence and Empowerment: Gandhian Philosophy in 21st Century'.

Paswan, Yogeshwar (2001), 'Government's Policies Towards Scheduled Castes in Bihar', Scheduled Castes In India', Ed. Birendra Kumar Singh, Maharaja Lakshmishwar Singh Research Society, Darbhanga (Bihar), pp. 21-61.

Prof. Kachroo, J.L. (1982), "Gandhi, Tagore, J. Nehru; Contribution and Thought," *Indian Culture Series,* Book Hive Publication, New Delhi, pp. 41-44.

Rao, P.V. Narasimha (1995), 'Vishwin Shatavdi Ke Yug Purush', pp. 11-14.

Ratanesh, Dr. Kumar (2007), 'Bharat Mein Dalit Andolan', Sodh Samiksha, ed. Prof. Jiwatesh Kumar Singh, J.P. Gramin Avan Shram Adhyayan Sansthan, Gautam Nagar, New Colony, Gannipur, Muzaffarpur (Bihar), pp. 58-59.

Renu, Prakash (1991), "Alpsankhyak Varg Vibhajan Tatha Jativad", *Ambedkar Ne Kaha Tha,* Publication Department, Ministry of Information and Broadcasting, Government of India, New Delhi.

Report (2007), 'Peace, Non-Violence, Empowerment: Gandhian Philosophy in 21st century', International Conference, New Delhi, July.

Roy, Surendra (2004), 'Gandhi's Significant Role in the Freedom Movement', 'The Independent India: A Political Glimse' (1947-2000), Yuvak Sansthan Prakashan, Kishanpur, Samastipur, Bihar, pp. III-IV.

Sen, Amartya (1998), 'Freedom of Choice'.

Sen, Amartya (1999), 'Development and Freedom'.

Sharma, Jai Narayan (2004) 'Gandhian Perspective of Rural Development,' *Journal of Gandhian Studies,* Ed. A.D. Mishra, Radha Publication, New Delhi.

Sood, Jyoti Prasad (1992-93), *Main Political Thinkers,* K. Nath and Company, Meerut.

Thakur, R.N. and Roy, Surendra (2007), 'Mahatma Gandhi and Satyagraha,' Indian Society of Gandhian Studies, New Delhi.

Thakur, R.N. and Roy, Surendra (2007), 'Relevance of B.R. Ambedkar and Gandhi', Political Economy of B.R. Ambedkar, J.P. Gramin Shrama Adhyayan Sansthan, New Colony, Gautam Nivas, Gannipur, Muzaffarpur (Bihar).

Upadhyaya, Hari Bhau (2005), 'Bapoo Katha (1920-1948),' Sarva Sewa Sangh Publication, Raj Ghat, Varanasi, June.

25

Economic Ideas of Gandhiji—Its Relevance

R.U. SINGH AND MAHESHWAR GOIT

The path of the liberalisation, privatisation and globalisation (LPG) that India adopted has definitely accelerated the growth of economy but it can neither ensure overall developments nor can guarantee the independence of Indian Industries. The solution lies in the Gandhian framework that focuses on the fulfilment of need and not the greed. The Gandhian formulation with regard to the economic system will not be dragging us backward rather it will carry us to progress. Gandhiji has been critic of modern civilisation but he agreed with everything which was not against humanity. Rudolph and Rudolph in "post-modern Gandhi" have rightly observed that Gandhiji set the agenda for post-modernism.

While Interpreting and re-interpreting Gandhiji one must analyse the economic extension of his thought in accordance with the place and time. Our circumstances do not allow us to ignore Gandhiji. There are number of dimensions in his thought. In many sense his thoughts are even more relevant today than his time.

INTRODUCTION

Mahatma Gandhi, the embodiment of truth and non-violence is the great thinker of modern times who added many new dimensions to the history of thought. He was not merely a philosopher of thinker rather a man of action who reacted with vigour to every problem—political, social and economic with truthful means. His thought is intensely practical and comprehensive. It is because of his multi-dimensional thought that the people around the world have remained engaged in exploring, explaining and evaluating the relevance of Gandhian thought for the last five decades. But the more we explore the Gandhism, the more we feel ignorant and thus get involved in knowing about Gandhian thought and its relevance to new economic policy of India.

Mahatma Gandhi was not conventional economist like Adam Smith, Alfred Marshall, J.M. Keynes, etc. He did not compose voluminous treaties on economic ideology. In his seminal essay *'Hind Swaraj'* and several lectures, articles and editorials in *'Young India'*, *'Harijan'* and *'Indian Opinion'*, he made references to the kind of economic system, he considered as ideal for India. He advocated certain policies with regard to the development of Indian agriculture, industries, swadeshi, etc. He did not present his economic ideas in any systematic manner and at one place, they have to be culled from innumerable passage occurring in his article interview, speeches and answer to the questions which are now available in 100 volume project named as *"The Collected Works of Mahatma Gandhi."*

RELEVANCE OF GANDHIAN ECONOMICS

In the new era of globalisation the production structure in world economy is undergoing a serious change. The computer technology has now spread in all forms of industrial production. The space and bio-technologies are on the threshold of opening up new ways of production. The industrial engineers now make a distinction between the existing nature of production, (large volume standardized production) and the growing new type of production known as "flexible production." The large volume standardized production is now on a continuous-decline. On the other hand, flexible production is registering a high rate of growth. It is flexible production that incorporates the new knowledge and technologies in electronics and other related fields. The effect of the changes in this production structure is fundamental. It involves nothing short of a new industrial revolution that is bound to change social institutions and moral values of the entire society. Looking at the global production system, this change is now in full swing. The success of Japanese and European economies lies in the fact that these economies have made the necessary institutional and related changes to facilitate the 'flexible production' system.

Further, the interesting thing about this new production system is that it requires a very different types of relations in the work place; cooperation and collaboration instead of competition in the large volume standardized production system. "In the emerging era of productivity, social justice is not incompatible with economic growth *but essential to it.* A social organisation promised on equity, security and participation will generate greater productivity than one premises on greed and fear. Collaboration and collective adaptation are coming to be more important to an industrialised nation's well-being than are personal daring and ambition. And at an even more fundamental level, the goals of prosperity and social justice can not validity be separated." To a large extent, the ideas of social justice, equity, participation, security, etc. are the very essential in Gandhian Economics. To promote flexible production and therefore prosperity, the economic policies have to follow, increasingly from the principles of Gandhian Economics.

GANDHIJI AND INDUSTRIALISATION

Gandhi saw the difficulties and dangers of indiscriminate industrialisation in under-developed countries which might result in the concentration of wealth in the hands of a few, or the creation of industrialised urban areas making for lop-sided development and exploitation. Gandhi also advocated that with growing industrialisation the same exploitative relationship between Britain and India would come to exist between India's cities and her country side.[1] Mahatma Gandhi was never against industrialisation rather he was against the 'craze' for large scale industrialisation which may make the reduction of poverty more difficult. Gandhiji knew about his attitude to machinery being much misunderstood. He, therefore, tried to clarify repeatedly his stand thus: 'My opposition to machinery is much, misunderstood, I am opposed to machinery which displaces labour and leaves it idle."[2] He further wrote, "What I object to is the craze for machinery not machinery as such. The craze is for what they call labour-saying machinery."[3] Elimination of mass poverty and unemployment in the shortest possible period was Gandhi's Central Concern and he believed in giving productive employment rather than 'doles' because, in his ideas "the supreme consideration is man"[4] not economic man of Adam Smith but a man with soul, and ethical values and therefore Gandhiji wrote "that economics is untrue which ignores moral values."[5] Hence emphasized to organize a network of small, cottage and village industries in the decentralised sector on a very wide basis. Gandhiji foresaw that modernisation would raise per worker capital requirements too rapidly and keep misery on the masses and urbanisation, equal to modern industrialisation, will impose excessive burdens of infrastructure build-up beyond the means of the poor nations. That is why Gandhi was in favour of "Production by masses" in place of the modern craze for "mass production."[6] He realised that the problem of India's economic development is not merely one of growth but also of rehabilitation and arresting of the growing drift towards urbanisation, a decentralisation of productive activities and an integration of rural and urban economics to ensure orderly production according to needs and therefore, pleaded for a decentralised system industry on a co-operative basis drawing the frontiers of the common man's world closer to him. This is reason that Prof. G.D.H. Cole, has accepted in 'A Guide to Modern Politics', the Gandhian campaign as a "practical attempt to relieve the poverty and uplift the standards of the Indian villagers."[7]

GANDHIJI AND ECONOMIC SYSTEM

The Gandhian concept of decentralisation and planning is reflected in his views on production, distribution, consumption and exchange. The Mahatma was in favour of "Production by masses" in place of the modern craze for "mass production." He favoured participative growth with social justice so that the benefits of production may trickle down to the millions of masses. The Mahatma favoured an appropriate middle technology which would help augment agricultural and industrial production for raising the per capita productivity without throwing people out of employment. Gandhi's concern for employment crystalised in his statement on the eve of independence on the purpose of planning as "real planning consisted in the best utilisation of the whole manpower of India." In the Gandhian scheme emphasis is laid on self-employment.

The whole programme of Mahatma Gandhi is built on the solid foundation of economic equality and distributive justice which never means possession of an equal amount of worldly goods by everyone. It means that every one will have proper house to live, sufficient and balanced food to eat and sufficient Khadi to cover himself. Gandhiji ceaselessly talked of meeting the basic needs of food, clothing and shelter for the last man of India. But equal distribution was not to be confused with crude equality. "The real implication of equal distribution is that each man shall have the where withal to supply all his natural needs and no more. To bring this ideal into being the entire social order has got to be reconstructed. A society based on non-violence cannot nature any other social ideal." Gandhiji asserted "The possession of inordinate wealth by individuals should be held as a crime against India's humanity."[10] He further observes, "My ideal is equal distribution, but so far as I can see it is not to be realised. I therefore work for equitable distribution."[11]

Mahatma's thinking about consumption was derived from his definition of civilisation, his faith redistribution as well as his commitment to be ideal of non-possession which God seekers must purpose. An aesthetically and hedonistically luxurious life was alien to the Gandhian ethos.

As Gandhi say, "He (who has made the ideal of equal distribution a part of his being) world reduce his wants to a minimum, bearing in mind the poverty in India."[12] According to Gandhiji civilisation in the real sense of the term, consists not in the multiplication of wants but in their deliberate and voluntary restrictions"[13].

In the ideal of "villagism", Gandhiji advocated barter system. Bapu was conscious of the blessings of money and the importance of monetary policy but he was equally apprehensive of the veil, peril and confusion that results from the dominance of money. In the Gandhian economy labour is the coin which may be bartered for an material things. When his self-sufficient village needs something which it cannot produce, it can easily exchange with the produce which has been grown in abundance at another place. Thus Gandhiji envisaged that trade will be the barter system. When objected that this is a revision to the primitive system of barter, Gandhi replied "Is not all international trade based on the barter system? On the whole the Gandhian view on technology, employment, growth and social justice is neatly expressed in the passage. "I want to save time and labour, not for a fraction of man kind, but for all. I want the concentration of wealth not in the hands of a few, but in the hands of all. Today machinery helps the few to ride on the backs of the millions. The against behind it is not the philanthropy to save labour but greed. It is against this constitution of thing that I am fighting with all my might."

Gandhi' new theory of trusteeship was put forth to remove the wide disparity between the rich and the hungry millions. He said that he would personally prefer decentralisation of power from the hands of the state, through and emphasis on trusteeship. He also believed that trusteeship could bring about a non-violent state. A harmonious relationship between labour and capital merge out of a trusteeship theory that placed emphasis on a balanced relationship between the rich and the poor.

GANDHIJI AND ECONOMIC PLANNING

Gandhian ideas of economic development are not the

outmoded concepts but are essentially rational and scientific concepts and in tune with modern economic themes regarding economic development of the developing countries like India. Though Gandhiji focused his attention mostly on the socio-economic problems present in India, but his analysis, vision and strategy bore relevance throughout the globe. But setting aside the world-wide aspect for the movement, even India is apparently no closer to 'Swaraj', than it was while under the British. Yet, on closer examination, we can see that Gandhij's work has not come to an end. His ideas, so often rejected, misunderstood, and neglected, are finding their way in the consciousness of the work and they are becoming popular and expanding. It is a movement that aims at nothing less than an ultimate transformation of the world a movement that is not likely to disappear until and unless peace on each becomes a reality.[9] Thus it becomes quite clear that if the Gandhian ideas are linked up with the broad functioning of our economic planning, we are sure to achieve the objectives of our plans.

As our ends are primarily related to eradication of countrywide poverty and unemployment, "our plans must be rooted in the condition that prevail in our land" and must "touch every living person in India" and "provide first the things the village need."[8] This can be possible only by adopting the Gandhian contents in our economic planning. But the success of even Gandhian way of planning is subject of certain conditions. This will require radical changes in the present system of planning and execution. First, planning process should be much from the bottom having the idea of decentralised planning and the plan must consider the needs and circumstances of each family which is below the poverty line. Additional avenues of employment within a reasonable distance must be provided to make full employment a reality. Second the executors or the administrative structure must be able to deliver to every family the basic benefits provides in the plan and participation of people through decentralised people's organisation must be secured in plan formulation and its implementation. Such an approach will need a total reorientation of the present administrative procedure and reorientation of the Panchayats in such a way that they may work as an economic and welfare unit rather than as its present shape being purely involved in political activities. This intends to have people-oriented micro-level sectoral planning with whole hearted support of the plan for the welfare of the masses.

If the plan of the country is prepared and implemented in the light of the Gandhian concepts giving appropriate priorities to the sectors relevant for developing the standard of life of the masses along with other allied sectors, the solution of the existing socio-economic problems will come nearer to our approach and the nation along with all its glamorous achievements, will be able to solve the basic problems of poverty, unemployment and inequality in the distribution of income and wealth which was the dream of the 'Father of Nation' for independent India.

TRUSTEESHIP

Trusteeship was the economic term Gandhi gave to the idea that all wealth should be treated as a national trust. The idea was born during the train journey form Johannesburg to St. Martizburg on the night of 7th June, 1893 while reading Raskin's 'Unto this Last'. The book changed the economic vision of 'Coolie Barrister' who was thrown out of the 1st class compartment bag and baggage, the incident changed the destinies of half of the people of the world.

The phoenix farm settlement and the Tolstoy farms were based on the principle of trusteeship. Gandhi said there should be minimum wage and ceiling on maximum the capitalist's property. Minimum has no meaning unless there is a ceiling on maximum. All economists today agree that trusteeship is the practical solution of present day malpractices in property and misdistribution of wealth. In fact, trusteeship is the only way to end capitalism without ending the capitalist who could be a trustee of his own wealth. For his won household expenses he would be entitled to a reasonable share.

It was not Gandhi idea to rob the rich or the rajas and the Maharajas to lead a life of penury. He only told them to voluntarily renounce their ownership. Why can't the head of the state tell his subjects that they are the real owners of the state property which is the only way to achieve socialism through democratic and non-violent means.

Gandhi always drew a distinction between the man and the system, it was an essential part of his non-violent approach. It was this approach which made him view his short comings rigorously and to be charitable in judging others. People accused Gandhi that he was the friend of the capitalists but the fact remains that nobody fought them harder. All he expected the rich to hold their riches and talents in trust and use them in the service of society. 'To insist on more' he said with a smile, 'would be to kill the goose that laid the golden eggs'.

Notes and References

1. Shephard, Mark, "Mahatma Gandhi: The Legacy", *Gandhi Marg*, April 1980, p. 31.
2. *Harijan*, 15 September 1946, p. 310.
3. *Young India*, 13 November 1924, p. 378.
4. Prabhu, R.K. and Rao, U.R., "The Mind of Mahatma Gandhi," Navajivan Publishing House, Ahmedabad, p. 234.
5. Kripalani, Krishna, 'All Men are Brothers, Navajivan Publishing House, Ahmedabad, p. 166.
6. Cole, G.D.H., Quoted in K. Thiagarajan, "Impact of Gandhian Economic on India's Economic Development", *Khadi Gramudyog*, March 1977, p. 270.
7. M.K. Gandhi: *Harijan*, 2 November, 1934.
8. Kumarappa, J.C., 'An Overall Plan for Rural Development, p. 3.
9. Shephard, Mark, "Mahatma Gandhi: The Legacy", *Gandhi Marg*, March 1983, p. 38.
10. Raj Krishna: Voluntary Action, Sept. 1978, Vol. XX, No. 9, p. 7.
11. *Ibid.*
12. *Ibid*
13. *Ibid.*, p. 8.

26

Economics of Mahatma Gandhi: Challenges and Development

G.M. BHAT AND SHABIR AHMAD PADDER

Modern world is faced with a multi-faceted economic crisis entailing poverty in the midst of plenty, insecurity of employment, alienation, erosion of moral values, uncontrolled urbanisation, environmental pollution, depletion of resources, ecological imbalance, inflation and other monetary and economic problems. The efforts to solve the problem by technological progress and exploitation of natural resources are further aggravating the situation. As a matter of fact, the problems are becoming more and more complex and gigantic day-by-day. One of the most important characteristics of the world economic problems of today is their inter-connectedness and inter-dependence. The problems act and interact upon each other, have positive feedback loops, and are not restricted to national boundaries. All these factors have gone a long way in increasing the magnitude and complexity of the problems. As a result, the traditional fragmentary economic solutions have been rendered quite ineffective in tackling these problems of a complex and global nature. As the Club of Rome holds, "The major problems facing mankind are of such complexity and are so inter-related that traditional institutions and policies are no longer able to cope with them, not even come to grips with their full content."[1]

The current economic crisis with all its complexity calls into question the very foundations of economics. The nature of the pressing economic problems that the world is facing today and the failure of the traditional economics to find a solution to them, necessitates a deep examination of the world-view underlying the entire economic thought. The solution to our problems cannot be found from within the existing theoretical frame-work, as the roots of the problems lie somewhere outside the system in the paradigm that bears upon the basic values and concepts of economics. In Schumacher's language, a deep study of meta-economics is required. "The study of economics is too narrow and too fragmentary to lead to valid insights, unless complemented, and completed by a study meta-economics."[2] *The present economic system contains the seeds of its own destruction. If the economic activity continues with the old methodology motivated by the traditional economic drives, the entire economic system is likely to meet a disastrous end. A study team at MIT (U.S.A.), under the guidance of Prof. Dennis Meadows, has concluded, "If the present growth trends in world population, industrialisation, pollution, food production and resource depletion continue unchanged, the limits to growth on this planet will be reached sometimes within the next one hundred years."*[3] *The restructuring of economics based on a new vision of reality is urgently required. It is in this connection that Gandhian Economics based on a fundamentally different paradigm becomes most relevant. Dr. V.K.R.V. Rao has observed, "Gandhi's ideas are beginning to command increasing attention in a world that is disillusioned by the working of both capitalism and communism and attracted by the possibility that the circle can be squared with economic growth, social justice, full employment, economic and social equality, political democracy, and individual freedoms all forming components of a harmonious new social order."*[4]

According to him, "the economic constitution of India and for the matter of that of the world, should be such that no one under it should suffer for want of food and clothing."[5] But he did not favour giving alms or doles and instead advocated 'Gospel of work' or 'Bread Labour' described in the Gita as Yajna. He tried to combine the secular and immediate needs with his philosophical approach to the entire development problem. He had a holistic conception of development—material, social, cultural and moral development. Hence, he wanted to create moral basis for Economic progress. To him, "true economics never militates against the highest ethical standard."[6] In Gandhi, man emerges at the centre of all economic or political development. Hence he challenged the technological basis of modern civilisation, which has caused environmental pollution. Where population pressure is too high to sustain on the per capita land available, it should not displace human labour. Where heavy and large-scale industries are inevitable it should be under producer's control. All production should be for consumption and not for Profit. Production and Consumption should be localised. Gandhi defined basic needs in terms of material and non-material needs. He did not accept multiplication of wants as the yardstick of progress. Hence he did not regard the western living standard as its ideal. It was an hindrance to man's spiritual or higher aspiration. Hence he was against indiscriminate large-scale mechanisation of life. All these points out towards Gandhi's relevance to the present predicament.

GANDHIJI AND SUSTAINABLE DEVELOPMENT

Gandhiji wanted to understand nature as an expression of God and tried to see life in everything breaking down even the customary distinction between the animate and the inanimate. He drew inspiration from the modern sacrifice researches. The idea of the continuity through different forms of being got confirmation even from Darwinian theory of evolution. But the Darwinion theory was taken by Gandhi as supporting the idea of gradual progress. Gandhi's call for

"Return to Nature", his fondness for naturopathy was an indication of this temper. Man has to learn to live in harmony not only with his fellows beings but with the entire nature—animate as well inanimate. That we should live together in peace is the basic ethics of all ethics. We are living in world divided politically, economically and racially. There are only a few rich nations. For example, U.S.A.. with a population of 6% consumes about 40% of world resources. The affluent nations within their specialised knowledge plunder the planet in the name of development. Cursed with poverty and illiteracy, the poor nations are constained to use Nature for their need. Hence the connect afford to conserve Nature when the rich nations are living a life of affluence. Unless the humanity has to perceive the prime need to develop on the principle of "One Earth" and "One World" with a spirit of sharing and just distribution of Nature's wealth cutting across the nationalistic boarders, we cannot achieve a sustainable development. Living with a sense division, separation and discrimination is detrimental to a health and meaningful life and the peaceful world.

Gandhi knew that the cause of the present chaos is exploitation not only of the weaker nations by the stronger, but of sister nations by sister nations. Economic equality is the master key to non-violent independence. At the root of equal distribution live the Gandhian principle of trusteeship. The wealth of the world is a common property. We are only its trustees. Hence, coal or mica of India or wheat grown in U.S.A. should be treated as common property of the world. India suffers from over-population where as Australia needs population. In short, if we can evolve an world economic order based on justice and need of the whole of humanity, there is less scope for strife. Nature produces enough for our wants but if we indulge in cruel exploitation of nature, we will face many problems including environmental disasters.

So the root cause of ecological imbalances and disasterless in our extravagant style of life. No doubt, nature produces enough for our wants but there is limitation to it. There is no limit to our desires. Excessive consumption or rather extravagance has been hall-mark of our civilisation. There should be self-restraint exercised in every sphere of life. If we go on increasing our wants, we shall need such instruments which can exploit natural resources more and more. Hence our unbridled desires for more and more comforts and luxuries implies that we should have a particular model of development and for that model of development, we need a particular technology. The modern sensate civilisation is the root cause of environmental problems. Gandhi has rightly said that "Nature has given enough to satisfy our needs but not our greed." He goes further to assert that "the world does not have sufficient things to meet the greed of a single person."[7]

Gandhiji and Industrializaiton

Gandhi saw the difficulties and dangers of indiscriminate industrialisation in under-developed countries which might result in the concentration of wealth in the hands of a few, or the creation of industrialised urban areas making for lop-sided development and exploitation. Gandhi also advocated that with growing industrialisation the same exploitative relationship between Britain and India would come to exist between India's cities and her country side.[8] Mahatma Gandhi was never against industrialisation rather he was against the 'craze' for large scale industrialisation with the help of indiscrimate technological modernisation which may make the reduction of poverty more difficult. Gandhiji knew about his attitude to machinery being much misunderstood. He, therefore, tried to clarify repeatedly his stand thus: 'My opposition to machinery is much misunderstood, I am opposed to machinery which displaces labour and leaves it idle."[9] He further wrote, "What I object to is the craze for machinery not machinery as such. The craze is for what they call labour-saving machinery."[10] Elimination of mass poverty and unemployment in the shortest possible period was Gandhi's central concern and he believed in giving productive employment rather than 'doles' because, in his ideas "the supreme consideration is man"[11] not economic man of Adam Smith but a man with soul, and ethical values and therefore Gandhiji wrote "that economics is untrue which ignores moral values."[12] Hence emphasized to organize a network of small, cottage and village industries in the decentralised sector on a very wide basis. Gandhiji foresaw that modernisation would raise per worker capital requirements too rapidly and keep misery on the masses and urbanisation, equal to modern industrialisation, will impose excessive burdens of infrastructure build-up beyond the means of the poor nations. That is why Gandhi was in favour of "Production by masses" in place of the modern craze for "mass production." He realised that the problem of India's economic development is not merely one of growth but also of rehabilitation and arresting of the growing drift towards urbanisation, a decentralisation of productive activities and an integration of rural and urban economics to ensure orderly production according to needs and therefore, pleaded for a decentralised system industry on a co-operative basis drawing the frontiers of the common man's world closer to him. This is reason that Prof. G.D.H. Cole, has accepted in 'A Guide to Modern Politics, the Gandhian campaign as a "practical attempt to relieve the poverty and uplift the standards of the Indian villagers."[13]

Salient Features of Gandhi's Multidimensional Views about Machinery and Technology

1. Machinery is not the end but the means for human happiness. Man is the supreme consideration. Machine is for man, not man for machine.
2. Gandhi challenged the technological basis of modern civilisation and so he posited an alternative to the industrial technique of today.
3. Any industrial technique must be geard to meet the basic human needs of food, clothing and housing.
4. Gandhi was not against development of industry provided: (a) it does not create unemployment, (b) it does not become an instrument of exploitation of man or nation, (c) it does not result in unlimited degradation of natural resources and resulting in pollution hazards, (d) it should not be used to concentrate wealth in the hands of a few

in total disregard to millions, (e) it should foster decentralisation as centralisation cannot be sustained and defended without adequate force, (f) Instead of mass-production, he preferred production by masses and hence his insistence upon rural industrialisation, cottage and small industries, (g) Machinery should help and ease human effort so he welcomed the use of machinery which turns waste land into arable and fertile lands and removes the drudgery of man, (h) Production should be localised, (i) where heavy and large-scale industries are inevitable, they should be under producer's control.

Modern technology and industrialisation has created manifold problems, not for one nation but for the whole world, and the entire humanity. Evils of unbridled industrialism has created crisis literature preoccupied with the theme of social disintegration and psychoneurotic disorders 'resulting from the growth of an over-centralised, over-mechanized industrial structure'.[14] Man, however, falliable and fallen, is much more than a machine.[15] Men have been entirely divorced from the world of nature.[16] This forced attainment of the human organism to the rigid and unnatural routines of the city, the factory and the machine has produced chronic, nerve-shattering tensions. There has been loss of permanent contact with natural elements, natural beings and rhythms has blunted and bifurcated sensibility.[17] Masses of men have been huddled into hideous over-crowded cities like cages of 'human spirit', which is a 'pathological phenomenon', the fountain source of divitalisation and delinquency. Modern techniques with excessive specialisation have deprived of all spontaneity, creative, aesthetic joy and all personal and human significance. Researches show over 60% workers suffered badly from boredom in the metallurgical industry.[18] Mechanisation and automation have reduced man to mere clog in the wheel, where men are corrupted and degraded.[19] The report of the Study of Conference on Human Problems of Industrial Communities[20] came to the conclusion that industry was not end in itself

UNESCO study complains of the lack of criminality satisfaction in modern culture.[21]

Production, Distribution, Consumption, Exchange and Employment

Gandhi was not a professional economist in the true sense of the term. But in a large and eventful life he had occasion to develop his economic ideas based on the situation in India. Gandhian economic theory provides a new and realistic approach to contemporary problems of poverty, hunger and degradation. Beginning with the position that exploitation is at the root of all violence, Gandhi builds his economic ideas in such a manner that avoids exploitation of man by man. His panacea is to do away with concentration of economic power by proposing economic decentralisation at various levels of the power hierarchy of the Indian society. Gandhi frequently asserted that "if India is to evolve along non-violent lines, it will have to decentralize many things."[22]

The Gandhian concept of decentralisation and planning is reflected in his views on production, distribution, consumption and exchange. The Mahatma was in favour of "Production by masses" in place of the modern craze for "mass production." He favoured participative growth with social justice so that the benefits of production may trickle down to the millions of masses. The Mahatma favoured an appropriate middle technology which would help augment agricultural and industrial production for raising the per capita productivity without throwing people out of employment. Gandhi's concern for employment crystallised in his statement on the eve of independence on the purpose of planning as "real planning consisted in the best utilisation of the whole man power of India." In the Gandhian scheme emphasis is laid on self-employment.

The whole programme of Mahatma Gandhi is built on the solid foundations of economic equality and distributive justice which never means possession of an equal amount of worldly goods by everyone. It means that every one will have proper house to live, sufficient and balanced food to eat and sufficient Khadi to cover himself. Gandhiji ceaselessly talked of meeting the basic needs of food, clothing and shelter for the last man of India. But equal distribution was not to be confused with crude equality. "The real implication of equal distribution is that each man shall have the wherewithal to supply all his natural needs and no more. To bring this ideal into being the entire social order has got to be reconstructed. A society based on non-violence cannot nurture any other social ideal."[23] Gandhiji asserted, "The possession of inordinate wealth by individuals should be held as a crime against Indian humanity."[24] He further observes, "My ideal is equal distribution, but so far as I can see it is not to be realised. I therefore work for equitable distribution."[25]

Mahatma's thinking about consumption was derived from his definition of civilisation, his faith in redistribution as well as his commitment to the ideal of non-possession which god seekers must purpose. An aesthetically and hedonistically luxurious life was alien to the Gandhian ethos. As Gandhi say, "He (who has made the ideal of equal distribution a part of his being) world reduce his wants to a minimum, bearing in mind the poverty in India."[26] According to Gandhiji civilisation in the real sense of the term, consists not in the multiplication of wants but in their deliberate and voluntary restrictions."[27]

In his ideal of "villagism", Gandhiji advocated barter system. Bapu was conscious of the blessings of money and the importance of monetary policy but he was equally apprehensive of the veil, peril and confusion that results from the dominance of money. In the Gandhian economy labour is the coin which may be bartered for any material things. When his self-sufficient village needs something which it cannot produce, it can easily exchange with the produce which has been grown in abundance at another place. Thus Gandhiji envisaged that trade will be the barter system. When objected that this is a revision to the primitive system of barter, Gandhiji replied, "Is not all international trade based on the barter system?[28] On the whole, the Gandhian view on technology, employment, growth and social justice is neatly expressed in the passage." I want to save time and labour, not for a fraction of mankind, but for all. I want the concentration of wealth not in the hands of a few, but in the hands of all. Today machinery helps the few to ride on the backs of the millions. The impetus behind it is not the philanthropy to save labour but greed. It is against this constitution of thing that I am fighting with all my might."[29]

Gandhi's new theory of trusteeship was put forth to remove the wide disparity between the rich and the hungry millions.[30] He said that he would personally prefer decentralisation of power from the hands of the state, through an emphasis on trusteeship.[31] He also believed that trusteeship could bring about a non-violent state. A harmonious relationship between labour and capital could merge out of a trusteeship theory that placed emphasis on a balanced relationship between the rich and the poor.

Decentralisation Features

(a) Government should provide suitable incentives to village crafts in the form of subsidies or remission of taxes in part or whole and institute prizes and other forms of recognition where greatest progress is achieved in this direction.

(b) Give local option to such units or regions as may wish in pursuit of the goal of self-sufficiency to protect themselves from the competition of heavy industry; to ban drink and drug evil, and the erection of power-driven machinery in their midst; and the import of mass-produced machine-made goods.

(c) Help them protect themselves from the vagaries of a fluctuating money economy by exempting them from the operation of intensive procurement drives and make it possible for them to meet a portion of their dues by payment in kind, which they should be allowed to retain in the area under experiment in order to carry out works and projects for their uplift.

Integrated Growth

The meaning of growth in Gandhian economics is good health, bright mind and spiritual richness. As Gandhiji had said, "The end to be sought, is human happiness combined with full mental and material growth. I use the adjective moral synonymous with spiritual."[32] However, the material and the moral influence each other and, therefore, the doctrine of economic growth cannot be viewed independently of spiritual growth and *vice versa*.

Gandhian economics, therefore, suggests a concept of 'integrated growth', comprising of a harmonious integration of both the spiritual as well as material growth. The outer material growth has to be a proper match to the inner spiritual growth. The material growth should never go against the spiritual growth. The material growth, should, however, never fall below the lower limit of providing the minimum parameters of the material growth keep changing according to the understanding of the Truth or the level of inner growth. In other words, economic growth is linked with the level of social consciousness, once the minimum needs of the society have been satisfied.

Sarvodaya: Welfare of All

In economic terms, Sarvodaya would mean that everyone without any exception must be assured a minimum standard of living, that is, a balanced diet, a decent house to live in, sufficient cloth and adequate educational and medical facilities. Provisioning of the minimum necessities of life for the masses is economic Swaraj which negatively speaking implies absence of all exploitation, deprivation and oppression. Gandhiji's attention was, however, especially captured by the last one on the socio-economic ladder, that is, the hungry, the poor, the exploited and the down-trodden. "The Swaraj of my dream is the poor man's swaraj,"[33] said Gandhiji, Swaraj is not 'Poorna Swaraj' until basic amenities are guaranteed to the poorest of the poor.

Maximum of moral welfare, and material welfare necessary for the same, is the principle welfare criterion in Gandhian holistic economics. However, the welfare criteria is to be applied to all without any exception and not just to the majority in a society. According to modern economics, the maximum happiness of the maximum number is the principle goal to be achieved. Accepting the 'Compensation principle', the welfare of a society is measure by the total amount of goods and services enjoyed by its people. An economy is said to be growing in welfare if its annual social product is increasing, even though it has millions of people who are hungry, illiterate and dying of disease and starvation. The holistic paradigm considers each individual to be an expression of wholeness, the Truth, the God. When one individual suffers, the whole society suffers. The suffering of a hungry, starving individual is indefinite and, therefore, it can never be compensated by making the others better-off in any way. There is unlimited potentiality in every human being, so even if one life whithers away without blossoming, there is an unlimited loss to the society.

Gandhian Contents in Indian Planning

Gandhian ideas of economic development are not the outmoded concepts but are essentially rational and scientific concepts and in tune with modern economic themes regarding economic development of the developing countries like India. Though Gandhiji focused his attention mostly on the socio-economic problems present in India, but his analysis, vision and strategy bore relevance throughout the globe. But setting aside the world-wide aspect for the movement, even India is apparently no closer to 'Swaraj', than it was while under the British. Yet, on closer examination, we can see that Gandhiji's work has not come to an end. His ideas, so often rejected, misunderstood, and neglected, are finding their way in the consciousness of the world and they are becoming popular and expanding. It is a movement that aims at nothing less than an ultimate transformation of the world a movement that is not likely to disappear until and unless peace on each becomes a reality.[34] Thus it becomes quite clear that if the Gandhian ideas are linked up with the broad functioning of our economic planning, we are sure to achieve the objectives of our plans.

As our ends are primarily related to eradication of countrywide poverty and unemployment, "our plans must be rooted in the condition that prevail in our land" and must "touch every living person in India"[35] and "provide first the things the village need."[36] This can be possible only by adopting the Gandhian contents in our economic planning. But the success of even Gandhian way of planning is subject of certain conditions. This will require radical changes in the present system of planning and execution. First, planning process should be much from the bottom having the idea of decentralised planning and the plan must consider the needs and circumstances of each family which is below the poverty line. Additional avenues of employment within a reasonable distance must be provided to make full employment a reality. Second, the executors or the administrative structure must be able to deliver to every family the basic benefits provided in the plan and participation of people through decentrlised people's organisation must be secured in plan formulation and its implementation. Such an approach will need a total reorientation of the present administrative procedure and reorientation of the Panchayats in such a way that they may work as an economic and welfare unit rather than as its present shape being purely involved in political activities. This intends to have people-oriented micro-level sectoral planning with whole-hearted support of the plan for the welfare of the masses.

If the plan of the country is prepared and implemented in the light of the Gandhian concepts giving appropriate priorities to the sectors relevant for developing the standard of life of the masses along with other allied sectors, the solution of the existing socio-economic problems will come nearer to our approach and the nation along with all its glamorous achievements, will be able to solve the basic problems of poverty, unemployment and inequality in the distribution of income and wealth which was the dream of the 'Father of Nation' for independent India.

CONCLUSION

Gandhian economics based on a holistic paradigm and ethical values like truth, non-violence, non-stealing, non-possession, Brahmacharya, equality, bread labour, Swadeshi and trusteeship, shows a radical departure from modern economics, Gandhiji equates 'well-being' or happiness of man with spiritual or moral elevation, and therefore, maintains that the basic goal of economics is not pursuit of unbounded materialism, but provision of optimal amount of goods and services in order to keep the body and mind in a fit condition so that through service, the highest potentiality of man may be realised. Truth requires that wants should be scientifically explored, pruned and regulated in the light of wholeness. Gandhian economics is, therefore, need-oriented and not want-oriented. Besides fulfilment of needs, Sarvodaya, equality, end of all deprivation and exploitation, creative work for all are some of the other basic 'ends' of holistic economics.

Growth is an ascent of consciousness. Since man is both physical as well as spiritual, and the physical is instrumental in unfolding the spiritual, growth is a function of material as well as moral factors.

Economic ends which are rooted in Truth must be achieved by holistic means only since there is an inviolable connection between the end and the means. The economic principles underlying Gandhian holistic economics are decentralisation, self-sufficiency, cooperation, equality, Swadeshi and trusteeship. The structure of a non-violent economy is composed of a number of decentralised, self-sufficient economic units. The economic unit is able to produce whatever is required with the help of local resources and is contented with whatever has been produced in local surroundings. Mutual help, cooperation and sharing among the various economic units is, however, not ruled out. Gandhiji was opposed to unlimited industrialisation and 'machinery' due to evils inherent in them. He suggested suitable limits to be imposed on them. Not only that, industrialisation and technological advancement must be within limits; the scale of operations must also be small. Technological progress and expansion of scale of production, without the accompanying spiritual advancement, inevitably leads to human degradation. Gandhiji advocated the promotion of handicrafts, village and small-scale industries and suggested that existing local technology must be revived and improved upon. There should be 'production by masses' instead of 'mass production' so that distribution can take place simultaneously with production, in order to ensure equality. Gandhiji was, however, willing to accept a few heavy and large scale industries with high technology in the national interest, provided they are under state control and are subservient to the needs of the village and small industries. He, thus, favoured a harmonious integration of industries with different technologies and capital intensities.

Economic ideas of Gandhiji regarding the system of planning, production, methods of management, involvement of the workers, the role of the owners, etc. are highly radical and require a serious thinking on our part. What we have adopted is the centralised system of planning, heavy reliance upon highly technical, capital-oriented heavy industrial growth increased role of state in the economic activities, etc. which are not close to the thinking of Gandhiji. The Community Development Schemes run by the Government half-heartedly, the Bhoodan movement initiated by Sri Vinoba Bhave, the Panchayat Raj system all have achieved only limited success or it would be better to say that such noble schemes have almost failed to click to bring about desired achievement in the country. The type of economic development which we have been able to achieve and the way we have achieved it and the result which we have attained are eye-openers. Even after about five and half decades of planned development we find that about half of the country lives below the poverty line and unemployment is rampant. Use of village industries products has not increased and with that the main source of occupation providing employment to millions is also dwindling. The craze for foreign goods is again on the increases. Use of simpler technologies for production, decentralised system of production providing more and more employment opportunities, development of self-reliant villages or integrated planned development of all the areas of the country are still not given proper attention. Even the minimum needs of our countrymen have not been fulfilled. The planners simply give lip-service to these vital aspects of development.

Notes and References

1. Cole, G.D.H., Quoted in K. Thiagarajan, "Impact of Gandhian Economic on Indian Economic Development", *Khadi Gramudyog*, March 1977, p. 270.

2. Donella H. Meadows, *et al., op. cit.*, p. 29.
3. Donella H. Meadows, *et al.*, The Limits to Growth, New York, Potomac Associates, 1974, p. X (2nd ed.)
4. E.F. Schumacher, Small is Beautiful, New Delhi, Radhha Krishna, 1977.
5. Fernandes, Angelo, "God's Rule and Mans Role", *Gandhi Marg*, March 1982, p. 699.
6. Gandhi, M.K., *Harijan*, 9.10.37.
7. Gandhi, M.K., *Young India*, 15.11.28.
8. *Harijan*, 15 September 1946, p. 310.
9. *Harijan*, Dec. 30, 1939, p. 391.
10. *Harijan*, Jan. 18, 1942, *Ibid.*, Vol. 75, 1979, p. 216.
11. Humford, Lewis, Condition of Man, p. 309 (Statement attributed to Pope Pias XI).
12. Huxley, Aldous, Science, Liberty and Peace, p. 23.
13. *Ibid.*
14. *Ibid.*
15. *Ibid.* p. 8.
16. *Ibid.*, p. 3.
17. "Industrialism and Happiness", Report prepared by J.C. Hunt, Aryan Path, April 1956, p. 167.
18. Kripalani, Krishna, 'All Men are Brothers', Navajivan Publishing House, Ahmedabad, p. 166.
19. Kumarappa J.C., 'An Overall Plan for Rural Development', p. 1.
20. Louis Fishcer: The Life of Mahatma Gandhi, p. 356.
21. Low, A.M., Science in Industry, p. 148, quoted by Rajkrishna, *Ibid.*, p. 11.
22. M.K Gandhi, Constructive Programme: Its Meaning and Place, Ahmedabad, Navjivan press, 1944, p. 18.
23. M.K. Gandhi: *Harijan*, 2 November, 1934.
24. Mahadeo Desai: In Defence of Machinery, *Young India*, June 22, 1935, pp. 91-92.
25. Maharajan, M., Economic Thought of Mahatma Gandhi, Discovery Publishing House, New Delhi, 1998, pp. 89, 90.
26. Mohan, R., Gandhian Economic System, *Vichar*, New Delhi, 1982, p. 62.
27. Prabhu, R.K. and Rao, U.R., "The Mind of Mahatma Gandhi," Navajivan Publishing House, Ahmedabad, p. 234.
28. Raj Krishna, Voluntary Action, Sept. 1978, Vol XX, No. 9, p. 7.
29. Rajkrishna, Human Values and Technological Change, Kashi: A.B. Sarva Seva Sangh Prakashan, 1958, p. 5.
30. Rajkrishna, Human Values and Technological Change, Kashi: A.B. Sarva Seva Sangh Prakashan, 1958, p. 91.
31. Rolt, L.T.C., "Science Run Mad", *Aryan Path*, Bombay, March 1956, p. 115.

32. Scott and Lynton, The Community Factor in Modern Technology, UNESCO Publications, pp. 29-30.
33. See B.S. Sharma, Gandhi as a Political Thinker, Allahabad, Indian Press Pvt. Ltd., 1956, p. 138.
34. Sharma, S.P., Gandhian Hoslistic Economics, Concept Publishing Company, New Delhi, 1992, pp. 20, 106-08.
35. Shephard, Mark, "Mahatma Gandhi: The Legacy', *Gandhi Marg*, March 1983, p. 38.
36. Shephard, Mark, "Mahatma Gandhi: The Legacy", *Gandhi Marg*, April 1980, p. 31.

27

Gandhian Economic Philosophy and its Relevance in the 21st Century

SHAKUNTLA GUPTA AND NISHA BHARGAV

Mahatma Gandhi was not a professional economist. He was not trained in pure economics, instead Gandhiji was formally trained in law which he hardly practiced.

His economic philosophy do not constitute well nit pure economic theory. It is the religious and social ideas adopted and developed by Gandhi, first during his period in South Africa from 1893 to 1914, and later of course in India. These ideas have been further developed by later 'Gandhians', most notably, in India, Vinoba Bhave and Jaya Prakash Narayan. Outside of India, some of the work of Martin Luther King Jr. can also be viewed in this light. Dr. Diwakar sum up Gandhi's thought in a few words: "The four words, truth, non-violence, Sarvodaya and Satyagraha and their significance constitute Gandhi and his teachings."

Gandhi's thoughts are truth and non-violence. In accordance with the principles of truth and non-violence, Gandhiji wanted to transform the individual and society. In his economic thought, Gandhi was greatly influenced by Ruskin's Book 'Unto This Last'. From this book, he learnt that the good of the individual is contained in the good of all. Further, Gandhi was also inspired by the ideas of Thoreau, Tolstoy and Kropotkin. Tolstoy's principles of simplicity, asceticism and equalitarianism become a part of Gandhi philosophy. Besides, India scriptures Gita and Upanishada and Indian Saints Kabir, Mira, Nanak, etc. left a deep influence on Gandhian mind. Gandhi was primarily interested in India. He was aware of the socio-economic consequences of the British rule in India and wanted to remedy the ills caused by the British rule. He wanted to rebuild Indian economy on a purely Indian pattern. Throughout his life, Gandhiji sought to develop ways to fight India's extreme poverty, backwardness and socio-economic challenges as a part of his wider involvement in the Indian independence movement. He was a champion of reforms in social and economic spheres. He wanted to restructure the social and economic life of the country.

Gandhian Economic Philosophy is a part of his general philosophy of life. Therefore, to understand Gandhian economic philosophy, we must have a clear idea of his philosophy of life. Gandhiji viewed life as a whole and not in its isolated compartments. Gandhian Philosophy is not only simultaneously political, moral and religious, it is also traditional and modern, simple and complex. It embodies numerous western influences to which Gandhi was exposed, but being rooted in ancient Indian culture and harnessing eternal and universal moral and religious principles, there is much in it that is not at all new. This is why Gandhi could say, "I gave nothing new to teach the world. Truth and non-violence are as old as the hills." Gandhiji is concerned even more with the spirit than with the form. If the spirit is consistent with the truth and non-violence, the truthful and non-violent form will automatically result.

Gandhian economic philosophy deals with certain principles of social economics, i.e. humanism, love and cooperation, non-violence, trusteeship, social justice, sattvik materialism, harmony, etc. It is on these principles, he wanted to build the ideal socialist society. Consistent with his economic philosophy discussed in the above mentioned principles, Gandhiji developed his economic ideas which are based on his vision of Swaraj and the philosophy of non-violence. In fact, Gandhiji's economic ideas are found scattered all over his writings and speeches which are relevant even after sixty years of independence. His economic ideas aim to promote spiritual development and harmony with a rejection of materialism. The paper focuses on Gandhiji's economic ideas of modern India and analyses the relevance of his philosophy to the problems and challenges posed by the present world that is globalised.

GANDHIJI'S ECONOMIC IDEAS

Economic Science and Economic Laws

Gandhiji never isolate economics from ethics. As per Mahatma Gandhi, true economists aim at material as well as moral progress of the society. Gandhi says, "Economics that hurts the moral well-being of an individual or a nation is immoral, and therefore, sinfull." Along with producing and increasing wealth, economics must also stand for social justice and moral progress. Economic laws which aim at material progress as well as social harmony and moral progress should be formulated in accordance with the higher laws of life/laws of nature.

In fact, the laws of economics which deal with the practical problems are not universal which are determined by the climatic, geological and temperamental conditions of the country need to be modified to the specific requirements of the country.

Consumption Behaviour

As per Gandhiji, money is required to satisfy certain basic requirements of life and the satisfaction of basic consumption requirements is the precondition for all progress. But it is not the end in itself. Man's aim is not to multiply worldly desires and engages his whole life in acquiring wealth to satisfy these wants. The goal of life is to control desires and transform it into liberation. Therefore, Gandhiji advices limiting of one's needs which according to him would help the individuals to achieve happiness. Gandhiji follows the Buddhist dictum that 'desire is the source of all sins'. Dr.

Das Gupta writes the 'concept of limiting of wants is a welfare economics'.

Gandhiji used the 'Swadeshi concept' to strengthen the consumption of indigenous or domestically produced goods. More so, Gandhi used this concept to abolish poverty and unemployment by encouraging decentralised consumer goods production system. Khadi represented the symbol of 'Swadeshi' movement said Gandhiji.

Self-sufficiency and Self-reliance

One of the important goals of Gandhian production scheme is the self-contented community. Each community should be able to satisfy the needs of its people and the production of each basic unit should be linked with the natural consumption requirements of those living in it. The scheme for production should not only be linked with the consumption needs of the people but also be synchronized with the availability of natural resources and human potentialities.

Foreign trade is not considered to be essential in the self-contented community of the Gandhian type. The consumption requirements of the people are such that they can be fulfilled by the commodities available with the community. There is no over-production and under-production as the aggregate supply is equal to aggregate demand. Imports in such a community are allowed only if there is surplus output of equal value to be exported in exchange.

Gandhiji's vision of 'Swaraj' was not only an instrument of achieving political freedom from the British rule but the symbol of achieving self-reliance and self-respect. For Gandhiji, Swaraj was a means of achieving the welfare and dignity of millions of villages of India.

The Sarvodaya Plan

Sarvodaya means all round well-being of all. It refers to many sided development of the whole of the community and advocates social ownership of the means of production, equitable distribution of income, elimination of discrimination of all kinds, universal brotherhood, peace and progress. The aim of the Sarvodaya plan is the establishment of Sarvodaya social order on the principles of non-violence, truth, love and cooperation which is to be established at the village level. In fact, the Gandhian struggle against poverty, unemployment starts from the village. The purpose was to bring all around development of the village and to make it self sufficient economic unit. Gandhiji's programme for the regeneration of Indian village include development of cottage and village industries, improvement in village sanitation, construction of village panchayat, self-sufficiency in basic requirements, removal of illiteracy, unemployment, poverty and abolition of caste system.

Science and Technology, Industrialisation and Scale of Production

Gandhiji sometimes blamed to be against science and technology but it is not so. He was not against large scale production but he was against starving people due to large scale production and against mechanisation leading to capitalism. Moreover, mechanisation and large scale production provides no solution to the problem of unemployment in the agriculture based over populated economies as is the case of India. Gandhiji pointed out that western type of industrial development shall not be an ideal for independent India because it is a source of exploitation and unhappiness. For the capitalists, in their effort to increase profits, tend to reduce wages which causes unrest among the workers.

Science and technology have produced destructive weapons, Gandhiji wanted science and technology for peaceful purposes. For Gandhiji, the consideration of man was supreme and that of science and technology was secondary.

Decentralised Development

Gandhi wanted to carry the production units to the homes of the masses, particularly, in villages. Therefore, he stressed the decentralisation of small scale production units to avoid concentration of large scale units in a few places. He emphasized the rehabilitation, development and expansion of cottage and village industries. Spinning and wearing was given the first place. Khadi according to Gandhi is the central industry on which all other village industries revolve which will remove unemployment, poverty from the villages and will make them self-sufficient economic units.

Labour Welfare

In Gandhian Philosophy, labour has been given greater importance as labour is both the means, and end of production and labour welfare is considered necessary precondition for bringing economic stability and social harmony. In an ideal society as envisaged by Gandhi, each individual must not simply get employment but also be provided with better working as well as living conditions. Security of employment and stability of wages is equally important for labour welfare.

Doctrine of Trusteeship

By trusteeship is meant that all those people who possess things as well as capabilities, abilities or other natural gifts, must hold these possessions as trustee for all others. Basically, Gandhiji suggested this doctrine as an answer to the economic inequalities of ownership and income a kind of non-violent way of resolving all social and economic conflicts which grew out of inequalities and privileges of the present social order.

According to Gandhi, man lives in society and all wealth is socially produced. Therefore, it must be equally distributed and nobody should be without food and clothing. The concentration of wealth in few hands is unjust. For this reason, Gandhiji advises limiting one's needs as excess wealth according to him causes unhappiness. In fact, Gandhiji was against exploitation of poor by capitalists. This can be avoided if the rich act as the trustees of the masses. With these views, he contemplated to solve the problems of poverty and unemployment. Gandhiji contended that the socialists society will be established through the doctrine of trusteeship. According to Gandhiji, the capitalists and the Zamindars will undergo a change of heart. They will consider themselves trustees of the wealth and property they possess.

There is no need of class war and physical liquidation of the capitalist class. Since the socialist goal is one of love and non-violence, it can be achieved only through peaceful means and not through hatred and war.

Satyagraha

The remaining central concept/idea in Gandhi's philosophy is Satyagraha. Satyagraha both as a philosophy and as a method of conflict-resolution was perfected and personalised by Gandhi. Satyagraha is itself a whole philosophy of non-violence. As a technique, Satyagraha was developed by Gandhi in South Africa to give the Indian population a weapon with which to resist the injustices being practiced upon it by the colonial government. But Satyagraha can be practiced in any cultural environment, provided the necessary ingredients are present. A Satyagraha campaign is undertaken only after all other peaceful means have proven ineffective. It involves applying the forces of both reason and conscience simultaneously.

GANDHIAN ECONOMIC PHILOSOPHY'S RELEVANCE IN THE 21ST CENTURY

Gandhian Economic thought based on truth, non-violence, dignity of labour and simplicity is more relevant today than what it was sixty years ago. The economics of Gandhi might also be described as the economics of non-violence. He opposed modern capitalism. To Gandhi, moral progress is more important than material progress. It is unfortunate that Gandhiji's ideas on village republics, on machinery, industrialisation, decentralisation, village Sarvodaya, bread labour, the doctrine of trusteeship have come in for a lot of criticism based on misunderstanding of the concepts and his basic philosophy. In fact, Gandhian thought have relevance for modern India. Recent contribution of eminent social scientists like M.L. Dantwala, B.N. Ganguli, Bhabatosh Dutta, V.K. Mehta, Raj Krishna, J.D. Sethi, etc. initiated discussion and rethinking on Gandhian economic ideas. Bhabtosh Dutta regarded Gandhian economics as an important part of Indian economic thought. Gandhian economic ideas have gained the interest and attention of an increasing number of people across the world. Some of Gandhi's closest supporters and admirers included industrialists such as Ghanshyam Das Birla, Ambalal Sarabhai, Jamnalal Bajaj and J.R.D. Tata who adopted several of Gandhi's progress ideas in managing labour relations. His social and economic Aganda continues to be relevant even today. In many Universities in the West, ethics is being taught in management courses. This is a welcome development.

Further, interest in Gandhian Economics has been re-enforced by the new problems of the world economy, the ecological and environmental imbalances, the alarm over the expansion of non-renewable resources, threat of widening gap between the rich and poor, cut-throat competition, increasing unemployment, growth of violence and threat of nuclear Holocaust, etc. The increase in political fanaticism, religious fundamentalism, economic deprivation and cultural homogenisation cannot be eliminated. They possess serious threat to the world. Gandhiji offers an exceptionally unique and outstanding ray of hope in such a situation.

GANDHIAN ECONOMIC PHILOSOPHY AND THE GLOBALISATION REGIME

Globalisation is an economic process of integrating the country's economy with the world economy through free trade and free enterprise. It indicates the desire to integrate nation-states within the overall framework of WTO. It is argued that this shall enable free flow of goods, capital and technology and thus globalisation becomes a motivating force for nations to develop themselves at a faster rate. Globalisation propagates global capitalist development process as a way out for maximisation of economic growth through which global poverty and inequalities may be addressed efficiency. Globalisation process is based on maximisation of economic efficiency, realizing more and more economies of scale, increasing factor productivity, increasing supply of factors of production, use of modern technology and organisational abilities, creation and augmentation of individual property, economic freedom, etc. Though there are potential benefits of the globalisation process but the social costs of globalisation are not less. The adverse social consequences of globalisation may be tackled through Gandhian social and ethical philosophies.

Gandhiji's economic and social ideas are relevant even in today's globalised world. In fact, the inadequacies of capitalists and communists forms of economic organisation make it imperative that a better system is evolved to structure the economic and social relationship of the people. Gandhiji views on industrialisation and its relation to employment and poverty are excellent ideas. He was very anxious to provide full employment to every able-bodied citizen of the country. He believed that this could be achieved only by organizing village and cottage industries in the countryside in an efficient manner. For him, any economic planning which did not fully utilize the idle manpower in rural areas could not be termed sound or rational. His idea of full employment is now widely recognized all over the world.

In the Indian context, the ideas of full employment and sustainable livelihood has been sought to be achieved by a growth process which is pro-poor and specifically targeted anti-poverty programmes for self-employment and wage employment. Our government has sought to promote rural industrialisation. Rural industrialisation (rural and village industries) have immense potential to generate new employment opportunities with relatively low level of direct investment. These industries depend on local raw material and labour force and meet the demand of the local area by adopting simple techniques. Rural industrialisation has also been pushed by government as a strategy to reduce regional disparities.

Gandhian concept of trusteeship shall provide us modified ethically sound globalisation model. Gandhiji gave the idea of trusteeship for business organisation. By propagating an ideal of trusteeship for business organisation, he attempts to evolve a comprehensive system of economic arrangement which eliminated ills of capitalists and state bureaucracy. Under trusteeship, he rejected both capitalism and statism as form of economic organisations as both were exploitative and based on violence. With trusteeship, he aimed at coordination between labour and capital in production of goods and services and in ownership of wealth. In fact, his idea of trusteeship is not only relevant to the industry but to the entire economy. It is a method of socialisation and community ownership of property. Though the ideal of trusteeship has not been practiced on a large scale, many variants of the theme have come to the force in recent years. Many industrial houses and industrial associations have expressed their willingness to take up social responsibilities.

Gandhiji's idea of decentralisation is being increasingly seen as counter poise to the ills of globalisation. In this regard, Gandhiji's idea of Panchayati Raj institutions which have been given a constitutional status with the 73rd and 74th Amendment Acts, assume greater significance. Gandhiji's idea of limiting human wants will not only help to increase welfare of the society but also to check the ruthless exploitation of natural resources.

The globalised world today has internalised violence in all aspects of life. Violence is being experienced in terms of ecological destruction, destruction of livelihood, social disintegration and an erosion of ethical and spiritual values. Mahatma Gandhi offered non-violent alternatives in the fields of politics, economy and science. He presented an alternative model of decentralised human scale, land-based, craft-oriented and spiritually sensitive decentralisation of governance, technology, production and distribution.

REFERENCES

Anjaria, J.J. (1944), *An Essay on Gandhian Economics*, Vora and Co., Bombay.

Ashaf, A. (1993), *Gandhian View of Sustainable Development*, 'Indian Journal of Public Administration', 39, No. 2, pp. 265-81.

Bhatia, H.L. (1978), *History of Economic Thought*, Vikas Publishing House, Pvt. Ltd., New Delhi.

Bawa, Vasant Kumar (1996), *Gandhi in the 21st Century: Search for an Alternative Development Model*, 'Economic and Political Weekly', 31, No. 47, pp. 3048-49.

Behari, Bepin (1963), *Gandhian Economic Philosophy*, Vora and Co., Bombay.

Bharathi, K.S. (1994), *Gandhian Approach to Rural Development*, Omson Publishing House, India.

Bhole, L.M. (1988), *A Gandhian Critique of Planned Development in India*, 'Gandhi Marg', 9, No. 10, pp. 611-20.

Charles, K.J. (1993), *Technical Progress in Gandhian Economy*, 'Gandhi Marg', 15, No. 3, pp. 323-33.

Chaturvedi, S.N. (1990), *The Relevance of the Gandhian Concepts of Rural Development*, 'Gandhi Marg', 12, No. 2, pp. 208-13.

Chaudhari, R. (1998), *Crises of Growth: A Gandhian Alternative*, 'Mainstream', 36, No. 4, pp. 9-13.

Dutta, Bhabatosh (1980), *Indian Economic Thought*, Tata McGraw Hill Publishing Co. Ltd., New Delhi, pp. 150-58.

Das Gupta, Ajit (1980), *A History of Indian Economic Thought*, Routledge, London, pp. 131-62.

Desai, S.S.M. (1987), *Development of Indian Economic Thought*, Himalaya Publishing House, Bombay.

Diwan, Romesh (1989), *Mahatma Gandhi and the Economics of Non-Exploitation*, 'International Journal of Social Economics', 14, No. 2, pp. 39-52.

Dutta, Dr. D.M. (1973), *Mahatma Gandhi Ka Darshan (Hindi)*, Bihar Hindi Granth Academy, Patna.

Ganguli, B.N. (1977), *Indian Economic Thought*, Tata McGraw Hill Publishing Co. Ltd., New Delhi.

Gandhi, M.K. (1969), *Mere Sapno Ka Bharat*, Sarva Seva Sangha Prakashan, Varanasi.

Gandhi, M.K. (1962), *Economic Though of Mahatma Gandhi*, ed. by J.S. Mathur and A.S. Mathur, Chaitanya Publishing House, Allahabad.

Gangrade, K.D. (1991), *Gandhian Ideal Development and Social Change: Theory and Practice*, Northern Book Centre, New Delhi.

Hejela, T.N. (1994), *History of Economic Thought*, Konark Publishers Pvt. Ltd., Delhi.

Kripalani, J.B. (1970), *Gandhi: His Life and Thought*, Publications Division, Govt. of India, New Delhi, pp. 366-81.

Narayan, Shiriman, ed. (1968), *The Selected Works of Mahatma Gandhi*, 1-6, Navajivan Publishing House, Ahmedabad.

Panditrao, Y.A. (1992), *Gandhian Approach to Economic Development*, Himalaya Publishing House, Bombay.

28

Gandhian Views: A Global Perspective and its Relevance

PUSHPA SINHA AND RATNA MITRA

India became open on the year 1991 by adopting Liberalisation, Privatisation and Globalisation. With Globalisation India started bringing various transparencies in her policies and programmes, various sector of the economies were opened for investment and various big multinational companies came in our market and began to capture the markets of India on one hand and tuned on the other hand it up the economy at par with the international level. Our growth rate has increased and our economy started booming.

Mahatma Gandhi, the man of vision can be quoted here who had visualised that every economy needs to be self-dependant, self-reliant and manageable once he had said, "I don't want my house to be walled in on all sides and my windows to be stuffed, I want the cultures of all lands to be blown about my house as freely as possible. But I refuse to be blown off my feet by any." Gandhiji was not an economist so his economic ideas are not present in well contented manner. Gandhi's economic ideas were in a sense a logical corollary of his political and moral principles such as swaraj, sarvodaya, truth and non-violence and the like based on these wider social principles. Gandhi derived his economic ideas which if brought together would give a picture of the economic system that he visualised. Hereby we are focussing on these Principles of Gandhiji, in context of Gobalisation.

SWADESHI, SARVODAYA, SWARAJ

Gandhiji believed in SARVODAYA, i.e. good of all. It was his desire that good should percolate even to the last of the socio-economic ladder, the poorest of the poor. It was in this context that this man of vision was influenced by the idea of swaraj and from it emerged the ideas of swadeshi and self-sufficiency and from the principles of truth and non-violence emerged a series of economic ideas like non-exploitation, non-possession, bread labour and soon all these ideas which infact have originated under different contexts formed the founding pillars of Gandhi's economics system.

Gandhi was of the opinion that main objective of the economic activities should be 'Sarvodaya'—the greatest good for all. The current economic philosophy of the world is misfit for the new concept of development that has taken over all the existing concepts of positive change like—Growth Proper and Development and is termed as sustainable development. The economic planning envisages improving the equality of life of people. In Indian perspective the quality of life is defined or redefined by the Gandhian Approach and has not only been widely accepted by most of Indians, but also by the rest of the world Economic justice in the best quality of life includes so many things.

Such quality of life cannot be attained through the new international Economic order which is ready to take over the world as a whole in the form of Globalisation, Eco-friendly development (sustainable development), Consumer-friendly markets and people-friendly society cannot be achieved if western management ignores Gadhian thinking. World Wealth Report 2005 presents a dark picture of fifteen years of Globalisation. According to the report, it widen the gap between rich and poor. It is a complete failure of globalisation in the field of the real economic justice like opportunity of equality, removal of poverty, generation of employment and improvement in the standard of living. Results of globalisation clears the fact that the main objectives of globalisation is not the welfare of the countries, but to exploit the natural resources, cheap labors, and cheapest and best talent of Developing countries. SARVE BHAVANTU SUKHINAH is economic justice in real sense. It can be achieved only by the guidelines of 'G' where 'G' stands for Gandhi not for Globalisation.

VIEWS ON SWADESHI

Gandhi's philosophy was the principle of 'Swadeshi' which means local self-sufficiency. This is the vision of Gandhi's vision of a free India. Maximum economic and political power including the power to decide what could be imported into or exported from the village would remain in the hands of the village assemblies. 'Swadeshi' avoids economic dependence on external market forces that could make the village community vulnerable. It also avoids unnecessary, unhealthy wasteful and therefore environmentally destructive transportation.

With the globalisation of the economy every nation would wish to export more and import less to keep the balance of payments in its favour. There would be perpetual economic crisis, perpetual unemployment and perpetually discontented, disgruntled human beings. The spirit of swadeshi is not against of globalisation, because in their ultimate aims there is no conflict between the two. The principle of local economy or swadeshi insists on minimizing the distance between the producer and the consumer. Swadeshi as conceived by Gandhi does not reject trade with other nations or communities into but it is opposed to an international order based solely on considerations of comparative advantage or a system that celebrates global trade for its own sake or for the sake of profit maximisation, in other words competitiveness. If the universal manpower is neglected and concentration of power finds the hands of the few who amassed fortunes at the expense of the many it will not be possible to banish poverty and degradation. Few general directions which we must bear in mind while developing our economy. Swadeshi and decentralisation are two words which can briefly summarize the economic policy suitable for the present circumstances. Centralisation and monopolisation have been the order of the day for all these years, knowingly or unknowingly. The planners have become prisoners of a belief that only large-scale, centralised industry is economic and hence without worrying about its ill-effects or knowingly but helplessly, they have continued in that direction. The same has been the fact. Swadeshi is ridiculed as old fashioned and reactionary. We proudly use foreign articles. We have grown over dependent upon foreign aid in everything from thinking management, capital methods of production technology, etc. to even the standards and forms of consumption. This is not the road to progress and development, we shall forget our individuality and become virtual slaves once again. The positive context of Swadeshi should be used as the cornerstone store for the reconstruction of our economy. Hence 'Swadeshi' is the only alternative left even in today's world for total socio-economic empowerment.

Infact we can see what that in this era of globalisation various problems are eating up Indian economy for example the recent purchase of acres of agricultural land by TATA motors in Nandigram which led to blood storming action as this act of selling agriculture land will throughout the farmers from there livelihood and in the long-run may give set back to the economy. We must think about here Gandhiji's idea of Swaraj. Though Swaraj was of first political weapon of Gandhiji but it actually acquired economic overtones gradually. It would be noted that the concept of swadeshi inculcated gradually in the minds of Indians the imperative and the value of village self-sufficiency both at the national and at the local village level. Thus he had given importace to localisation. He later used this concept along with the other economic idea, viz. decentralisation as a technique of building an economic system which was purely Indian and mass based.

His belief that India lived in villages led him to propound the concept of village Swaraj which among other things envisaged village self-sufficiency. Presently in the era of globalisation, India is following this path as we are not able to accomodate the migrating population from village to the big towns and cities so what we need to do is to provide all the required infrastructural and basic facility in the village itself. Which is actually being alone through PURA that is providing urban ammenities in rural areas?

Gandhi insisted that it is "the labour which is the current coin not metal." Any person who can use his labour has that coin and has health. He quoted bread labour implies that each should do physical labour to satisfy his ordinary wants and therefore although machine has its place, it should not be allowed to displace the necessary human labour. It is also true in present contest that is in a population abundant economy labour saving technology will not work as it would create more and more unemployment which is always an obstacle for a developing economy like India. Gandhian views on production. As for production, Gandhi stood for village production even of those goods that can be made at a lesser cost in the cities. He was particularly concerned at the way the sale of mill cloth deprived Indian farmers of a useful seasonal occupation, village production would reduce unemployment. He promoted Khadi and Village Industry which use less capital per worker and after produce more output directly and indirectly per unit of capital.

GANDHIAN VIEWS ON GLOBLISATION AND ITS RELEVANCE

Gandhi argued that both capital and labour represent power and are mutually dependent on each other what is therefore called for is not class struggle but class collaboration. Both must act as trustees aiming at the welfare of the whole community instead of their respective class interest capital should assist labour in production and labour must be co-sharer in the administration of industry. The economics of Ghandiji was of simple living and high thinking. According to Gandhi simple living or limited wants would neither invite aggression nor itself be tempted to commit aggression. Limiting wants would mean limiting production and this is fully in keeping with the Gandhian principle of labour intensive decontrolled production. Are we prepared for this? It is possible in today's competitive world to live and run a subsistence economy when other notions are constantly raising their standards of living and increasing production?

Gandhiji was advocating use of nominal level of resources available and that is what means sustainable development, what we are talking about today that is using the resources given to us in such a manner that the next generation may also use it and those free gift of nature as provided to the humanity for seeking their growth and ignoring Gandhian thinking would not let achieving eco-friendly development, consumer-friendly market, and people-friendly society. Thus we should follow Gandhian ideas as guidelines and then move further in the path of development.

GANDHIAN THEORY OF DISTRIBUTION AND TRUSTEESHIP

The Gandhian view of distribution can be dissented under two heads. In his earlier view he followed Ruskin's concept as absolute equality. In his book "Survodaya" (Gujarat translation of Ruskin's Unto the Last) Gandhi claimed no work is superior or inferior and there should be equal payment.

In his second view Gandhi came to accept a concept of equality which would be compared to the Marxian concept of "from each according to his ability, to each according to his need." Gandhi now insisted on living wage. In return for getting tiring wage every worker was duty bound to do some work that is what Gandhi meat by bread labour—a term be borrowed from Tolstoy. In other words, no man was to be given meals free.

But is the era of globalisation and corporate culture the satiation points of people is increasing and what Dunsen Berry called 'Demonstration Effect' that is imitating the living style of upper section is ruling in the society.

The concept of Trusteeship is one of the components of the Gandhian economic order. This has assumed special importance in view of the new world economic order popularly known as Globalisation, Privatisation and Liberalisation. There as the later concept promotes economic individuation to the extent of exploiting the poor and the downtrodden the Gandhian approach stands for protecting the interest of the marginalised. Thus the Gandhian approach also stands security to promote good will and co-operation between the rich and the poor. Gandhi evolved his theory to neutralize economic views as propounded by communism and rank capitalism as promoted by western economic system.

Gandhi believed that all property belonged to God. Nobody was infact, the owner of the natural productive resources at his or her disposal. Infact, she or he is a manager or trust to be exact. If a person has got vast riches then, in the opinion of the Gandhi he is entitled to only that portion of the riches which are enough to fulfil his needs. That is why Gandhiji used to say that one must get according to his needs and must to person, State or Nation according to his capacity. No doubt this concept seems to have been borrowed from Marxism and yet the credit to bring the concept into vogue goes to Gandhi, of course this give an impetus in promoting his concept of trusteeship also. The need of the time is to revive this embracing economic concept for the benefit of one and all. The galloping speed of the Globalisation bound to harm the small economics of the world including that of our country too. By corporate and multinationals are on the way to squeeze out the small economics of the poor nations and thereby render them destitute ultimately. This has already happen in a few countries of Latin America like Venezuela and Brazil. The question is why the globalisation does/do? The answer would be simply that it is self-centered.

CONCLUSION

In the present scenario where the prevalence of corruption raise strong obstacles and inhibition to development we are highly in need of moral boost up for which we have to adcpt Gandhian model of growth which is based on spirituality, morality and ethical background and so, it is Gandhian prescriptions for economic diseases found in India was relevant, is relevant, and will be relevant, for the future generation.

It is true that Gandhian economic concepts were not contained well, thought out and well planned books written with a scholar's patent effort but his six basic concepts essential to Gandhian economics are found in his speech, short notes, etc. These six basic concepts are the following: *first,* avoidance of mechanisation and encouragement of cottage industries especially spinning and weaving; *second,* improvement of rural small scale agriculture; *third,* making the village community as much self-sufficient and self-reliance as practicable; *fourth,* decentralisation of the administrative and economic structures; *fifth,* reducing income inequalities by raising the income level among the poor and by changing the attitude and motivation of the rich; and *sixth,* ensuring that capitalist and big businessman serve as 'trustees' for the whole community.

Presently, it is presumed that globalisation provides unhindered flow of goods, resources and capital across regions and countries based on comparative market efficiency and most efficient utilisation of world resource. More than one and half decade has passed since the process of globalisation was initiated and our economy has went through many changes in different sectors of the economy leading to mass scale unemployment of labour force and concentration of wealth in the few hands never be advantageous.

A look over the various variables of growth and development show that the process of globalisation in India has enabled it to achieve high growth rate, increment in agricultural and industrial production, a rising standard of living but for millions of people residing in rural areas it has delivered no progress at all, unemployment in general and in rural sector in particular has increased. Globalisation has failed to provide work to millions of hands and food to equal number of people in rural India.

It has also lead to excessive consumerism resulting in more environmental pollution, more emission of green house gases and rapid depletion of natural resources, increasing poverty and inequality, widening gap between rich and poor countries, globalisation of agriculture causing rural impoverishment increasing food insecurity and many others.

These adverse social consequences of globalisation may be tackled with Gandhian model of growth in Mahatma's words. "Economics that he art moral well-being of an individual or a nation are immoral and therefore sinful."

He realised long before that any wholesome transfer of western technology without due regard to local conditions and requirements could never be conductive to healthy development of Indian villages.

What is needed is interpretation of economics from Gandhian point of view, i.e. not consider economics as a tool of meeting unlimited wants with limited resources but limiting our wants according to limited resources.

Self-reliance and self-governance, his basic principles are answer to Indian farmer's crises driven cries today. These principles will ultimately help us to achieve environmentally sustainable development and production.

According to Gandhi, "Happiness is not only bodily Welfare" In *Hind Swaraj* Gandhi writes, "Civilisation in the real sense of term consists not in the multiplication of the wants but in the deliberate and voluntary reduction of wants. This alone promote real happiness and contentment and increase capacity for service. The mind in the restless bird, the more it gets, the more it wants and still remains unsatisfied."

For Gandhi basic materials wants of human-being must be satisfied because staving cannot talk of god. Gandhian opposes seeking more often the minimum required because it led to greet which destroys human values like honesty, high thinking and led to increase and more production which in turn has resulted in exploitation state control and centralism to those who except simple living or subsistence living as the highest value what Gandhi says is certainly relevant even today. But how many would except the principle of an economy of limited wants limiting production in this era of globalisation and competitive production is a mother to think about.

REFERENCES

Dhawan, Gopinath, The Political Philosophy of Mahatma Gandhi.
Gupta, M.G., Gandhism Redefined.
Mishra, G.P. and Das, B.C., Gandhi in Today's India.
Patu, V.T., Studies on Gandhi.
Singh, Ramjee, Gandhi and the Modern World.
Sinha, S.N., Gandhian Philosophy of Sarvodaya.
Verma, M.M., Gandhi's Technique of Mass Mobilisation.

29

Concepts of Social Justice and Equity in Gandhian Perspective

Dalip Kumar and Venkatesh Sharma

I. INTRODUCTION

History of human civilisation is the story of incessant struggle for conquest, subjugation and subordination by the advantage as well as the story of fight against atrocities, exploitation and injustice by the disadvantaged lot. The concept of social justice and equity has always been on the centre stage. It has been the topic of study by economic thinkers from Aristotle to Plato, to Herbert Spancer, Hayak, Robert Nozic, Karl Marx, Gandhi, Sahajanand and all those great souls who pursued the passion to ameliorate the conditions of those who have been the victims of social discrimination and injustice. The present paper tries to peep through the aspects of social justice. The paper contains themes which explain the thoughts on Gandhian Perspective of justice and equity, justice for gender equity, justice for Indigo Peasants in Champaran, Justice against untouchability and justice related to communal conflagration. The paper is an honest and sincere attempt to reflect the ideas of social justice in the contemporary contexts.

Economic thinkers have been studying, from ancient times the concept of social justice and equity. Aristotle called economic equality wrong. Kautilya said that the state will perform its economic duties in such a way that the economic interest of the weaker section will not suffer. Marxism gives top priority mainly to the economic justice. The meaning of economic justice embraces the ideas of equal opportunities to the citizens to earn money and to use this money for the satisfaction of the necessities of their lives. Not only this, economic justice implies that the society should help its helpless class, which can not earn money. In fact, realisation of the dream of economic justice is necessary so that all should be equal participants in the property and income of the nation, and the national property should not be allowed to be concentrated in a few hands and major part of the society is not debarred from it.

Justice has been considered as elastic and dynamic concept varying from time to time, from people to people, according to prevailing conditions, traditions, religious beliefs and above all the philosophy of life. There have been wars, struggles, revolutions and social movements that were inspired by the idea of justice and equity. The concept of justice is intricately associated with religion, morality, equity, liberty, law, property, politics and the economic system. In determining the rank of a nation in the scale of political civilisation, no test is more decisive than the degree in which justice is actually realised in its judicial, administrative and social, economic and political life both as between one private citizen and another as well as between private citizens and wielders of governmental authority.

Basically, there are two schools of thought regarding the major task for political thinkers to realize justice in a society. One school represents the Marxists, socialists and neo-liberals. This school concentrates on the principle of social justice. Thinkers like Herbert Spencer, F.A. Hayek, and Robert Nozic propound the other school. It believes in the realisation and distribution of Justice according to one's own merit. In this approach, the inherent merit of a person becomes the criteria for the extent of the allocated Justice. Plato conceived the idealist theory of justice, which emphasized the moral element in justice. To him, justice is a virtue to be cultivated by society through subordination of the irrational masses of producers to the brave class of warriors and rational class of philosopher-rulers. Aristotle opined that different people should be treated differently and that difference in treatment should be proportionate to the degree to which individuals differ in relevant respects. This is the geometric concept of Justice.

The liberal concept of justice focussed on its legal and political dimensions, which is based on the condition that "Rule of Law" is distinguished from the "Rule of Man". Equity in law and the equal protection of laws are two judicial principles enshrined in the Anglo-Saxon Judicial System.

Entitlement theorists of Justice conceived justice within the framework of a limited state or a police state. Herbert Spencer advocates the "principle of survival for the fittest" in any social system. On this basis, he prevents the state from performing "the protective function and from perpetuating positive discrimination which will suppress the merit and will be against the law of natural selection."

Friedrick Hayek and Milton Friedman also believe in a negative state or a minimal state. He rejects the concept of social justice which can be given a meaning only in a directed or a "Command Economy" in which all major economic decisions are taken by the state and all processes of production and distribution are controlled by the state. He takes the meaning of Justice as equal opportunity to all citizens but the concept of social justice puts burden over able to carry on the unabled in a negative sense.

Robert Nozick favours the principle of non-interference in the economic affairs. He supports Right to Property, survival of meritocracy and the function of the state only as a Night Watchman. He does not want any reward to be given undeserving.

In the concept of the theory of distributive justice, John Rawls tries to work out general principle of distribution which will justify the class difference which any state is bound to produce whether capitalist or non-capitalist. Rawls has provided an alternative theory of justice, which tries to transform the capitalist state into a welfare state. He believed that the changes in the market economic system would pave the way for the change in the basic structure of the society. He accepts that even after the change, there would remain two classes in society, but the poor section can lead a happy life due to the drastic changes made in a class divided society.

Adam Smith was the first to look into the question of justice and equity in course of material progress. He said that the rapid material progress leads to degeneration of ethical and humanitarian values resulting into prosperity of minority at the expense of the majority.

Karl Marx dreamt of a classless and stateless society free from exploitation and oppressions. But in reality, Marxist ideas proved to be only utopian. After the collapse of Socialist states, revival of Capitalism and the on going communication revolution, the world has become a "Global Village." In the changed scenario, the question of equity and justice seems to be a matter of great concern.

Sahajanand has explained that "the Kisan movement in reality are relentless wars against hunger, poverty, servitude and humiliation. The movement raised its voice against capitalism and landlordism because these two institutions are the most formidable allies of these principal enemies of Kisans. (Kumar, 2005) In fact, landlords and capitalists are exploitative forces which are solely responsible for the poverty and servitude of the Kisans. The landlords and capitalists on the other hand uphold the institutions of feudalism and capitalism. Therefore, in-fighting against feudalism and capitalism Kisans are compelled to fight against landlords and capitalists. If only the landlords and Capitalists withdraw their support from these institutions they at present stand by the Kisans opposition to the Landlords and the Capitalist will automatically come to an end." (Sahajanand, 1938)

Amartya Sen contributed a lot to the concept of human values and societal well-being from the roots of classical economic theory and gave them fresh dimensions in terms of tangible observable and qualitative indicators of development. He considers the causes of famine as "entitlement failure" due to imperfect delivery mechanism in poor societies. His thoughts paved the way for new researches in the analysis of entitlements, capabilities, hunger, famines, and liberty and public actions. Famines are the result of lack of employment opportunities, low purchasing power, lack of literacy and lack of health facilities to the poors. As a lover of freedom and true humanist, Prof. Sen supports liberalised and market-friendly economy and suggests for the rapid spread of primary education, sustainable improvement of health care and women's empowerment. He focuses on the poor not as objects of pity requiring charity but as disempowered group needing empowerment. (Thakur and Kumar, 2007)

II. JUSTICE AND EQUITY IN GANDHIAN PERSPECTIVE

Justice and Equity in Gandhian Perspective can be explained under following heads:

(a) Justice for self-respect of Indians in South Africa
(b) Justice for Gender Equity
(c) Justice for Indigo Peasants in Champaran
(d) Justice against Untouchability
(e) Justice Related to Communal Conflagration

A. Justice for Self-respect of Indians in South Africa

Gandhi expressed his wish in the following words: "I want to bring about an equalisation of status. My ideal is equal distribution, but so far as I can see, it is not to be realised. I, therefore, work for equitable distribution. (Gandhi, 1963) The direct task of the village *swaraj* is to create economic equality so that one could uphold one's own dignity as a human being. Economic disadvantages in a society used to force an individual to accept sub-human conditions of living and it was difficult for a person to escape such an inferior position. Instead, all must have equal opportunity; everyone should be able to fulfil his or her human wants. By equality, what Gandhi meant was equal status and not equal division of social wealth. Whenever he referred to equal wages for all services, his emphasis was not on the wage but on equal respect for all professions. As everyone should strive to fulfil only his or her needs and be satisfied with that, the distribution of wealth was not a question to be specifically considered. He emphasized the co-operative and collective use of society's wealth. Special talents of any particular member of the society should be treated as his gifts to the society for serving the poors and the needy. Thus, every member of a non-violent society should give great importance to the welfare of all. They should be ready to sacrifice their self-interests for the common interests of all. Everyone is free to choose his profession according to his aptitude and temperament to fulfil the social needs. Vocations should be chosen not for one's personal advancement, but for the good of society as a whole. On the contrary, in practice we opt for a profession that will fetch us money, power and status, which endangers society. For example, if one who does not have an aptitude for taking care of sick persons, chooses to become a doctor or a nurse, what good can the society expect?

Justice has come to the stage of being a fair and truthful enquiry into truth by way of some definite procedure laid down by the organised community through its government. Gandhi, a barrister trained in England had his own view about the law, lawyers and the justice according to law. His view of justice is bound up with 'tyaga' (sacrifice, renouncing) and 'tapasy' (suffering, austerity). He looked at justice as a whole virtue and not as a specific virtue. Two distinguishing features of Gandhi's position on justice are, firstly, he paid special attention to the elimination of poverty and exploitation of peasants and rural areas, and secondly, he highlighted the conflict between justice and modern progress. (Atri, 2007)

Mahatma Gandhi was a man of great depth, very well aware of his shortcomings. His book, "My Experiments with Truth" gives an intimate insight into how he developed into the world figure that he became, from the humble beginnings of a law student. Gandhi's idea of Justice and equity was wider and more comprehensive. For him, true economics stands for social justice, which promotes good of all equally including the weakest. His concept of Trusteeship is an ideal measure to reduce inequality and poverty, which perpetuate injustice. It is based on the higher moral principles of service to others. He had the dream of establishment of an exploitationless society without any bloodshed.

The 1910 Allahabad Congress expressed its appreciation of the struggle waged by the Indians in South Africa. The 1911 Congress congratulated Mohandas Karamchand Gandhi and the Transvaal Indian community. The 1913 Karachi Congress passed a resolution admiring the heroic endeavors of Mr. Gandhi and his followers and their unparalleled sacrifices in their struggle for the maintenance of the self-respect of Indians and the redressal of Indian grievances. Thus, neither Gandhi nor his programme of non-violent action, which was individual-based in character but involved groups of men and women dedicated to the cause of Indians in South Africa, was no stranger to Indian National Congress.

Mahatma Gandhi was to stay in South Africa for over twenty years. The Indians who had been living in South Africa were without political rights, and were generally known by the derogatory name of 'coolies'. Gandhi was to emerge as the leader of the Indian community, and it is in South Africa that he first coined the term satyagraha to signify his theory and practice of non-violent resistance. In his book *"Satyagraha in South Africa"* he gave details about the struggles of the Indians to claim their rights, and their resistance to oppressive legislations and executive measures, such as the imposition of poll tax on them, or the declaration by the government that all non-Christian marriages were to be construed as invalid. Ghandi's struggle in South Africa was not against the Africans as such, it was mainly against the British and their treatment of the non-whites in general and the Indians in particular. This was the struggle for justice and right.

Within days of reaching South Africa, and while traveling from Durban to Johannesburg, a journey of 24 hours by train and horse buggies, Gandhi had his first experience of racial discrimination. Just three hours into his journey, the conductor came to examine the tickets. Although Gandhi had a First Class ticket, he was asked by the conductor to move to other coach, because the South African Railway did not allow colored people to travel in First Class. Gandhi refused to move and was eventually thrown out of the train at night, on a small station up in the mountains, during the peak of winter! Soon after reaching his destination, Gandhi called a meeting of the local East Indians. He began studying their situation and representing their rights for fair treatment in the courts. Throughout that year Gandhi worked equally hard on two fronts: fighting the authorities on legal grounds for the elimination of discrimination, and educating the Indians to become better citizens. In the meantime he also devoted a good deal of his time working on the case, for which he had been engaged, and succeeded in negotiating a mediated settlement.

In 1914, Gandhi secured an agreement from the Natal government that promised the alleviation of anti-Indian discrimination. As a result of Gandhi's campaigns, the South African government made a number of concessions to the Indian people living there: the honor of South Africa was saved and a new history written by the Satyagrahis. On two occasions in South Africa, Gandhi had forced the British authorities to repeal oppressive laws and inhumane practices regarding Indian indentured labour in the Natal province.

In 1930, in protest against the government's salt tax, Gandhi and his followers began their famous 200-mile Dandi March to extract salt from the sea. This drew the wrath of the British, who again imprisoned Gandhi. While imprisoned, Gandhi would begin to fast in protest. This drew anger and resentment from the British who knew that should Gandhi die while wrongly imprisoned, there would be far-reaching and grave repercussions from the people of India.

B. Justice for Gender Equity

In India the role of women in home has always been exalted but it did not mean a division of work with women inside and men outsides homes. There is a very large participation of women in agriculture and other non-farm activities, while there is natural demand for work in urban areas also as women find their family costs increasing under inflation. Gandhi felt that no movement could be successful if half of the human face remained passive and neutral to it. Gandhi wanted women, not to be just mothers and wives but equal partners in social life. He defended the role of women as not just 'a sex object' but respectful companions having a rightful social identity. Gandhi was thus for priority to women in jobs or status but no favour. He was, therefore, against reservation for women but not against priority. This was the Gandhian norm of equal justice. Gandhi also meant that feminist movement could not be an exclusive movement for women but a part of general movement for social justice and equality (Sinha, 2002).

Mahatma Gandhi was a ceaseless crusader of women's equality. He brought the women out of their homes and made them equal participants in all walks of life—social as well as political. His entourage always consisted of several women and many of his closest associates were women. Gandhiji claimed that a woman is completely equal to a man and practiced it in strict sense. Thousands and millions of women, educated and illiterate, house wives and widows, students and elderly participated in India's freedom movement because of his influence. For Gandhiji, the freedom fight was not political alone; it was also an economic and social reform of a national proportion.

Gandhiji always advocated a complete reform which he called *"Sarvodaya"* meaning comprehensive progress. He believed that the difference between men and women was only physical and has expressed several times in his writings that in many respects especially those of tolerance, patience, and sacrifice the Indian woman is superior to the male. You will discover this when you read his articles from *"Young India"* and *"Harijan."* During the 40 years of his political career, he only found more reasons to deepen his faith in what he wrote. He never had a specific program for women, but women had a integral role to play in all his programs. I feel that this is one of the reasons why women participated in his programs so overwhelmingly. Gandhiji declared that there is no school better than home and there is no teacher better than parents. He said men and women are equal, but not identical. "Intellectually, mentally, and spiritually, woman is equivalent to a male and she can participate in every activity." He wanted women to outgrow the traditional responsibilities and participate in the affairs of nation. He criticized Indian's passion for male progeny. He said that as long as we don't consider girls as natural as our boys our nation will be in a dark eclipse.

He declared that protecting women's honor was important and as holy as protecting cows. His book, "Women and Social Injustice" contains discussions of very deep thoughts and solutions on the topic. He felt that after India became free, the system of temple women (*Devadasis*) and brothels must be abolished. Even though on paper we have abolished the system of Devadasis, rampant exploitation of women as sex servants still continues. There was no way Gandhiji could have predicted modern ways and means of prostitution (call girls, phone sex, etc.) but he certainly identified its social evil and tried to fight it.

Gandhiji formulated India's freedom struggle as a comprehensive plan for women's development. Even though a lot of inequalities remain in our society, there is a fundamental agreement that men and women are equal.

Under Gandhi's leadership thousands of women took leading roles in several movements. Gandhi never considered women to be unfit for any position or task. Because of Gandhi's support, women's groups were formed all over India and there was hardly a week when Gandhi did not address a women's group. It was mainly because of Gandhi that the first Cabinet of Independent India consisted of two women ministers. Gandhi expressed his wish in the following words: "To call women the weaker sex is a lie; it is man's injustice to women." He also said about the equity for women. "The wife is not the husband's slave but his companion and his help-mate and an equal partner in all his joys and sorrows—as free as the husband to choose her own path."

C. Justice for Indigo Peasants in Champaran

It was thus natural that when the British colonised India, many of them started indigo plantations in Bihar and nearby. The exploitation and cruel maltreatment of native workers by these white planters forms an important part of the saga of India's freedom movement. In a repeat of this some sixty years later, Mahatma Gandhi spoke out about the inhuman treatment of the Champaran Peasants and ignited the nation into a non-violent battle for freedom. Thus Indigo is India and India, Indigo.

Gandhi arrived at Champaran to lead an agitation against extortionist British indigo planters. "We may look at Mr. Gandhi as an idealist, a fanatic or a revolutionary according to our particular opinions," wrote Bettiah's sub-divisional officer W.H. Lewis to his commissioner on April 29, 1917, "But to the raiyats he is their liberator, and they credit him with extraordinary powers. He moves about in the villages, asking them to lay their grievances before him, and he is daily transfiguring the imaginations of masses of ignorant men with visions of an early millennium." (Dasgupta, 1997)

Gandhi organised a team of devoted activists, inspired and united the people and wrote and published detailed reports about the atrocities in the region. The people refused to pay taxes and organized protests, fully bracing themselves for arrests and seizures of property. Gandhi himself was arrested by police in Champaran, but the outcry that followed was worse for the authorities. The whole nation was outraged, hundreds of thousands of people protested all over Bihar and Gujarat and Gandhi had to be released.

While we will not hesitate to advise the Kisans, when the movement comes, to suspend payment of taxes to the Government, it is not contemplated that at any stages of non-cooperation we would seek to deprive the zamindars of their rent. The Kisan movement must be confined to the improvement of the status of the Kisans and the betterment of the relations between the zamindars and them (Gandhi, 1921).

D. Justice Against Untouchability

I consider untouchability to be a heinous crime against humanity. It is not a sign of self-restraint, but an arrogant assumption of superiority. (*Young India*, Dec. 8, 1920)

The period 1931-34 marked the most important crossroad both in Gandhi's own life as well as in the annals of the Indian national movement. Coming shortly after the high-water mark of mass participation attained by the Salt

Satyagraha, his year-long campaign against untouchability (1933-34) was not only perhaps the most intensely and passionately carried out of all his campaigns, but one which also provided the occasion for Gandhi to work out his wider economic and constructive programmes. Gandhi also strove to raise the status of untouchables, the caste whom everybody avoided. He gave them the name *harijan*, or "children of God", and launched the weekly paper *Harijan*, which was published in English and Hindi. In an attempt to persuade the orthodox Hindus to wipe out the "plight of untouchability", Gandhi undertook fast in the summer of 1933 for three weeks. In order to promote village self-sufficiency, Gandhi popularized hand spinning and made know *khadi*, hand-spun cloth, the "liver of freedom." However, Gandhi's rejection of the Industrial Revolution wasn't supported by some of his most close friends, like Jawaharlal Nehru. Gandhi began the publication of a weekly paper, *Harijan* ("Children of God"), which was meant to educate the Indian people about the evils of Untouchability.

Gandhi's campaign against Untouchability had touched the masses, and his fasts had revived their affections for him. Gandhi saw his "constructive programs" as attempts for removing Untouchability.

It is a wrong to destroy caste because of the outcaste, as it would be to destroy a body because of an ugly growth in it or of a crop because of the weeds. The outcasteness, in the sense we understand it, has therefore to be destroyed altogether. It is an excess to be removed, if the whole system is not to perish. Untouchability is the product, therefore, not of the caste system, but of the distinction of high and low that has crept into Hinduism and is corroding it. The attack on untouchability is thus an attack upon this 'high-and-lowness'. The moment untouchability goes, the caste system itself will be purified, that is to say, according to my dream, it will resolve itself into the true Varnadharma, the four divisions of society, each complementary to the other and none inferior or superior to any other, each as necessary for the whole body of Hinduism as any other.

A new twist to the civil disobedience movement came in September 1932 when Gandhi, who was in Yeravda Jail, went on a fast as a protest against the segregation of the so-called "untouchables" in the electoral arrangement planned for the new Indian constitution. It was in reaction to the 'Communal Award' announced by the British Prime Minister McDonald. It was spontaneous outrage, against the British Policy of 'divide and rule.' Uncharitable critics described the fast as a form of coercion, a political blackmail. Gandhi was aware that his fast did exercise a moral pressure, but the pressure was directed not against those who disagreed with him, but against those who loved him and believed in him. He did not expect his critics to react in the same way as his friends and co-workers, but if his self-crucifixion could demonstrate his sincerity to them, the battle would be more than half-won. He sought to prick the conscience of the people and to convey to them something of his own inner anguish at a monstrous social tyranny. The fast dramatized the issues at stake; ostensibly it suppressed reason, but in fact it was designed to free reason from that mixture of inertia and prejudice which had permitted the evil of untouchability, which condemned subjected millions of Hindus to humiliation, discrimination and hardships.

The news that Gandhi was about to fast shook India from one end to the other. September 20, 1932, when the fast began, was observed as a day of fasting and prayer. At Shantiniketan, poet Tagore, dressed in black, spoke to a large gathering on the significance of the fast and the urgency of fighting an age-old evil. There was a spontaneous upsurge of feeling; temples, wells and public places were thrown open to the "untouchables." A number of Hindu leaders met the representatives of the untouchables; the Poona Pact was signed by Gandhi and depressed class leader Dr. B.R. Ambedkar, an alternative electoral arrangement was agreed upon which received the approval of the British Government before Gandhi broke his fast.

More important than the new electoral arrangement was the emotional catharsis through which the Hindu community had passed. The fast was intended by Gandhi "to sting the conscience of the Hindu community into right religious action." The scrapping of separate electorates was only the beginning of the end of untouchability. Under

Gandhi's inspiration, while he was still in prison, a new organisation, Harijan Sevak Sangh was founded to combat untouchability and a new weekly paper, the *Harijan,* was started. Harijan means "children of God"; it was the name given by Gandhi for the "untouchables."

After his release Gandhi devoted himself almost wholly to the campaign against untouchability. On November 7, 1933, he embarked upon a countrywide tour which covered 12,500 miles and lasted for nine months. The tour evoked great enthusiasm for the breaking down of the barriers which segregated the untouchables from the rest of the Hindu community, but it also provoked the militancy of the orthodox Hindus. On June 25, while Gandhi was on his way to the municipal hall in Poona, a bomb was thrown at his party. Seven persons were injured, but Gandhi was unhurt. He expressed his "deep pity" for the unknown thrower of the bomb. "I am not aching for martyrdom," he said, "but if it comes in my way in the prosecution of what I consider to be the supreme duty in defence of the faith I hold in common with millions of Hindus, I shall have well earned it."

Gandhi's fast had aroused public enthusiasm, but diverted it from political to social issues. In May 1933, he suspended civil disobedience for six weeks. He revived it later, but confined it to himself. A year later he discontinued it; this was a recognition of the fact that the country was fatigued and in no mood to continue a campaign of defiance. These decisions disconcerted many of his adherents, who did not relish his moral and religious approach to political issues, and chafed at his self-imposed restraints. Gandhi sensed the critical mood in the Congress party and in October 1934, announced his retirement from it. For the next three years, not politics but village economics was his dominant interest.

E. Justice Related to Communal Conflagration

During these years Gandhi was also much distressed by the rise of communal tension. To some extent this increased tension was attributable to the elections to the legislatures. The religious minorities were allowed to elect their representatives only from a purely communal electorate, from which adherents of all other religions were excluded. It was only natural that Muslim candidates should raise religious issues which could make the widest and easiest appeal to a largely illiterate electorates. It so happened that from 1937 onwards it suited the All India Muslim League, under the leadership of M.A. Jinnah, to whip up religious feeling. The League had done badly in the elections, but it sought to retrieve its position by launching a tirade against the Congress and Gandhi. Gandhi was alleged to be 'Enemy Number One' of the Muslim community and the British Governors were accused of conniving at a systematic oppression of the Muslim minority by the Hindus. Vague and exaggerated accusations were made about "atrocities" on the Muslims.

The Muslim League's antagonism to the Congress acquired a progressively sharper edge. Jinnah began even to question the suitability of a democratic system of government for India, in 1940 came out with the theory that Hindus and Muslims were two separate nations and the Muslim nation needed a 'homeland' of its own in the north-west and north-east of the sub-continent. The Muslim League embarked upon the 'two-nations theory' which was total falsification of history of people of India.

Gandhi's reaction to the two-nation theory and the demand for Pakistan was one of bewilderment, almost of incredulity. Was it the function of religion to separate men or to unite them? He described the two-nation theory as an "untruth"; in his dictionary there was no stronger word. He discussed the attributes of nationality. A change of religion did not change nationality; the religious divisions did not coincide with cultural differences. A Bengali Muslim, he wrote, "speaks the same tongue that a Bengali Hindu does, eats the same food, has the same amusements as his Hindu neighbour. They dress alike. His (Jinnah's) name could be that of any Hindu. When I first met him, I did not know he was a Muslim."

To divide India was to undo the centuries of work done by Hindus and Muslims. Gandhi's soul rebelled against the idea that Hinduism and Islam represented antagonistic cultures and doctrines, and that eighty million of Muslims had really nothing in common with their Hindu neighbours.

And even if there were religious and cultural differences, what clash of interests could there be on such matters as revenue, industry, sanitation or justice? The differences could only be in religious usage and observances with which a secular state should have no concern.

At a time when tension was mounting, it was imperative that the country should have a strong and stable government at the centre. The Cabinet Mission had failed in the formation of a national interim government. In July 1946, the Viceroy, Lord Wavell, once again took the initiative and called upon Jawaharlal Nehru to form the Government. Jinnah, who was approached by Nehru, refused to cooperate, was bitterly critical and announced that August 16 would be observed by the Muslim League as "the Direct Action Day." On that day Calcutta witnessed a communal riot, the scale and intensity of which had never been known in living memory. "The Great Calcutta Killing" touched-off a chain reaction of violent communal explosions in East Bengal, Bihar and the Punjab.

As the news of disturbances in Bengal came through, Gandhi cancelled all his plans and decided to leave for the riot-affected areas. In East Bengal he noticed how fear, hatred and violence had come to pervade the countryside. He toured the villages, saw things at first hand, and tried to lift the issue of peace from the plane of politics to that of humanity. Whatever the political map of the future, he pleaded, it should be common ground among all parties that standards of civilised life would not be thrown overboard.

In the *Round Table Conference* held in 1932, the then British Government accepted the demand of the *Dalits* for separate electorate. The basis of that demand was the fact that the *Dalit*s are not Hindus but a separate nation. Gandhi started his '*fast unto death*' against that plan and sabotaged it. It was a thunderous blow to the cause of the emancipation of the *Dalit*. Gandhi, however, showed great respect to the *Dalits* when he made them comparable to the cows who have divine position in Hinduism. He said: "*Majority of Harijans (Dalits) can no more understand the presentation of Christianity than my cows (Gandhi).*

Gandhi's presence acted as a soothing balm on the

villages of East Bengal; he eased tensions, assuaged anger and softened the communal frenzies. In March 1947, he left for Bihar where the Hindu peasants had wrecked a terrible vengeance on the Muslim minority for the misdeeds of the Muslim majority in East Bengal. In Bihar, Gandhi's refrain was the same as in East Bengal: the majority community must repent and make amends; the minority must forgive and make a fresh start. He would not accept any apology for what had happened, and chided those who sought in the misdeeds. Of the rioters in East Bengal, a justification for what had happened in Bihar. Civilised conduct, he argued, was the duty of every individual and every community irrespective of what others did.

Alarmed by the increasing lawlessness, Lord Wavell brought the Muslim League into the Interim Government. The formation of the coalition between the Congress and the League fanned political controversy instead of putting it out. The Constituent Assembly had been summoned to meet on December 9, 1946, but the Muslim League refused to participate in its deliberations. The constitutional impasse looked complete when in the last week of November at an eleventh hour bid to bring the parties together, the British Government invited Wavell, Nehru, Jinnah, Liaquat Ali and Baldev Singh to London. The discussion proved to be abortive, but the British Government issued a statement to clarify the points at dispute. Though this clarification largely met its objections, the Muslim League did not lift its boycott of the Constituent Assembly.

The year 1947 dawned with the darkest possible prospects on the political horizon. To check the drift to chaos, Clement Attlee, the British Premier, came to the conclusion that what was needed was a new policy and a new Viceroy to carry it out. He announced in the House of Commons on February 20, 1947 that the British Government definitely intended to quit India by June 1948, and if by that date the Indian parties did not agree on an all-India constitution, power would be transferred to "some form of Central Government in British India or in some areas to the existing Provincial Governments." Simultaneously it was announced that Lord Mountbatten would succeed Lord Wavell as Viceroy.

The British withdrawal had been decided and dated by the February 20th statement. Lord Mountbatten arrived in India in March and one of his first acts, as Viceroy was to invite Gandhi for a discussion. The Mahatma interrupted his peace mission in Bihar and travelled to New Delhi. During the next few weeks it became evident that a solution of the political deadlock would be sought through the division of India. The Muslim League led by Jinnah was adamant, but there was also a re-orientation of the Congress attitude towards partition. Hitherto the Congress had insisted that partition should, if at all, follow and not precede political liberation, that there could be "no divorce before marriage." But the few months of stormy courtship in the Interim Government had cured Nehru, Patel and other Congress leaders of the desire for a closer union with the Muslim League. In the spring of 1947, the choice seemed to them to be between anarchy and partition; they resigned themselves to the latter in order to salvage three-fourths of India from the chaos, which threatened the whole.

III. CONCLUSION

To conclude, it can be summarised that the concept of social justice is a dynamic concept which changes in context of time and place. Politico-economic thinkers have their prescriptions in their own distinct styles and contents Gandhian perspective of social justice and equity tries to find the solution at the moral and ethical levels. His concept emanates from the inner conscience which believes that all men and children of one and only one God.

References

Atri, Ajit (2007), *Gandhi's View of Legal Justice*, New Delhi, Deep and Deep Publications, 2007.

Dasgupta, Swapan (1997), Journeys in Time, *India Today*, August 18, 1997.

Gandhi, M.K. (1921), "The Zamindar and the Ryots", *Young India*, Vol. III (New Series) No. 153, 18 May.

M.K. Gandhi, *Christian Missions: Their Place in India*, (Ahmedabad. n.d.), p. 58.

Gandhi, M.K. (1963), *Village Swaraj*, compiled H.M. Vyas, Ahmedabad: Navajivan, p. 37.

Kumar, Dalip (2005), "Justice and Equity for the Peasants of Jharkhand: A Swami Sahajanand Saraswati's View", Published in *Indian Economic Journal,* Conference Volume, 88th Annual Conference at Andhra University Visakhapatanam.

Sahajanand, S. (1938), All India Kisan Sabha, 3rd Session, Presidential Address by Swami Sahajanand Saraswati at Commilla, 13-15 May.

Sinha, Priyam Kumar (2002), 'Empowerment of Women in Panchayats: Some Gandhian Norms' published in the book *Economics of Total Revolution*, edited by K.K. Sinha, Economic Association of Bihar, Special Conference issue.

Thakur, Anil K. and Dalip Kumar (2007), *Economic Thoughts on Justice and Equity*, Deep and Deep Publications, New Delhi, pp. xvii-xxx.

30

Mahatma Gandhi's Realisation of Democracy, Non-violence and Governance (1869-1948)

Arjun Singh

Gandhiji was born, brought up in a background when revolt of 1857 against the British Raj in India got failed and India was deprived of freedom for another ninety years. Suppression, loot, killing of innocent people and freedom fighters, curbing of democratic rights of people were being followed by the British Government. Divide and Rule was a open policy of the British in multilingual, multireligious, multicultural India. Famines occurred frequently due to lack of rain and wrong food policy of the Government. Jalianwala Bag massacre in 1919 broke all previous records of mass killings of innocent Indians.

However inspite of all this the Britishers were able to raise a loyal class of Zamindars, Rai Bahadurs, Raisahibs, politicians, officers, industrial rich people, merchants which never joined freedom struggle and helped the Britishers always because of which it took another ninety years to get independence on August 15, 1947 with the massive sufferings of people, freedom fighters all of sorts at patriots.

Gandhiji joined and lead freedom movement in India. He stayed in South Africa for 20 years and received a great experience of his struggles and actions there. He founded upon Truth, Non-violence the basic values of religion. He was much influenced by his family atmosphere, western literature, Gita, Ramayana, Bible and some of his friends known to him.

He has given quite a number of thought provoking concepts like, *Trusteeship, Swadeshi, Sarvodya,* Bread labour, Self-sufficiency, Satyagraha, Democracy, Non-violence and Governance, etc. In this small piece of paper his ideas about democracy, non-violence and governance have been put forward and critical scientific analysis is made.

GANDHIAN DEMOCRACY, NON-VIOLENCE AND GOVERNANCE

Famous statement of president Abraham Lincoln should be remembered in relation to democracy. He described democracy as the government of the people by the people for the people. Gandhi described, "democracy must in essence mean the art and science of mobilizing the entire physical, economic and spiritual of all the various sections of the people in the service of the common good of all"[1] (*Harijan,* 27th May, 1939). He said, "Swaraj of people means the sum total of the swaraj (self-rule of individual)"[2] of individual. He understood Swaraj a form of real democracy for India. "To safeguard democracy the people must have keen sense of independence, self-respect and their oneness and should insist upon choosing as their representatives only such persons as are good and true."[3] He believed in qualified adult franchise. He said that lunatics, loafers, very old people and very young people should not have the right to vote, of the remaining, he said only those who are educated should be allowed to vote."[4]

He wrote in *Harijan* on 12th January, 1947, "Do not depend on military and the police help. You have to uphold democracy, and dependence on the military and the police are incompatible."[5] The government was the best in which government least. He said, "In case of emergency the government may take by force the wealth of the individuals but that in such cases the minimum force has to be applied."[6]

He wrote in *Harijan* on April 20, 1940, "But it must be realised that the reform cannot be rushed. If it to be brought about by non-violent means. It can only be done by education both of the haves and the have-nots. The farmer should be assured that they never will be forced used against them. They have-nots must be educated to know that no one can really compel them to do anything against their will and they secure their freedom by learning the art of non-violence, i.e. self-suffering"[7], Gandhi used the word socialism which appeared synonymous with his democracy. But Gandhi's socialism of a different kind devoid of centralisation violence and untruth. He said, "I am socialist enough. But he would not like to be labeled as socialist."[8] He was in favour of using minimum force by the State. One should exercise power himself and upon himself he said. He held the view that private ownership was less injurious than the violence of the State and power based upon love was a thousand times more effective and permanent that the one derived from fear of punishment. He liked individual freedom but unrestricted individualism was the law of the beast of jungle. Willing submission to social restraint for the sake of well-being of the whole society, enriched both the individual and the society of which one was members he argued. He wanted to achieve freedom and democracy through non-violence. "In a democracy that I have envisaged, a democracy established by non-violence, there will be equal freedom for all. Every man will be his own master."[9] (Gandhiji's correspondence with the Government 1942-44, Ed 1945). Gandhiji was against socialism through violence. He was in favour of socialism through non-violence methods only. He put forward his doctrine of 'Trusteeship' against exploitative capitalism. But till Trusteeship was not followed he was against use of any kind of violence against capitalism *vis-à vis* rich people. He said, "It is my firm conviction that if the State suppressed capitalism by violence, it will be caught in coils of violence, itself and fail to develop non-violence at anytime."[10] True democracy could be represented in his 'Trusteeship' economic order according to him. He thought that road to Trusteeship was easy and short. He further added, "I cannot accept benevolent or any other dictatorship as neither will the rich vanish nor will the poor protected. Some men will certainly be killed and some poor men will be spoonfed. As a class, rich will remain and the poor also, inspite of dictatorship labeled benevolent. The real remedy lies in non-violent democracy. Otherwise spell true education of all. The rich should be taught doctrine of stewardship and the poor of self-help."[11] (*Harijan*, 8th June, 1940). Thus according to him rich and poor would remain for ever.

Concerning freedom of speech and freedom of the press he spoke, "Liberty of speech means that it is unassailed, even when the speech hurts liberty of the press can be said to be truly respected only when the press can comment in the severest terms upon and even misrepresent matters, protection against misrepresentation or violence being secured not by an administrative gagging, not by closing down the press but punishing the real offender, leaving the press itself unrestricted."[12] He was admirer of Britain and held the view, "There is one country today in which people are allowed to enjoy a great deal of freedom to express their views for or against the ruling party. That country is England."[13] He favoured violence of the State number of times if it was for self-realisation, ethical and moral grounds, i.e. curbing rebellion of the poor people, army and strikes of labourers and peasants which seemed violent according to his thinking. About strikes he said, "Sympathetic strikes must be taboo until it is conclusively proved that the affected men have exhausted all the legitimate means at their disposal."[14] (*Harijan*, Aug. 11, 1946). So he favoured and disfavoured strikes. In a true democracy there would be no provision for strikes of any kind for any purpose. He believed in classes cooperating each other but never believed in class struggle.

Gandhiji was in favour of equality of nations and equal opportunity to all human beings as well. In a interview on April 1st, 1939 he said, "we do not want full freedom like frog in the well. On terms of equality we want to establish friendship of Britain and India for ever."[15] Gandhiji was against mechanical equality, "We do not want to produce a dead equality where every person becomes or is rendered incapable of using his ability to the utmost possible extent. I therefore suggest that my advice that moneyed men may earn their crores (honestly, only of course) but so as to dedicate them the service of all is perfectly sound."[16]

Gandhi was not a trained economist, sociologist or philosopher or academician in the accepted form. He was not a *Rishi* or *Sadhu*. He never made any *Guru*. Some western literature, Indian thinking, family atmosphere and a few friends around him influenced him deeply and acted as Guru to him. Every of his philosophy came out of his working experience. He made his foundation upon ancient ideas of religion and spiritualism. Every of his ideas came through truth, non-violence, *brahmacharya*, realisation of self and God. He was full of idealism. He never cared for logic or consistency or reasoning which were scientific in nature. He developed his own science through his religion and own thinking which suited him. "He used to say that he did not care for consistency, and he said that what appeared to be correct. That is why he said one thing today and an another the next day. He advised to accept his latest utterances."[17]

He gave number of concepts like his renowned doctrine trusteeship, *sarvodaya, swadeshi, satyagrarah,* bread labour, use of machinery, on labour, welfare other than Pareto optimality, self sufficiency, rural development through small scale and cottage industries, his philosophy of wants, decentralisation social change, change of hurt, right to work and democracy, etc.

He visualised that all his economic social, political, cultural ideas and upliftment were workable only under the democracy which he realised and advocated and nowhere else. Actually this was a prerequiste for all other actions to follow in a State for all sorts of economic, social and individual development.

But during last years of his life he experienced opposite which he taught. Thousands of people were killed during Hindu-Muslim, riots in 1946, 1947 and 1948. He saw all-round untruth, corruption, opportunism, casteism and communal haterdness, nepotism, regionalism. Gandhi wrote in 1939, "To day our democracy is chocked by our internecine strife. We are torn by dissensions-dissensions between Hindus and Muslims, Brahmans and non-Brahmans, congressmen and non-congressmen. It is no easy task to evolve democracy out of this mobocracy."[18] A few days before his death observing rot set in individual of an organisation like the Indian National Congress he said, "Our moral standards are going down at such a rate that I can now see why our *satyagraha* fights in the past lacked the real content and were reduced to serve passive resistance of the weak. The only chance of savings the congress is in having as president one who will act with firmness and impartiality in the midst of growing welter of confusion, otherwise the congress will disintegrate, rather than that fate should overtake it, it is much better to dissolve it."[19]

But what did happen! The congressmen being the major group ignored all his advice and got opportunity to grab power and money. Thus lived in despair and was a heart broken man. It was this disappointment that made him to say that he had no desire to live for 125 years. A person who struggled throughout his life for achieving freedom was so disappointed of events and mentality that he preferred to remain absent of the biggest event his life. On midnight of August 14, 1947 transfer of power took place and Jawaharlal Nehru was sworn as first Prime Minister of India by Lord Mountbatten, Gandhiji was in Calcutta and slept through the event."[20] This was really very serious.

Gandhiji developed his own tools and thinking to serve masses. He was farsighted and lead independence struggle. He floated number of ideas through experience. His experiments of *Satya, Ahimsa, Brahmacharya, Charkha, Khadi, Swadeshi* remained successful for awakening of masses. He thought always good of all in religious manner.

But his analysis about the materialistic world were not scientific and rational and therefore he lived in dualism and sometimes even neutral. A humble, critical and scientific approach is needed in this regard.

All educated congressmen voted on January 29, 1939 for president of Congress party in which one of the most educated and brilliant man Subash Chander Bose got 1580 and Pattabhi Sitarammaya 1377 votes. Subhash got elected democratically but Gadhiji could not digest, his ego got clashed in undemocratic manner and he said that Sitarammaya's defeat is my defeat. Subash felt too much this behaviour and could not keep himself in Congress.

He favoured and disfavoured strikes. At one place he said, "True is that such a strike should be spontaneous and not on manipulated and should be characterised by perfect cooperation" but this could never be possible. He himself lead a few strikes which he thought proper and left in between with fear of violence.

He believed in Varanvyavastha[21] strongly. This provided base for casteism which posed threat to democracy.

"He helped the British war effort with men and money. Before Jalianwala Bag massacre in 1919, he was a cooperator." In 1899 Boer South African war started and 1906 heavy taxes were imposed upon Zulu tribal community and they became rebel. Gandhi organized an ambulance corps and fought for the Government in which thousands of Zulu tribes were killed. "He was not averse to helping the British"[22]. He had a big praise for the British Empire and the *vice-versa.* He fought against the Policy of suppression and exploitation of the British and he launched non-cooperation movement in 1920 and Civil Disobedience movement in 1930, Quit India movement in 1942. Even then he had a sense of cooperation with the British always. "Sometime Gandhiji's peaceful approach and philosophy was though of as a weak policy. Gandhi had requested Churchill on July 17, 1944 to repose trust and faith in him. Its request was ignored and good treatment was not given to the congress[23]. He remained always in hope for good treatment by the British. He favored violence on moral grounds like of Lord Krishna preaching for violence in Mahabharta and Lord Rama in Ramayana keeping this kind of morality and ethics in mind he helped and cooperated the British Government in and South African Government to suppress Julu rebellion. But he never liked violence by any individual or any group of workers and peasants and soldiers rebellion in any situation. Udham Singh killed Michel O'Dyre a person responsible for Jalianwala Bag Massacre Gandhiji reacted, "Every Indian should be ashamed of this incident like me and he should feel happy that life of another three gentle Englishmen is saved."[24] This hand of action has been received as a great ethics, morality and pride of every Indian like *Rama* killing *Ravna* and *Arjuna* killing *Duryodhana*. But not acceptable to Gandhiji with the same thinking he never recognized actions of Bhagat Singh, Rajguru, Sukhdev and other revolutionaries in great service of humanity and the nation doing extreme sacrifice in prime youth. Every Indian feels proud of them with all sincerity and honesty except a few true Gandhian in the country. "Sitarammaya wrote that Bhagat Singh's name was equally famous to Gandhi after hanging of Bhagat Singh on March 23, 1931. Government intelligence has written that at that time Bhagat Singh got established himself as a main political figure even more than Gandhi."[25] His thought in relation to violence against women were "In the face of kidnapping a woman does not have to surrender herself to the kidnappers. She should be ready to end her own life but not be violent to the person kidnapping her. It may convert him."[26] But suicide has never been solution to any problem like this according to top thinkers of the world. He had similar some backward thoughts for women.

He was against use of machinery. Because Industrialisation breeded violence, concentration of power and replaced labour and hindrance in freedom and liberty of labour and encouraged slavery. In relation to Economics he said that the Bible or the Gita contained more economics that a hundred books, text books on economics.[27] How far it is true; let economists themselves think and decide.

It was often said that he could change his heart only and half of his close associate and right hand Jamanalal Bajaj one of the biggest cotton trader of central India. This has been admitted by Gandhi himself.

Jawarhar Lal Nehru his ideal successor used to oppose him tooth and nail regarding his *khadi* movement, *swaraj*, industrialisation, religion-based politics and number of other ideas but always surrendered before Gandhi. Gandhi declared, "Jawaharlal will be may successor. He says what is in his mind but acts as I wish.[28] Subhash had doubts about efficacy of Gandhian approach. Swadeshi and boycott were quite opposite in Gandhi's thinking and were used side by side.

CONCLUSION AND PRESENT DAY GOVERNANCE

Gandhi was an utopian socialist. He got successful in awakening the masses of India for independence. He was in favour of welfare of the whole human beings. Religion was his politics and *vice-versa*. He worked for realisation of self, self-purification and realisation of God. His experiments with truth, non-violence and *brahmacharya* were found useful. He was successful in reading Indian psychology upto much extent. Truth and non-violence were found to have for reaching implications for future.

Inspite of all this, he lived in despair in his last years of life. He developed his own sense of working, own ego to satisfy, developed his own science of thoughts based on religion and spiritualism. He preached democracy, non-violence, truth and laws of good governance always. Yet he observed corruption, casteism, communal riots, violence, opportunism, untruth behavior, violence, moral degradation in a big way.

He lacked scientific analysis of cause of things in the material world. Therefore, he was full of contradictions, illusions, dualism and only therefore he was never consistent in his writings, speeches and actions. He said one thing today and another tomorrow. He was for welfare of all, i.e. rich and poor, rulers and the ruled, haves and have-nots, suppressor and the suppressed. He worked and struggled for poor masses of India and had close affinity with the rich class. He preached class cooperation and discarded scientific class struggle.

Presently same dualism, contradiction and illusion are seen in Indian politics. Though India is developing at a fast rate a great welcome but casteism, communalism, corruption, nepotism, opportunism, moral degradation, crimes against women and children specially, all time shameful terrorism by fundamentalists, scandals, police crimes, farmer suicides are increasing even at a faster rate. Gandhiji was intelligent enough to smell in advance. Mass defection, cheating the voters in a big way and unruly behavior in assembly and parliament is noticed in a big way. Imperialism is spreading its feet in India and imperialistic tendencies are flaired up.

The very scientific conclusions of imperialism are; policies of mass exploitation of resources for profits only, violence through puppet military dictators in different regions of the world, killing lakhs of innocent people and ruining nations (Vietnam, Korea, Afghanistan, Iraq, Chili, etc.) and to a great fun in the name of maintaining peace and democracy. Looting and empowering the nations through use of men, material, money, machinery and all kinds of cheap methods are another proved attributes of Imperialism.

Though good growth and all round development is seen during past decades in India and on the globe gap between rich and poor in nations, gap between rich and poor among nations is on rampant increase which is another attribute of capitalistic and imperialistic policies and a big cause of frustration in India. All these tendencies which Gandhiji noticed are to be fought with if any iota of democracy is to realize. Gandhiji wanted peace on the earth through his truthful and non-violent ways and so in India. He will be remembered for his struggles and services for awakening of masses to achieve freedom of the nation and freedom of individual as well.

Notes and References

1. Mehta, J.K. (1985), "Gandhian Thought", Ashish Publishing House, New Delhi-26, Chap., Gandhian Democracy for Self-realisation. p. 167.
2. *Ibid.* p. 169.
3. *Ibid.* p. 170.
4. *Ibid.* p. 171.
5. *Ibid.* p. 173.
6. *Ibid.* p. 175.
7. *Ibid.* p. 175.
8. *Ibid.* p. 176.
9. *Ibid.* p. 177.
10. *Ibid.* p. 180.
11. *Ibid.* p. 190.
12. *Ibid.* p. 182.
13. *Ibid.* p. 77.
14. *Ibid.* p. 188.
15. Birla, G.D. (1955) Bapu-3, p. 269.

16. Ref. I, p. 189.
17. *Ibid.* p. 183.
18. *Ibid.* p. 240.
19. *The Hindu,* August 15, 2007, Independent India at 60 from the achieves of the Hindu.
20. Ref. I, p. 189.
21. Gaur, V.P. (1977), 'Mahatma Gandhi: A study of his message of Non-Violence', Sterling Publishers Pvt. Ltd., AB/9, Safdarjang Enclave, New Delhi-16, p. 42.
22. *Ibid.* p. 5.
23. *Ibid.* p. 59.
24. *CWMG*-71, p. 391.
25. Sitaramayya, B. Pattabhi (1947), "The History of Indian National Congress", p. 456.
26. Ref. I, p. 68.
27. Ref. I, p. 13.
28. *CWMG*-75, p. 248.

31

Gandhian Thought in 21st Century: Relevance and Limitations

SUNIL KUMAR

"The mother earth provides sufficient for the need of the people but not for greed."

The contribution of Mahatma Gandhi to the theory of economic planning and dvelopment can hardly be described in words. Gandhi was a rare admixture of a great humanist, a master strategist, a veteran politician and a down to earth economist. Above all Gandhi was realist as well as pragmatist who saw not only the present generation but also posterity.

Gandhian thought is non-compartmentalised rather he held the synthetic and holistic view of the man, society and nature but man was the main thrust of his consideration.

Science of economics is in crisis. Rarely would an economist not talk about the crisis while dealing with contemporary issues. When a science is in crisis, it begins to question its own philosophical assumptions and methods and begins a search for alternative paradigms. Unfortunately, the century old reign of positivist economics which included famous models and their numerous versions such as neo-Keynesian, Keynesian and even Marxian economics, lost track of its philosophical assumptions. The disease of economic science have spread to other social sciences also. Technological revolution created more problems instead of solving them. The science for economics ceased to be dismal, it rather became an art of rat race. J.K. Galbraith talked about private affluence and public poverty as the central crisis of the developed capitalist system. It has been of no help to modern economists for raising the discipline of economics to the level of science to keep the value out of their analysis. Values without philosophy lead to vulgarisation of theory and corruption of practice.

If new wants can be generated at a rate faster than the existing ones are satisfied, not only will there be a feeling of deprivation and poverty but society would be obliged to become an arena of rat race among the human beings.

Explosion of knowledge and rapid progress in technological development, instead of solving the old problems, are creating new ones. Technology has taken the shape of Philosophy and it threatens to become the supreme value. Technology is also looked upon as the answer to crisis created by technology itself. But by changing the structure of production, labour force and demand, technology has also eroded many old economic theories and paradigms. This crisis is getting circular and the curve of economics is a vicious circle.

Notwithstanding all the developments in the field of science and technology human organisation lags behind in capturing and controlling their essence. On the contrary, human beings are becoming victims of science and technology. The greater the thrust of new innovation, the greater the threat of human enslavement. There is bound to be reaction towards total anti-technology which is equally dangerous. To remove an old misunderstanding, it must be affirmed that Gandhi was neither anti-science nor anti-technology.

There are limits within which science and technology can be neutral. Once those limits are crossed, science and technology will become 'Frankenstine mosters'.

In the backdrop of above discussion and focus on the basic transformation that economics undergoes with the fresh metaphysical outlook, credit goes to Gandhi. Not supprisingly, the radical formulation is reflected in Gandhian elements in terms of swadeshi, bread labour, Apparigrah or non-possession, trusteeship, non-exploitation and equality which from the core of Gandhian economic thought.

During the last few decades, the global economy has been in perpetual crisis. The International monetary system is under stress. There has been energy cirsis leading to rethinking about the mode of production and energy-induced technological development. The dialogue between the North and South is more and more full of conflict and suspicion. Capitalist system is suffering from stagflation and persistently high levels of uneployment accompanied by increasing number of poor, hungry and malnourished people. The future is not optimistic.

In the words of the Global 2000 Report to the U.S. President: "If the present trends continue, the world in 2000 will be more crowded, more polluted, less stable ecologically and more vulnerable to disruption than the world we live in now. Despite greater material output, the world's people will be poorer in many ways than they are today."

The crisis in global economy and in economic theory have precipitated a number of fresh ideas. The basic proposition is that the thought and practice of Gandhi also provide a fruitful area for fresh thinking specially in the changed scenario of the world. It is a fact that Gandhian ideas present a complete basis of economic theory. One point should be clearly borne in mind that Gandhian Economics and thought, in spite of its emphasis on the local level, relates to the global economy. In other words, global issues are necessary for the solution of local problems. This follows from the following Gandhian proposition: (1) there is an elite-mass contradiction in every society, and (2) the national elites exploit national masses and international elites exploit masses all over the world. It can easily disrupt and destroy a society operating on Gandhian ideas elsewhere. Ramesh K. Diwan and Shushila Gidwani,[1] have suggested that there are six basic concepts that are essential in Gandhian economics. These are all related to each other. There is no hierarchy among them. These are equally important. They are:

(i) Swadedhi, (ii) bread labour, (iii) aparigrah or non-possession, (iv) trusteeship, (v) non-exploitation, and (vi) equality. A votary of swadeshi will carefully study his environment and try to help his neighbours wherever possible by giving preference to local manufacturers, even if they are of an inferior grade or cheaper in price than things manufactured elsewhere. But even swadeshi like any other good thing, can be ridden to death if it is made of fetish. To reject foreign manufacturers merely because they are foreign, and to go on wasting time and resources in the promotion in one's country or manufacturers for which it is not suited, would be criminal folly and negation of the swadeshi spirit.

Throughout Gandhi's writings run the thread of the improtance of work in men's personal growth. The doctrine of bread-labour was inspired by Ruskin, Tolstoy and the Gita. In *Young India*, 10 October, 1921, Gandhi asserts:

"I cannot imagine anything nobler or more rational than that, for say, one hour in the day, we should do all the labour that the poor do, must do and thus identify ourselves with them and through them, with all mankind. It asserts not only the dignity of labour but also avoids alienation which create classes leading to tension, conflict and distrust.[2]

The economic laws have discussed value-in-use and value-in-exchange but in the present day society value-in-threat has engulfed all other considerations. It is imperative for creating power base which is ultimately supported by them.

People concerned about the deprivation and poverty of a large part of humanity question such values of materialism, rationalism and selfishness. Gandhi argued for a different set of values.

To quote:

> "The moral law also requires that the strong men of a community or nation should regard it as their paramount duty to protect the weak and the oppressed. If all men realise the obligation of service, they would regard it as a sin to amass wealth and then, there would be no inequalities of wealth and consequently no famine or starvation."

The concept of non-possession is based on a different morality on the idea that all human beings are equal and that person is not to be exploited by another. The principle of aparigrah is an answer to the problems created by the acquisitive society. This society has set impressive records in the expansion of productive capacity, advances in technology, exploitation of resources, affluence and abundance of goods and services. But the same society has also generated severe strains and stresses on life and powerful tendencies towards the degradation of the total environment, social, economic, ecological, political and last but not the least moral. This is not accidental, it is quite natural. Gandhi has serious doubt the ability of modern societies to serving on its resent course. To corroborate Gandhi the Limit to Growth Study, 1972 asserts:

> "If the present growth trend in world population industrialisation, pollution, food production and resource depletion continue unchanged, the limit to growth on this planet will be reached some time within next one hundred years. The most probable result will be a rather sudden and uncontrollable decline in both population and industrial output."[3]

Similarly, the Cocoyoc Declaration of 1974 observes:

> "The failure of the world society to provide a safe and happy life for all is not caused by any present lack of physical resources. The problem today is not one of physical shortages but of economic and social maldistribution and misuse of these resources. We believe that ways of life and social systems can be evolved that are more respectful of the whole planetary environment. The road forward does not lie through the dispair of doom watching not through the easy opportunism of successive technological fixes."[4]

TRUSTEESHIP

Gandhian thought argues that in virtually every society

there is an elite mass contradiction. Generally, the elites exploit the masses, consequently every society is divided into two sub-societies. The elites, consisting of small part of population, are politically powerful, economically rich and by and large urbanised while masses are exploited, politically powerless, economically poor and generally rural-based.[5] These two societies exist side by side. Privileges are the main characteristics of the elite society.

The Gandhian solution involves, *inter alia*, the concept of trusteeship. Trusteeship is based on the idea that "what belongs to me is the right to an honourable livelihood", no better than enjoyed by millions of others. The rest of my wealth belongs to the community and must be used for the welfare of the community. Here trusteeship implies relationship between privilege and power or the access to power and also involves decentralisation.

Finally, the two elements or non-exploitation and equality can be either explicitly or implicitly encountered throughout the discussion of Gandhian economic thought. Thus the decomposition and analysis of separate aspects and elements of Gandhi's economics, although necessary, is not without problems due to the interrelated and holistic nature of Gandhian thought.

Equality meant to Gandhi primarily two things: First, everybody has a basic right to live, is to meet the basic needs and live a dignified life integrated in community with one's fellow. He was averse to doles and charity. He advocated guaranteed employment for everybody who wants to work. Secondly, equality is absence of exploitation. He endorsed non-exploitative capital-labour relation as well as non-exploitation of manual by intellectual labour and above all, non-exploitation of the countryside by the city. Now it is clear that the core of Gandhi's economic thought has to be seen in the wider context of his view of human nature reflecting the whole of psychology, philosophy and religion. His system represents a radical departure from the mainstream of economic thought. It becomes remarkably coherent and logical as soon as we accept the axiomatic premises of his world view. Here equality means equality of opportunities open to all in order to be self-supporting and finally self-reliant.

Gandhi observes that democracy and violence cannot go together. The capitalist society is exploitation personified and the essence of all kinds of exploitation is violence. In order to root out exploitation, therefore, non-violent society or state is to be established. Such a society, of necessity, must be based on economic freedom and equality because without economic equality there can exist no real political democracy. Centralisation breeds violence and essence of non-violence is decentralisation. He advocated such decentralisation of economic and political power in the form of, more or less, self-sufficient and self-governing village communities.

In short, the above principles of Gandhian economy are the only practical and rational solution of various ills that harass the modern world. They point out the middle path between blood-thirsty capitalism and freedom-thirsty socialism.

Gandhian thoughts are economically viable, politically sound, sociologically desirable and ecologically sustainable. The use of violence both invites and suppresses further use of violence, but finally the violent victor is himself vanquished by the power unleashed by him or he becomes a victim of his own institution of violence, allowing the means to swallow the ends (Pakistan and Bangladesh).

The question of relevance of Gandhian thought in the 21st century appears to be absurd as it is universal and relevant for all times to come. But the forces which operate in the national and international fields, it has become imperative to rethink about Gandhian thought. When society is in trouble and deep distress, it has to find out the ways to extricate itself from the crisis. Every revolution has a child in its womb and when revolution succeeds, the child is born and by the passage of time the child attains maturity and ultimately devours the mother. This is exactly true in case of U.S.S.R.

Similar development of science and technological revolution has created situation which is posing problem even for the survival of mankind in terms of its destructive power and all engulfing impact. Now it is being realised by individual thinkers and various institutions that the present mode of production which is energy-based and technologically-induced is not sustainable in the long run. Nuclear catastrophe like Bhopal Gas Tragedy, Chernobyl Nuclear Blast in Russia, rising temperature on this planet, hole in the ozone layer, ecological disruption and environmental pollution are posing challenges before the survival of human civilisation and existence of mankind. This is true globally and India cannot escape from the final destruction even if it may not be responsible to a great extent.

India presents a different picture as it suffers from absolute poverty, structural unemploment, disparities in the wealth and income and consequent social tension, conflict and unrest. This destabilises social structure and administrative set-up. To cap it all, it is rendering the political system irrelevant. Then all the channels for the redressal of genuine grievances are disrupted people are constrained to resort to direct action which generates extremism, terrorism and subversive activities. Ultimately the very foundation of nationhood is threatened. This is the realistic assessment of existing scenario of India. After independence, process of politicisation of crime was started as it was beneficial for the politicians and ultimately it resulted in the criminalisation of political system. Muscle and money power became the main ingredients of not only political system rather it engulfed the administrative structure as well. Consequently corruption has been institutionalised. Instead of inbuilt provision of justice, equity and fair distribution, there is in-built provision of corruption in the process of development itself. Less said is better in the present scenario of the country. In this context Gandhi's views are pertinent. Gandhi said:

> "A violent and blood revoution is a certainty one day unless there is a violuntary abdication of fiches and the power that riches give and sharing them for common good."[6]

Almost similar opinion was expressed by Dr. B.R. Ambedkar in his speech in the Constituent Assembly:

> "On the 26th of January, 1950, we are going to enter into a life of contradictions. In politics we will have equality and in social and economic life we will have inequality. How long shall we continue to live this life of contradiction? How long shall we continue to deny equality in our social and economic life? If we contiunue to deny it for long, we will do so only by putting our political democracy to peril. We should remove this contradiction at the earliest possible moment or else those who suffer from inequality will blow up the structure of political democracy which this Assembly has so laboriously built up."[7]

The above assertions remind the government to be aware of its responsibility for not only for the present generation but also of the well-being of the future generation and Gandhi nearly fits in this scheme in terms of long-term survival of mankind with peace and prosperity.

The task, then for the governments of the developing countries is to reorient their development policies in order to attack directly the personal poverty of the oppressed and depressed segments of the society. This the government can do without abandoning their goal of vigorous overall economic growth. But they must be prepared to give greater priority to establishing growth targets in terms of essential human needs. Such a reorientation of social and economic policy is primarily a political task, and the developing countries must decide for themselves if they wish to undertake it. It is obvious that there is no rational alternative to moving towards policies of greater social equity. The situation cannot be ignored when the highly privileged are few and desperately poor are many, and when the gap between them is worsening rather than improving, it is only a question of time before a decisive choice must be made between the political costs of reform and the political risk of rebellion. That is why policies specifically designed to reduce the deprivation among the poorest 40 per cent in developing countries are prescriptions not only of principle but of prudence. Social justice is not merely a moral imperative. It is a ploitical imperative as well.[8]

Mahbub Ul Haque is of the opinion that time has come when we have to take decisive stand to serve the people and thereby the nation as well.

> "I have always believed that those who make a virtue out of institutional conformity and loyalty serve their institution far more poorly than those who are willing to express their dissent and pay the necessary price for it.[9]

In India Gandhi paid the price in terms of his life for the conviction which he held and opinion expressed. Thus principles upheld by Gandhi offer solution to the present predicament of mankind and his views were shared by E.F. Schumacher, Myrdal, Laski, King Martin Luther, etc. Not only in India, he is now remembered all over the world and people think, Gandhian thought will lead the humanity to peace and prosperity. There is no rational alternative to Gandhian principles for the salvation of humanity and solution of the problems on long-term and sustainable basis. Let us hope and pray for the peace and prosperity of mankind.

If there is one single issue on which there is unanimity among the otherwise badly divided intelligentsia of this country, it is the profound nature of the moral crisis of contemporary Indian society. This was termed as crisis of conscience by Rajendra Pur. There are many dimensions to this crisis, rampant and incrasingly visible corruption, decline in ethical standard among the individuals as well as social groups and classes, rapid erosion of morality in public life, collapse of number of institutions that could be termed guardians or Social "Conveyor belts" of morality.

This crisis consists not so much in a generalised degradation of ethical norms in society, as in the absence of a coherent, consistent and viable morality, both individual and public, and hence the prevalence of moral chaos. Praful Bidwai called it acquisitive hedonism.[10]

Acquisitive individualistic hedonism represents the most important of the many moral doctrines that hold sway over Indian society in particular the one-fifth of the population that comprises its best represented, most powerful, most articulate, relatively more privileged elite social strata. This doctrine puts pleasure above all other possible criteria of what is morally right, the individual pursuits of material pleasure is justified. In reality, callousness and cynical unconcern for social consequences of one's pleasure maximising actions, indeed for any aspect of social reality, are the usual concomitants of hedonism.

This kind of acquisitive culture has distorted the economy and society. Prof. K.N. Raj has recently analysed as an essential duality the Indian "Twin nation" in which co-exist a low-growth near subsistence-level majority economy and a high-growth near subsistence-level majority economy and a high-growth minority elite sector marked by a sharp rise in expendable incomes that fuels the consumer boom. Credit-induced consumption has replaced austerity and Gandhian ideals in India. Consumerism has become all pervasive and it is disrupting the social cohesion and structure.

Then question arises what is the wayout. If nothing can be done, then the situation is irretrievable. But where there is a will, there is a way, Gandhi offers solution.

If we take the holistic view of man and society, hopes can be rekindled amidst doom and dispair. According to Gandhi, economics, ethics and religion constitute an indivisible whole. Economics is the science of human welfare, hence, its goal ought to be Sarvodaya, the welfare of all. The supreme consideration has to be man. The huamn welfare economics focusing on what Gandhi called the human element, implies the crucial importance of decentralised social economy. Finally, economics has to respect the law of Swadeshi.

Humanistic aproach is needed for the eradication of all the ills which affect mankind all over the world. Even today there is no real physical scarcity of resources to feed the mankind and to keep them in peace and happiness provided the leaders of the world think, work and consider the world as single homogeneous unit. The concentration of economic and political power will be avoided, tension relaxed and unrest and other social ills finally, eliminated making this planet safe, happy, peaceful and harmonious for the entire mankind. Crisis is our own creation hence, we have to solve it amicably.

In the changing global scenario, modernisation is inescapable even for the third world country like India but rational and selective approach to technology is essential. In the words of Plato, poverty results from increase of man's desires, not from diminution of his property. A new approach based on Schumacher's philosophy of appropriate technology advocating the Small is Beautiful certainly caught the people's imagination. It is pragmatic also for the poor country. His assertion confirms Gandhian concept of self-sufficiency and work for all. He advocated production by masses as against mass production. This implies that appropriate technology should be basic component of development strategy and where necessary capital-intensive technology may be preferred but selectively in the larger interest of the nation. Man being the main focus reiterated by Gandhi, there is no escape from this strategy in India. This is empirically proved on the basis of Planned Process of economic development. Principle of justice and equity cannot be ignored in the larger interest of the people.

Ideologies are almost always lonely, more adored and admired than followed. Similarly, Gandhi has been more worshipped than followed. Political ideologies are no substitute for self-realisation. One example may suffice the purpose. Atheist Jinnah created theocratic Pakistan while religious Gandhi created secular India. This is mainly due to inner and self-realisation and not due to ideology.

Notes and References

1. Ramesh Diwan and Shushila Gidwani, Elements in Gandhian Economics, *Gandhi Marg*, Vol. I, August 1979.
2. *Young India*, 10 October, 1921.
3. Limit to Growth Study, 1972.
4. The Cocoyoc Declaration of 1974.
5. Ivan Ilich, Employment, Growth and Basic Needs: A One World Problem, New York.
6. Mahatma Gandhi: Constructive Programme, Its Meaning and Place, pp. 20-21.

7. Dr. B.R. Ambedkar, Speech in the Constituent Assembly on 25th of November, 1949.
8. Robert McNamara, Annual Speech to the Boar of Governors, September 1972.
9. Mahbub Ul Haque, Poverty Curtain, Oxford University Press, Cal. 1978, p. 6.
10. Praful Bidwai, Acquisitive Hedonism, *The Times Magazine*, November-December, 1988.

32

Relevance of Gandhian Economic Thoughts in the Context of Present Economic Problems of Indian Economy

N. Sharma and Aniruddha Kumar

Billions of words have been written on Mahatma Gandhi, his life and works but the discussion in this paper will touch only a few basic issues relating to the relevance of Gandhian economic ideas in the context of present economic problems prevailing in Indian economy. An attempt has been made in this paper to enquire into the causes of the present, miserable state of affairs of the weaker sections of the population, living particularly in rural areas, in spite of the concerted efforts made under different plans since the very inception of planning in India, adopting the concept of mixed economy, supported by huge plan outlays, modern production technology along with noble objective to initiate "a process of development which will raise the living standards and open out to the people new opportunities for a richer and more varied life." (First Five Year Plan, p. 7)

In the first decade of the twenty-first century, under the banner of 'Globalisation', the world economy claims for such outstanding achievements in all sectors which the world has never achieved in the past. The sound of drum beating beyond eye sight is always pleasant but the visible drum beating sounds unpleasant. Globalisation is just like drum beating pleasant to hear but the reality is that whole of world has reached the point of crises today. Abject poverty, mass unemployment, mounting inflation, environmental pollution, regional imbalances and the insecurity of under-developed countries are prevailing. Not only the under-developed countries but the capitalistic advanced countries have not also been able to eradicate the poverty. The environmental pollution has posed a threat to the health and sanitary conditions have increased the social cost of production. People are becoming impatient and are looking for an economic system that is alternative for both socialism and capitalism.

Among the leading names of modern history that of Mohandas K. Gandhi is respected by many men for his association with principle, nationalism and pacifism. (Paul. F. Power, 1960) The whole world recognized him as the greatest personality of the twentieth century. Once, the great Nobel-prize winning scientist, Sir Albert Einstein spoke on Gandhiji, "Generation to come, will scarcely believe that, such a one as this, ever in flesh and blood, walked upon this earth." Various political scientists, economists, sociologists and spiritualists have studied Gandhi's political, economic, social, religious and spiritual concepts. Some of these scholars are of the view that Gandhi's ideas are pragmatic and always relevant irrespective of time and places. But some others are of the view that his ideas are completely irrelevant and inapplicable in this age of scientific and technological progress. There may be contrary views on Gandhism but one thing is certainly beyond doubt that Gandhism presents a new, dynamic, revolutionary, and rational approach to the existing political and socio-economic problems. Shriman Narayan says, "the more I think about diverse problems facing India at present, the more I feel convinced that Gandhian approach alone will be able to solve our difficulties on a lasting basis." (Shriman Narayan, 1970)

I. INDIA'S EXISTING SOCIO-ECONOMIC CONDITION

Before making a discussion on the relevancy of Gandhian economic ideas in the context of economic problems it would not be improper to throw some light on the general background of the strategy and techniques which the Indian planners adopted for solving the economic problems and the results thereof. It is a fact that India is one of the few countries of the world where expertise in the techniques of planning has been developed to a rather sophisticated extent with all the modern statistical analysis. It is also a fact that the path followed on the advice of the development model makers has created a modern sector of the economy which has earned us a place among the top ten industrialised nations of world. Our economic planners show the positive impact of the economic reforms. The economic reforms have increased the pace of India's integration with the world economy. Inward, Foreign Direct Investment India grew from about US $ 100 million in 1991 to over $ 15. 7 billion in 2006-07. Exports as a percentage of GDP have grown from less than 6 per cent in 1990-91 to almost 13 per cent in 2005-06. Private sector participation across industry sectors aided by financial market reforms has lead to increase in the market capitalisation as a percentage of GDP from 13 per cent in 1990 to close to 100 per cent levels now. (Narayana N.R. Murthy, 2007)

Going by the data on the human developmental indicators, India has met reasonable success in the past fifteen years. Poverty has been reduced, primarily because of increase in per capita income. Life expectancy has gone up from less than 60 years in 1991 to close to 65 years now. Literacy rates have gone up from 52 per cent in 1991 to 62 per cent in 2006. One of the significant outcomes of the reforms was the realignment of the contribution of sectors. Services sectors saw its contribution to GDP now from 41 per cent in 1990-91 to 56 per cent in 2007. At the time of independence the contribution of agriculture to the economy was 56 per cent but now it contributes less than a fifth of the national GDP. (Narayana N.R. Murthy, 2007) While we talk of India rocking towards becoming a rich nation fueled by over 9 per cent annual growth, what finally matters is how well the common men feel. Though economic indicators are positive for our country the livelihood indicators in rural areas, do not suggest a very rosy picture, which gets reflected in the social face of India, which we discuss here. Even after 60 years of independence and developmental planning, the rural population in India does not find themselves in the mainstream of development across the country. The livelihood indicators of our rural areas are lower than even some of our neighbouring countries. The basic issues of health care, sanitation, comparable quality of education, employment and overall quality of life remain a serious consideration in policies and programmes of national and provincial governments.

Widely-used and accepted international definition of sustainable development is: 'development which meets the needs of the present without compromising the ability of future generation to meet their own needs'. Globally we are not even meeting the needs of the present let alone considering the needs of future generations. (A.K. Rajvanshi, 2004)

Optimism about the growth of national economy is rife. However, as there is so much of data to aver that India is on fire, there is abundant data to show that there are several potholes that could derail the ambitious growth plans of India. India has over 350 million people who earn less than $ 1 a day; this number is more than the population of India in 1947. Adult literacy rate is at 61 per cent, about 151 million people don't have access to proper drinking water and almost half the children below five years are under weight. Several estimates put the number of unemployed in India around 250-300 million. Every year we are adding about 35-40 million new job-seekers to the massive figure. Against this, the country has been able to generate hardly three million jobs a year. 65 per cent of the population is still dependent on agriculture. In terms of corruption, India is ranked among the most corrupt. A recent study from Goldman Sachs, which forecast that India could Sustain Eight per cent growth until 2020, clearly stated that this would require better education and less red tape. (*Yojna,* August 2007)

II. WHAT DID THE PLANNERS MISS?

The planners in India have missed the real perspective of the Indian economy and to quote Gunnar Myrdal, "The main reason for slow development in India is that Indian planners have deviated from the fundamentals of Mahatma Gandhi's rationalistic plans. (G. Myrdal, 1973) Our planners adopted highly capital-intensive technology based on sectoral development planning model ignoring Gandhian planning model based on labour-intensive technology. The result of not adopting Gandhian model is that even after six decades of developmental planning greater mass of humanity is being plunged into destitution and unemployment. Gandhiji was of the view that "any plan which exploits the raw material of a country and neglects the potentially more powerful manpower is lopsided and can never tend to establish human equality. Real planning consists in the best utilisation of the whole manpower of India and the distribution of the raw products of India in her numerous villages instead of sending them outside and rebuying finished articles at fabulous prices (M.K. Gandhi, 1947) The results of the India's five year plans indicate that there is something fundamentally lacking in the strategy and process of planning. It may be precisely because in our type of mixed economy "planning is outwardly patterned after the soviet Model but its basic ingredients are those of the western economics." Our planners who are of the view that a mixed economy is basically different from capitalist mode of production are greatly mistaken. The adoption of Soviet type of planning, within a democratic framework, has prevented the planners over the past six decades from giving serious attention to the Gandhian concepts which are extremely relevant to the Indian situation. Our planners have still strong faith in the economic theories, models and approaches and policies as advanced by the Western economists even when they do not have relevance to our problems. The Indian planners are still in illusion and are mistaken. They have doubts even now in Gandhian way of planning for the solution of the emerging socio-economic problems. It is evident from the fact that they adopt Gandhian peacemeal and as a programme in place of giving these items high rank among the basic priorities. This is what our planners missed and are missing.

III. THE GANDHIAN ECONOMIC IDEAS

The Economic portion of Gandhi's vision was based on a set of interrelated concepts. Gandhian economics was meant to set-up 'Swaraj' or 'Sarvodaya' society. The word 'Swaraj' is a sacred word, a Vedic word, meaning self-rule and self–restraint, and not freedom from all restraints which 'independence' often means. (M.K. Gandhi, 1931) Gandhi's motto for his philosophy of social classes was 'Sarvodaya' the welfare of all. (Paul. F. Power, 1960, p. 43) 'Swaraj' or 'Sarvodaya' society has been characterized by simplicity, self-sufficiency and self-reliance. Gandhi's 'Swaraj' embodies multifaceted constructive programmes and lays heavy emphasis on co-operative and equitable social relations and strives for a renewal and a development of localised economy and village industries and rehabilitation of handicrafts. Gandhiji insisted that village should have economical necessities. The development of agriculture through decentralisation and self-reliant activities which promote a self-sufficient economy and rural industries constitute the core of Gandhian economics. He believed in 'production by masses' instead of more mass production by machines. He opinionated that this was the only guarantee that a village could remain free and outsiders fully entitled to the return his labour and not be robbed of his right and share in the produce. Gandhi's concept of true Swaraj is man-centered, non-exploiting, decentralised, simple village economy providing, for full employment to each one of its citizens on the basis of voluntary co-operation and working for achieving self-sufficiency in its basic requirements of food, clothing and other necessities of life. (M.K. Gandhi, 1930)

The concept of 'trusteeship' is another important economic idea of Gandhiji. He believed that modern economic systems rooted as they are in self-indulgence, multiplicity of wants and divorce of ethics from economics are large-scale, mechanized, centralised, complicated organisation. (H.M. Vyas, 1962, p. XVI) They are disfigured by unemployment, under-employment, pauperism, exploitation, a mad race for capturing markets and conquering lands for raw materials. Competitions, conflicts and class wars corrode the social fabric. Therefore, he gave his own indigenous solution to the problems faced by the society. He hoped for and planned for a change of heart to create an environment in which the employer and employee and rich and the poor would work together as one in the service of the nation without exploiting anyone, instead benefiting everyone. In this context Gandhiji advocated for the principle of 'trusteeship' whose true implementation was difficult in practice which he himself felt. However, he believed that Indian condition, persuasion or conversion was clearly the better way to coercion or confiscation, which creates ill will animosity, wasteful war, instead of increasing wealth by common effort to be shared by agreement in fair proportions. He frequently asserted that economic equality is the master key to non-violent independence. The contrast between the palaces of New Delhi and miserable hovels of the poor, labouring class can not last one day in a free India in which the poor will enjoy the same power as the richest in the land. A violent and bloody revolution is a certainty one day unless there is a voluntary abdication of riches and the power that riches give and sharing them for the common good. Therefore, he wrote, "I adhere to my doctrine of trusteeship in spite of the ridicule that has been poured upon it. It is true that it is difficult to reach. So is non-violence difficult to attain. But we made up our minds in 1920 to negotiate that steep ascent. (H.M. Vyas, 1961, p. 18)

Gandhiji was against the indiscriminate industrialisation in under developed countries. It causes concentration of wealth in the hands of a few, or the creation of industrialised urban areas making for lop-sided development and exploitation. Gandhiji advocated that with growing industrialisation the same exploitative relationship between Britain and India would come to exist between India's cities and her country-side. (Mark Shepherd, 1980) Mahatma Gandhi was never against industrialisation rather he was against the 'craze' for large scale industrialisation with the help of indiscriminate technological modernisation which may make the reduction of poverty more difficult.

Gandhi was not a professional economist. He developed his economic ideas keeping in view the economic situation of Indian economy. His economic theory provides a new and realistic approach to contemporary problems of poverty, hunger and degradation. Beginning with the position that exploitation is at the root of all violence, Gandhi builds his economic ideas in such a manner that avoids exploitation of man by man. His panacea is to do away with concentration of economic power by proposing economic decentralisation at various levels of the power hierarchy of the India's society. Gandhiji very often asserted that "if India is to evolve along non-violent lines, it will have to decentralize many things." (J.N. Lal, 1970, p. 146) Khadi and village industries were one of the important economic ideas of Gandhiji. He always laid greater stress on khadi and village industries and frequently asserted that these industries had capacity to correct the regional imbalances by initiating industrial activities on dispersed basis in the most neglected, backward and inaccessible areas, where perhaps large scale sector is unable to penetrate. In short, such rural industry could provide employment, increase incomes, slow down migration to cities and increase the supply of goods and services to the farmers at lower cost and generally stimulate rural and regional development. Gandhiji had great honour for Khadi. As Gandhiji said, "Khadi is the sun of the village solar system. The planets are the various industries which can support Khadi in return for the heat and the substance they derive from it." (*Journal of Gandhian Studies,* 1980) He was happy that the 'charkha' was a simple machine which would bring solace to the poverty stricken people. He felt that without the spinning wheel there was no Swaraj. "My sole claim for khadi" he had written "is that it offers an immediate practicable and permanent solution to the twin problems of enforced illness and chronic starvation." (*Journal of Gandhian Studies,* 1980)

Gandhi in his theory of technical progress has said that man should not be subservient to technology, rather technology should remain controlled in the service of man, to reduce him drudgery and to help solve his material problems. He did not treat technology as neutral nor as an exogenous element. He was definitely opposed to technological determinism. As he says, "what I object to the craze for machinery not machinery as such. The craze is for what they call labour saving machinery. Men go on "saving labour" till thousands are without work and thrown on the open street to die of Starvation." (*Young India*, November 13, 1924) He further pointed out that "My machinery must be of the most elementary type which I can put in the homes of the millions."

V. GANDHI MORE RELEVANT TODAY

Critics used to say, Mahatma Gandhi does not belong to the twenty-first Century, meaning thereby that with old fashioned ideas, he belonged to the twentieth century. But there are many people who say that Gandhi is becoming more and more relevant, not only for India, but for the whole world. Nirmala Deshpande, President of *Harijan* Sabha Samiti and follower of Gandhism says, "with present phase of globalisation, which can not be stopped, India needs to look into the evil effects of globalisation. We can not allow our fellow citizens to starve, to lose their employment, and to become destitute. It is Gandhi's Charkha, that can save us from this predicament." (Nirmala Deshpande, 2002) Prof. K.D. Gangrade says, "Gandhi is believed to have greater relevance in the present world of modern science and technology which has produced geographical neighbourhood but the distance between man and man has increased." (K.D. Gangrade, 2002) Pollution is one of the biggest problems that we are facing today. Air is polluted, water is polluted, land is polluted. Why? because the mind of man is polluted. Gandhiji was aware that with all the advancement of science and technology, attention needs to be given to the mind of man also, which is the domain of spirituality.

A search for eco-friendly, pollution-free technology, takes one to charkha and village industries Gramodyoga. Charkha is symbol of eco-friendly and pollution-free technology. It also provides employment to millions and millions of people, with negligible investment.

Modern world seems to be much more attracted by

violent technology while non-violent and soft technology repels the modern world. But of late even in the west there is a trend towards intermediate technology. It is now realised everywhere that labour saving, capital intensive, highly sophisticated technology transfer of mass production has no relevance to the Less Developed Countries (LDCs) where there is plenty of labour, little capital, lack of technical sophistication and elaborate infrastructure.

The relevance of Gandhian economic ideas can be expressed by a story of the drowning boy and the philosopher or a leader. When the philosopher was lecturing him, the boy cried: "take me out of the water first." Similarly, lectures enough, meetings enough, papers and books enough; where is the man who will lend us a hand to drag us out? where is the man who really loves us? where is the man who has sympathy for us? Ah! That man is wanted and that is Gandhi, the greatest human being of the twentieth century. He is no more on this earth but his thoughts are relevant, and will remain relevant and only the honest implementation of his programmes can drag the drowning world out of the sea of globalisation. Sriman Narayan, has gone up to the extent to say with conviction that "instead of being medieval and out-of-date, Bapu's ideas are even ahead of times and economic and political compulsions would inevitably force us to revert to them for resolving some of the paradoxes that intrigue us today. (Sriman Narayan, 1977) Gandhian philosophy is so relevant that American universities have inserted his philosophy in the course of studies. Gandhi had never visited America.

VI. CONCLUSION

The planned economic development of six decades and adoption of western model of development could not get rid of poverty, unemployment, and destitution, thus, it is clear that present model of development is not suitable to Indian economy. To conclude, we can assert that Gandhian ideas of economic development are not the outmoded concepts but are essentially rational and scientific concepts and in tune with modern economic themes regarding economic development of the developing countries like India. So our planners should make a rethinking on the process of economic development. Therefore, we can conclude that Gandhian economic thought may be described as pragmatic humanistic economy because it is based on realistic approach of life with emphasis on human value and human dignity. If we adhere to the ideals of Mahatma Gandhi, we may be sure that the country will survive for many more centuries and its philosophy will make a healing of nations and bringing of people together. Lastly, may the life of and teachings of Bapu be a bacon of hope and courage to all of us.

References

Government of India, Planning Commission, First Five Year Plans, p. 7.

Power, Paul F., Gandhi on World Affairs, Public Affairs Press, 419, New Jersey Avenue, S.E. Washington 3, D.C., 1960, p. 1.

Murthy, Narayana N.R., 'The Path: Long Travelled and the Journey Adhead', *Yojna*, Special Issue, Vol. 51, August 2007, p. 103.

Rajvanshi, Anil, K., 'India Shining Needs Sustainable Rural Development, Project Monitor, May 15-31, 2004, Issue on India Vision 2020.

Gandhi, M.K., *Harijan*, 23 March, 1947, p. 79.

Gandhi, M.K., *Young India*, 19 March, 1931, p. 38.

Power, Paul F., Gandhi on World Affairs, p. 43.

Gandhi, M.K., 'Village Swaraj' (Compiled by H.M. Vyas), Navajivan Publishing House, Ahmedabad, 1962, p. XVI.

Gandhi, M.K., 'Constructive Programme' (Compiled by H.M. Vyas), 1961, p. 18.

Shephared, Mark, "Mahatma Gandhi: The Legacy", *Gandhi Marg*, April 1980, p. 34.

Quoted in J.N. Lal, "Gandhian Democracy and Its Relevance", in the Relevance of Gandhi to our Times, New Delhi, 1970, p. 146.

Journal of Gandhian Studies, 1980, Vol. 7, p. 192.

Young India, November 13, 1924, pp. 85-86.

Deshpande, Nirmala, 'Gandhi More Relevant Today', Vol. 46, *Yojna*, October 2002, p. 11.

Gangrade, K.D., 'Gandhi's Eternal Relevance', *Yojna*, Vol. 46, October 2002, p. 7.

Narayan, Sriman, "Relevance of Gandhian Economics", *Journal of Gandhian Studies*, Allahabad, Vol. 17, October 1977, p. 25.

33

Gandhian Economic Philosophy: Its Resilience and Survival in the 21st Century

UGRA MOHAN JHA AND AMRENDRA KUMAR SINGH

The Gandhian view of development is based on a philosophy fundamentally different from the ideas and principles animating the western model of development. Gandhian model is indigenous. It is a product of Indian soil. It hears the imprint of local conditions and needs. The market model of development has emanated from Adam Smith and Ricardo. The welfare model of development has sprung from J.M. Keynes. The socialist model of development has come from Europe—from St. Simon, Robert Owen, Proudhou and Karl Marx. The socialist model is not homogeneous model. It has a variety of colour and complexion but all of them agree in one point that they are European in origin. It was left to the miraculous and spectacular of greyly of Mahatma Gandhi to evolve a theory of development suited to particular conditions and circumstances of India. The European views are grounded essentially upon industrialisation. Industrialisation is backdrop to all the European theories.

R.C. Vermani has to say this thing on this point, "The Gandhian view of development is radically different from the western model of development. It was based upon his metaphysical idealism with emphasis on the supremacy of ethical values and a moral approach to the problem of development. It was a plan of political, social and moral reconstruction and a critique of the western model of development-based essentially."[1]

The proponents of western model of development approach the problem from an economist's point of view. For them the paramount consideration was economics. They felt that economic factors constituted the core of development. In the opinion of Gandhiji development based on economics and economics alone was no real development. Gandhiji adhered steadfastly to the view that real development was a moral development. Development takes place when a person pursues truth. This pursuit of truth passes through the highways of love and non-violence. Truth left to itself is sterile. When it is suffused with love and accompanied by non-violence it performs miracle.[2]

Before embarking upon the detailed and deep exposition of his views it is essential that we should know the man. In India he is known as Mahatma—a high souled person or a lofty soulest man. Albert Einstein has this to say about Mahatma Gandhi, "Generation to come, will scarce belief that such a man as this, ever in flesh and blood walked upon this earth." I.G. Patel calls him "articulate and spectacular. He was the most remarkable man to come out of India in many generations—who was more than half saint and (it is empting to say—'defying logic as Gandhi did so often) more than half politician'. No world figure was more familiar than Gandhiji in the last years of his life—clad in loin cloth and half humorously surveying the scene or the people around him. All his life he has been a vegetarian and he never touched wine. He was a total abstainer from alcohol. He commanded respect as politicians who was more than a politician. He was more than an artist in expediency. He was a man devoted to his own people. At the same time he was also devoted to all of mankind. All his actions and principles flowed from these principles of his life. He admired Thoreau and forged the art of civil disobedience from him. Thoreau was an American naturalist. Like him he was a tender human being but when it came to the dignity of the individual and honour of the country nobody was more resolute and more determined. His classic and characteristic essay—civil disobedience—inspired Mahatma Gandhi in his campaign of resistance against English rule in India. He was the real spokesman of the Indian masses.

Primarily and basically he was an idealist. Views vary whether material development means real development but Gandhiji tenaciously held that if there was a conflict between material development and moral development, the former has to be eschewed and abandoned and moral development should he embraced. He was deadly apposed to the view that material development leads to moral development. If there is material development it does not mean that there is moral development but if there is material degeneration below a certain level it can produce moral degeneration. He writes "No one has even suggested that grinding pauperism can lead to anything else than moral degeneration.[3] If there is utter destitution or deprivation it bound to generate moral decay. At the same time Gandhiji held the view that material upliftment could not be abolished altogether. There must be a minimum material advance. Beyond this, the material development comes in conflict with moral development. In short be supported material development if it was morally justifies and if it eliminated penury. A person must have a certain minimum assortment of material goods and services. Need was the basis of Gandhiji's thinking. If a person wants more than his "need" it becomes greed and greed is antithetical to human values. Honesty is the first casualty in this condition. High thinking is given a go-bye. If a person wants more and more material goods, his wants can be satisfied only by increasing production. If production is increased it is bound to lead to exploitation and the state control. There will be centralisation of the economy and Gandhiji was against centralisation of power and authority. He believed in devolution of power. He succinctly points out that "the greater the position of riches the greater was the moral turpitude."[4]

Gandhiji had a clear cut criterion to judge an economic policy. If any economic policy was detrimental to the moral health of an individual or to the moral health of the nation that economic policy was immoral. If it was immoral, it was sinful also. Gandhiji never assessed development in terms of money. He never considered development in the light of any monetary unit.

At the same time Gandhiji stubbornly clung to the view that if a society is to be established in an orderly manner, such a society must assure to the people a minimum standard of living. If this minimum standard of living is taken away from the people there cannot be concord or harmony or tranquility in it. In a well ordered society livelihood is secured to all and it is a basic thing in the world. Livelihood is a generic word and it comprehends victuals, raiment, housing and education. The general idea about development is that if a society has increasing numbers of millionaires it is said to be developing more and more. Gandhiji differed from such a view. According to him development does not mean augmentation of the number of the opulent and the effluent but negation of starvation. In accordance with the theory and understanding of Gandhiji the concept of development includes happiness as its necessary component. In fact development is synonymous with happiness in his eyes. If development leads to happiness it is development par excellence and if it does not lead to happiness it is worthless and futile. Gandhiji defines happiness in a particular manner. Physical comforts and amenities are necessary parts of happiness but they do not constitute the nodel point of happiness. Gandhiji says, "civilisation in the real sense of the term consists not in the multiplication of wants but in the deliberate and voluntary reduction of wants. This alone promotes real happiness and contentment and increases capacity for service. The mind is a restless bird. The more it gets the more it wants and still remains unsatisfied."[5]

Thus we find that the views of Mahatma Gandhi are diametrically opposed to the views held by modern economists and the inclination harbored by the teeming millions of the country. The scratch for material well-being is good and desirable and even necessary but if it disregards moral conditions and standpoint it has to be rejected because it is in contradiction to the divine order and arrangement. Thus the problem of material development *versus* moral development can be reduced to the problem of defining happiness and formulating a standard as creating an ideal for measuring the attainment of happiness. The general tenor of Gandhiji's thought is that the root of happiness lies not in materialism but in spiritualism. In the universe of real development the pursuit of truth counts and if there is pursuit of truth it leads to the sanctuary of god. If a person descries divinity and places himself in its lap the result is the real happiness. The reduction of wants should not be made under compulsion or under duress or under the tyranny of circumstances. If a person reduces wants because he has no other alternative to follow or if he is compelled to cut down his wants it will not lead to happiness. The reduction of wants must be voluntary and it must be deliberate. Only then it shall have a value in the Gandhian moral universe. A person must adopt and embrace what Gandhiji calls voluntary poverty. It is this voluntary poverty that gives contentment to a person and promotes real happiness. If the goal of a person is not the pursuit of truth but the pursuit of wealth, be swerves from the path of rectitude and goes stray from the ideal of real development. Gandhiji believes that not only the religious books and scriptures but the entire history of human civilisation bears testimony to the fact that the real or ideal form of development is moral and not material and that the standard of morality is nothing but the standard of truth.

The essence of the views of Mahatma Gandhi boils down to two propositions. First, if a society is poor materially then development, for such a society, means that material conditions should be improved. Development means a progress towards an ideal by which each and every member of the society is given goods material in nature. If society lacks material goods, steps must be taken to make material goods available to all. Secondly, if there is a society in which there is superfluous wealth then development in this case means hoping off the superfluity. Persons in such a society are not faced with the problem of increasing production because production is not needed what is needed is cutting down production and renouncing the already existing superfluous goods. Development here means destroying superfluous goods and stopping their production. If this theory is applied on a global scale the result will be that the goods found in abundance in European Union and the USA should be either destroyed or transferred to the poor developing countries whose people are suffering from malnutrition, undernourishment and scarcity of goods vitally needed by the people. Thus we find that the theory of development of Gandhiji is the theory of social equilibrium. If a society has more than its store of goods should be reduced and if a society has scarcity, its stores of goods should be increased by further production. The social equilibrium can be achieved by resort to individual and social reformation.

It can also be achieved through various physical mental and social rules. It can also be secured by improvement in the material progress through cottage industries, spinning wheels and village upliftment. "Development is a complex web of moral, material and social relationship. The moral basis of this development lies in truth, Ahimsa, Brahmacharya, non-possession, non-stealing, fearlessness, swadeshi, bread-labour, toleration of face, vegetarianism, nature cure and simplicity in life. At social level it means equality of human beings, removal of untouchability, prohibition, education, communal harmony, equilibrium between city and village. The material basis of development lies in increasing wealth through village and cottage industry, decentralisation of economic production and redistribution of wealth between labour and capital through trusteeship."[6]

GANDHIAN ECONOMIC THOUGHT

There is something undying and imperishable in Gandhian concept. Simplicity, Non-violence and Bread labour are three elements which constitute the edifice of Gandhian concept

Simplicity

The first fundamental principle of Gandhiji's economic

thought was his emphasis on 'simple living and high thinking'. A practical idealist as he was Gandhi diagnosed the real and the deep malady of modern civilisation and by pointing out the remedy for that disease, he was not behind but ahead of his times. He was of the opinion that western civilisation attached more importance to material welfare and maintains that the goal of progressive individual or nation should be the ever increasing accumulation of physical comforts and material luxuries. As Gandhiji pointed out: "the true test of modern civilisation lies in the fact that people living in it, make bodily welfare the object of life." Gandhiji maintained that more economic affluence would not be able to secure a balanced life for the Indian masses. While every attempt should be made to secure a minimum standard of living for all citizens, India should not imitate the highly developed mechanistic civilisation of the west. He was of the opinion that "maximisation of satisfaction can be brought about only my limitation of wants." On another occasion Gandhiji pointed out: "we notice that the mind is a restless bird; the more it gets, the more it wants and still remains unsatisfied. A man is not necessarily happy because he is rich or unhappy because he is poor. The rich are often seen to be unhappy, the poor to be happy. Observing all this our ancestors dissuaded us from luxuries and pleasures"[7]. Apart from the moral and psychological values of simplicity in life, Gandhiji also discouraged reckless pursuit of wealth by means of rapid industrialisation because without maximum self-dependence through manual labour, human life would get intricately involved in the chain of economic serfdom. To him a progressive economic system should lead to greater simplicity through fuller life.

Non-Violence

The creation of a non-violent democratic society was another foundation on which Gandhian economic order is built. Under Gandhiji's economic order, there would be no room for exploitation of man by man in any form. Gandhiji held that violence, in any form, would not lead to any kind of lasting peace and economic reconstruction. True democracy and real growth of individual personality would be possible only in a non-violent society. Violence breeds greater violence and whatever is gained by force needs to be preserved by using greater force. Gandhiji did not subscribe to the Machiavelli and philosophy that end justifies means. In order to conserve the purity of the end, Gandhiji advocated right means for the attainment of the end. A capitalistic order is based on the exploitation of human labour which, according to Gandhiji, is violence.[8] "Machine is the handmaid of capitalism; it ousts human labour and concentrates wealth and power in the hands of a few. Wealth is thus accumulated by violence." To eschew violence and exploitation of human labour, Gandhiji advocated rural based decentralised economic order. Speaking about the suitability of a rural-based economic order for Indian, Gandhiji said, "I suggest that if India is to evolve along non-violent lines, it will have to decentralize many things. Centralisation cannot be sustained and defended without adequate force. Simple homes from which there is nothing to take away require no policing; the palaces of the rich have strong guards to protect them against dacoits. Rurally organized India will run less risk of foreign invasion than urbanized India will equip with Military, Naval and Air force." Therefore, under the non-violent economic order of Gandhiji, there would be no scope for exploitation because production would be for immediate use and not for distant profitable market.

Bread Labour

The third fundamental principle on which the Gandhian economic order is based in his insistence on manual labour. To Gandhiji, physical labour is the law of nature and its continued negligence was mainly responsible for the economic malady of India. Gandhiji said, "we are destroying the matchless living machines, i.e. our own bodies, by living them to rest and trying to substitute life-less machinery for them."[9] Gandhiji was of the opinion that poverty and unemployment, found in rural India, were to certain extent of our own making, our own neglect of manual labour. There was enough employment in rural India provided all would work with their hands and feet honestly. Gandhiji believed in the dignity and sanctity of labour and for him, "No labour is too mean for one who wants to earn an honest penny. The only thing is the readiness to use the hands and feet that God has given us."[10] The economics of bread – labour was the living way of life. Bread-labour means that every man had to labour with his body for his food and clothing. Gandhiji felt that much of the exploitation and conflict in society was due to the fact that some powerful individuals avoid physical labour and throw their burden on others. If society was to be non-violent, all must be involved in physical labour for earning their bread. Consequently Gandhiji advocated 'production by masses' as against 'mass production'. Gandhiji says, "under my system, it is labour which the current coin, not metal. Any person who can use his labour as that coin is wealthy. He converts it into cloth, he converts his labour into grain. If he wants paraffin oil, which he cannot himself produce, he uses his surplus grain for getting the oil. It is exchange of labour on free, fair and equal terms, hence it is no robbery. You may object that it is a reversion to the primitive system of barter. But it is not at all international trade based on the barter system."[11]

Charkha Technique

To Gandhiji India's Independence meant not merely political freedom but a general liberation from the social and economic injustices suffered by the Indian rural folk. Gandhi's concept of Swaraj for India coincided with his concept of emancipation of Indian rural masses from the clutches of poverty, unemployment, exploitation and illiteracy. Gandhiji firmly believed and therefore often repeated that "India lives not in a handful of her big cities but in her seven lakh villages. So long with his efforts for securing political freedom from the British yoke, Gandhiji evolved his constructive programme for village Swaraj." After his return from South Africa in the year 1919, Gandhiji undertook a tour of India which was an eye-opener for him as he came face to face with the social and economic conditions under which the Indian rural masses existed. The dire poverty and the enforced idleness of the Indian rural folk pained him. The hungry skeleton like figures of Indian rural masses, clad in dirty clothes, living in unsanitary dwellings constructed in 'a dunghill', idling away their time in enforced unemployment for over six months in a year, victims of age old social evils and exploitation from the urban rich, not knowing what to do for their sustenance, began to haunt the mind of Gandhiji. He gave vent to his sad feelings at the plight of Indian villagers in these words, "I have indeed wept to see the stark poverty and unemployment in our country."[12]

Gandhiji's deep anguish at the appalling poverty found among the Indian rural folk of his times is also revealed through these words: "The human bird under the Indian sky gets up weaker than when he pretended to retire. For millions it is an eternal vigil or an eternal trance. I have found it impossible to soothe suffering patients with a song from Kabir the hungry millions ask for one poem—invigorating food. They cannot be given it. They must earn it. And they can earn only by the sweat of their brow."[13] Gandhiji could find out for himself that India's rural poverty was due to the depletion of Indian villages and due to a policy of extreme centralisation of production which was controlled by a few urban rich. He was also convinced that India was one of the few nations in the world which had retained some of her ancient institutions inspite of onslaughts from western civilisation. He felt that some adaptations that suited Indian culture were necessary if the old patterns were to be saved under the impact of the western policy of mechanisation of production. Gandhiji, therefore, advocated the revival of Indian village industries, which became extinct under the British rule, for the economic reconstruction of Indian rural society.

Being a practical economist, Gandhiji had the perspicacity to see that there is an inexhaustible supply of natural resources spread all over the length and breadth of India at the doorsteps of the people. All that was needed for the economic reconstruction of Indian rural society was to mobilize the labour, skill and unutilised time of the rural families by presenting to them a simple technique which could be put to practical use without any elaborate training. It was Gandhiji's claim that under the given conditions there was no quicker way of providing the Indian rural masses, their basic requirements of food and clothing except by enabling them to utilize their idle time and labour through a system of village industries aided by simple tools, to supplement their income. The tool to be offered to the rural families should be simple, inexpensive and within the economic capacity of them to own, understand and operate independently silting in their homes.

It was with this view that Gandhiji offered his Charkha —the spinning wheel—as a symbol of decentralisation and emancipator of Indian rural masses. He believed that the Charkha technique was the only means of guaranteeing full employment to a large number of rural families. Introducing his Charkha technique for the economic reconstruction, Gandhiji said: "The message of the spinning wheel is much wider than its circumference. Its message is one of simplicity, service of mankind, living so as not to hurt others creating an indissoluable bond between the rich and the poor, capital and labour, the prince and the peasant. The larger message is naturally for all. It is not an attempt to spiritualize the machinery because that seems to me an impossible task—but to introduce, if it is at all possible, a human or humane spirit among the men behind the machinery. The movement of the spinning wheel is an organized attempt to displace machinery from the state of exclusiveness and exploitation and to place it in its proper state."[14]

Gandhiji's economic thought, Swadeshi was a key concept. It must now merely an economic doctrine but also carried ideological implications. In his Swadeshi movement, Gandhiji saw at once not only the economic salvation of rural folk but also an answer to the psychological and political problems of the nationalist movements. He defined the concept of Swadeshi in these words, "Swadeshi is that spirit in us which restricts us to the use and service of our immediate surroundings to the exclusion of the more remote. Thus as for religion in order to satisfy the requirements of the definition, I must restrict myself to my ancestral religion. That is the use of my immediate religious surroundings. If I find it defective, I should serve it by purging it of its defects. In the domain of politics I should make use of the indigenous institutions and serve them by curing them of their proved defects. In that of economics, I should use only things that are produced by my immediate neighbours and serve those industries by making them efficient and complete where they might be found wanting."[15] For Gandhiji Swaraj meant an undeterred economic life for the Indian masses which his Charkha Offered to them. Gandhiji, therefore, linked his Charkha technique of rural reconstruction with his Swadeshi concept.

RELEVANCE OF GANDHIAN CONCEPT IN THE 21st CENTURY

We have the expression that King is dead and long live the King. It means that the King is physically dead and therefore non-existent but Kingship continues to exist. Kingship is an institution which is not dependent on the physical existence of a particular person who happens to be the King. We have another expression that Caesar is dead but Caesarism grows larger than life and acquires more and more strength as days roll on. When Julius Caesar was assassinated it was thought that Caesar's method of acting had come to a dead end but the march of events after his death demonstrated that Caesar has caught the imagination of the people and has become more and more influential and potent in the lives of the Roman people.

Now can we say that after the assassination of Mahatma Gandhi his philosophy and approach became more and more pervasive and acceptable? In fact Gandhiji was physically eliminated by a mad and desperate and misguided young man but that should not have been end of Mahatma Gandhi's philosophy. Physical death does not matter for a great man who has made history in his life. What is important is his ideology. Does his ideology live after his death? This is a very crucial question. It is distressing and tragic to learn that Gandhian ideology was systematically eroded and undermined after his death. His ideology was denigrated and defiled by so-called followers. Mahatma Gandhi has been replaced by Dr. Manmohan Singh, a bureaucrat turned politician. Hence Gandhiji is dead and the Gandhian philosophy has also been buried in oblivion.

Mahatma Gandhi lives on not in and through his

ideology but he has been declared a national asset under the National Emblem Act. Under this Act the name or the pictorial representation of the Mahatma or the word Gandhi may only be used on calendars and that too only if the calendars are not for advertising purposes. But outside India Gandhi has become a brand and is being used recklessly for commercial purposes. Gandhi restaurants are found everywhere. They are found from Amsterdam to New York. In some of the cases a Gandhi restaurant is complete with a bar and elaborate non-vegetarian. A gymnasium in New York used Gandhi in an advertisement which said that while Gandhi was undoubtedly great, he could have done better with triceps. Even in India the marketers have drawn on his legacy. A salt named Dandi Namak has been launched. Apart from theses examples we find that Gandhiji has become a monuments in India and we can see sparrows sitting on the monuments. At one time Gandhiji himself has said: "Everyone is eager to garland my photos but no one wants to follow my advice." This has proved to be prophetically true. He has become an icon and the trouble with the icon is that once dead, their relevance quickly decays and their image becomes fixed in popular memory. Gandhiji lives in offices of India and in the stone images. The image of Gandhiji is buried inside history books in chapters nobody in the country and the Government cares to read or rewrite.

Yet the core idea of Gandhiji is not to be found in physical things and manifestation. His ideas have guided the nations of movements like the Narmada Bachao Andolan or of men like Martin Luther King Jr., Nelson Mandela and Steven Biko. The core idea of Gandhiji lies on his principles of ethical action, self-reliance and ability to draw strength from within oneself. In fact it is not the man, but the ideas of Gandhi which are extremely relevant. Let us look at special interest group. They may not bear the name of Gandhi but they draw inspiration from the ideas of Gandhi. We can say that in many parts of the world where substantial numbers are beginning to turn against globalisation and greed, Gandhi is once again becoming a relevant figure. The interest in him is not merely from a sociological, philosophical or intellectual perspective. His ideas are liberally drawn upon by management thinkers in the west. His ideas are used in subjects as diverse as conflict management, negotiation skills, management ethics and corporate leadership programmes.

Stephen Covey devotes an entire chapter to learning from Gandhiji. The management thinker, Tom Peters, the author of In Search of Excellence points out—"I would like to believe that the average Indian and American should have, both, a little bit of Gandhi and a little bit of Washington in them. They should not be simply willing to obey the rules. Gandhiji's ability to find unique and seemingly impractical solutions to daunting problems is being examined and appreciated extensively. Gandhiji was the inventor of outrageous experiments. Why can't be apply him to conflict negotiation situation and see how he would have tackled globalisation or the Kashmir problem? What we need to do is to reinvent Gandhiji and apply him in modern context."

The central driving idea of Gandhian approach is to derive moral strength from truth. Gandhiji extracted from truth, not just righteousness but also the strength to change the world. The adherents of Gandhian approach, therefore, must know how to change the depressed rural economy into a flourishing one. Gandhiji gave Indians belief in themselves. He stood for finding joy in what one had. He advocated non-violent actions in the face of injustice. The marvellous thing in him was to convert his idea into inspiration and to communicate to the stratified masses of India. He was the master of the articulate symbol. "Be it his attire that collapsed all he stood for into a single vivid image (The Naked Fakir), the charkha which symbolised self-reliance at both national and individual levels, or the use of salt, an emotionally resonant symbol, as the pivot of proletarian protest, Gandhi's life is a crash course in semiotics."[16]

Gandhi is too tolerant of the rich for leftists, too proletarian for rightists, too tolerant for the religious right and too religious for secularists. Gandhi's appeal at home was most powerful when India was feeling downtrodden and victimized and today when India is more often portrayed in the international media as the aggressor than the victim, the arrogant winner rather than the humble loser, the biggest and most successful of the emerging nations rather than a submerging economy, the figure of Gandhi seems rather out of place. It is rather hard to square the image of Bapu crouched by his charkha with that of Azim Hasham Premiji grinning next to Bill Gates.

The surest ground of resurgence and revitalisation of Gandhian approach is the urgent necessity to deal with ecological degradation and environmental dangers. Population explosion, climate change, global warming, vanishing forests, loss of bio-diversity, falling water resources and necessity of sustainable development are the key areas which confront and control this troubled and passionate planet—the earth. It is a mater of serious consideration whether earth's natural systems will be able to sustain such an alarming and menacing growth at all in times to come. How many people can the earth support at the level and rate of consumption of natural resources? The world population was 2.5 billion in 1950 and now it is 6.1 billion. According to an estimate the world population will zoom to 9.4 billion. The question is whether the earth and its natural resources will be able to cater to the needs of the mushrooming population. For too long global economics has remained rooted in environmental exploitation. The ruthless exploitation of nature and its resources has resulted not only in pollution of the atmosphere but also in the poisoning of healthy soil through the dumping of hazardous and toxic waste often in the Third World. Furthermore, seas, much more than rivers or lakes are now having eutrophication (over fertilisation due to excessive inflow of phosphates and nitrates). Air, soil, water and even buildings are facing acidification due to unchecked and highly complex chemical reactions involving man-made substances, viz. sulphar dioxide, nitrus oxide and ammonia. These environmental aspects and impacts have caused damage that is not only globally widespread but also irreversible to a great extent.

When Johannesburg World Summit 2002 took place, *The Times of India* in an editorial on September 6, 2002 remembered Gandhiji and wrote—

> "Hammering out international protocols on environment is the protracted and polemical process.

> On what can individual citizens do? In practical terms very little. In moral terms, perhaps a lot. Mahatma Gandhi used the boycott of Videshi (foreign) goods against the pollutant of colorisation. Sunder Lal Bahuguna and his followers saved trees with Chipko movement. NRIs in the United States forced the Golden Agch to turn contrite when they boycotted beef-tallow polluted French pries. When international celebrities espoused animal rights, animal products became both unfashionable and illegal. Green consciousness has to sprout from within first: from the individual, to the community, to the national and international levels."

Here is the victory of Gandhian approach. Gandhiji is remembered when the world economy has reached cul-de-sac and the problems become insoluble.

The current state of world economy also demands Gandhian approach. The world is living now under the undisputed domain of a particular system of production. What is the result? The incomes of 358 persons in the world are equal to the incomes of 270 crores of the people. During 2nd World War 25,200 persons were killed daily from 1939 when the war began in 1945 when it ended after killing lakhs of innocent persons of Hiroshima and Nagasaki. On one hand, crores of people die of starvation per year and on the other hand 36 million sheep were killed in Australia. Mountains of butter and cheese were thrown in the sea off Holland and Denmark. Lakhs of cows were slaughtered in the USA and 20 lakh chickens were killed in Malaysia. And all these took place only to prevent the world price of these commodities from sliding to the Bottom of the trough of the world economy.

Wars are recurrent features under this system. In 1st world war 21,000 dollars was spent to kill one person. In 2nd World War 2 lakh dollars was spent to kill one person. In Korean War 5,70,000 dollars was spent to kill one person. But 200 crores of people cannot buy medicines to save their lives. And what is most horrible is that 250 crores of people have no access to pure drinking water as a result of which people die of avoidable water-borne diseases. All these facts underline and spotlight the necessity of adopting Gandhian approach. If this approach is not adopted the alternative is the end of humanity and therefore the end of modern civilisation.

The state of Indian economy also demands that Gandhian approach be adopted. The Indian economy has been tied to global chariot. Hence India has been made dependent on the twists and turns of world economy. Our country has been now under the control of international economic forces and therefore the country's self-reliance has been dangerously undermined. Indian economy will sink if the global economy sinks but when the global economy swims it is not necessary that the Indian economy may sail out of backwaters. In 1999 the price of coffee was Rs. 58 per Kg. but in 2000 it has crashed to Rs. 30 per Kg. The price of black pepper was Rs. 2600 per Kg. but in 2000 it dipped to Rs. 1300 per Kg. Coconut was selling at Rs. 10 per piece in 1999 but its price nosedived to Rs. 2 per piece. Our country' economy has been made open for exports and imports. The result is that small and marginal farmers are sure to be eliminated. It is this section of agricultural population that is the core of the Indian economy and it is this section again which is the special focus of Gandhian approach. America sells wheat at a price 46 per cent less than the cost price and the European Union sells at a price 34 per cent less than the cost price. If these agricultural goods enter Indian markets, Indian farmers will be wiped out of existence. Hence if the people of this country are to be saved they must be made to adopt and follow the Gandhian principle.

It is true that Gandhian approach is to be applied on the global scale, some modifications have to be introduced and affected. Gandhiji believed in the village unit. In this case then entire globe should be regarded as a village and the entire world production should be carried on in keeping with Gandhian ideas and ideals. The USA is regarded as the world's richest and most prosperous country but it remains the truth that poverty is America's most persistent and serious problem. It is more prevalent in the USA than in most of the rest of civilised world. In 1990 33.6 million Americans were poor and they constituted 14 per cent of the population.

This level of poverty remains inspite of the fact that the government made stupendous effort to reduce it. Gandhian approach is needed even for the American people. The farmers in America are not happy. They are sunk in the debt to the tune of more than 200 billion dollars. Hence considered from all points of views it seems that Gandhian approach is the only way—out of poverty, inequality and threat to humanity itself.

Notes and References

1. R.C. Vermani, An Introduction to Political Theory, p. 463.
2. Unnithan, J.K.N., Gandhi and Social Change, Rawat Publication 1979.
3. Tendulkar, D.G., Life of M.K. Gandhi, Vol. I, p. 236.
4. Tendulkar, D.G., Life of M.K. Gandhi, Vol. I, p. 237
5. Tendulkar, D.G., Life of M.K. Gandhi, Vol. I, p. 238
6. Tendulkar, D.G., Life of M.K. Gandhi, Vol. I, p. 280.
7. Unnithan, J.K.N., Gandhi and Social Change, p. 32.
8. M.K. Gandhi, *Hind Swaraj*, Ahmedabad, Navjivan Publishing House, 1946, p. 87.
9. Shriman Narayan, Principles of Gandhian Planning, Allahabad, Kitab Mahal, 1960, p. 20.
10. *Harijan*, 30.12.1964.
11. *Young India*, 17.12.1927.
12. *Harijan*, 17.12.1936.
13. *Harijan*, 19.12.1936.
14. M.K. Gandhi, The Great Sentinel, Ahmedabad, Navjivan Publishing House, 1946.
15. *Young India*, 1937, p. 321.
16. *Economic Times*, 2 October 2002.

34

Relevance of Gandhian Rural Economic Philosophy in Twenty-first Century: India and its Challenges

S. Rengarajan and R. Raj Kumar

INTRODUCTION

'Simple Living and High Thinking' of Gandhi's principle now challenged with 'High Living and Simple Thinking' in the sphere of rural population in India. Rural India is in agrarian crisis which has its roots with the collapse of the rural economics, and unemployment leading to out-migration of the asset-less is grown. The minimum support price mechanism is not operative for most commodities. There is a tendency to make profit out of the poverty at every level of the livelihood security system. Sometimes it is terribly wrong in the country side.

The peasantry (farmers) in some parts of our country is resorting to extreme measures (suicides). The adversities are repeated due crop failures caused by unpredictable climatic variations, unbearable rising cost of cultivation and frustration in the minds of farmers due to increasing debt burden. Meeting the challenges of rural reconstruction becomes formidable and priority task in this situation. Small farmers holding less than two hectares of land accounting nearly 80 percent of holdings in India. As agriculture is the very basis of livelihood security especially in developing countries, it is important to focus on increasing its productivity. There have to be a job-led growth, instead of the jobless growth that we have currently, as famine by work lead to famine of income. *Food insecurity: a great threat to human secure.*

GANDHIAN RURAL ECONOMIC PHILOSOPHY

Gandhi was not a theorist, but a practical man, dealt with practical problems. He felt that the problems of poverty, disease, ignorance and inertia did not admit of being postponed to a distant date. The ideas of Gandhian rural economic philosophy are listed below. (Nanda, 1958)

(i) Revival of village economy as whole which acquired a new urgency.

(ii) Exploitation of the village in the interest of the town was a species of violence, and their economic and social resuscitation as a *sine qua non* for freedom from foreign rule.

(iii) Fostering village industries could create employment and pump purchasing power into the village.

(iv) Indian villagers could be educated out of inertia by bands of selfless worker infiltrating into the village.

(v) As the food habits of Indian masses were responsible for their undernourishment, the Indian scientists to pursue research into Indian diets in the contexts of Indian conditions.

(vi) In a country where the hands too many and the work too little machinery could only add to unemployment and poverty. Gandhi was not favoured mass production but favoured production by masses and at the same time welcomed simple tools and instruments.

(vii) Decentralisation of production in thousands of villages was closely linked with the decentralisation of political power and it was basic to ideal of a non-violent society.

(viii) The ideal Indian village was of a 'republic', independent of its neighbours for its vital wants yet interdependent in other ways.

REVIVAL OF RURAL ECONOMY

Gandhi's own activities and those of the Congress, the Indian National Congress in October 1935 authorised the formation of All India Village Industries Association, unaffected by and independent of the political activities of the Congress. This was for revival and encouragement of the village industries and the moral and physical advancement of the village. Ever since 1915 Gandhi entered public life, he had been pleading for a new deal for the village. To solve the problem of rural poverty, he began to think for the revival of the village economy as a whole. He appealed to the town-dwellers to find a substitution to the articles of daily consumption which were manufactured in India and abroad and insisted to find a substitute for it from the village-broom for brush, kikar tooth stick for tooth brush and gur for factory sugar.

Now in India the government has allowed MNCs in retail trade. As economy is advancing in the service and manufacturing sector that much the rural sector is not advancing. The rural people are migrating to urban areas in search of employment opportunities. The migrant residents of the cities immediately go for retail trading activities such as vegetables, fruits, etc. for their subsistence. The MNCs in the above retail trade will affect these poor people who depend on these for their subsistence. Gandhi's opinion on substitute for manufactured goods in India and abroad from the village only for giving employment opportunities for rural people. This was also a reason for the protest by some organisations against MNCs entering in retail trade in India.

VILLAGE EXPLOITATION

Gandhi assessed the Indian village population which accounted for 85 percent of the total population. Their economic and social resuscitation was a *sine qua non* for freedom from foreign rule. And also expressed for the benefit of the town the exploitation of the villages is a species of violence. The wide differences emerged in the economic standards and amenities between the town and the villages had to be bridged he asserted. The Special Economic Zone (SEZ) Act, 2005 in India is expected to give a big push to exports, employment and investment in SEZs. For expediting the process of industrialisation the promotion of SEZs is an attempt to deal with infrastructural deficiencies, procedure complexities and bureaucratic hassles. The competitive advantages of zones may be explained with the framework of the cluster approach. These zones offer a number of benefits such as, (i) tax incentives, (ii) provision of standard factories/ plots at low rents with extended lease period, (iii) provision of infrastructure and utilities, (iv) single window clearance, v)simplified procedures, and (vi) exemptions from various restrictions that characterize the investment climate in the domestic economy. (Aggarwal, 2006)

The company will simply relocate to SEZs to take advantage of the tax concessions being offered and little net activity will be generate. This policy would cause a revenue loss of Rs. 939,000 million over the next four year. If annual average of this four-year figure is drawn, it comes out to be Rs. 23,475 million, which is about 6.7 percent of the central government's total revenue receipt during 2005-06. The act will lead to a large scale land acquisition by developers, displacement of farmers, meagre compensation and no alternative livelihood to them. If SEZs is built on prime agricultural land, it will result in serious implications for food security. The minimum required procession area is 35 percent and the rest 65 percent is make use of by the promoters for the real estate development and speculation indiscriminately. As on now seven states account for 80.6 percent of approvals, the SEZ will aggravate regional disparities. The industrial backward states of Bihar, North-East and Jammu and

Kashmir do not have a single approval. The sectoral break of SEZs approval shows that the largest number of approvals (61 percent) has been in the IT sector. There was a farmers' resistance to the industry being set-up in Nandigram, a village in West Bengal. It evoked violence resulted in some deaths that clearly show the farmers' fear and apprehension. Since the act came into effect in February 2006 and the total number of formal approvals granted has reached 339, of which 126 have so for been notified.

Gandhi opposed the exploitation of the villages in the interest of the town which was species of violence. Now the government has announced that in the process of setting up of SEZs, acquisition of land should be carried out only by the private promoters and also not the fertile land acquired for SEZs. The government should ensure that land givers should be benefited by giving adequate share in emerging industries in the SEZs or employment opportunities. The state will first to satisfy the interest of the farmers who are going to lose their traditional source of income. Provision of job opportunities to avoid exploitation may also be preferable.

INCLUSIVE GROWTH

Providing universal coverage with the median wage, adjusted for inflation, lower now than in 1980, most middle class families cannot afford additional taxes. In contrast, the top tenth of one percent of earners today makes about four times as much as in 1980, while those higher up have enjoyed even large gains (Robert H. Frank, 2007). Historically unprecedented economic growth in India during the last decade of reform will continue to remain exclusive, leave poverty, and malnutrition unaffected and lead to growing social tensions unless unshaped by democratic political process. For inclusive growth it must be minimally 'trickled down' to the poor. If the gains of growth accrue largely to the rich, the government is able and willing to redistribute a fraction of them to the poor through an appropriate fiscal policy. But the recent evidence government continue to offer endless tax sops to the rich (SEZs being only the latest instance of it), and it is unwilling to increase allocation for such redistributive development programmes as National Rural Employment Guarantee Scheme. Their allocation remains stagnant while employment stagnated over one and half a decade since the reforms begun. The real output of the non-agricultural part of the economy, which was expected to provide new jobs, grew by a factor of four: the same number of workers produced four times as much output due to automation of production process. (Srivastava, 2007)

HEALTH CHALLENGES

Nutrition was another problem on which Gandhi wrote and spoke frequently. He realised that nutrition as a problem of the Indian masses with something of a stock that apart from their poverty. Their food habits were responsible for their undernourishment. The deficiency of vitamins was an inexcusable when green leaves were available for picking. He requested chemists and starve in order to give an ideal diet for their poor countrymen. The UN Millennium Development Goals aim at reduction of hunger and poverty by half by 2015. But today, hunger and deprivation affect about 260 million people in the country. India is home to 40 percent of the world's underweight children. Iron deficiency anaemia is estimated to affect 75 percent of children under age of five; 57 percent of the same age group suffers from vitamin A deficiency. Under-nutrition in women of reproductive age contributes significantly to child hunger. Consequently 30 percent of the babies weigh less than 2.5 kg at birth leading to multiple handicaps in later life, including in cognitive ability (Swaminathan, 2007). The underutilised crops, such as, millets, ragi, bajra, and jowar are rich in micronutrients and minerals and should be referred as 'nutritious cereals' and not as coarse cereals as is being done now. The imports of pulses and oil seeds serve as indicators of our failure to launch a green revolution in dryfarming areas, in spite of having the technologies and resources to do so. It is human tragedy of vast dimensions where millions of children, women and men are condemned to a life of malnutrition and poverty. If we were to achieve a second green revolution covering rainfed areas, the first important requisite is opportunity for assured and remunerative marketing for dryland farm products such as pulses, oilseeds, millets, vegetables, fruits, milk and meat (Swaminathan, 2006).

MECHANISATION AND DECENTRALISATION

In *Hind Swaraj*, while criticizing machinery, mills and industrial civilisation, Gandhi elaborated his ideas on machinery relating them to his fundamental doctrine of non-violence. Mechanisation tends to concentrate the production of wealth in a few hands. In a country where the hands are too many, and the work too little, machinery would lead to unemployment and poverty. Gandhi did not favour mass production because the free enterprise often made the rich richer and poor poorer, but favoured production by masses. Even Gandhi welcomed simple tools and instruments which lightened the burden of millions of cottages' without atrophying the limbs of man. He wanted decentralisation of production in thousands of villages closely linked with the decentralisation of political power which was basic to Gandhi's ideal of a non-violence society. Only in small communities, producing for local needs and free from glaring inequalities, could there be a democracy based on human rather than material relationships. Industrial Revolution led to exploitation of the many by a few. Exploitation is an essence of violence. Rural economy eschew exploitation altogether.

According to Edward Luce of London's *Financial Times,* the Tata Steel plant in Jamshedpur the India's largest private sector steel company employed 85,000 workers to produce one million tonnes of steel worth $800 million in 1991. But it churned out five million tonnes worth $4 billion, employed only 44,000 people. This shows that the output multiplied five times, whereas the employment got halved. Stephen Roch, the Chief Economist of Morgan Stanley, gave real picture of kirloskar plant, Pune where one worker mans 27 machines. The Indian government's Economic Survey (2006-07) indicates between 1991 and 2004 the number of people employed in the organised private sector grew by a meagre 0.6 million from 7.7 million in 1991 to 8.3 million in 2004. The number of people employed in the organised sector as a whole including public sector fell from 26.7 to 26.4 million in the same period. (Srivastava, 2007)

This situations cited above in India indicate the Gandhi's idea on mechanisation and decentralisation. Mechanisation leads to the concentration of wealth in few hands by avoiding the employment opportunities of the people in India. As the employment opportunities dwindled, the benefits of increased production went to the industrialists. The decentralisation aims at as Gandhi evolved production by masses in different locations in India, not mass production as enunciated by different SEZs which are pro-rich. This will not create an ideal non-violent society in India (e.g. Nandigram violence caused many deaths in West Bengal).

CONCLUSION

Gandhian Economics is based on rural foundations. Economics that hurts the moral well-being of a nation is immoral. Gandhi was not theorist, but a practical man, dealing with practical problems. He asserted that the problems of poverty, disease, ignorance and inertia did not admit and being postponed to a distant date. Gandhi dealt with humanitarian approach in rural economic philosophy. Revival of village economy, exploitation of the village in the interest of the town was a species of violence and their economic and social resuscitation as a *sine qua non* for freedom from foreign rule. Fostering village industries could create employment and pump purchasing power into the village. Indian villagers could be educated out of inertia by bands of selfless workers infiltrating into the village. As the food habits of Indian masses were responsible for their undernourishment, the Indian scientists should pursue research into Indian diets in the contexts of Indian conditions. In a country where the hands are too many and the work too little, machinery could only add to unemployment and poverty. Gandhi did not favoured mass production but favoured production by masses and at same time welcomed simple tools and instruments. Decentralisation of production in thousands of villages is closely linked with the decentralisation of political power, the basic to ideal of a non-violent society. The ideal Indian village is of a 'republic', independent of its neighbours for its vital wants yet interdependent in other ways.

Development must be equitable if it is to be sustainable. The time has come to distinguish development sharply from exclusive growth. A "careful transition" from agriculture to industry, with people support will be a model. The transition from agriculture to industry was inevitable in capitalist or socialist society. It would not be able to hold on to agricultural success unless industries were developed.

References

Aggarwal, Aradhana (2006), "Special Economic Zones: Revisiting the Policy Debate", *Economic and Political Weekly*, XLI(43) and (44), November 4, 2006.

Nanda, B.R (1958), "Mahatma Gandhi: A Biography," Oxford University Press, Oxford, New Delhi, pp. 371-82.

Frank, Robert H (2007), "Trickle-down' theory doesn't hold up", *The Hindu*, English Daily, April 13.

Srivastava, Aseem (2007), "Why this growth never trickle down," *The Hindu*, English Daily, March 20, p. 18.

Swaminathan, M.S (2007), "Dealing with the agrarian crisis," *The Hindu*, English Daily, May 28.

Swaminathan, M.S (2006), "Avoiding an unequal social bargain", *The Hindu*, English Daily, July 6, 2006.

35

Mahatma Gandhi: His Journalistic Venture and Rural Reconstruction

RAGHUBANSH SINGH

Very few great men have displayed such a versatile life and character as Mahatma Gandhi. No aspect of human life has been left untouched by him. To quote Late Prime Minister Nehru, "To him life was an integrated whole, a closely woven garments of many colours." However, an aspect of the career of Mahatma Gandhi that has been ignored concerns his life and experiences as a Journalist. Gandhiji had a wide experience as a journalist. He worked as a correspondent and editor, folded copies and set types, wrote editorials and features and reviewed books. He was an editor for more than thirty years. During this period he edited four weekly news-papers—*Indian Opinion, Young India, Navajivan* and *Harijan*.

GANDHIJI'S JOURNALISTIC VENTURE

Gandhiji went to England to study Law in 1898. While in London, he for the first time read a newspaper. News paper reading was a maiden experience for him. To quote

Gandhiji: "In India, I never had read a newspaper." Newspaper were not only a source of information and amusement to him, but they produced a strong temptation in him to write articles and see his name and articles printed in the newspaper. Luckily he got an opportunity to write articles for the journal entitled "Vegetarian"—an official organ of the London Vegetarian Society. These are his earliest writings on record. Three years of continuous writing articles on Indian diets, festival, customs, etc. enlarged his scope of writing and made him a matured and accomplished journalist.

In 1893 Gandhiji went to South Africa after getting an offer from a client to defend his case. In South Africa Mahatma Gandhi began his journalistic career as a correspondent. Shri Dadabhai Naoroji, leader of the Indian community in England started the publication of a journal in 1890 dealing mainly with topics of Indian interest. Gandhiji became the journal's South African's correspondent. He started ventilating the grievances of Indians living in South Africa. Subsequently, Gandhiji, who offered his services serving the sick and the wounded during Boer wore war in 1899, gained the first hand experience of the battle field. He recorded these experiences for publication in *Times of India*, Bombay.

The London Vegetarian society provided him with a forum to write for newspapers, the political situation in South Africa transformed him into a conscientious journalist. For Gandhiji journalism was "a means for the study of humen nature in all its casts and shades." Gandhiji defined the aim of journalism in his Autobiography as such. "One of the objects of newspaper is to understand popular feeling and give expression to it, another is to arouse among the people certain desirable sentiments, and the third is fearlessly to express popular defects."

Gandhiji used the power of the press to propogate his ideas and views. In South Africa he needed to own a paper and a press to disseminate his views to the public. Sri Madanjit Vyavaharik as a political co-worker of Gandhiji in South Africa, established a press in Durban in 1889. Gandhiji exhorted Madanjit to start the publication of a weekly journal. Thus a journal entitled 'The Indian Opinion' came into existence and its first issue was out in May 1898. The main idea behind the publication of a weekly was to prepare the Indians in South Africa for struggle against injustice and racial discrimination. On its publication Gandhiji wrote "I believe that a struggle which chiefly relies on internal strength, cannot be wholly carried on without a newspaper, it is also my experience that we would not perhaps had educated the local Indian community nor kept Indians all over the world in touch with the courses of events in South Africa in any other way, with the same case and success, as through the Indian opinion." The first editorial—ourselves was written by Gandhiji. He was writing incessantly in the Indian opinion to boost up the morals of Indians in South Africa and preparing them for satyagraha.

Gandhiji returned to India in 1913. He wanted political emancipation of his country first as that would make people politically conscious. He believed that masses once awakened cannot rest till social and economic problems were fully resolved. For awakening the masses, Gandhiji needed a paper to transmit his ideas, as he wrote "Newspaper, if well edited, could became a most powerful vehicle to transmit our ideas in coincise manner."

While the ideas of launching a paper was taking shape in his mind, the First World War ended and instead of self-rule India got Rowlett Act. There was a mass upheaval in the country against this black Act. Gandhiji was very much in the midst of the movement. And as a protest. An unregistered weekly the *Satyagraha,* under the editorship of Gandhiji, started publication from April 7, 1919. Mass upheaval continued and very soon the Jallianwalla Bagh massacre took place. Leaders were stunned at this development. The weekly *Satyagraha* was not registered according to law. Gandhiji wrote, "It is not our intention to break for all times the law governing the publication of a newspaper. Consequently, the weekly, The *Satyagraha* was temporarily suspended after its May 6, publication.

However, the void created by the cessation of *Satyagraha* was filled by the publication of a Journal entitled the *Young India.* A band of Gujarati young men started the publication of a English weekly, the *Young India* and the editorship of the *Young India* was offered to Gandhiji. The Gujarati monthly, the *Navajivan* was also placed at his disposal.

Gandhiji soon made his personality felt through the columns of *Young India* and *Navajivan*. He got a medium to preach what he believed. He turned these two weeklies into views papers. Gandhiji said, "they enabled me freely to ventilate my ideas and to put heart into the people."

Gandhiji was detained and put behind bars during the civil disobedience movement. While lodged in Poona prison, he was thinking a terms of a new journal. It would be devoted to the castes of untouchables. With the help of G.D. Birla, the new weekly entitled 'The *Harijan*' first appeared on April 11, 1933. Gandhiji was conducting the weekly from the prison. The *Harijan* became the mouth piece for *Harijan* movement and rural reconstruction. Gandhiji said, "since the *Harijan* movement has a world-wide significance and seeks the sympathy of whole humanity, it is necessary to keep the world acquainted with its implications and problems." The paper he made it clear would highlight all efforts for the removal of unsociability. The *Harijan* was a newspaper. Gandhiji explained now a newspaper differs from a newspaper. "Let it be known that *Harijan* is a newspaper as distinguished from a newspaper. People buy and read it not for amusement but for instruction and regulating their daily conduct. They literally take their weekly lessons in non-violence."

EDITOR PAR-EXCELLENCE

Gandhiji was an editor par-excellence. Truth, pole star of Gandhiji's life and philosophy permeated his writings. This helps explain the absence of exaggerated accounts in his papers, "publication of false news is a crime against humanity", he wrote. For a motto he favored this "*Young India* will be stale when truth becomes stale." He weighted every adjective or adverbs before writing. "I cannot recall a word in my articles written in Indian opinion, or down without thought or deliberation or a word of conscious exaggeration or any thing merely to please." He wrote,

Gandhiji in a short "what is Journalism?" wrote in *Indian Opinion* in Jaunary 19, 1907, "we have always necessitated the one test of journalism is that it gives facts to the people. My writings cannot be poisonous, they must be free from anger. There can be no room for untruth in my writings." Thus Gandhiji's insistence on truth prevented him from using unwanted words. Yet he expresses what is in his mind quite explicitly.

Another great quality of Gandhiji's writings which stands very prominently is clarity. His writings are top the point and in unambiguous language. It is thus evident that his writings are characterized by deep thinking and constant self-examination. He had a clear thinking and knew well what he was going to write. He would put forth his ideas and argument in simple and short sentences. Of his writings, the late Prime Minister Nehru wrote, "The language was always simple and to the point and seldom was an unnecessary word used." The fact that Gandhiji wrote from the core of his heart made the writings all the more absorbing. A few examples of this writings are worth mentioning. Lokamanya Tilak passed away on August 1, 1920. Obituary written by Gandhiji was unsurpassed, "A great among men has fallen. The voice of the lion is hushed. His patriotism was a passion with him. He knew no religion but love of his country. His courage never failed him. It is blasphemy to talk of such a man as dead."

This style was a complete departure from the one which was in practice in India during the early period of the twentieth century. The eminent writers of those years were writing in Macaulayan style. These writings were heavy in form and content. Sentences were usually complex and long. For an average reader they were difficult to understand. But Gandhiji wrote in utilitarian, simple, clear and direct language. Gandhiji, though himself not a literateur, his writings are many times masterpiece of literature. For they excel those of literary savants. The writings of Mahatma Gandhi are the documents of an age. They wrought beyond the power at any sword to conquer. Single-handed and single-minded, this man turned the tides of history. So every would be said and wrote will be remembered for every.

Gandhiji revolutionized the English writing of this countrymen. Younger generation of writers got inspired by this style. Not only the contributors of the *Young India* or the *Harijan*, but those of other papers started writing in simple English. A new class of English writer emerged in India. Thus the individuality of Gandhiji comes through his style completely confirming Walter Pater's Phrase "the style is the man."

STRESS ON RURAL UPLIFT

Apart from the language and the style, the contents of his writings were more important. Writing to him was not an art but rather a practical medium of expression. The prestige of the Gandhiji paper was largely due to the purpose he proclaimed. The subject matter he treated was down to the earth. Gandhiji was able to divert the attention of the journalists from glittering lift or the cities to the stark reality of the villages. He impressed on them the fact that India lives in her villages. The journalist therefore, should devote more time and energy in highlighting the problems of the villages and their inhabitants. On 29 August 1946, Gandhiji wrote in the *Harijan*, "I wanted to have a programme at rural reconstruction. So that "During Hill" villages could be converted into "Tiny Garden." My mission is to build Indian society based on the village system and I believe if villages Perish, India would Perish." For Gandhiji "The first and most important programme was the resurgence of villages." Addressing a literary society in Gujarat on November 2, 1936 Gandhiji questioned "For whose sake are we going to write? Not certainly, for the great gentry of Ahmedabad. They can afford to engage literary men and have great libraries in their homes. But what about the peasants at the well who with unspeakable abuses is goading his bullocks to pull the leader buckets. Our literary men will pour on Kalidas and Bahavabhum and English authors. I want them to go to villages, study them and given them some thing life giving."

Gandhiji introduced a new era in the realm of Indian journalism. He succeeded in putting the villages on the wider convas of journalism. From 1920, Gandhiji had been in the center of Indian Freedom movement. But despite his deep involvement in Indian politics, Gandhi through his impressive article and future focused the attention of the countrymen on vital issues like Swadeshi, spinning, *Harijan* rigorously omitted political news. Even the India Act, 1953 which introduces a Federal system did not receive any coverage in the *Harijan*. On the other hand, it published more and more articles on rural industries. In the *Young India* Gandhiji wrote "village economy cannot be complete without the essential village industries such as handwriting, hand pounding, oil processing, tanning, hand spinning and weaving, etc. when we have become village minded we will not imitate the West, but we should develop a true national taste in keeping with the vision of New India in which pauperism, starvation and idleness will be unknown."

The weeklies edited by Gandhiji practiced an exciting venture in journalism by not accepting advertisements. Gandhiji had boundless faith in conducting his weeklies without advertisements. He believed acceptance of advertisements would compromise the independence of a paper and also restrain the editor in expressing views. Gandhiji's objection to advertisement was also based on economic grounds. Advertisements cost money and hence they unnecessarily enhance the price of the products. Indian poor people cannot afford to pay higher price for a commodity. The money spent on advertisement was sheer waste. This can be better utilised for the benefits of the poorer section of the society. Gandhiji also opposed advertisements on ethical moral grounds. Advertisements some times were indecent, immoral and also a total lies.

Gandhiji believe that a paper without advertisement must pay its way from some other sources. The subscriber must buy for ideas and make a venture success. Gandhiji's own weeklies did not operate entirely on the revenue from circulation. The production costs were met by the job-work accepted by the press. This added source of revenue balances the lack of advertisements.

Gandhiji strongly believed that the economic fate of the country depended heavily on the rural economy. The villages were the center of Gandhiji's economic thought. He wrote in the *Harijan*. "The farmers, the cattle breeders and the artisans are the main pillars of social and economic life of India." This is why, despite his distaste and dislike for the advertisements, Gandhiji's weekly gave adequate space to propagate any new things which would help to boost the rural economy. He would advertise, on his own, the improved oil crusher which could crush more oil, he would give due publicity through his weeklies to hand hounding machine for husking more vitaminous rice with minimum efforts. Any improvement in the art of cultivation or methods of spinning and weaving would get adequate space in these weeklies for publicity.

Gandhiji saw Khadi as the base for rural prosperity. He wrote in his weekly "Not on the clatter of arms depends the revival of India's prosperity and true independence. It depends most largely upon re-introduction in every hone the music of spinning wheel. It gives sweater music and is more profitable than the execrable harmonium concertina and accordion." And hence Gandhiji made full uses of his weeklies to popularize khadi among the Indian people. Anything which was supposed to benefit the rural masses got full publicity in his journal. In the *Harijan*, Gandhi wrote, "I would be no party to the advertisement of tooth-brushes even when they are made in India. I should declare my preference for the tooth-stick. I am convinced that 'neem' and 'babul' sticks were more useful to India's teeming millions than the brushes." In the opinion of Gandhiji the main aim of journalism is to provide service to the people. As such he did not hesitate in giving publicity to, through columns of his paper, anything which Gandhiji was convinced would bring about immense good to the rural people.

FREEDON OF THE PRESS

Gandhiji fought vigorously for freedom of press which was to him "a dear privilege." Right from his appearance on the India political horizon, he had emerged as the champion of the freedom of expression and the liberty of the press. He wanted fearless editors. He wanted to keep up the moral at a time when the British government was imposing all sorts of restrictions on the freedom of the press. He appealed to every editor to stick to his own conscience and independent judgment. He always pleaded with the British Government to free the press from all administrative controls. He felt that an important task before the country was to restore the liberty of the press. For him "the restoration of free speech, free association and free press was real Swaraj."

Gandhiji's weekly suffered under the press rules and restrictions. He wrote that it was better publish a newspaper then to bring them out under all kinds of restrictions imposed by the government. During the Non-co-operation Movement Gandhiji was exhorting the people to fight injustice and tyrannical rule of the British government. He felt that the alien government had no right to govern. In the *Young India* he wrote, "An India prostrated at the feet of Europe can give no hope to humanity. An India awakened and free has a message of peace and goodwill to goaning world." The British government was deeply perturbed by such inflammatory writings of Gandhiji. Gandhiji's imprisonment for six years for writing three editorials in *Young India* symbolise his dedication to freedom of the press. The editorials were. "Tamperint with loyalty" (Sept. 19, 1921), "The puzzle and its solution" (Dec. 15, 1921) and "Shaking the Manes" (Feb. 21, 1922).

In 1939 the Press Act of 1910 was revived through on ordinance promulgated by the then Viceroy. The Press Act of 1910 had made it mandatory for the publishers to furnish heavy security for registration of their Newspapers. Gandhiji vehemently opposed this ordinance. He urged the pressmen and the publishers to refuse to furnish security and if they were called upon to do so, either to cease publication or to challenge the authorities to confiscate their press. The Navajivan Press did not furnish the security and hence their Press was forfeited. And in 1932 Gandhiji's two weeklies the *Young India* and the *Navajivan* ceased their publication rather than to surrender to governmental restriction.

The start of the Second World War in Septemebr 1939 led to a serious confrontation between Gandhiji and the British government. India was involved in the war against anti-fascist forces without consulting the Congress Party. Gandhiji felt how could a colony help in other nations' fight for freedom, when it was itself enslaved. Thus Gandhiji as a protest decided to initiate a limited Satyagraha on an individual basis by a few selected individuals in every locality asking people not to support the war effort either through men or material. In October 1939, the government imposed censor on publication of news pertaining to Individual Satyagraha. Opposing the censorships, Gandhiji wrote in the *Harijan,* "I cannot function freely if I have to send to the press Advisor, at New Delhi, every line, I write about 'Satyagraha'. The three weeklies have been conducted in the interest of truth. But cannot serve that interest if editing has to be done under threat of prosecution. Liberty of press is a dear privilege, I am unable to reconcile myself to an order whose infringement will carry its own consequences." The *Harijan* served such purges by voluntarily closing its publication for six years. Gandhiji wrote in the *Harijan* "The suspension must continue while the gagging lasts. It constitutes a Satyagrahi's respectful protest against the gag."

To sum up, Gandhiji's genius was not primarily political and religious. The journalist in him was bold, courageous and conscientious. He was a journalist of the first rank and a great editor. Gandhiji is immortal through his journalistic venture.

References

Agarwal, S.N., Gandian Plan of Economic development for India.
Bhattacharya, S.N., Mahatma Gandhi—The Journals.
Diwaker, R.R., Glimpses of Gandhiji
Fischer, Louis, We are with Gandhi.
Gandhi, M.K., My experiment with Trust.
Gandhi, M.K., Rebuilding our villages.
Nehru, Jawaharlal, Autobiography.
Publication Division, History of Journalism in India.
Saxena, K.S., Gandhi Centenary Papers.
Winslow John, Journalism in Modern India.

Index